Asian Yearbook of International Law

# Asian Yearbook of International Law

*Volume 21 (2015)*

BRILL
NIJHOFF

LEIDEN | BOSTON

The Development of International Law in Asia-Korea (DILA-KOREA), as the secretariat of DILA, is responsible for the management of DILA along with the Asian Yearbook of International Law and Asia Pacific Ocean Law Institutions Alliance. DILA-Korea has generously provided financial support so that Volume 21 (2015) is available as open access.

The Library of Congress Cataloging-in-Publication Data is available online at http://catalog.loc.gov
LC record available at http://lccn.loc.gov/93643886

Typeface for the Latin, Greek, and Cyrillic scripts: "Brill". See and download: brill.com/brill-typeface.

ISBN 978-90-04-34454-9 (hardback)
ISBN 978-90-04-34455-6 (e-book)



This book is printed on acid-free paper and produced in a sustainable manner.

Printed by Printforce, the Netherlands

# Asian Yearbook of International Law



VOLUME 21 (2015)

The titles published in this series are listed at *brill.com/ayil*

# Foundation for the Development of International Law in Asia (DILA)

DILA was established in 1989, at a time when its prime movers believed that economic and political developments in Asia had reached the stage at which they would welcome and benefit substantially from a mechanism to promote and facilitate exchanges among their international law scholars that had failed to develop during the colonial era.

The Foundation was established (a) to promote the study of and analysis of topics and issues in the field of international law, in particular from an Asian perspective; and (b) dissemination of knowledge of, international law in Asia; promotion of contacts and co-operation between persons and institutions actively dealing with questions of international law relating to Asia.

The Foundation is concerned with reporting and analyzing developments in the field of international law relating to the region, and not primarily with efforts to distinguish particular attitudes, policies or practices as predominately or essentially "Asian". If they are shown to exist, it would be an interesting by-product of the Foundation's essential function, which is to bring about an exchange of views in the expectation that the process would reveal areas of common interest and concern among the States of Asia, and even more importantly, demonstrate that those areas of interest and concern are, in fact, shared by the international community as a whole.

# The Asian Yearbook of International Law

Launched in 1991, the Asian Yearbook of International Law is a major internationally-refereed yearbook dedicated to international legal issues as seen primarily from an Asian perspective. It is published by Brill under the auspices of the Foundation for the Development of International Law (DILA).

When it was launched, the Yearbook was the first publication of its kind, edited by a team of leading international law scholars from across Asia. It provides a forum for the publication of articles in the field of international law, and other Asian international legal topics. The objects of the Yearbook are two-fold. First, to promote research, study and writing in the field of international law in Asia; and second, to provide an intellectual platform for the discussion and dissemination of Asian views and practices on contemporary international legal issues.

Each volume of the Yearbook contains articles and shorter notes, a section on State Practice, an overview of the Asian States' participation in multilateral treaties and succinct analysis of recent international legal developments in Asia, as well as book reviews. We believe this publication to be of importance and use to anyone working on international law and in Asian studies.

In keeping with DILA's commitment to encouraging scholarship in international law as well as in disseminating such scholarship, its Governing Board decided to make the Yearbook open access and is available through Brill Open.

# Contents

## *Notes and Commentaries*



## *Legal Materials*

## *Literature*



## *DILA Events*

# Editorial Note

The 2015 edition (volume 21) of the *Asian Yearbook of International Law* marks a major milestone in the history of the Yearbook and the Foundation for the Development of International Law in Asia (DILA) which authorized the publication of the Yearbook. Because this is the 21st volume, it gives us, the Editorial Board, the chance to recognize the tremendous efforts that went into the production of the first 20 volumes which spanned the years of 1991 to 2014 and provides an opportunity to remind us of the purpose of the Yearbook to first, to promote research, study and writing in the field of international law in Asia; and second, to provide an intellectual platform for the discussion and dissemination of Asian views and practices on contemporary international legal issues.

Volume 21 also represents a homecoming of sorts as the Yearbook has returned to Brill|Nijhoff as the publisher of the Yearbook. When the Yearbook was launched in 1991 with the publication of volume 1, Martinus Nijhoff Publishers, now an imprint of Brill, published the Yearbook. Founding General Editors Ko Swan Sik, J.J.G. Syatauw, and M.C.W. Pinto were all at The Hague at the time of the establishment of the Yearbook and naturally, Martinus Nijhoff became the publisher not only because of the convenience of Nijhoff's offices in The Hague, but also because of its prestigious history and commitment to international law publications. Martinus Nijhoff published volumes 1 through 11 while Routledge then published volumes 12 through 15. Given the desire of DILA to make the Yearbook widely available, especially to students and scholars of international law in Asia, Volumes 16 through 20 were made open access with the Yearbook being published by DILA in collaboration with Handong International Law School located in South Korea.

The decision to move the publication of the Yearbook back to Brill was undertaken by DILA's Governing Board on December 7, 2016 at its meeting in Tokyo subsequent to the 2016 DILA International Conference. The basis of this decision was to give the Yearbook the opportunity to utilize Brill's global reach with its wide access to libraries and institutions around the world and its marketing prowess with regard to international legal publications. The Governing Board also recognized that the scholarship and information found in the Yearbook would likely be difficult to access in hardcopy form for Asian students and scholars. Therefore, the commitment was made by DILA-Korea, the secretariat of DILA, to financially support making the Yearbook open access so that the full contents of the Yearbook would be made available for downloading without cost through Brill's website for the Yearbook. Volume 21 is the first volume of the Yearbook that will be available as open access through Brill with the hope that eventually all of the Yearbook's volumes will be accessible without cost.

## 1 Main Articles

The main articles of volume 21 concern the South China Sea Arbitration between the Philippines and China that commenced in 2013 and decided in 2016 focusing on the implications of the decision of the arbitral tribunal on territorial and maritime disputes in Asia.*

The first article by Ted L. McDorman of the University of Victoria in Canada is entitled "The South China Sea Arbitration: Selected Legal Notes." Professor McDorman examines the South China Sea Arbitration between the Philippines and China specifically focusing on the legal status of the 2016 Award; the decision of the Tribunal that possessed jurisdiction to deal with the subject-matter of the dispute regarding the legal status of specific maritime features as rocks and islands since it did not concern territorial sovereignty or maritime boundary delimitation; and finally, the Tribunal's decision on the merits where it ruled that it had jurisdiction to decide upon China's historic rights claims and the nine-dash line.

The second article is from Hsiao-Chi Hsu of National Taiwan Normal University who discusses "The Political Implications of the South China Sea Ruling on Sino-Philippine Relations and Regional Stability." Professor Hsu looks at the South China Sea Arbitration by examining the political implications of the arbitral panel's decision in favor of the Philippines on the foreign policy of the Philippines and on the prospects for regional stability.

Thi Lan Anh Nguyen of the Diplomatic Academy of Vietnam follows with the "Award of the Republic of Philippines v. the People's Republic of China Case: Legal Implications on the South China Sea Disputes." Dr. Nguyen observes that the Tribunal's conclusions as to the legal status of the low tide elevations and the impossibility of drawing the archipelagic

* The main articles that are included in the Yearbook were presented as part of a conference entitled "The Aftermath of the South China Sea Arbitration: International Law, Politics, and Security Perspectives" held on 18 – 19 July 2016 in Taipei, Taiwan and the 2016 DILA-Korea and KIOST International Conference entitled "South China Sea Arbitration and Beyond Territorial and Maritime Disputes in East Asia" held on 5 – 6 October 2016 in Seoul, Korea. Special thanks go to Dustin Kuan-Hsiung Wang, Professor of the Graduate Institute of Political Science of National Taiwan Normal University, who organized the conference in Taipei.

baselines for the Spratlys indicate that the scope of sovereignty disputes has been significantly reduced between the Philippines and China. She also notes that the decision addressed important issues regarding marine environmental protection and the safety of navigation. She hopes that the award has created a new legal status quo in the South China Sea.

Jacques deLisle of the University of Pennsylvania in the United States discusses the "International Political Implications of the July 2016 Arbitration Decision in the Philippines-PRC Case Concerning the South China Sea: the US, China and International Law." He notes that the decision in the Philippines-China arbitration was fully consistent with the legal-political position of the United States in that (1) there was no position taken on the questions of sovereignty over disputed maritime features; (2) the rights to freedom of navigation and overflight and access to maritime commons in the South China Sea were asserted and protected; (3) the parties were insisted to follow international law and in particular, UNCLOS; and finally, (4) there was a call on the claimants to use peaceful means to address their disputes. In regards to China, while China's response to the arbitral decision was predictably negative and consistent with their long-standing position, China faces the situation where it is being accused of being an international scofflaw and a revisionist in its approach to major components of the international legal and political order. Professor deLisle then looks at the implications of the decision for international law and expresses concern that if China ignores the decision, this will prevent China from integration into the mainstream international legal system which will result in the Tribunal's decision being a hollow victory for law.

Alan H. Yang of National Chengchi University in Taiwan continues with his article, "South China Sea Arbitration and Its Implication for ASEAN Centrality". In his article, he argues that the final award of the Tribunal will not put an end to the dispute, but will rather legally socialize China's actions in the South China Sea. Professor Yang believes that the decision will lead to a more divided ASEAN and a more fragmented regional community. He looks at strategic conditions of the South China Sea from the perspective of ASEAN noting that ASEAN has failed to secure unity among its member States. He also goes on to examine the policy implications for ASEAN of the Tribunal's decision.

Terence Roehrig of the U.S. Naval War College follows with "Caught in the Middle: South Korea and the South China Sea Arbitration Decision." He notes that while the disputes over the South China Sea and the Tribunal's decision do not have a direct impact on South Korean interests, it does increase the chance that South Korea will have to take a side on the matter. Professor Roehrig points out that the decision could affect South Korea's maritime disputes with China, Japan, and North Korea. He observes that South Korea has been relatively successful in balancing its competing interests, but notes that depending on how the dispute between the Philippines and China evolves, and more importantly, the future of Sino-U.S. relations, South Korea may have some increasingly difficult choices to make concerning international law, maritime security and its relations with China and the United States.

The next article is by Leszek Buszynski of the Australian National University entitled "Law and Realpolitik: The Arbitral Tribunal's Ruling and the South China Sea". Professor Buszynski contextualizes China's response to the Tribunal's decision against it in light of the tension between international law and realist notions of international relations. He notes that while the perception may be that powerful States are able to ignore international law and not comply with its standards, there are consequences for non-compliance. He examines China's response to the Tribunal's award and its domestic impact and the effect it has on ASEAN and its member States. He concludes by noting that by rejecting the Tribunal's ruling, China is creating greater uncertainty in maritime affairs when the resort to force to settle disputes will become more likely. From his perspective, the consequences for China, a major trading country with a strong interest in the security of maritime trade, would be that it faces the consequences of a deterioration in maritime security first. He believes that Beijing should assume the responsibilities commensurate with its economic weight and support a maritime order based on law and the legal principles that sustain it.

Eiichi Usuki of Daito Bunka University in Japan looks at "China's Three Distinctive Assertions under the 'Nine-dash-line' Claims and the Annex VII Arbitral Tribunal's Interpretation of Article 121 Regarding an Island and Rocks under the 1982 UN Convention on the Law of the Sea." Professor Usuki examines the historical background of the South China Sea to provide a context to understand China's nine-dash line claim. He then goes on to analyze the Arbitral Tribunal's characterization and evaluation of the nine-dash line claim. Given the Tribunal's decision against China, Professor Usuki looks at the implications of the ruling for China and ASEAN. He comments on the Tribunal's standards for determining maritime features such as rocks and islands under UNCLOS and what this means for Japanese claims.

The last of the main articles is by Chie Kojima of Musashino University in Japan entitled "South China Sea Arbitration and the Protection of the Marine Environment: Evolution of UNCLOS Part XII through Interpretation and the Duty to Cooperate." Professor Kojima discusses the contributions of the South China Sea Arbitral Award to the development of international marine environmental law. First, she analyzes the evolutionary interpretation of Part XII of the UNCLOS in the light of other treaty regimes, namely the Convention on Biological Diversity (CBD) and Convention on International Trade in

Endangered Species of Wild Fauna and Flora (CITES). Second, she looks at the Arbitral Tribunal's interpretation of Article 206 of UNCLOS on environmental impact assessment (EIA) and the duty to communicate the results of an EIA in the context of the duty to cooperate enshrined as a fundamental principle under Part XII of UNCLOS.

## II Notes and Commentaries

The main articles are followed by notes and commentaries that examine the State practice of Asian countries in more depth. Xiangxin Xu, Guobin Zhang, and Guifang (Julia) Xue look at "China's Deep Seabed Law: Towards 'Reasonably Appropriate' Environmental Legislation for Exploration and Exploitation of Deep Sea Minerals in the Area." Next, Kanami Ishibashi of Tokyo University of Foreign Studies in Japan examines "Further Developments in Fukushima and Other New Movements for Implementing International Human Rights Law in Japan." Eonkyung Park and Taegil Kim of Kyung Hee University follow with an examination of the "Status and International Cooperation Aspects of Air Quality Control Laws and Policies in Korea." Finally, Kyu Rang Kim and Seong Won Lee of Inha University Law School in Korea present "The Waste You Left Behind: Polluter Liability as Tort."

## III Legal Materials

The Yearbook from its inception was committed to providing scholars, practitioners, and students with a report on Asian State practice as its contribution to provide an understanding of how Asian States act within the international system and how international law is applied in their domestic legal systems. The Yearbook does this in two ways. First, it records the participation of Asian States in multilateral treaties; and second, it reports on the State practice of Asian States.

### 1 *Participation in Multilateral Treaties*

From the very first volume of the Yearbook, the Multilateral Treaties section has recorded the participation of Asian States in open multilateral lawmaking treaties which mostly aim at world-wide adherence during the calendar year that corresponds to the particular year of the Yearbook. Karin Arts of the International Institute of Social Studies, Erasmus University Rotterdam in The

Hague, Netherlands has compiled and edited this section since the 1994 edition of the Yearbook up to the present volume.

### 2 *State Practice of Asian States in the Field of International Law*

The State Practice section of the Asian Yearbook of International Law is intended to offer readers of the Yearbook an outline and summary of the activities undertaken by Asian States that have a direct bearing on international law. The national correspondents, listed in the table of contents, who have undertaken the responsibility to report on State practice in their respective countries commit themselves to give the readership of the Yearbook a comprehensive snapshot of what States are doing in relation to international law during the calendar year that corresponds to the particular year of the Yearbook. The intention is not to provide a commentary on Asian State practice of international law, but to describe how these States are applying international law in their domestic legal systems and in their foreign relations. This task is all the more challenging given the increasing relevance of international law throughout the region and the abundance of State practice that is seen year after year.

## IV Literature

### 1 *Book Review*

The Yearbook seeks to review manuscripts that focus on the international legal issues that impact the Asian region. For this edition of the Yearbook, Dr. Lowell Bautista of the University of Wollongong School of Law and of the Board of Editors gives his review of *Asia-Pacific and the Implementation of the Law of the Sea: Regional Legislative and Policy Approaches to the Law of the Sea Convention* edited by Seokwoo Lee and Warwick Gullett and published by Brill.

### 2 *Bibliographic Survey*

From the first volume (1991) to the fourteenth volume (2008), the Yearbook has provided information on books, articles, notes, and other materials dealing with international law in Asia, broadly defined to give the readership of the Yearbook a simple way to find scholarship about international legal issues in Asia. Originally, it was referred to as the "Bibliography of International Law Concerning Asian Affairs" the first of which was drafted by J.J.G. Syatauw. From volume 9 (2000), this section was referred to as "Survey of International Law Literature Published in [calendar year] Relevant to Asian States" and continued in that format until volume 14 (2008). From volume 15 (2009) through volume

16 (2010), the section was omitted. From volume 17 (2011), it was revitalized and renamed "International Law in Asia: A Bibliographic Survey" and has been included ever since. Dr. Bautista has prepared the bibliography for the 2015 edition.

## V DILA Activities

The 2015 edition of the Yearbook reports on the activities undertaken by DILA in 2015, namely the annual DILA International Conference and DILA Academy and Workshop that were held on 16 and 17 October 2015 on the campus of Hasanuddin University at the Faculty of Law in Makassar, Indonesia.

Finally, in recognition of the past 20 volumes of the Yearbook, a list of the main articles that have been published from volume 1 to volume 20 has been provided to recognize the depth and breadth of scholarship that the Yearbook has been privileged to publish.

We hope to continue and build on the excellence that has been established by the previous editorial boards of the *Asian Yearbook of International Law* with this 2015 edition and beyond. Here's to another 20 volumes of the Yearbook!

*Seokwoo Lee*, Inha University Law School
Co-Editor-in-Chief

*Hee Eun Lee*, Handong International Law School
Co-Editor-in-Chief

# *Articles*

# The *South China Sea Arbitration*: Selected Legal Notes

*Ted L. McDorman*[1]

## I Introduction

All international disputes are by their nature political. Opting to utilize international third-party adjudication to resolve or be a step in the resolution of an international dispute, while rarely pursued by States, does not alter the political nature of the dispute. International courts and tribunals, however, generally only deal with the legal questions and the related facts. As a result, where States accept to utilize third-party adjudication to resolve a dispute, they essentially accept to depoliticize the matter in dispute and to focus on the legal issues. At the macro-level, the *South China Sea Arbitration*[2] was a situation where China viewed the subject matters in dispute as political and beyond the jurisdiction and competence of the Tribunal established pursuant to the United Nations Convention on the Law of the Sea[3] at the request of the Philippines.[4] The Philippines characterized the subject matters in dispute as that of interpretation and application of the LOS Convention, a legal matter, and thus, within the jurisdiction of the Tribunal.

In most situations, the lack of mutual consent to utilize international third-party adjudication prevents its use.[5] However, the LOS Convention provides for compulsory adjudication of disputes concerning the interpretation and application of the Convention, subject to a number of exceptions.[6] As China

1 Faculty of Law, University of Victoria, Victoria, British Columbia.

2 *In the Matter of the South China Sea Arbitration* (the Philippines and China), *Award on Jurisdiction and Admissibility* (29 October 2015) and *Award* (12 July 2016), on the website of the Permanent Court of Arbitration at www.pca-cpa.org.

3 United Nations Convention on the Law of the Sea, opened for signature 10 December 1982, 21 I.L.M. 1261 (entered into force 16 November, 1994). [Hereinafter, LOS Convention].

4 Philippines, *Notification and Statement of Claim*, 22 January 2013, *South China Sea Arbitration*, Philippines Memorial, Vol. III, Annex 1, on the PCA website, *supra* note 2.

5 See: JAMES CRAWFORD, BROWNLIE'S PRINCIPLES OF PUBLIC INTERNATIONAL LAW 718 (2012).

6 LOS Convention, *supra* note 3, Part XV.

 | DOI 10.1163/9789004344556_002

and the Philippines are both parties to the Convention, the first stage of the LOS Convention dispute settlement process in the *South China Sea Arbitration* was whether the Tribunal had the jurisdiction to examine the merits of the Philippine submissions.

China declined to participate in the establishment of the Tribunal or to participate or appear before the Tribunal.[7] In deciding not to participate, China has followed a small number of States which have similarly declined to participate in cases before the International Court of Justice,[8] as well as the more recent non-participation by the Russian Federation in the LOS Convention procedures in the *Arctic Sunrise Case* brought by the Netherlands.[9] As noted by Merrills: "The cases in which the [International] Court's competence to handle politically charged disputes has been questioned have all been referred unilaterally and involved a basic disagreement as to how the dispute should be characterized."[10]

The Tribunal in the *South China Sea Arbitration* ultimately held that it had jurisdiction to consider the merits of almost all the subject-matter claims

---

7 See: China, *Note Verbale No. (13) PG-1039*, 19 February 2013, in Philippines Memorial, Vol. III, Annex 3 and China, *Note Verbale 29 July 2013*, in Philippines Memorial, Vol. III, Annex 4, on the PCA website, *supra* note 2.

8 See: *Fisheries Jurisdiction Case* (Germany v. Iceland), *Jurisdiction*, [1973] I.C.J. Reports 43 and *Merits*, [1974] *I.C.J. Reports* 175; *Fisheries Jurisdiction Case* (United Kingdom v. Iceland), *Jurisdiction*, [1973] I.C.J. Reports 3 and *Merits*, [1974] I.C.J. Reports 3, where Iceland did not appear; *Nuclear Test Case* (Australia v. France), [1974] *I.C.J. Reports* 253 and *Nuclear Test Case* (New Zealand v. France), [1974] I.C.J. Reports 457, where France did not appear; *United States Diplomatic and Consular Staff in Tehran*, [1980] *I.C.J. Reports* 3, where Iran did not appear; and *Case concerning Military and Paramilitary Activities in and against Nicaragua Case* (Nicaragua v. United States), *Jurisdiction*, [1984] I.C.J. Reports 392 and *Merits*, [1986] I.C.J. Reports 14, where the United States did not appear at the merits phase.

9 See: Russian Federation, *Note Verbale No. 11945*, 22 October 2013 delivered to the Netherlands, which states that "the Russian Side does not accept the arbitration procedure under Annex VII … initiated by the Netherlands … and does not intend to participate in the proceedings before the International Tribunal for the Law of the Sea in respect of the request of … the Netherlands for the prescription of provisional measures," available on the website of the International Tribunal for the Law of the Sea (ITLOS) at www.itlos.org. See further: *The "Arctic Sunrise" Case* (Netherlands v. Russian Federation), *Provisional Measures Order*, 22 November 2013, available on the ITLOS website; *The "Arctic Sunrise" Arbitration* (Netherlands v. Russian Federation), *Award on Jurisdiction*, 26 November 2014 and *Award on the Merits*, 14 August 2015, on the PCA website, *supra* note 2.

10 J.G. MERRILLS, INTERNATIONAL DISPUTE SETTLEMENT 170 (2005).

made by the Philippines[11] and overall, accepted the claims and arguments on the merits asserted by the Philippines.[12]

The short and long-term consequences, if any, of the *Arbitration* on the relations among and the actions of China, the Philippines and the other States with a clear interest in the South China Sea remain for the future but will be dictated largely by political and strategic considerations.

This contribution will focus on legal issues and matters, specifically those concerning: first, the legal status of the 2016 *Award*; second, the decision of the Tribunal that the subject-matter of the dispute regarding the legal status of certain maritime features as rocks or islands was within the jurisdiction of the Tribunal as this subject matter did not deal with territorial sovereignty or maritime boundary delimitation; and finally, the decision of the Tribunal that it had jurisdiction to deal with China's historic rights claim and the nine-dash line and the decision on the merits on this matter.

## II Legal Status of the Award[13]

As noted above, there are two parts of the *Award*, the first dealing with the question of whether the Tribunal had jurisdiction over the subject matter of the Philippine submissions and, second, the Tribunal having decided it had jurisdiction to deal with most of the Philippine submissions, the merits of the submissions made by the Philippines.

In respect of the jurisdiction of the Tribunal to deal with the subject matter of the Philippine submission, the LOS Convention, Article 288(4) provides: "In the event of a dispute as to whether a court or tribunal has jurisdiction, the matter shall be settled by decision of that court or tribunal." Thus, pursuant to the LOS Convention, a court or tribunal has the competence (jurisdiction) to decide whether it has jurisdiction (competence) to determine whether both States involved have consented to have a tribunal deal with a disputed matter. This wording follows the Statute of the International Court of Justice, Article 36(6) that: "In the event of a dispute as to whether the Court has jurisdiction,

---

11 *Award, supra* note 2, at para.1203, for the exception, see para. 1203(6)(a).

12 *Ibid.*, at para. 1203(B).

13 Part of this section has been drawn, with modification, from: T.L. McDorman, *The South China Sea Arbitration and the Future of the Law of the Sea Convention Dispute Settlement Regime* a paper prepared for the International Conference on the South China Sea Disputes and International Law, hosted by Soochow University School of Law, Taipei, Taiwan, April 2016.

the matter shall be settled by the decision of the Court."[14] In addition and of direct relevant to the *South China Sea Arbitration* is the last sentence of Annex VII, Article 9 of the LOS Convention which deals with the non-appearance of a State before a tribunal established pursuant to the LOS Convention: "Before making its award, the arbitral tribunal must satisfy itself not only that it has jurisdiction over the dispute but also that the claim is well founded in law."

As already noted, the *South China Sea Arbitral Tribunal* found that it had jurisdiction to consider the merits of almost all of the claims made by the Philippines and decided in favour of the Philippines on the merits.[15]

The LOS Convention, which is the basis of the relevant international law regarding the creation, operation, jurisdiction and results of the South China Sea Arbitral Tribunal is very clear in Annex VII, Arbitration, Article 11 that: "The award of the arbitral tribunal shall be *final and binding* and without appeal .... It shall be complied with by the parties to the dispute." (emphasis added)

Based on this, there is no argument to be made that non-participation or non-appearance by a State changes or effects the "final and binding" nature of the *Award*. Moreover, while China has asserted both after the release of the 2015 *Award on Jurisdiction* and the 2016 *Award* that the *Awards* are "null and void" and have "no binding force,"[16] there is no legal basis in the LOS Convention for such assertions. Moreover, there is little international legal support for the view that State-to-State arbitration awards (as opposed to international commercial arbitration awards, which typically involve a commercial party and a State) can be determined, particularly unilaterally, to be null and void and thus not legally binding. Nevertheless, as a counter argument to the above, the United States expressed the view that regarding the decision of the International Court of Justice in the 1984 *Nicaragua Case*,[17] that the Court had jurisdiction to hear the merits of the dispute, that:

---

14 Statute of the International Court of Justice, on the website of the International Court of Justice at <icj-cij.org>.

15 *Award, supra note* 2, at para.1203, for the exception, see para. 1203(6)(a).

16 China, *Statement of the Ministry of Foreign Affairs on the Award on Jurisdiction and Admissibility of the South China Sea Arbitration by the Arbitral Tribunal Established at the Request of the Republic of the Philippines*, 30 October 2015, on the Ministry of Foreign Affairs of China website at www.fmprc.gov.cn/mfa_eng/zxxx_662805/t1310474.shtml and *Statement of the Ministry of Foreign Affairs on the Award of 12 July 2016 of the Arbitral Tribunal Established at the Request of the Republic of the Philippines*, 12 July 2016, on the Ministry of Foreign Affairs of China website at www.fmprc.gov.cn/nanhai/eng/snhwtlcwj_1/t1379492.htm.

17 *Nicaragua Case, supra* note 8.

> [I]t is not enough to claim that, just because Article 36(6) of the Court's statute says that it *may* decide jurisdiction, the Court, indeed, *did* have jurisdiction in this particular dispute. No court, including the International Court of Justice, has the legal power to assert jurisdiction where there is no basis for that jurisdiction. (emphasis in original).[18]

China has further stated that it "neither accepts nor recognizes" the *Award*.[19] There is a modest practice of States having opted not to accept or recognize, and thus not comply with, decisions of the International Court[20] and in the case of the Russian Federation, with the decisions of International Tribunal for the Law of the Sea (ITLOS) and the tribunal established pursuant to the LOS Convention.[21] As noted by Merrills, adjudications that involve both legal and significant political matters where the latter remains unaddressed are "unlikely to be respected."[22]

## III The Rocks-or Island Legal Status of Features: The Issue of Jurisdiction

It was the position of the Philippines that the Tribunal had jurisdiction to determine whether certain insular features in the South China Sea were rocks or islands for the purposes of ocean jurisdiction entitlement, even though these features were subject to territorial sovereignty disputes, as this involved interpretation of the provisions of the LOS Convention.[23] Further, the Philippines asserted that the territorial sovereignty dispute with China was "entirely irrelevant to the Tribunal's jurisdiction" since at no point would the Tribunal be

18 U.S. Statement, 3 November 1986, U.N. General Assembly, reproduced in United States, *Department of State Bulletin* (January 1987), Vol. 2118, at p. 83.

19 China, *Foreign Ministry Statement*, 12 July 2016, *supra* note 15.

20 Four cases have been identified as being ones where a State has "openly and wilfully chosen to disregard" a decision of the International Court. CONSTANZE SCHULTE, COMPLIANCE WITH DECISIONS OF THE INTERNATIONAL COURT OF JUSTICE 271 (2004) and see: MALCOM N. SHAW, INTERNATIONAL LAW 1104 (2008). The cases are: Albania in the *Corfu Channel Case*, [1949] I.C.J. Reports 4; Iceland in the *Fisheries Jurisdiction Case*, *supra* note 7; Iran in the *Hostages Case*, *supra* note 8 and the United States in the *Nicaragua Case*, *supra* note 8.

21 *Arctic Sunrise Case*, *supra* note 9.

22 MERRILLS, *supra* note 10, at 171.

23 *Award on Jurisdiction*, *supra* note 2, at para.140.

required to express a view on the extent or existence of China's sovereignty[24] and that "there is no need to determine sovereignty before considering the existence of maritime entitlements … of features in the South China Sea" since the legal of a maritime feature as a rock or an island is a matter of objective determination unrelated to sovereignty.[25]

China in a "Position Paper" issued on 7 December 2014,[26] put forth a number of arguments concerning the jurisdiction of the Tribunal. For the purposes here two were of importance. China argued that the heart of the dispute between it and the Philippines concerned questions of territorial sovereignty and that such questions did not involve disputes respecting the "interpretation or application" of the LOS Convention as set out in Article 288. Second, as an alternative, was the argument that the rock or island subject matter of the dispute concerned maritime boundary delimitation and that as a result of China's Article Declaration of 26 August 2006,[27] such subject matter was exempted from the compulsory adjudicative jurisdiction under the LOS Convention pursuant to Article 298(1)(a)(i).[28]

There had been a number of international adjudications involving maritime boundary delimitation and territorial sovereignty disputes.[29] In the *Eritrea-Yemen Arbitration* is an example of the sequential approach taken in these cases where the parties agreeing to utilize a two-stage approach for the Arbitration with the territorial sovereignty issue dealt with in the first stage and the delimitation issues (including the legal of maritime features) dealt

24 *Ibid.*, at para. 141.

25 *Ibid.*, at para. 144.

26 China, *Position Paper on the Matter of Jurisdiction in the South China Sea Arbitration Initiated by the Republic of the Philippines*, 7 December 2014, available on the website of the Ministry of Foreign Affairs of China at www.fmprc.gov.cn/nanhai/eng/snhwtlcwj_1/t1368899.htm.

27 China, *Declaration of 25 August 2006*, available on the U.N. Division for Ocean Affairs and the Law of the Sea (DOALOS) website at www.un.org/Depts/los/index.htm.

28 LOS Convention, *supra* note 3, Article 298(1)(a)(i): 1. When signing, ratifying or acceding to this Convention or at any time thereafter, a State may, without prejudice to the obligations arising under Section 1, declare in writing that it does not accept any one or more of the procedures provided for in Section 2 with respect to one or more of the following categories of disputes: (a)(i) disputes concerning the interpretation or application of articles 15, 74 and 83 relating to sea boundary delimitations, or those involving historic bays or titles, ….

29 See, for example: *Maritime Delimitation and Territorial Questions between Qatar and Bahrain*, [2001] *I.C.J. Reports* 40; *Territorial and Maritime Dispute between Nicaragua and Honduras in the Caribbean Sea* (Nicaragua v. Honduras), [2007] I.C.J. Reports 659; and *Territorial and Maritime Dispute* (Nicaragua v. Colombia), [2012] I.C.J. Reports 624; 40 Honduras (2012).

with in the second stage.[30] However, none of the above cases arose pursuant to the compulsory dispute settlement regime in the LOS Convention and, thus, none of the cases raised questions respecting the jurisdiction of a court or tribunal established pursuant to the provisions of the LOS Convention. Thus, the *South China Sea Arbitration* was the first time that an international court or tribunal, without the direct consent of the States through a special agreement, was asked to assess the legal status of maritime features as rocks or islands that were subject to a territorial sovereignty dispute. It was also the first time a court or tribunal had to deal with an Article 298(1)(a)(i) declaration.

In reaching its conclusion that it had jurisdiction to determine the rock or island status of the contested features, the Tribunal stated that it: "does not accept ... that it follows from the existence of a dispute over sovereignty that sovereignty is also the appropriate characterization" of the Philippine claims.[31] The Tribunal took the view that:

- none of the Philippine Submissions required "an implicit determination of sovereignty;"
- any decision it reached on the Submissions would not advance or detract from either State's sovereignty claims;
- the resolution of the Philippines' claims did not require the Tribunal "to first render a decision on sovereignty;" and
- the "actual objective" of the Philippines' claims was not to advance its position in the Parties' dispute over sovereignty.[32]

In regard of China's alternative position on the characterization of the dispute as one relating to maritime boundary delimitation, the Tribunal did not accept China's assessment stating that it was "not convinced that ... the dispute is properly characterized as relating to maritime boundary delimitation;" and that: "It does not follow ... that a dispute over an issue that may be considered in the course of a maritime boundary delimitation constitutes a dispute over maritime boundary delimitation itself."[33] More specifically, the Tribunal commented that "the existence of an entitlement to maritime zones is distinct from a dispute concerning the delimitation of those zones in an area where

30 See: *Award of the Arbitral Tribunal in the First Stage between Eritrea and Yemen* (*Territorial Sovereignty and Scope of the Dispute*), 9 October 1998, *Reports of International Arbitral Awards*, Vol. XXII, at 209–332 and *Award of the Arbitral Tribunal in the Second Stage between Eritrea and Yemen* (*Maritime Delimitation*), *Reports of International Arbitral Awards*, Vol. XXII, at 335–410.

31 *Award on Jurisdiction*, *supra* note 2, at para. 152.

32 *Ibid.*, at para. 153.

33 *Ibid.*, at para. 155.

entitlements overlap" and pointed out that "... a dispute over claimed entitlements may exist without overlap, where – for instance – a State claims maritime zones in an area understood by other States to form part of the high seas or the Area for the purposes of the Convention."[34] This was followed by the comment that:

> [T]he Philippines has challenged the existence and extent of maritime entitlements claimed by China in the South China Sea. This is not a dispute over maritime boundaries. The Philippines has not requested the Tribunal to delimit any overlapping entitlements ...[35]

As "the Tribunal does not consider the disputes between the States to be about maritime boundary delimitation," the Tribunal decided that Article 298(1)(a)(i) of the LOS Convention was not applicable to deprive the Tribunal of jurisdiction to determine the rock-or-island status of the contested features.[36]

The Tribunal's characterization of the dispute as not being about territorial sovereignty was premised on the view that the Tribunal had not been asked, nor saw it as necessary in considering the relevant submissions of the Philippines, to engage in any way in making a determination of territorial sovereignty. Similarly, the Tribunal's characterization of the dispute as not involving maritime boundary delimitation was premised on the view that the Tribunal had not been asked, nor saw it as necessary in considering the relevant submissions of the Philippines, to engage in formal maritime boundary delimitation.

The Tribunal's approach was that if it was not directly required or called upon to determine a territorial sovereignty dispute or to formally delimit a maritime boundary, that the Tribunal was not interfering in or prejudicing the territorial sovereignty of either State or interfering in or prejudicing maritime boundary delimitation. The Tribunal was not troubled by what States may "perceive" as an interference in a territorial sovereignty/territorial integrity matter or that an important element of a State's sovereignty over a maritime feature (as the coastal State) is its assessment and assertion of the legal status

34 *Ibid.*, at para. 156.

35 *Ibid.*, at para. 157.

36 *Ibid.*, at para. 366. For a perspective suggesting a broader meaning of the "disputes concerning the interpretation or application of articles 15, 74 and 83" wording in Article 298(1)(a)(i) than was adopted by the Tribunal, see: Chris Whomersley, *The South China Sea: The Award of the Tribunal in the Case Brought by Philippines against China – A Critique*" 15 CHINESE JOURNAL OF INTERNATIONAL LAW (2016) (in press).

of a maritime feature for the purposes of maritime boundary delimitation discussions with neighboring coastal States (or before a court or tribunal). This approach by the Tribunal appears to turn the classic law of the sea principle that the "land dominates the sea" on its head.[37]

## IV The Nine-Dash Line and Historic Rights[38]

The principal jurisdictional question concerning the nine-dash line and possible Chinese historic rights therein was whether such a claim was captured by the wording of LOS Convention, Article 298(1)(a)(i) "... disputes ... involving historic bays or title."[39] China had not directly raised the "historic bays or title" exemption in the December 2014 "Position Paper."[40] The principal issue on the merits was the relationship between the historic rights asserted by China as existing within the nine-dash line and the rights of the Philippines based on the LOS Convention in areas where the claimed historic rights were in areas beyond China's 200 nm exclusive economic zone (EEZ) or continental shelf and within the EEZ/continental shelf of the Philippines.

To deal with both the jurisdictional and merits questions, it was necessary for the Tribunal to assess what was being claimed by China within the nine-dash line, in other words, what was "the nature of any historic rights claimed by China" within the nine-dash line.[41] The Tribunal stated that: "It is for China to determine the scope of its maritime claims."[42] However, the Tribunal noted that this was "complicated by some ambiguity in China's position"[43] and commented in both the *Award on Jurisdiction* and the *Award* that China had not

37 For a more detailed view, see: Bing Bing Jia, *The Principle of the Domination of the Land over the Sea: A Historical Perspective on the Adaptability of the Law of the Sea to New Challenges*, 57 GERMAN YEARBOOK OF INTERNATIONAL LAW 1–32 (2014).

38 Part of this section has been drawn, with modification, from: T.L. McDorman, *The 2016 South China Sea Arbitration: Comments on the Nine-Dash Line and Historic Rights* a paper prepared for the "Public International Law Colloquium on Maritime Disputes Settlement" sponsored by the Chinese Society of International Law, Hong Kong, July 2016. For an excellent analysis of this aspect of the South China Sea Arbitration, see: Sophia Kopela, *Historic Titles and Historic Rights in the Law of the Sea in the Light of the South China Sea Arbitration*, 48 OCEAN DEVELOPMENT AND INTERNATIONAL LAW (2017) (in press).

39 *Award on Jurisdiction, supra* note 2, at para.152 and *Award, supra* note 2, at para. 171.

40 China, *Position Paper, supra* note 26.

41 *Award, supra* note 2, at para. 171.

42 *Ibid.*, at para. 206.

43 *Ibid.*, at para. 180.

"expressly clarified the nature and scope of its claimed historic rights" or "the meaning of the 'nine-dash line'".[44] China, having chosen not to participate in the proceedings and thus not present to make its claims clear, the Tribunal determined that "it necessarily falls to the Tribunal to ascertain, on the basis of conduct" what was the content of China's historic rights assertion within nine-dash line.[45] The Tribunal undertook an examination of China's statements and actions to assess what it was the China was claiming as being historic rights,[46] concluding "that China claims rights to living and non-living resources within the 'nine-dash line' but (apart from the territorial sea generated by any islands) does not consider that those waters form part of its territorial sea or internal waters."[47]

The Tribunal undertook a modest review of the relevant international cases and commentaries that shed light on the meaning of the terms historic rights, waters and title.[48] The conclusion reached was that there was a recognizable usage made of the terms.[49]

> The term "historic rights" is general in nature and can describe any rights that a State may possess that would not normally arise under the general rules of international law, absent particular historical circumstances. Historic rights may include sovereignty, but may equally include more limited rights, such as fishing rights or rights of access, that fall well short of a claim of sovereignty. "Historic title", in contrast, is used specifically to refer to historic sovereignty to land or maritime areas. "Historic waters" is simply a term for historic title over maritime areas, typically exercised either as a claim to internal waters ...[50]

The examination of the term historic title in Article 298(1)(a)(i) centered on the wording in the 1958 Convention on the Territorial Sea and Contiguous Zone[51] and the 1982 LOS Convention. Both Conventions recognized the existence of "historic bays" (aligned with historic waters[52]), albeit in a round-about manner,

---

44 *Ibid.*, at para. 180 and *Award on Jurisdiction*, *supra* note 2, at para. 160.

45 See: *ibid.*, at para. 206.

46 See: *ibid.*, at paras. 172–187, 200 and 207–214.

47 *Ibid.*, at para. 214 and see para. 232.

48 *Ibid.*, at paras. 218–225.

49 *Ibid.*, at para. 225.

50 *Ibid.*

51 Convention on the Territorial Sea and Contiguous Zone, opened for signature 29 April 1958, 516 U.N.T.S. 205 (entered into force October 10, 1964).

52 See: *Case Concerning the Land, Island and Maritime Frontier Dispute* (El Salvador/Honduras: Nicaragua Intervening), [1992] I.C.J. Reports 351, at para. 383.

where it is stated that the juridical bay provisions in the Conventions do not apply to historic bays.[53] Neither the 1982 nor the 1958 Convention provides any indication of when historic claims to waters exist, such as historic bays, or the consequence of waters being historic.[54] The same can said of "historic title" found in Article 12(1) of the 1958 Convention and Article 15 of the LOS Convention with one exception, where historic title exists it has the consequence that the rule of applying an equidistance line where territorial seas overlap is not applicable. As well, and noted above, Article 298(1)(a)(i) provides an exercisable exemption from compulsory adjudication pursuant to the LOS Convention where the subject matter of the dispute concerns "historic title."

The Tribunal took the view that "historic title" wording in the 1958 Convention was tied directly to the historic terminology used in the 1951 *Anglo-Norwegian Fisheries Case*,[55] where the area in question was "an area of sea claimed exceptionally as internal waters"[56] and that this was understood as being the meaning of historic title in Article 298(1)(a)(i) – "claims to sovereignty over maritime areas derived from historical circumstances"[57] – historic waters.

Having determined that China was claiming historic rights and not historic waters, the Tribunal concluded that the Article 298(1)(a)(i) exception to compulsory adjudication was not available as regards China's historic claims.[58]

While questions can be raised, the Tribunal has clarified the meaning and consequences that attaches to historic rights, historic waters and historic title such that States will be well aware of the legal effect of the use of the differing terms particularly in the context of Article 298(1)(a)(i).

As already noted, the principal issue on the merits was the relationship between the historic rights asserted by China as existing within the nine-dash line and the rights of the Philippines based on the LOS Convention.

As the Tribunal makes clear:

> The Convention does not include any express provisions preserving or protecting historic rights that are at variance with the Convention. On the contrary, the Convention supersedes earlier rights and agreements to the extent of any incompatibility. The Convention is comprehensive in setting out the nature of the exclusive economic zone and continental

53 LOS Convention, *supra* note 3, Article 10(6) and Territorial Sea Convention, *supra* note 51, Article 7(6).

54 *Case Concerning the Continental Shelf* (Tunisia/Libya), [1982] I.C.J. Reports 18, at para. 100.

55 *Fisheries Case* (United Kingdom v. Norway), [1951] I.C.J. Reports 116.

56 *Award, supra* note 2, at para. 221.

57 *Ibid.*, at para. 226.

58 *Ibid.*, at para. 229.

> shelf rights of other States within those zones. China's claim to historic rights is not compatible with these provisions.[59]

Interestingly, the Tribunal referenced the statement of a Chinese delegate made during the negotiation of the fishing provisions of the LOS Convention that resolutely opposes the idea of historic fishing in another State's EEZ commenting that this position is "incompatible" with China's historic rights claim.[60]

The Tribunal also referenced the 1984 *Gulf of Maine Case*[61] where the United States argued that historic fishing rights had a role to play in the delimitation of 200 nm zones and the International Court response that as the waters in question where previously high seas that no special rights could accrue where the fishers in question were simply exercising a high seas right open and available to all.[62]

Beyond fishing rights, the Tribunal, albeit in a different section of the *Award*, noted the difficulty of the possibility of any kind of historic right as regards the resources of the continental shelf given the recent (1960s) development of significant offshore oil and gas activities.[63] Note might also have been made that the continental shelf regime dating back to the 1958 Continental Shelf Convention[64] was premised on preventing States from be able to assert an historic right to shelf resources where that shelf was the natural prolongation of another State.[65]

The overall view of the Tribunal was that:

> It is simply inconceivable that the drafters of the Convention could have gone to such lengths to forge a consensus text and to prohibit any but a few express reservations while, at the same time, anticipating that the resulting Convention would be subordinate to broad claims of historic rights."[66]

59 *Ibid.*, at para. 246 and see also para. 261.

60 *Ibid.*, at para. 252.

61 *Case concerning Delimitation of the Maritime Boundary in the Gulf of Maine Area* (Canada/United States), [1984] I.C.J. Reports 246.

62 *Award, supra note* 2, at para. 256 and see further at para. 270.

63 *Ibid.*, at para. 270.

64 Convention on the Continental Shelf, 499 U.N.T.S. 311.

65 See: T.L. McDorman, *Rights and Jurisdiction over Resources in the South China Sea: UNCLOS and the 'Nine-Dash Line* in S. JAYAKUMAR, T. KOH AND R. BECKMAN, eds., THE SOUTH CHINA SEA DISPUTES AND THE LAW OF THE SEA 159 – 160 (2014).

66 *Award, supra* note 2, at para. 254.

Thus, the Tribunal concluded that as the LOS Convention "leaves no space for an assertion of historic rights,"... "China's claim to historic rights to the living and non-living resources within the "nine-dash line" is incompatible with the Convention...."[67]

The Tribunal's support of the primacy of the LOS Convention in the areas of fisheries and continental shelf resources is reassuring and may be an important result in preventing the reopening of fisheries disputes internationally and bilaterally.

The decisions on jurisdiction and the merits of the Tribunal regarding the nine-dash line and China's claimed historic rights are based are based on a specific package of evidence. If China were to produce new or different evidence or perhaps clarify using different terminology what is being claimed within the nine-dash, then a reassessment of the *Award* might be necessary. Perhaps in anticipation of this, the Tribunal indicated what evidence would be required to sustain a claim of a historic right arising where the waters or activity were, prior to the LOS Convention, subject to high seas freedoms.[68]

## V Conclusion

This diverse article has touched upon three aspects of the *South China Sea Arbitration*. First, the legal status of the *Award* is clear – it is binding on both China and the Philippines. Nevertheless, there is a small practice of States that have rejected such binding decision. Second, the Tribunal in determining whether it had jurisdiction to deal with many of the Philippine submissions drew a sharp distinction between the entitlement of an insular feature to either 12 or 200 nm and both the question of the territorial ownership of the feature and maritime boundary delimitation. It is uncertain whether this legal distinction accords with the legal/political understanding held by States of the relationship between the rocks-islands difference and territorial sovereignty and maritime boundary delimitation. Third, the Tribunal clearly and correctly rejected the idea, presented to them in the form of China's nine-dash line, that a State a party to the LOS Convention can have historic rights to fish or to the resources of the seafloor within the 200 nm zone of another State.

67 *Ibid.*, at para. 261.

68 See: *ibid.*, at paras. 265–272.

# The Political Implications of the South China Sea Ruling on Sino-Philippine Relations and Regional Stability

*Hsiao-Chi Hsu*[1]

## 1 Introduction

On 12 July 2016, the Arbitral Tribunal at the Permanent Court of Arbitration (PCA) in The Hague released its ruling on the South China Sea (SCS) arbitration case brought by the Philippines against China, indicating that the latter's expansive maritime claims in this area have no "legal basis." This decision triggered complex responses from a variety of countries. China immediately issued its rejection of the ruling, calling it "null and void."[2] The United States (U.S.), a major ally of the Philippines, called on both parties to abide by the ruling, arguing that the panel's decision is "legal and binding."[3] However, while it was successful in this legal battle, the Philippines issued a complicated response. Immediately following the PCA's press release, Philippine Secretary of Foreign Affairs Perfecto Yasay Jr. responded by expressing Manila's welcome of the ruling. He also noted the Philippines' strong "respect for this milestone decision as an important contribution to ongoing efforts in addressing disputes in the South China Sea." Unlike the U.S., Yasay did not urge China to comply with the ruling. Rather, he called on "all those concerned to exercise *restraint* and *sobriety*."[4] The Philippine Presidential Communications Office then announced the government's plan to study the decision and release "a complete and thorough interpretation" of it in five days, while Presidential Spokesperson

---

1 Assistant Professor, Graduate Institute of Political Science, National Taiwan Normal University, Taipei.

2 Associated Press, *China rejects ruling on South China Sea as "null and void"*, INQUIRER.NET (Manila, 13 July 2016), available at http://globalnation.inquirer.net/141037/china-rejects-ruling-south-china-sea-null-void.

3 Agence France-Presse, US: South China Sea ruling "legal and binding", INQUIRER.NET (Manila, 13 July 2016), available at http://globalnation.inquirer.net/141051/us-south-china-sea-ruling-legally-binding.

4 *Full Text: DFA Secretary Yasay Statement on West PH Sea Ruling*, INQUIRER.NET (Manila, 12 July 2016), available at http://globalnation.inquirer.net/140968/full-text-dfa-foreign-affairs-perfecto-yasay-west-philippine-sea. Emphasis added by the author.

Ernesto Abella reiterated Manila's promise to "exercise restraint and sobriety."[5] The government's prudent response was in stark contrast to the Filipino public's excitement over the arbitration result, but consistent with the newly inaugurated President Rodrigo Duterte's desire to seek improvements in his country's relations with China. In fact, just days before the decision, Duterte had stated that he did not want to "taunt" Beijing or "flaunt" the SCS ruling.[6] However, the Philippines' arbitration victory has resulted in an increasing uncertainty over the future of Sino-Philippine relations and regional stability. On the one hand, the ruling infuriated the Chinese government and instigated nationalist sentiment in both countries, making foreign policy concession on the SCS issues more difficult and costly. On the other hand, the ruling might further increase SCS stakeholders' desire to participate actively in maritime competition. These factors make the situation in the SCS more complicated and difficult to predict. To explore the impact of the arbitration, this paper offers a preliminary analysis of its political implications on Philippine foreign policy orientation and on regional stability in the SCS area.

## II The Background of the South China Sea Arbitration

The reason prompting the Philippines to file the SCS arbitration was the ongoing dispute over the Spratly/Nansha Islands. There are indications of potentially rich reserves of natural resources such as oil and natural gas in the SCS. As such, territorial disputes—especially those between China and Vietnam and China and the Philippines—have become increasingly contentious over the past decade. Being a country highly dependent on energy imports, the Philippines has been eager to secure the sources and reduce the costs of its energy supply by controlling more oil and gas resources in the SCS. This was especially apparent after the country's economic losses due to the 2008 global financial crisis and since the rapid oil price surge in 2010. The conflict of interests between Manila's desire for natural resources in the SCS and China's maritime expansion, thus, further exacerbated their bilateral frictions. Besides economic and energy considerations, former President Benigno Aquino III (2010–2016)

5 Nestor Corrales, *PH gov't to release interpretation of UN ruling in 5 days*, INQUIRER.NET (Manila, 13 July 2016), available at http://globalnation.inquirer.net/141065/ph-govt-to-release-interpretation-of-un-ruling-in-5-days.

6 Raul Dancel, *Filipinos Cheer Hague Ruling On South China Sea With Funny Memes*, THE STRAIT TIMES (Singapore, 13 July 2016), available at http://www.straitstimes.com/asia/se-asia/filipinos-cheer-hague-ruling-on-south-china-sea-with-funny-memes.

considered the modernization of the Philippine air force and navy a policy priority to better protect national interests. To achieve this goal, Aquino saw a closer relationship with the U.S. necessary for enhancing military support from Washington.[7] The U.S. policy of seeking "strategic rebalance" in Asia since 2010 further complicated the regional situation by encouraging the Philippine president to take a tougher stance toward China. As a result, Sino-Philippine relations have significantly deteriorated and territorial conflicts between the two sides have escalated in recent years.

The conflict between China and the Philippines reached a dangerous point when the two countries engaged in a series of military confrontations over the Scarborough Shoal/Huangyan Island in 2012. On 8 April 2012, a Philippine surveillance plane detected eight Chinese fishing vessels entering the disputed waters. The Philippine naval vessel BRP *Gregorio del Pilar* attempted to arrest the Chinese fishing crews two days later, but was blocked by two Chinese maritime surveillance ships.[8] The tensions quickly escalated, as both sides continued to send more ships into the disputed area in order to protect their territorial claims. The military standoff finally came to an end in June 2012, when the Philippines withdrew its military forces from the area. China, however, has retained its presence on and control over the island. The Aquino administration strongly criticized this result, but finally admitted that a return to the shoal was impossible by the end of the year. It then turned to the International Tribunal for the Law of the Sea (ITLOS) under the United Nations Convention of the Law of the Sea (UNCLOS), Annex VII, to address the SCS disputes.

The Philippines initiated the arbitration by sending the "Notification and Statement of Claim on West Philippine Sea" to the Chinese government in January 2013. China responded with a "note verbale", which rejected the Philippine claims and returned its notification. China insisted on settling their SCS disputes through bilateral negotiation, but the Philippines continued its legal pursuit. A five-member Arbitral Tribunal was later formed to hear the case with the PCA acting as the registry in the proceedings.[9] In response, China reiterated its rejection to accept the arbitration and to participate in the proceedings. As the deadline to submit its counter-memorial to the Philippines'

---

7 Kaicheng Lin, *Changes in the Philippines' South China Sea Policy*, 3 FORUM OF WORLD ECONOMICS & POLITICS 60, 62 (2015) (in Chinese).

8 Ely Ratner, *Learning the Lessons of Scarborough Shoal Reef*, THE NATIONAL INTEREST (21 November 2013), available at http://nationalinterest.org/commentary/learning-the-lessons-scarborough-reef-9442.

9 Permanent Court of Arbitration, *Arbitration between the Republic of the Philippines and the People's Republic of China: Arbitral Tribunal Establishes Rules of Procedure and Initial Timetable*, 27 August 2013, available at http://www.pcacases.com/web/sendAttach/227.

approached, China issued a "Position Paper of the Government of the People's Republic of China on the Matter of Jurisdiction in the South China Sea Arbitration Initiated by the Republic of the Philippines". The document argues that the PCA lacks jurisdiction in the SCS case since "[t]he essence of the subject-matter of the arbitration is the territorial sovereignty over several maritime features in the South China Sea, which is beyond the scope of the Convention and does not concern the interpretation or application of the Convention."[10] However, on 29 October 2015, the Tribunal released its "Award on Jurisdiction and Admissibility" regarding the SCS case. The panel decided that "it does have jurisdiction with respect to the matters raised in seven of the Philippines' Submissions" and thus would "convene a further hearing on the Philippines' claims." The other eight submissions in the claims would also be considered further in the following proceedings.[11] The final decision of the arbitration came out on 12 July 2016, which was in favor of almost all the claims made by the Philippines. It not only rejected China's nine-dashed line claim and historical rights in the SCS, but also supported the Philippines' claim that none of the features in the SCS qualifies as an island entitled to an exclusive economic zone (EEZ) of 200 nautical miles. Its conclusion that the Taiwan-governed Taiping Island (Itu Aba) does not fulfill the requirements of an "island" according to Article 121(3) of UNCLOS was especially controversial and thus was met with strong criticisms from both Taipei and Beijing. Due to the high level of sensitivity of the SCS disputes, the ruling immediately attracted heated discussions about its legitimacy and legality, as well as its political and security implications in the SCS region.

## III Political Implications of the South China Sea Arbitration on Philippine Foreign Policy

When considering the domestic political implications on the Philippines of the SCS ruling, several factors should be taken into consideration: the current administration's foreign policy position, rising nationalist sentiment in the

10 Ministry of Foreign Affairs of the People's Republic of China, *Position Paper of the Government of the People's Republic of China on the Matter of Jurisdiction in the South China Sea Arbitration Initiated by the Republic of the Philippines*, 7 December 2014, available at http://www.fmprc.gov.cn/mfa_eng/zxxx_662805/t1217147.shtml.

11 Permanent Court of Arbitration, *The South China Sea Arbitration* (*The Republic of the Philippines v. The Republic of China*), 29 October 2015, available at http://www.pcacases.com/web/sendAttach/1503.

country, China's response to the ruling, and the U.S. policy position in the East and South China Seas. These factors will influence the direction of Manila's China and U.S. policies in general, and its SCS policy in particular.

## 1 *Duterte's Foreign Policy Position*

The current administration's foreign policy orientation plays the most important role in shaping the country's SCS policies. Unlike Aquino's pro-U.S. orientation, Duterte sees a friendly relationship with China as a priority for his country's foreign policy. In early 2016 during the presidential campaign, when most candidates were reluctant to provide details of their China policy positions in front of rising anti-China sentiment among the public, Duterte was one of just two candidates who publicly expressed a willingness to "explor[e] joint development agreements with China."[12] After winning the election, Duterte has continued to emphasize the importance of economic cooperation with China and has on several occasions expressed his intention to "reevaluate his country's close ties with Washington."[13] Against this backdrop, the Philippine victory in the SCS ruling seemed to create a diplomatic inconvenience as opposed to being an asset for the new president. This can be clearly demonstrated by the administration's cautious response to the SCS ruling right after its announcement—so noticeable that it immediately drew close attention on domestic social media. For instance, Foreign Affairs Secretary Yasay's lukewarm responses to the ruling during his press conference were strongly criticized and mocked. A picture of his "gloomy face", posing a striking contrast to his country's legal victory, became broadly circulated and discussed on the internet.[14] The foreign secretary's somber reaction reflects the Duterte administration's dilemma regarding the SCS ruling. On the one hand, Duterte wants to maximize his country's economic and trade benefits by reestablishing good relations with China as soon as possible. To pursue this goal, he has tried to de-escalate the SCS disputes since taking office. On the other hand, however, the Philippines' sweeping victory in the SCS arbitration will most likely

---

12 Richard Javad Heydarian, *Tale of Two Nations: How Philippines Election Will Impact Manila's China Policy*, ASIA TIMES (Hong Kong, 11 April 2016), available at http://www.atimes.com/article/tale-of-two-nations-how-philippines-election-will-impact-manilas-china-policy/.

13 Eric Baculinao, *Philippines President Rodrigo Duterte, Asia's 'Trump,' Eyes Closer China Ties*, NBC NEWS (New York, 30 June 2016), available at http://www.nbcnews.com/news/world/philippines-president-rodrigo-duterte-asia-s-trump-eyes-closer-china-n600886.

14 Janvic Mateo, *Netizens ask: Why So Sad, Yasay?*, THE PHILIPPINE STAR (Manila, 14 July 2016), available at http://www.philstar.com/headlines/2016/07/14/1602694/netizens-ask-why-so-sad-yasay.

create greater political hurdles for Duterte to make significant concessions over the disputes considering the public's strong support of the ruling and the possibility that his political enemies might use the issue to attack him. Therefore, how to break the country's diplomatic stalemate with China without giving up its victory in the SCS arbitration poses a difficult challenge to the new administration.

Duterte's strategy to cope with this dilemma was to seek direct talks with China first. His decision to designate former president Fidel V. Ramos as special envoy to China paid off. Ramos' meetings with "old friends" in Hong Kong successfully broke the bilateral stalemate and eventually led to Duterte's official visit to Beijing.[15] This was an important foreign policy success for the president, for he was able to obtain significant economic benefits from China during his trip. To demonstrate its welcome of the president, China lifted its restrictions on the importation of Philippine fruits that had been in place since the 2012 conflict over the Scarborough Shoal/Huangyan Island. It also expressed interest in increasing its imports of Philippine agricultural and aquaculture products.[16] After the restoration of bilateral relations, the Duterte administration became more open to expressing its willingness to set aside the SCS for the sake of good relations with China.[17] While this policy attitude has resulted in a gradual increase of domestic criticism, there is no sign that the current government might consider a different path at this point.

## 2 *Rising Domestic Nationalism*

A second factor that might shape the SCS ruling's political impact is the growing anti-China sentiment among Filipinos. According to a survey conducted by the Social Weather Stations, Filipinos have expressed a decline in trust of China during the past five years: the net trust (% of much trust minus % of little trust)

---

15 Cris Larano, *Philippines' Duterte Asks Ex-President to Begin Talks in South China Sea Dispute*, THE WALL STREET JOURNAL (New York, 15 July 2016), available at http://www.wsj.com/articles/philippines-duterte-wants-ex-president-ramos-to-meet-with-china-on-maritime-dispute-1468520651; Associated Press, 'Ramos arrives in Hong Kong, talks China ties', the *Philippine Star* (Manila, 9 August 2016), available at http://www.philstar.com/headlines/2016/08/09/1611719/ramos-arrives-hong-kong-talks-china-ties.

16 Louise Maureen Simeon, *China Lifts Import Ban on Philippine Bananas*, THE PHILIPPINE STAR (Manila, 7 October 2016), available at http://www.philstar.com/business/2016/10/07/1630958/china-lifts-import-ban-philippine-bananas.

17 Jim Gomez, *Duterte Says He'll Set Aside Sea Feud Ruling against China*, THE PHILIPPINE STAR (Manila, 17 December 2016), available at http://www.philstar.com:8080/headlines/2016/12/17/1654340/duterte-says-hell-set-aside-sea-feud-ruling-against-china.

dropped from +17 in June 2010 to −45 in June 2015.[18] Along with ongoing territorial disputes, such anti-China sentiment made foreign policy one of the important issues during the 2016 presidential campaign. The Philippines' victory in the SCS arbitration might once again stir anti-China sentiment. For instance, according to news reports, the word "Chexit", an abbreviation of "China exit" which was similar to "Brexit" for the British exit from the E.U., quickly became a popular topic on Twitter in the Philippines.[19] This development suggests that anti-China sentiment might become a factor that the Duterte administration has to take into consideration when handling the SCS disputes in particular, and its relations with China in general.

Domestic support for the SCS ruling might play a role in explaining the fluctuations in the Duterte administration's early responses to it. Two days after the release of the ruling, the Philippine Department of Foreign Affairs issued a statement on the eve of the biennial Asia-Europe Meeting (ASEM) Summit on 15–16 July, indicating that Yasay would discuss "the Philippines' peaceful and rules-based approach on the South China Sea and the need for parties to respect the recent decision of the Arbitral Tribunal" in the summit.[20] Although Yasay still did not urge China to respect the ruling, the fact that he raised the SCS issues in his speech displayed a firmer stance by the Philippines compared to its initial somber reaction on 12 July. Then, however, on 22 July in a speech in Buluan, Maguindanao, Duterte hinted that the Philippines could set aside the SCS ruling as Ramos suggested in exchange for the resumption of bilateral talks with China. He emphasized that the restoration of bilateral relations would benefit the southern island economically. "It's China that has money, not America. America doesn't have money", the president said.[21] Later on, Yasay again brought up the SCS disputes in the 2016 ASEAN Ministers' Meeting

18 Social Weather Stations, Second Quarter 2015 Social Weather Survey, available at https://www.sws.org.ph/pr20150709b.htm.

19 Voltaire Tupaz, *#CHexit: Filipinos Celebrate PH Victory over China*, THE RAPPLER (Manila, 12 July 2016), available at http://www.rappler.com/move-ph/139492-chexit-filipinos-celebrate-ph-victory-china.

20 Agence France-Presse, *Philippines Urges Beijing to 'respect' Sea Ruling*, THE STAR (Manila, 14 July 2016), available at http://www.thestar.com.my/news/regional/2016/07/14/philippines-urges-beijing-to-respect-sea-ruling/; Agence France-Presse, 'Beijing Faces S. China Sea Rebuke At Europe-Asia Summit', *ABC News* (New York, 15 July 2016), available at http://news.abs-cbn.com/overseas/07/14/16/beijing-faces-s-china-sea-rebuke-at-europe-asia-summit.

21 Paterno Esmaquel II, *Duterte Hints He Can Set Aside Hague Ruling For China Talks*, THE RAPPLER (Manila, 23 July 2016), available at http://www.rappler.com/nation/140660-duterte-ramos-hague-ruling-talks-china.

(AMM) on July 25, saying that he hoped a joint communique after the meeting would address the issue. He stressed that the ruling is "final and binding to all parties concerned, a clearly established fact…[with] significant implications for the entire region, not just the coastal States bordering the South China Sea."[22] Duterte also once told the press that "[w]hen the time comes for negotiations, we will not go out of the arbitral award".[23] The above incidents show a high degree of inconsistency in the Duterte administration's attitudes toward the SCS ruling, which seem to reflect the government's difficulty in reconciling its China policy position with its SCS arbitration victory. However, as the two countries began to restore their diplomatic relationship, the Duterte administration became more clear and consistent in its SCS position—to downplay the disputes for the sake of better bilateral relations unless further conflict emerges. This policy principle can be further demonstrated by the Philippine's low-profile response to a U.S. report finding China's installation of "anti-aircraft and anti-missile weapons" on its artificial islands in the South China Sea in early January 2017.[24]

Domestic public opinion continues to disagree with Duterte's current approach of handling the SCS disputes. According to a survey conducted by the Pulse Asia Research Institute from 6 to 11 December, 84 percent of the Filipinos agree (with 44 percent saying 'very much agree' and 40 percent 'agree') with the statement that "the government should assert its right on the West Philippine Sea as stipulated in the decision of Permanent Court of Arbitration."[25] Although the government has been aware of the public's sentiment toward the SCS disputes, it nonetheless has not been affected by it. Two reasons might have contributed to this. First, foreign policy has not been considered a prioritized national issue by most Filipinos, as Philippine law scholar Jay

---

22 Recto Mercene, *Yasay Hammers on PCA Decision on South China Sea in Rallying ASEAN vs China*, BUSINESS MIRROR (Manila, 25 July 2016), available at http://www.businessmirror.com.ph/2016/07/25/yasay-hammers-on-pca-decision-on-south-china-sea-in-rallying-asean-vs-china.

23 Alexis Romero, Pia Lee-Brago, and Marvin Sy, *FVR's China Mission: No Hard Proposals, Just Dialogue*, THE PHILIPPINE STAR (Manila, 4 August 2016), available at http://www.philstar.com/headlines/2016/08/04/1609949/fvrs-china-mission-no-hard-proposals-just-dialogue.

24 Associated Press, *Philippines protests China's weapons installation on islands*, THE PHILIPPINE INQUIRER (Manila, 16 January 2017), available at https://globalnation.inquirer.net/151709/philippines-protests-chinas-weapons-installation-islands.

25 Kristen Angeli Sabillo, *8 in 10 Filipinos Want PH to Assert Rights in South China Sea—Pulse Asia*, THE PHILIPPINE INQUIRER (Manila, 27 January 2017), available at https://globalnation.inquirer.net/152106/8-10-filipinos-want-ph-assert-rights-south-china-sea-pulse-asia.

Batongbacal observes.[26] Therefore, while the public has strong support for the SCS ruling, it is less likely that they will act on it unless the issue becomes critical to their well-being. Second, the public might have concerns about Duterte's handling of the SCS disputes, but the president's popularity remains sound—over 80 percent during the last quarter of 2016.[27] Under these circumstances, the Duterte administration remains less influenced by the public's enthusiasm with the SCS victory. However, the extent to which this situation will endure will depend on future development of Sino-Philippine relations. If talks with China fail to generate substantial economic and political benefits to its country, the Duterte administration might have to face growing domestic dissatisfaction and be forced to answer to the public's anti-Chinese sentiment. The president's domestic opponents might also try to exploit such nationalism as a political weapon by that time. But currently, public opinion seems to play only a limited role.

## 3 *The China Factor*

The third factor that shapes the SCS ruling's political impact on the Philippines is China's future approach to the SCS disputes. Beijing has responded negatively to the SCS ruling, despite continuing to emphasize a willingness for negotiations and joint development. It released a number of statements and documents to refute the decision and to clarify China's position on the SCS.[28] These materials shed some light on how China would handle the SCS disputes after the arbitration. On the one hand, political statements made by Chinese officials display a strong resentment towards the SCS ruling. For example, China's Ministry of Foreign Affairs (MFA) issued a statement calling the award "null and void" and as having "no binding force" and further emphasized that "China neither accepts nor recognizes it."[29] MFA Spokesperson Lu Kang also

26 Kristen Angeli Sabillo, *Disconnect? Duterte Admin Foreign Policy vs. Public Sentiment*, THE PHILIPPINE INQUIRER (Manila, 27 January 2017), available at https://globalnation.inquirer.net/152137/disconnect-duterte-admin-foreign-policy-vs-public-sentiment.

27 Kristen Angeli Sabillo, *Duterte Approval Rating at 83%—Pulse Asia*, THE PHILIPPINE INQUIRER (Manila, 6 January 2017), available at http://newsinfo.inquirer.net/859906/duterte-approval-rating-at-83-pulse-asia.

28 Feng Zhang, *South China Sea Arbitration Award: Breathtaking (But Counterproductive)*, THE NATIONAL INTERESTS (16 July 2016), available at http://nationalinterest.org/blog/the-buzz/south-china-sea-arbitration-award-breathtaking-17004.

29 Ministry of Foreign Affairs of the People's Republic of China, *Statement of the Ministry of Foreign Affairs of the People's Republic of China on the Award of 12 July 2016 of the Arbitral Tribunal in the South China Sea Arbitration Established at the Request of the Republic of the Philippines*, 12 July 2016, available at http://www.fmprc.gov.cn/mfa_eng/wjdt 665385/2649_665393/t1379492.shtml.

questioned the Arbitral Tribunal's lawfulness and again emphasized China's "steadfast position of not accepting nor participating in the arbitration case and not accepting nor recognizing the so-called award."[30] This position was also reiterated by President Xi Jinping and Foreign Minister Wang Yi. Wang made a strong statement criticizing the SCS ruling as "completely a political farce staged under legal pretext."[31] Vice Foreign Minister Liu Zhenmin further indicated that the precondition to resume bilateral negotiations is for the Philippines to give up the ruling.[32] On the other hand, however, in the two policy documents, "Statement of the Government of the People's Republic of China on China's Territorial Sovereignty and Maritime Rights and Interests in the South China Sea" and "China Adheres to the Position of Settling Through Negotiation the Relevant Disputes Between China and the Philippines in the South China Sea", the Chinese government did not consider a hawkish approach a priority in handling the SCS disputes.[33] On the contrary, besides emphasizing Beijing's willingness to settle the SCS disputes through negotiation and avoid confrontation, these two documents also only briefly mention the term of "nine-dashed line". This might indicate the Chinese government's "intention to

30 Ministry of Foreign Affairs of the People's Republic of China, *Foreign Ministry Spokesperson Lu Kang's Remarks on Japanese Foreign Minister's Statement on the Award of South China Sea Arbitration initiated by the Philippines*, 12 July 2016, available at http://www.fmprc.gov.cn/mfa_eng/xwfw_665399/s2510_665401/2535_665405/t1380245.shtml.

31 Ministry of Foreign Affairs of the People's Republic of China, *Remarks by Chinese Foreign Minister Wang Yi on the Award of the So-called Arbitral Tribunal in the South China Sea Arbitration*, 12 July 2016, available at http://www.fmprc.gov.cn/mfa_eng/wjdt_665385/zyjh_665391/t1380003.shtml.

32 In response to a question raised by a CNN reporter regarding whether there would be a precondition for resuming bilateral talks between Beijing and Manila, Liu said that "China expects the new Filipino government to cooperate and recognize that the ruling is nothing more than a piece of waste paper and cannot be enforced. China hopes that the Filipino side will set aside the award and return to the negotiation table". See Paterno Esmaquel II, *China Rejects Talks With Ph If "Based On Ruling"*, THE RAPPLER (Manila, 13 July 2016), available at http://www.rappler.com/nation/139724-china-philippines-bilateral-talks-hague-ruling?utm_source=twitter&utm_medium=referral&utm_medium=share_bar

33 Ministry of Foreign Affairs of the People's Republic of China, *Statement of the Government of the People's Republic of China on China's Territorial Sovereignty and Maritime Rights and Interests in the South China Sea*, 12 July 2016, http://www.fmprc.gov.cn/mfa_eng/wjdt_665385/2649_665393/t1379493.shtml; *China Adheres to the Position of Settling Through Negotiation the Relevant Disputes Between China and the Philippines in the South China Sea*, 13 July 2016, available at http://www.fmprc.gov.cn/mfa_eng/wjdt_665385/2649_665393/t1380615.shtml.

seek regional peace and stability".[34] This suggests that although Beijing strongly rejected the arbitration result, an escalation of bilateral confrontation is not of its best interests.

Nonetheless, China's prudence in handling the SCS disputes faces two challenges: one from the external environment and another from its domestic politics. Externally, the SCS ruling undermines the moral prestige and legality of China's maritime claims and thus might encourage other claimant States to take similar legal action. Vietnam is one of those countries likely to do so, considering that Sino-Vietnam relations have also experienced serious deterioration since 2011. Anti-China sentiment is much higher in Vietnam than in the Philippines, as demonstrated by the disastrous anti-China protests over China's oil rig in 2014. Against this backdrop, Vietnam has been very supportive of and has closely followed the Philippines' arbitration case against China. Moreover, like the Philippines, Vietnam has cultivated close military ties with the U.S. After the SCS ruling came out, Vietnam was one of the few ASEAN States that immediately welcomed it. Manila's victory opens a window of opportunity for Hanoi to address its maritime disputes with China via international law. Other stakeholders in this region or even in the East China Sea (ECS) might also want to do the same. The fact that Vietnam, Malaysia, Indonesia, Thailand and Japan all sent observers to the arbitration hearings demonstrates these States' strong interest in the case. Thus, there is a distinct likelihood of an increase in the legal battles in this region.

Internally, just like the Philippines, the Chinese government also faces public pressure when addressing the SCS disputes. As a result of rising nationalism over the past decade, the public has become more interested in and sensitive about their country's foreign policy behavior and international situation. Protests against foreign enterprises and threats to boycott or boycotts of foreign products can often be seen when other countries are considered misbehaving diplomatically toward China.[35] The 2012 Chinese boycott against Japanese products was especially influential, and caused significant damage to the latter's economy. A similar case can also be found in the Sino-Philippine conflict over the Scarborough Shoal/Huangyan Island in the same year. However, while strong nationalist sentiment could sometimes increase the

---

34 Feng Zhang, *South China Sea Arbitration Award: Breathtaking (But Counterproductive)*, THE NATIONAL INTERESTS (16 July 2016), available at http://nationalinterest.org/blog/the-buzz/south-china-sea-arbitration-award-breathtaking-17004.

35 Two earlier examples of this include CNN's negative reports on and French President Jacques R. Chirac's criticism of the Chinese government's handling of the 2008 Tibet riots, as well as Japan's nationalization of the disputed Diaoyu/Senkaku Islands in 2012.

Chinese government's credibility to signal its resolve to stay firm when handling diplomatic disputes, they also constrain the government's policy choices by increasing the costs of compromises.[36] Aware of this, Beijing has been cautious in handling domestic frustration over the SCS ruling. Hours before the ruling came out, the Beijing municipal government issued an emergency notice stating that the city is in a "state of alert" and asking law enforcement to increase its security forces to prepare for "unexpected events" for a week.[37] This appears to be an effort to prevent the recurrence of incidents like the 2012 anti-Japanese riots. To avoid an outburst of extreme nationalism, the central government also closely monitored internet discussions and took action to delete internet posts "calling for military action against the U.S. or the Philippines to defend China's territorial claims".[38] While these measures demonstrate the government's capability in containing public discourses and behavior, they also reveal the growing importance of nationalism in Chinese foreign policy.

Considering the international and domestic pressures discussed above, it would be risky for the Chinese government to make too many compromises over the SCS issues, since a softer position might encourage more legal challenges from other stakeholders in maritime disputes and make the government look weak in front of the its people. As a result, although Beijing and Manila have the incentive to build closer ties, substantial progress on addressing the territorial disputes will remain difficult and the SCS ruling will continue to complicate their bilateral relationship.

## 4 *The U.S. Factor*

The last factor is Washington's attitude toward the SCS disputes and Sino-U.S. competition in the area. Although the U.S. strongly supports the SCS ruling, the Duterte administration's eagerness to rebuild diplomatic ties with China makes it more difficult for Washington to seek further Philippine cooperation on this issue in the short run. Future U.S.-Philippine relations might also become more dynamic than they were during the Aquino administration.

36 Jessica C. Weiss, Powerful Patriots: Nationalist Protest in China's Foreign Relations (2014) 4. Also see James Reilly, Strong Society, Smart State: The Rise of Public Opinion in China's Japan Policy (2011).

37 J. Michael Cole, *Beijing in "State of Alert" Ahead of Key Ruling on South China Sea*, The News Lens (Taipei, 12 July 2016), available at http://international.thenewslens.com/article/44063.

38 Bethany Allen-Ebrahimian, *After South China Sea Ruling, China Censors Online Calls for War*, Foreign Policy (12 July 2016), available at http://foreignpolicy.com/2016/07/12/after-south-china-sea-ruling-china-censors-online-calls-for-war-unclos-tribunal/?wp_login_redirect=0.

However, despite Duterte's desire for economic benefits from China, maintaining its ties to the U.S. remains necessary for his country's security interests. But currently, Duterte's top priorities are economic development and a war on drugs. Therefore, improvements of Sino-Philippine relations would be more urgent for the president than strengthening military cooperation with the U.S.

On the U.S. side, although Washington continues to insist that it does not take sides on sovereignty disputes in the SCS, its strong support of the ruling and emphasis on the freedom of navigation shows a significant increase in its interests in the region. This in evinced by an official document published by the Bureau of Oceans and International Environmental and Scientific Affairs in 2014, which explicitly refutes China's nine-dashed line claim and historic rights in the SCS.[39] While it is not in Washington's interests to encourage confrontation, ensuring the Arbitral Tribunal's ruling is recognized and respected by concerned parties is strategically important for it contain China's maritime expansion. Therefore, during then Secretary of State John Kerry's first visit to the Duterte administration in July 2016, Washington tried to push Manila to base its future negotiations with Beijing on the SCS ruling.[40] Further complicating the U.S. influence on the Philippine's SCS policy is the conflict between the Obama and the Duterte administrations regarding the latter's radical anti-drugs policy. Duterte made several verbal attacks against Obama publicly and threatened to sever Manila's close ties with Washington.[41] It is still unclear how the new president, Donald Trump, will handle U.S.-Philippine relations. Unlike Obama, Trump does not see a problem with Duterte's violent anti-drugs campaign. This different attitude seems to create an opportunity for the two old allies to amend their deteriorated relations since Duterte took office. However, as the Trump administration considers SCS policy a strategic priority, it will be risky to get too optimistic about the future developments of the relationship between the two sides in the short term. In other words, while bilateral disagreements over moral issues between Washington and Manila are likely to

---

39 Bureau of Oceans and International Environmental and Scientific Affairs, Limits in the Seas: China's Maritime Claims in the South China Sea (2014), available at http://www.state.gov/documents/organization/234936.pdf.

40 Estrella Torres, Leila B. Salaverria, *Duterte: PH-China Talks to Be Based on Int'l Law*, The Philippine Daily Inquirer (Manila, 25 July 2016), available at http://globalnation.inquirer.net/142080/duterte-ph-china-talks-to-be- based-on-intl-law.

41 Richard C. Paddock, *Rodrigo Duterte, Pushing Split With U.S., Counters Philippines' Deep Ties*, The New York Times (Manila, 26 October 2016), available at https://www.nytimes.com/2016/10/27/world/asia/philippines-duterte-united-states-alliance.html?_r=0&module=ArrowsNav&contentCollection=Asia%20Pacific&action=keypress&region=FixedLeft&pgtype=article.

reduce, escalating Sino-U.S. tensions in the South China Sea might nonetheless further complicate Duterte's foreign policy choices. As a result, the triangular relations among the three actors will become even more dynamic in the future, and the SCS arbitration will continue to play a role in it.

The four factors discussed above are crucial for understanding how the SCS ruling will influence the Philippines' handling of its maritime disputes with China and how Sino-Philippine relations might develop in the post-arbitration era. So far, President Duterte's pro-China orientation seems to play the most important role in shaping the Philippines' responses to the arbitration result. China's rejection of the SCS ruling and future policy behavior—also constrained by the SCS ruling—in the region will also influence the extent to which Duterte is willing to cooperate on the SCS issue. Washington's attempt to pressure Duterte into firmly upholding the SCS ruling might not be effective unless it can provide higher levels of substantial economic benefits to the Philippines. Domestic political opinion is currently the least influential factor by far. Its impact, however, might be more significant if Duterte's power position becomes unstable in the future. Under such circumstance, the president might be more likely to turn to nationalist sentiment to consolidate his domestic support and defend himself from possible attacks by his political opponents. As a result, a tougher SCS policy position and firmer emphasis on the SCS ruling might emerge.

## IV Regional Political Impact of the South China Sea Ruling

Other than influencing Sino-Philippine relations, the SCS ruling might also have significant regional impact by causing more diplomatic friction in the SCS. As mentioned earlier, the ruling might amplify other SCS stakeholders' ambition to seek more active participation in the maritime competition. For instance, besides urging China to abide by the SCS ruling, Australian Foreign Minister Julie Bishop responded to the SCS ruling by emphasizing that her country would continue freedom of navigation exercises in the region. In return, Beijing issued a harsh warning to Canberra, urging it to "carefully talk and cautiously behave."[42] This tough response reflects China's anxiety about rising challenges in the SCS in the post-arbitration period. To deter potential challenges to its national interests in the region, the Chinese government might try

42 Matthew Carney, *China Warns Australia: Stay out of the South China Sea or Risk Damage to Bilateral Relations*', ABC NEWS (New York, 15 July 2016), available at http://www.abc.net.au/news/2016-07-15/china-tells-australia-stay-out-of-the-south-china-sea/7631492.

to demonstrate a strong resolve by accelerating its military buildup and increasing its military activities. For instance, days before the ruling came out, China conducted a series of military drills from 5 to 11 July. Later, in response to the SCS ruling, it has threatened to impose an SCS air defense identification zone (ADIZ). While these military actions signaled Beijing's resolve to defend its national interests, they also increased the sense of insecurity among surrounding States. Indonesia, for instance, has begun to take action in response to rising regional tensions. After the SCS ruling was announced, Indonesian Defense Minister Ryamizard Ryacudu said in an interview that Jakarta will "sharply strengthen security around its South China Sea islands where there have been clashes with Chinese vessels."[43] Ryacudu's remark reflects an assertive change in his country's maritime policy regarding the escalating Sino-Indonesian conflict over fishing rights in the waters near the Natuna Islands. Indonesia's responses to the SCS ruling might offer some insights for understanding future Sino-Philippine relations in the long-term. Like the Philippines, Indonesia is eager to obtain more trade opportunities and financial investments from China to improve its infrastructure. Nonetheless, such economic needs do not prevent it from pursuing a tougher position in the SCS.[44] This shows that economic interests do not necessarily supersede security concerns, especially when these two concerns are intertwined.

However, China's biggest challenges come from two non-claimants in the SCS—the U.S. and Japan. Despite the U.S. efforts to reduce tensions by urging stakeholders in the region to exercise restraint,[45] it is pushing for compliance with the SCS ruling, emphasis on freedom of navigation, and actions to strengthen security cooperation with its East and Southeast Asian allies

---

43 Agence France-Presse, *Indonesia Details Defense Plan after South China Sea Ruling*, THE RAPPLER (Manila, 13 July 2016), available at http://www.rappler.com/world/regions/asia-pacific/indonesia/bahasa/englishedition/139609-indonesia-defense-plan-south-china-sea-ruling.

44 Keith Johnson, *Can Indonesia Afford a Fish War With China?*, FOREIGN POLICY (8 July 2016), http://foreignpolicy.com/2016/07/08/can-indonesia-afford-a-fish-war-with-china/.

45 Lesley Wroughton and John Walcott, *U.S. Launches Quiet Diplomacy to Ease South China Sea Tensions*, REUTERS (London, 14 July 2016), available at http://www.reuters.com/article/us-southchinasea-ruling-usa-idUSKCN0ZT2TY. The U.S. has also tried to calm China by avoiding to discuss the ruling directly. Therefore, when National Security Advisor Susan Rice visited China and met with Xi Jinping on July 25, their discussions did not focus on the SCS issues. Rather, she emphasized that it is in America's interest to see China succeed and that it is important for both powers to work together to address major global issues. See Gillian Wong, *Susan Rice Visits China*, U.S. NEWS (Washington, 25 July 2016), available at http://www.usnews.com/news/world/articles/2016-07-25/obama-aide-visits-china-after-south-china-sea-ruling.

all continue to raise Beijing's security concerns. The long-term hostility and distrust by the Chinese government and people toward the U.S. only deepened after the SCS ruling. Complicating the situation is the announcement of the location of U.S. deployment of the Terminal High Altitude Area Defense (THAAD) system in South Korea,[46] which further convinces China of America's intentions of containment.

Like the U.S., Japan also welcomed the ruling and called on both sides to abide by it. Being a stakeholder in the disputes over the Diaoyu/Senkaku Islands in the East China Sea, Japan's position on the SCS issues is highly sensitive to China. Beijing has considered Tokyo's effort to enhance its security linkages with Manila and Hanoi in recent years a strategic move aimed at containing China's maritime expansion. Therefore, as Japanese Prime Minister Shinzo Abe and Chinese Premier Li Keqiang discussed the SCS ruling during the ASEM summit in Mongolia, Li reiterated China's rejection and bluntly told Abe to "exercise caution in its own words and deeds, and stop hyping up and interfering."[47] Nonetheless, for Japan, it would be impossible to give up the benefits of the ruling. Therefore, to increase its influence in the region, Japan announced a decision to increase its defense attaches in the Philippines and Vietnam to boost its security relations with these two countries.[48] Japanese Foreign Minister Fumio Kishida also visited President Duterte and Secretary Yasay to build closer ties with the Philippine leadership.[49]

Drawing on the above analysis, it seems reasonable to argue that when faced with more ambitious challengers in both the South and East China Seas, China would have little choice but to pursue a military deterrence strategy. The purposes are two-fold: externally, Beijing needs to demonstrate its capability to protect its national interests in the South and East China Seas to deter

46 Reuters, *China Stands Ground on THAAD, Senkakus as It Advances toward Control of West Pacific*, THE JAPAN TIMES (Tokyo, 10 August 2016), available at http://www.japantimes.co.jp/news/2016/08/10/asia-pacific/china-stands-ground-thaad-senkakus-advances-toward-control-west-pacific/#.V7COh_l95hE.

47 Sue-Lin Wong and Terrence Edwards, *China Tells Japan to Stop Interfering in South China Sea*, REUTERS (London, 15 July 2016), available at http://www.reuters.com/article/us-southchinasea-ruling-idUSKCN0ZV06F.

48 Jiji, *Japan to increase defense attaches in Philippines, Vietnam*, THE JAPAN TIMES (Tokyo, 11 August 2016), available at http://www.japantimes.co.jp/news/2016/08/11/national/politics-diplomacy/japan-increase-defense-attaches-philippines-vietnam/#.V7COkfl95hE.

49 Minoru Satake, *US, Japan Court Duterte over South China Sea Dispute*, NIKKEI (Tokyo, 11 August 2016), available at http://asia.nikkei.com/Politics-Economy/International-Relations/US-Japan-court-Duterte-over-South-China-Sea-dispute.

potential challengers; domestically, the Chinese leadership cannot afford to look weak and incompetent in front of its own people when addressing the SCS disputes. Against these backdrops, China's continuation of military build-up and more frequent military operations in the two seas will be inevitable in the post-SCS-arbitration era, as demonstrated by the situations following the announcement of the Arbitral Tribunal's decision. On the same day of the ruling, two Chinese civilian aircraft landed at Subi and Mischief Reefs. On August 2, Chinese navy conducted a live-fire military drill in the East China Sea. On August 6, the Chinese air force flew bombers and fighter jets over the Spratly/Nansha Islands for "combat patrol" for a show of strength.[50] On the same day, Japan issued a protest against China after spotting a fleet of three armed Chinese coastguard vessels and 230 fishing boats sailing close to the disputed Diaoyu/Senkaku Islands.[51] Satellite photographs also reveal that China seems to be constructing reinforced aircraft hangars on the disputed Fiery Cross, Subi and Mischief Reefs.[52] These military actions seem to suggest a deterrence intention. However, for its neighbors, these actions could mean increased military threats that need to be met with greater defense capability and maybe stronger U.S. military support. The result will likely be a security dilemma in the region, as all parties' defensive intentions lead to an arms race and increasing prospect of military conflict.

## V Conclusion

The SCS ruling creates opportunities and challenges for a variety of States, including both claimants and non-claimants in the region. While it is difficult to predict future development, this paper discusses some possible political influences of the ruling on Sino-Philippine relations and regional stability. The ruling's influence on the Philippines' SCS policy will be determined by four important factors, although with varying degrees of influence: the Duterte administration's foreign policy orientation, the rising anti-China sentiment

50 Max Lewontin, *Why Did China Fly "Combat Patrols" over The Spratly Islands?*, THE CHRISTIAN SCIENCE MONITOR (Boston, 6 August 2016), available at http://www.csmonitor.com/World/Asia-Pacific/2016/0806/Why-did-China-fly-combat-patrols-over-the-Spratly-Islands.

51 Kiyoshi Takenaka and Osamu Tsukimori, *Japan Protests after Chinese Coastguards and Fishing Boats Sail near Disputed Islets*, REUTERS (London, 1 August 2016), available at http://www.reuters.com/article/us-japan-china-islands-idUSKCN10G1KP.

52 CSIS, *Build It and They Will Come: China Preps Spratlys for Military Aircraft*, (1 August 2016), available at https://amti.csis.org/build-it-and-they-will-come/.

among Filipinos, China's responses to the ruling, and Sino-U.S. competition in the SCS. Manila's mixed responses to the ruling during the first few days after its announcement suggest that although Duterte prefers better ties with China, the public's anti-China sentiment might have stopped him from making substantial compromises to his Chinese counterpart too fast. Eventually, however, Duterte chose to cope with the ruling's challenge by prioritizing the economic benefit of restoring Sino-Philippine relations over the SCS issue. His determination to pursue close ties with China has to a great extent reduced the SCS ruling's direct impact on Philippine foreign policy. But the degree to which the Sino-Philippine reconciliation will go will have to depend on China's future policy moves in the South China Sea. As the SCS ruling might increase Beijing's sense of insecurity and its cost to make compromises, the room for mutual cooperation on the SCS disputes between China and the Philippines is rather limited. This limitation would in turn raise the uncertainty of their bilateral relations in the long term. Continuous Sino-U.S. competition is also key to the Philippines' SCS policy, as it will define the extent to which the Philippines has to strike a balance between its economic interests and security needs. At the regional level, the SCS ruling put China on the defensive and thus might increase the instability in the SCS as the regional hegemon now sees a heightened need to demonstrate its military capabilities and resolve. As tensions continue to intensify, risks of armed confrontation will also increase. Therefore, the SCS ruling's political impact might be most significant and dynamic at this level.

# Award of the Republic of Philippines v. the People's Republic of China: Legal Implications on the South China Sea Disputes

*Thi Lan Anh Nguyen*[1]

## I Introduction

Initiated in January 2013, after more than three years, on 12 July 2016, the Arbitral Tribunal established in accordance with Annex VII of the UN Convention on the Law of the Sea (UNCLOS) issued its final award on the case over some aspects of the South China Sea (SCS) disputes between the Philippines and China. Whether one likes it or not, the South China Sea case marked the first attempt to settle the differences between the parties by peaceful means within the current rules-based order. The legal arguments of both parties to the case, the reasoning and conclusions of the arbitral tribunal carry enormous legal implications for the SCS disputes. This paper will first summarise the subject matter, procedural aspects and the conclusions of the award in the case filed by the Philippines against China. It then analyses the legal implications of the award on substantive and procedural aspects of the SCS disputes. With regard to the substantive aspect, the paper will examine the impacts of the award on both the sovereignty and maritime disputes in the SCS. In respect of the procedural aspect, the paper will explore the contribution of the award to dispute settlement and management of the SCS disputes.

## II Summary of the SCS Arbitration Awards

The arbitration case between the Philippines and China was unilaterally initiated by the Philippines under Annex VII of UNCLOS on 19 January 2013. In its position paper dated 7 December 2014, China challenged the jurisdition of the Arbitral Tribunal.[2] The Arbitral Tribunal treated China's rejection as a plea

1 The views expressed in this paper are strictly those of the author and do not necessarily reflect any official position of the Diplomatic Academy of Vietnam.

2 Available at: http://www.fmprc.gov.cn/mfa_eng/zxxx_662805/t1217147.shtml.

DOI 10.1163/9789004344556_004

concerning its jurisdiction and decided to bifurcate the proceedings.[3] Accordingly, the first hearing was held from 7 to 13 July 2015 to address jurisdiction and admisibility. In the award on jurisdiction issued on 29 October 2015, the Tribunal concluded that it had jurisdiction over 7 among 15 submissions of the Philippines, 7 others would consider the jurisdiction and admisibility in combination with the merits and 1 submission was requested for further clarification.[4] The second hearing was convened from 24 to 30 November 2015 on the merits and resulted in the final award on 12 July 2016.[5]

In the first award, in order to conclude on jurisdition and admissibility, the Tribunal addressed three issues, including the nature of the disputes between China and the Philippines, the procedural requirements for the Philippine submission and the limitations and exceptions under Articles 297 and 298 of UNCLOS.

Regarding the nature of the disputes, China argues that the subject-matter of the arbitration initiated by the Philippines is territorial sovereignty over several maritime features in the SCS, therefore, is beyond the scope of the dispute settlement procedure provided for under UNCLOS.[6] The Tribunal denied the arguments of China and supported the submissions of the Philippines on the basis of the existence of the disputes between the two parties as a question of interpreation of UNCLOS. Accordingly, the Tribunal held that submissions number 1 and 2 of the Philippines reflected the disagrement between the two parties on interpreting "historic rights" under UNCLOS.[7] Submissions 3 to 7 constitute the differences in understanding and applying UNCLOS on the legal regime of maritime features and their maritime entitlements in the SCS.[8] Submissions 8 to 14 are related to the interpretation and application of UNCLOS on actitivities concerning hydrocarbon exploration, exploitation, fishery, construction at sea and marine environment protection.[9] The Tribunal also elaborated that the disputes between the two parties consist of several components and the existence of disputes on territorial sovereignty will not rule out the disputes on other aspects. In this case, addressing the submissions of the

3 The fourth press release of the Arbitration, available at: https://www.pcacases.com/web/sendAttach/1298.

4 AWARD ON JURISDICTION AND ADMISSIBILITY, para. 413, available at: https://www.pcacases.com/web/sendAttach/1506.

5 The eighth press release of the Arbitration, available at: https://www.pcacases.com/web/sendAttach/1521 (hereafter referred to as JURISDICTION AWARD).

6 Part II, POSITION PAPER OF CHINA, 7 December 2014.

7 Paras. 164–168, JURISDICTION AWARD.

8 Paras. 169–172, JURISDICTION AWARD.

9 Paras. 173–177, JURISDICTION AWARD.

Philippines will neither require the Tribunal to conclude on sovereignty issues, nor consolidate sovereignty claims of any parites.[10] The Tribunal also rejects the assimilation between maritime entitlement and maritime delimitation.[11]

Concerning the procedural requirements, the Tribunal reviewed all multilateral and bilateral agreements between Philippines and China, such as the 2002 Declaration on the Conduct of Parties in the SCS (DOC), the 1976 Treaty of Amity and Cooperation (TAC), the Convention on Biological Diversity (CBD), the Convention on International Trade of Endanger Spices (CITES), among others, and concluded that the two parties neither made any options on dispute settlement means, nor ruled out the possibility of settling their disputes under UNCLOS.[12] The Tribunal also recognized that the Philippines has completed their obligations on the exchange of views.[13] The Tribunal, therefore, endorsed the right of the Philippines to submit the case before Arbitration established under Annex VII of UNCLOS.

With respect to the limitations and exceptions under Articles 297 and 298 of UNCLOS, the Tribunal adknowleged the Statement made by China in 2006 in accordance with Article 298 and concluded that submissions 4, 6 and 7 concerning legal status of maritime features and submissions 3, 10, 11 and 13 concerning Scarborough, traditional fishing rights, maritime environment protection and safety of navigation were excluded from the exception of Article 298.[14] Meanwhile, submissions 1 and 2 on the nine-dashed line, submission 5 on the ownership of Mischief Reef and Second Thomas Shoal, submissions 8, 9, 12 on Chinese activities conducted in the exclusive economic zone (EEZ) and continental shelf of the Philippines and submission 14 on exaggeration of the disputes contain the interelation between jurisdition and substances, thus are left to be addressed in combination in the merit hearing.[15]

In the merit award, the Tribunal delivered comprehensive conclusions on three major issues, namely the maritime entitlement of the nine-dashed line, legal regime of maritime features and the legality of a handful activities conducted by China in the SCS.

In clarifying the maritime entitlement of the nine-dashed line, the Tribunal drew the distinction between the concepts of historic bays, historic waters,

10 Paras. 148–153, JURISDICTION AWARD.

11 Para. 155–157, JURISDICTION AWARD.

12 Paras. 212–229, 241–251, 265–296, 281–289, 299–302, 307–310, and 317–321, JURISDICTION AWARD.

13 Paras. 332–352, JURISDICTION AWARD.

14 Paras. 400, 401, 403, 404, 407, 408 and 410, JURISDICTION AWARD.

15 Paras. 390–396, JURISDICTION AWARD.

historic titles and historic rights under customary international as well as under UNCLOS and concluded that historic titles in Article 298 of UNCLOS referred to claims of sovereignty over maritime areas derived from historical circumstances.[16] The Tribunal also examined various official statements, legislation and conduct of China in the SCS to explore the nature of maritime claims resulted from the nine-dashed line of China. The fact that China still respects the freedom of navigation of others and Chinese fishery has never been conducted exclusively in the waters within the nine-dashed line led to the Tribunal's conclusion that China neither claimed historic title, historic water, nor historic bay over the waters of the SCS. What China claims is rather a constellation of historic rights short of title.[17] However, as UNCLOS is currently the only systematic source of international law to distribute maritime rights and obligations to coastal States, the Tribunal concluded that China's claims to historic rights, or other sovereign rights or jurisdiction, with respect to the maritime areas of the SCS encompassed by the relevant part of the nine-dashed line are contrary to UNCLOS and without lawful effect to the extent that they exceed the geographic and substantive limits of China's maritime entitlements under UNCLOS.[18]

Concerning the legal regime of some maritime features in the SCS, the Tribunal first relies on the definition provided for under Article 13 of UNCLOS, data on tidal ranges, the Schofield Report,[19] nautical surveying and sailing directions to clasify maritime features into low and high tide features. As a result, the Tribunal concluded that of the nine maritime featured submitted by the Philippines, six maritime features, namely Scarborough Shoal, Cuarteron Reef, Fiery Cross Reef, Johnson Reef, McKennan Reef, and Gaven Reef (North) remain above water at high tide and are accordingly high-tide features. In their natural condition, five maritime features, namely, Hughes Reef, Gaven Reef (South), Subi Reef, Mischief Reef, and Second Thomas Shoal are exposed at low tide and submerged at high tide and are accordingly low-tide elevations. Among them, Hughes Reef lies within 12 nautical miles of the high-tide features on McKennan Reef and Sin Cowe Island, Gaven Reef (South) lies within

16 Para. 226 of the Arbitral Tribunal Award on the Merits, available at: http://www.pcacases.com/pcadocs/PH-CN%20-%2020160712%20-%20Award.pdf (hereafter referred as the MERITS AWARD).

17 Para. 229, MERITS AWARD.

18 Para. 278, MERITS AWARD.

19 C. SCHOFIELD, J.R.V. PRESCOTT & R. VAN DER POLL, AN APPRAISAL OF THE GEOGRAPHICAL CHARACTERISTICS AND STATUS OF CERTAIN INSULAR FEATURES IN THE SOUTH CHINA SEA, Annex 513, MERITS AWARD.

12 nautical miles of the high-tide features at Gaven Reef (North) and Namyit Island, and that Subi Reef lies within 12 nautical miles of the high-tide feature of Sandy Cay on the reefs to the west of Thitu.[20]

The Tribunal then addressed the maritime entitlement of some maritime features in SCS by applying Article 121 of UNCLOS. The legal regime of maritime features has long been a subject of controversy due to the ambiguity of the wording of Article 121 as well as diverse State practices. In this case, the Tribunal takes a decisive approach in providing a comprehensive interpretation. The Tribunal has interpreted all the words and phrases contained in Article 121(3), namely "rocks", "cannot", "sustain", "human habitation", "or", "economic life of their own" based on their ordinary meaning. It also clarified the context of Article 121(3) in relation with the object and purpose of UNCLOS and the *travaux préparatoires* of the Convention and stated that Article 121(3) serves as a limitation to prevent the expanded jurisdiction of the EEZ from rocks going too far. Overall, through 76 paragraphs, the Tribunal made nine important conclusions on the interpretation of Article 121(3). Among them, the most two important points are (i) the status of a feature is to be determined on the basis of its natural capacity, without external additions or modifications intended to increase its capacity to sustain human habitation or an economic life of its own and (ii) the determination of the objective capacity of a feature is not dependent on any prior decision on sovereignty.[21] The Tribunal also further finds the support for its interpretation from relevant State practice.[22] Applying such interpretation to the original, natural and geographical conditions of the Spratlys, the Tribunal concluded that none of the high-tide features in the Spratly Islands, including Itu Aba, can generate entitlements to an EEZ or continental shelf.[23] The Tribunal also clarified that the Spratlys cannot be treated as an archipelago and from which to draw straight baselines.[24]

As to the activities conducted by China in the SCS, the Tribunal held five important conclusions. First, the Tribunal determined that China has violated the sovereign rights and jurisdiction of the Philippines over its EEZ and continental shelf by interfering with the Philippines' petroleum exploration and seismic survey at the Reed Bank, applying the 2012 moratorium on fishing in the area north of 12°N latitude and through the Hainan Regulation, preventing fishing by Philippine vessels at Mischief Reef and Second Thomas Shoal and

20 Paras. 382–384, MERITS AWARD.

21 Para. 551, MERITS AWARD.

22 Paras. 552–553, MERITS AWARD.

23 Para. 646, MERITS AWARD.

24 Paras. 573–576, MERITS AWARD.

constructing installations and artificial islands at Mischief Reef without the authorization of the Philippines.[25] Through the operation of its marine surveillance vessels in tolerating and failing to exercise due diligence to prevent fishing by Chinese flagged vessels at Mischief Reef and Second Thomas Shoal, China also failed to exhibit due regard for the Philippines' sovereign rights with respect to fisheries in its EEZ.[26] The conclusion of the Tribunal based on the earlier rejection of any maritime entitlement of the nine-dashed line as well as the limited maritime entitlement of the maritime features of the Spratlys. Accordingly, as both Mischief Reef and Second Thomas Shoal are located within 200 nautical miles of the Philippines' coast on the island of Palawan and are located in an area that is not overlapped by the entitlements generated by any maritime feature claimed by China, between the Philippines and China, Mischief Reef and Second Thomas Shoal form part of the EEZ and continental shelf of the Philippines.[27]

Second, the Tribunal held that China, through the operation of its official vessels at Scarborough Shoal from May 2012 onwards, failed to respect the traditional fishing rights of Philippine fishermen.[28] The conclusion given was based on the recognition that Scarborough Shoal has been a traditional fishing ground for many nations, including the Philippines, China (including Taiwan) and Vietnam.[29]

Third, the Tribunal confirms that China, through its toleration and protection of, and failure to prevent Chinese fishing vessels engaging in harmful harvesting activities of endangered species at Scarborough Shoal, Second Thomas Shoal and other features in the Spratly Islands as well as its island-building activities at Cuarteron Reef, Fiery Cross Reef, Gaven Reef (North), Johnson Reef, Hughes Reef, Subi Reef and Mischief Reef, violated its obligation concering protection and preservaton of the marine environment.[30]

Fourth, the Tribunal stated that China, by virtue of the conduct of Chinese law enforcement vessels in the vicinity of Scarborough Shoal, created serious risk of collision and danger to Philippine vessels and personnel, violated its obligation to maintain safety at sea.[31]

Finally, the Tribunal found that China, in the course of the arbitral proceedings, aggravated and extended the disputes between the parties concerning

25 Para. 716, MERITS AWARD.
26 Para. 757, MERITS AWARD.
27 Para.647, MERITS AWARD.
28 Para. 814, MERITS AWARD.
29 Para. 805, MERITS AWARD.
30 Paras. 992–993, MERITS AWARD.
31 Para. 1109, MERITS AWARD.

maritime entitlement at Michief Reef, as well as the legal status of maritime features and its marine environmental protection obligations through its dredging, artificial island-building, and construction activities.[32]

## III Implications on the Scope of the SCS Disputes

The SCS disputes consist of two layers: (1) territorial disputes over sovereignty of maritime features and (ii) maritime disputes over maritime entitlements and rights. The awards in the SCS arbitration case, although binding only upon the parties to the case, i.e. the Philippines and China, produce significant implication in limiting the scope of the SCS disputes.

Parties to the disputes in the SCS lodge various sovereignty claims over the maritime features in the SCS. Vietnam claimed the whole Paracels and Spratlys by an official statement made by its protectorate, France, in 1933,[33] then by the official Declaration of South Vietnam at the San Francisco Conference of 1951,[34] and the official statements made by the united Vietnam since 1975.[35] China made the first offical claim over the Paracels, Spratlys and Macclesfield Bank (which is said to include Scarbrough) in 1951 through the statement of the Foreign Minister of the People's Republic of China, Zhou Enlai.[36] The Philippines claimed sovereignty over the Kalayaan Island Group (a large number of features in the Spratlys) by the issuance of Presidental Decree No. 1956 on 11 June 1978[37] and Panatag (Scarborough) Shoal on the basis of State practice of Spain during the colonial period.[38] Malaysia claimed several maritime

32 Para. 1181, MERITS AWARD.

33 For full text of the French statement see OFFICIAL JOURNAL OF THE REPUBLIC OF FRANCE, 26 July 1933, 7837.

34 Letter dated 3 July 2014 from the Permanent Representative of Vietnam to the United Nations addressed to the Secretary-General of the United Nation, UN documents, A/68/942, available at <http://undocs.org/A/68/942>.

35 Ibid.

36 Para 33 of the Paper entitled *China Adheres to the Position of Settling Through Negotiation the Relevant Disputes Between China and the Philippines*, issued on 13 July 2016, available at <http://www.fmprc.gov.cn/mfa_eng/zxxx_662805/t1380615.shtml>.

37 PRESIDENTIAL DECREE NUMBER 1596, full text available at <http://www.gov.ph/1978/06/11/presidential-decree-no-1596-s-1978/>.

38 PHILIPPINE POSITION ON BAJO DE MASINLOC (SCARBOROUGH SHOAL) AND THE WATERS WITHIN ITS VICINITY, 18 April 2012, full text available at: <http://www.gov.ph/2012/04/18/philippine-position-on-bajo-de-masinloc-and-the-waters-within-its-vicinity/>

features of the Spratlys based on the continental shelf map of 1979.[39] Brunei also used a map on the EEZ and continental shelf published in 1987 and 1988 to claim sovereignty over Louisa Reef.[40] All parties, nevertheless, have not yet clarified the legal status of claimed maritime features. All claims, except those of Brunei, was made to groups of features and it seems that there is neither distinction made for sovereignty over high tide or low tide features. This is confirmed by Chinese straight baselines drawn over the Paracels similar to archipelagic baselines method,[41] oath taking ceremony at James Shoal (a low tide elevation) and construction building on Mischief Reef (a low tide elevation concluded by the SCS arbitration that is located on the continental shelf of the Philippines), etc. These practices show that claimants in the SCS lodge sovereignty claims over both low tide and high tide features as well as the waters between the features.

The SCS Award, echoed the conclusions of previous judgment and affirmed that low tide elevations are not subject to sovereignty claims. It stated that "[n] otwithstanding the use of the term 'land' in the physical description of a low-tide elevation, such low-tide elevations do not form part of the land territory of a State in the legal sense. Rather they form part of the submerged landmass of the State and fall within the legal regimes for the territorial sea or continental shelf, as the case may be. Accordingly, and as distinct from land territory, the Tribunal subscribes to the view that low-tide elevations cannot be appropriated, although 'a coastal State has sovereignty over low-tide elevations which are situated within its territorial sea, since it has sovereignty over the territorial sea itself.'"[42] In the possibility of treating the maritime features as a group and drawing archipelagic baselines, the Tribunal takes a clear view that any application of straight baselines to the Spratly Islands in this fashion would be contrary to UNCLOS.[43] This conclusion is made based on the interpretation of Article 7 of UNCLOS on the application of straight baselines, in cross reference

39 The map was published under the name of Peta Baru and supported by no official sovereignty statement. For further, see Asri Salleh, Che Hamdan Che Mohd Razali and Kamaruzaman Jusoff, *Malaysia's policy towards its 1963–2008 territorial disputes*, 1(5) JOURNAL OF LAW AND CONFLICT RESOLUTION 107 (2009) 111–113.

40 Similar to Malaysia's claim, the map has not been supported by official sovereignty statement. For further information, see Daniel J. Dzurek, *The Spratlys Island Dispute: Who's on first?* 2(1) MARITIME BRIEFING (1996) 22.

41 DECLARATION OF THE GOVERNMENT OF THE PEOPLE'S REPUBLIC OF CHINA ON THE BASELINES OF THE TERRITORIAL SEA, 15 May 1996, available at http://www.un.org/Depts/los/LEGISLATIONANDTREATIES/PDFFILES/CHN_1996_Declaration.pdf.

42 Para. 309, MERITS AWARD.

43 Para. 577, MERITS AWARD.

with Articles 46 and 47 on archipelagic baselines. The Tribunal also examined relevant State practices and held that "[n]otwithstanding the practice of some States to the contrary, the Tribunal sees no evidence that any deviations from this rule have amounted to the formation of a new rule of customary international law that would permit a departure from the express provisions of the Convention."[44]

The two important conclusions of the Tribunal on the legal status of low tide elevations and the impossibility of drawing archipelagic baselines for the whole Spratlys indicates that at least between China and the Philippines, the scope of sovereignty disputes has been significantly reduced. For example, Mischief Reef, Second Thomas Shoal and Reed Bank are no longer subject to sovereignty disputes between China and the Philippines. The Tribunal made a firm conclusion that they belong to the continental shelf of the Philippines. If this approach is followed by other claimants, the scope of the sovereignty disputes in the SCS, accordingly will be narrowed to only high tide features and low tide features which are located within 12 nautical miles of the high tide features. Other low tide elevations located beyond 12 nautical miles off a coast will be freed from disputes, their fates will be decided according to the legal regime of the respective seabed where they are located.

In terms of maritime disputes, the disagreements in the SCS come from three different maritime entitlements generated from the main coastlines of the littoral States, maritime features and the nine-dashed line. First, maritime zones generated from the coastlines of littoral States in accordance with UNCLOS may create overlapping maritime jurisdictional entitlements due to the adjacent and opposite locations of relevant States. These overlaps, after the Award, remain the same as these are outside the jurisdiction of the Tribunal and the Tribunal is unable to address maritime delimitation.

The second is the maritime zone generated from the mid-ocean maritime features in the SCS, of which, due to their geographical locations, if such belong to one country, may lead to significant overlapping with other littoral States. China, in fact, claims not only the sovereignty over the whole of the Spratlys, but also the EEZ and continental shelf for this group.[45] This leads to a series of incidents in the SCS in asserting sovereignty, sovereign rights and jurisdictions, including, for example, the severing of towed cables attached to Vietnamese

---

44 Para. 576, MERITS AWARD.

45 NOTE VERBALE FROM THE PEOPLE'S REPUBLIC OF CHINA TO THE SECRETARY-GENERAL OF THE UNITED NATIONS, No. CML/8/2011 (14 April 2011), available at: http://www.un.org/depts/los/clcs_new/submissions_files/mysvnm33_09/chn_2011_re_phl_e.pdf.

survey ships by Chinese vessels and the encounter between China and the Philippines at Reed Bank in 2011, the opening of nine oil blocks in Vietnam's EEZ for bidding by a Chinese State oil company and the Scarborough standoff in 2012, the deployment of the Chinese drilling vessel HYSY-981 into Vietnam's EEZ and Chinese oath taking at James Shoal in 2014, and frequent fishing incidents, etc. The Tribunal also clarified that all of the high tide features of the Spratlys have no EEZ or continental shelf. This approach may apply by analogy to the Paracels, a similar group with the Spratlys in terms of geography and historical usage. As a result, maritime disputes generated by the maritime features in the SCS will be significantly reduced and confined within 12 nautical miles of the high tide features.

The third maritime entitlement from the nine-dashed line has never been fully clarified by China, but could be some kind of "sovereignty over adjacent waters and sovereign right and jurisdiction over relevant waters"[46] or "rights and relevant claims over the SCS ... formed in the long course of history."[47] This may result in up to 80% of the maritime zones in the SCS to be in dispute. In the Merits Award, the Tribunal clearly denied the possibility of using the nine-dashed line to generate historic rights, or other sovereign rights or jurisdiction

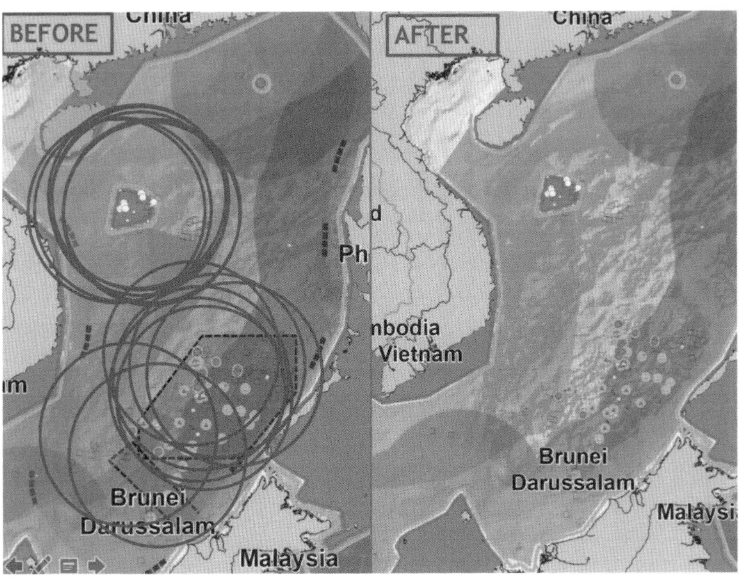


46 Para. 2, NOTES VERBALE OF CHINA, 7 May 2009. The attached map was the nine-dashed line map.

47 Foreign Ministry Spokesperson Jiang Yu's Regular Press Conference on 15 September 2011 http://www.fmprc.gov.cn/eng/xwfw/s2510/t860126.htm.

in the SCS. This means the nine-dashed line will no longer be a source of maritime disputes in the SCS.

Permanently removing the source of maritime disputes from the nine-dashed line, limiting the maritime entitlement from the maritime features, the Tribunal Awards have drawn a much simpler and brighter picture for the SCS where the scope of maritime disputes has been significantly reduced as follows:

## IV Implications on the SCS Dispute Management and Settlement

The case is an opportunity for the parties in the SCS disputes to review all available dispute settlement mechanisms. As between China and the Philippines, the Tribunal reviewed the application of the dispute settlement mechanism provided under various treaties, including the TAC, DOC, the UN Charter, as well as other bilateral and multilateral statements. The provisions of these treaties and documents clearly indicate that China, the Philippines and other parties to the SCS adhere to the principle of settlement of disputes by peaceful means.

The TAC provides that "in case disputes on matters directly affecting [the parties] should arise, especially disputes likely to disturb regional peace and harmony, they shall refrain from the threat or use of force and shall at all times settle such disputes among themselves through friendly negotiations."[48] It further stipulates that "[n]othing in this Treaty shall preclude recourse to the modes of peaceful settlement contained in Article 33(1) of the Charter of the United Nations. The High Contracting Parties which are parties to a dispute should be encouraged to take initiatives to solve it by friendly negotiations before resorting to the other procedures provided for in the Charter of the United Nations."[49] The DOC also confirms that "[t]he Parties concerned undertake to resolve their territorial and jurisdictional disputes by peaceful means, without resorting to the threat or use of force, through friendly consultations and negotiations by sovereign States directly concerned, in accordance with universally recognized principles of international law, including the 1982 UN Convention on the Law of the Sea."[50] This means that despite the favourable emphasis on negotiation, the parties are still open for any peaceful settlement means, including those from judicial processes. Along this line, in the Awards, the Tribunal also confirms that the provisions from relevant treaties and statements

48 Article 13, TAC.

49 Article 17, TAC.

50 Para. 4, DOC.

do not create a binding agreement between the parties to solely settle the SCS disputes through negotiation. They neither exclude the application of the dispute settlement mechanism provided for under Part XV of UNCLOS.[51]

Under Part XV of UNCLOS, the parties must follow the general provisions of Section 1. Accordingly, exchange of view is a precondition in order to invoke the compulsory procedures under Section 2. The Awards made significant clarifications on the fulfilment of such obligations. The Tribunal quoted the dictum in *Chagos Marine Protection Area*[52] and *Artic Sunrise*[53] cases to specify that Article 283 of UNCLOS requires an exchange of view on the means by which the Parties' dispute will be settled and that this obligation is met. An exchange of view in this context does not require negotiations with regard to the subject-matter of the disputes.[54]

Before the case between the Philippines and China, another country in the region already invoked the procedures of Part XV of UNCLOS. Malaysia on 4 July 2003 unilaterally submitted a case concerning land reclamation by Singapore in and around the Straits of Johor. During the proceeding, Malaysia also made a request for provisional measure by the International Tribunal for the Law of the Sea (ITLOS). The case later ended in September 2005 by an award recognizing the settlement agreement reached by the parties. In the case between Philippines and China, the Tribunal not only endorsed the dispute settlement mechanism provided for under Part XV of UNCLOS as an alternative for peaceful settlement of the parties concerned but also concluded that the arbitral tribunal established under Annex VII of UNCLOS had jurisdiction over most of the submissions of the Philippines. These practices suggest that dispute settlement mechanism under UNCLOS serves as a feasible means for the parties to settle certain aspects of the SCS disputes. Given the complexity of the disputes and the current deadlock in negotiations, the success of the land reclamation case between Malaysia and Singapore and the arbitration between Philippines and China show the effectiveness of the dispute settlement system with the purpose to uphold international law[55] and open an alternative for the parties in their attempts to settle the SCS disputes through peaceful means.

---

51 Paras. 212–229, 241–251, 265–296, 281–289, 299–302, 307–310, and 317–321, JURISDICTION AWARD.

52 *The Chagos Marine Protected Area Arbitration* (Mauritius v. United Kingdom), 2015, available at <http://www.pcacases.com/web/view/11>.

53 *The Arctic Sunrise Arbitration* (the Netherlands v. the Russian Federation), 2015, available at <http://www.pcacases.com/web/view/21> (accessed on 10 November 2016).

54 Paras. 332–352, JURISDICTION AWARD.

55 Yoshifumi Tanaka, *Reflections on the Philippines/China Arbitration: Award on Jurisdiction and Admissibility*, 15 THE LAW AND PRACTICE OF INTERNATIONAL COURTS AND TRIBUNALS 305 (2016) 325.

Notwithstanding significant conclusions to narrow the SCS disputes and facilitate dispute settlement, the sovereignty and maritime delimitation issues remain unresolved as these two issues fall outside of the compulsory dispute settlement mechanism under UNCLOS. Pending dispute settlement, this raises the question for dispute management in the SCS. At the moment, due to different interpretations and application of UNCLOS, parties to the SCS dispute impose various measures to enhance their claims. These activities are a source of further complication of the disputes and threats to marine environment protection and preservation, safety of navigation and good order at sea. The Award on the merits, in the way it examined the legality of various activities of China in the SCS, has provided legal basis for the conduct of parties in the SCS. Accordingly, as the nine-dashed line cannot be used for maritime claims and the maritime features of the Spratlys can only generate limited maritime entitlement, activities of one State conducted within the EEZ and continental shelf of other littoral States, generated from their mainland, will constitute violations of UNCLOS. This may facilitate the process of building of a list of what activities are permitted and which ones are prohibited, an important matter in the drafting a code of conduct for the parties in the SCS.

Moving beyond activities which are considered legal within the maritime zones, the Award addressed two other important aspects regarding the marine environment protection and safety of navigation. As to the marine environment, the Tribunal sought assistance from expert reports,[56] which provide a factual picture of current devastation and damage of the marine environment and the cause of such a situation in the SCS. The preservation of the marine environment is further highlighted as an international obligation regardless the legal regime of maritime zones. The Award provides a harmonised application of such obligation from provisions of UNCLOS, CBD, CITES and FAO Code of Conduct for Responsible Fisheries.[57] The considerations of the Tribunal, therefore, pave the way for cooperation and management for marine environment

56 Dr. rer. Nat. Sebastian C.A. Ferse, Professor Peter Mumby, PhD and Dr. Selina Ward, PhD, *Assessment of the Potential Environmental Consequences of Construction Activities on Seven Reefs in the Spratly Islands in the South China Sea* (26 April 2016) (referred as Ferse Report), Professor John W. McManus, *Offshore Coral Reef Damage, Overfishing and Paths to Peace in the South China Sea* (rev. ed., 21 April 2016) (referred as McManus Report), Professor Camilo Mora, Dr. Iain R. Caldwell, Professor Charles Birkeland, and Professor John W. McManus, "*Dredging in the Spratly Islands: Gaining Land but Losing Reefs*, 14(3) PLoS BIOLOGY (31 March 2016) (referred as Mora Report), Professor Kent E. Carpenter, *Eastern South China Sea Environmental Disturbances and Irresponsible Fishing Practices and their Effects on Coral Reefs and Fisheries* (22 March 2014) (referred as Carpenter Report).

57 Paras. 939–996. MERITS AWARD.

protection and preservation in the SCS. This becomes a more urgent need given the rich biodiversity and marine environment of a semi-enclosed sea like the SCS.

Regarding safety of navigation, at the moment, due to the competing claims, vessels from different forces, including law enforcement, navy as well as private sectors operate within the narrow sea of the SCS, which pose a high risk for safety of navigation. Reports from experts providing assistance to the Tribunal during the arbitral proceedings confirm this risk.[58] The conclusions of the Tribunal on this issue affirm that operation of law enforcement vessels in a dangerous manner constitute a violation of the obligation provided for under UNCLOS and the Convention on the International Regulations for Prevention of Collisions at Sea (COLREGS). The situation in the SCS and the conclusions of the Tribunal stress the need for cooperation for safety of navigation in the SCS. For example, an initiative for expanding the application of the Code for Unplanned Encounters at Sea (CUES) to law enforcement vessels is under discussion for its application in the SCS.

In addition, the conclusions of the Tribunal on the maritime entitlement of maritime features of the Spratlys as well as the nine-dashed line reveal that the high sea and international seabed likely exist in the SCS. This possibility also further facilitates other sea users to enjoy *mare liberum* freedom of navigation, overflight, commerce and fisheries.[59] It also raises the need for cooperation to preserve the freedom of the high seas as well as coordinate with the International Seabed Authority to manage the exploration and exploitation of the resources in the deep seabed of the SCS.

## V Conclusion

With more than 700 pages, the two awards of the Arbitral Tribunal established in accordance with Annex VII of UNCLOS in the case between Philippines and China mark the first successful attempt of using a judicial measure to settle certain aspects of the SCS disputes. Upon the submission of the Philippines on January 2013, the Tribunal bifurcated the arbitral proceeding to address the procedural and merit aspects of the case. The statements of the Tribunal

58 Allen Report, Captain Gurpreet S. Singhota, *Report of the International Navigational Safety Expert appointed by the Permanent Court of Arbitration*, The Hague, The Netherlands (15 April 2016).

59 George K. Ndi, *Philippines v China: assessing the implications of the South China Sea arbitration*, AUSTRALIAN JOURNAL OF MARITIME & OCEAN AFFAIRS (2016) 14.

on jurisdiction and admissibility provide a positive confirmation on jurisdiction of the Tribunal, thereby, prove that judicial method can be used as a feasible solution facilitating dispute settlement in the SCS. On the merits of the case, the conclusions of the Tribunal produced significant impacts on freeing the majority of the maritime spaces in the SCS from disputes. Relying on the awards, the parties possess firm legal basis to clarify the scope of sovereignty and maritime disputes in the SCS disputes. The reasoning of the Tribunal also provided a guideline for the conduct of the parties in the SCS, which will facilitate the process of management of the disputes and foster cooperation for marine environment protection and safety of navigation. The arbitrators have completed their roles producing a landmark award for the SCS and the result has opened new chapters, creating a new legal status quo in the SCS. It is now up to the parties to seize the given opportunities to turn a hotspot into a sea of cooperation based on good faith and the rule of law.

# Political-Legal Implications of the July 2016 Arbitration Decision in the Philippines-PRC Case Concerning the South China Sea: The United States, China, and International Law

*Jacques deLisle*[1]

## 1 Introduction

The international political and legal implications of the 12 July 2016, unanimous decision in the Philippines vs. China international arbitration case concerning the South China Sea (SCS)[2] vary significantly among the major affected interests. For the United States, the decision reads, in many ways, as an affirmation of what have been core legal elements of US policy and strategy toward the contested maritime region and China's claims and actions therein. The panel's ruling, thus, augured basic continuity in the US approach. But, the tribunal's decision nonetheless put the US to complex and difficult choices. The challenges for the US stemmed partly from China's mostly predictable reaction (a sharp rejection of the award and its legitimacy) and were compounded by the Philippines' surprising backing away from its legal victory (following Rodrigo Duterte's ascension to the presidency). Donald Trump's unexpected win in the US presidential election generated further complications and more uncertainty, given the new US administration's evident disdain for its predecessor, skepticism toward established approaches in many aspects of US foreign policy, and early moves that sent mixed signals and suggested a lack of understanding of, or concern with, international legal issues relevant in the SCS.

For China, the decision was a stunning repudiation of many of its key legal arguments and much of its behavior in the disputed SCS region. The tribunal's ruling, thus, portended a continuation of the strongly negative stance that China had adopted toward the proceedings as well as the substance of the

1 University of Pennsylvania and Foreign Policy Research Institute.

2 PCA Case No. 2013-19, South China Sea Arbitration between the Republic of the Philippines and the People's Republic of China, Award, 12 July 2016 ("South China Sea Arbitration Award (Merits)").

Philippines' claims before the decision. Beijing's initial responses to the arbitral award were in this familiar vein. Still, the panel's sharply adverse judgment put Beijing to more difficult political calculations about how to respond—choices that Beijing had not had to face (at least in full or publicly) before the panel's award. Manila's post-decision shift to a more accommodating position ameliorated, but hardly eliminated, these challenges for China.

For international law—a concededly more abstract "affected interest"—the arbitral decision constituted a noteworthy resolution of several contentious doctrinal issues, and a strong assertion of the reach and capacity of international legal rules and formal dispute resolution procedures. But, here too, the broader and longer-term implications are more ambiguous and ambivalent. The sweep and ambition of the panel's decision came with risks that the apparent "victory" for international law would prove fleeting or illusory, and perhaps even perverse. China's stern rejection, the Philippines' striking downplaying, the evident limits to what the US is able or willing to do, and vulnerabilities inherent in international legal rules and institutions all contribute to serious doubts about whether the tribunal's ruling will be, in the end, a win for international law and legal institutions.

## II The United States

For the US, the arbitration decision was remarkably in line with the central legal components of US policy toward the SCS disputes and toward China's approach to the issues at stake in those disputes. The principal law-related features of US policy date to the middle 1990s, and were framed partly in response to an earlier round of escalating tensions in the region.[3] The version of the policy in place at the time of the Philippines-China arbitration had been set forth authoritatively by then-Secretary of State Hillary Clinton in 2010–11, during the early phases of the most recent phase of heightened frictions over SCS issues.[4]

Major holdings in the Philippines-China arbitration decision are fully consistent with—and supportive of—four main elements of the US legal-political

3 US Department of State, *Daily Press Briefing*, 10 May 1995, available at: available at: http://dosfan.lib.uic.edu/ERC/briefing/daily_briefings/1995/9505/950510db.html.

4 See, for example, *Hillary Clinton Statement on the South China Sea*, 22 July 2011, available at: https://2009-2017.state.gov/secretary/20092013clinton/rm/2011/07/168989.htm.
*Remarks at Press Availability* (*Hillary Clinton*), 23 July 2010, available at: http://china.usc.edu/remarks-press-availability-secretary-clinton-july-23-2010.

position: (1) not taking a position on questions of sovereignty over disputed landforms and lesser features in the SCS (none of which is the object of US claims to territorial sovereignty or maritime rights to be derived therefrom); (2) asserting and protecting rights to broad freedom of navigation and overflight and access to the maritime commons in the SCS area; (3) insisting that all parties follow international law, including particularly the law of the sea rules in UNCLOS, which the US regards as, in most respects, reflective of binding customary international law; and (4) calling on rival claimants to use peaceful means to address their disputes and to eschew coercive or destabilizing measures.[5] The first two of these positions concern relatively specific legal points that are highly salient in the fraught international politics of the SCS region. The third and fourth address broader matters of legal and related political principles. The third also largely subsumes the second.

These components of the US position align with Washington's broader political objectives in East Asia. The US agenda in the region includes: maintaining regional peace and stability, reassuring allies and friends of the reliability of the US's commitments, and maintaining a significant US role and presence, militarily, politically, and economically. On each of the elements, the arbitration decision's congruence with US positions is clearest on issues over which the US and China disagree and which are also the issues of greatest regional political and strategic significance for the US.

*First, the US has not taken a position on the question of who has sovereignty over disputed landforms in the SCS.* This stance has allowed the US to avoid "taking sides" on the issues that have been most fraught and most conflict-provoking in the region. It has enabled the US to focus on other legal issues relevant to US interests and systemic values (such as freedom of access, peace and security, and so on), and to deflect China's arguments that the US has no legitimate role in the SCS because it does not, and cannot, have any claim to sovereignty over any landforms or to coastal State rights over maritime zones.[6] At the same time, the

5 These positions, which are addressed sequentially in this section, are articulated in many official US sources, including those cited in the immediately preceding two footnotes.

6 People's Republic of China Ministry of Foreign Affairs, *The Issue of the South China Sea* (June 2000) § 3; "China Opposes Attempts to Internationalize South China Sea Disputes," XINHUA, 28 September 2011, available at: http://news.xinhuanet.com/english2010/china/2011-09/28/c_131165615.htm; "Ministry of Defense: Outside Intervention Not Welcome," XINHUA, 31 July 2012, available at: http://news.xinhuanet.com/english/china/2012-07/31/c_123503297.htm; *Yang Jiechi Gives Interview to State Media on the So-Called Award by the Arbitral Tribunal for the South China Sea Arbitration*, 16 July 2016, available at: http://www.chinaembassy.org/eng/zt/abc123/t1382060.htm ("certain countries outside the region, driven by their own agenda, have frequently intervened in the South China Sea").

US's agnosticism on questions of sovereignty has left Washington free to insist that it can and should play a pivotal role in the region to protect US interests, and to provide international public goods. Among the US's more prominent active measures have been freedom of navigation operations, military reconnaissance, and other measures by the US Navy that challenge China's claims or possible claims to impede open access to the SCS area. (In principle and likely in practice, the US would extend these methods to States other than China if they were to pursue a course akin to that which China recently had been pursuing to increase dominion over the SCS, such as undertaking extensive land reclamation, building port facilities and landing strips, denying other States' ships access to disputed areas, harassing US military ships, and so on.)

The arbitration tribunal's decision is consistent, and resonates, with the "agnosticism on sovereignty, but opposition to enclosure" element of US policy. The panel made clear that it purported not to make any decisions on territorial sovereignty, recognizing that such questions were beyond its purview because they lie outside the law of the sea and, thus, the tribunal's jurisdiction as an UNCLOS-based dispute resolution body. (The panel here rejected a version of this argument from China, which claimed that the tribunal lacked jurisdiction over the Philippines' claims as a whole because—on Beijing's account—none of Manila's arguments about maritime zones and maritime rights could be resolved without straying into issues of sovereignty.)[7]

This could have meant that the panel would forego addressing the Philippines' challenge to China's expansive claims to maritime rights, and thus would have said little that aligned with the US's opposition to China's expansive jurisdictional claims. After all, the valuable rights over maritime zones that were the focus of the Philippines' claims in the arbitration proceeding, and that are the principal source of economic and strategic value in the SCS disputes more generally, derive from sovereignty over territory. But the panel took a different tack, accepting its lack of authority to address territorial sovereignty but nonetheless issuing extensive decisions on the merits rejecting Beijing's claims of rights over the contested sea areas (essentially on the grounds that none of the landforms or maritime features, even if under Chinese sovereignty, could support the maritime zones and rights China asserted).

The tribunal's distinction between territorial sovereignty issues that were beyond its reach and maritime rights questions that were largely within its

7 PCA Case No. 2013-19, South China Sea Arbitration between the Republic of the Philippines and the People's Republic of China, Award on Jurisdiction and Admissibility, 29 October 2015 ("South China Sea Arbitration Award (Jurisdiction and Admissibility)") ¶¶ 151–154.

reach dovetailed with US positions, which distinguish between territorial sovereignty questions in which the US does, and must, acknowledge it has no direct interest, and the law of the sea issues in which the US sees important national and systemic interests in relatively open seas. In addition to providing indirect legal reinforcement for the US's long-standing and politically sage disjunction between sovereignty and maritime rights, this feature of the tribunal's decision may enhance the US's credibility in arguing that China should respect and implement international law—which now includes the arbitration decision's rejection of Chinese positions that threaten open seas norms—while maintaining that the US is not using support for the arbitral award to "interfere" in questions of sovereignty, which are especially neuralgic and provocative for China.[8]

*Second, the US has insisted on respect for rights of freedom of navigation and overflight in the SCS.* These principles, which the US has articulated and implemented primarily in response to challenges—clear, perceived, or potential—from China, serve and reflect major US interests in the SCS region: protection of international trade in which the US has a large economic stake and in which its friends and allies in the region have an even greater stake, and freedom of operation for the US Navy in a strategically—as well as economically—vital region.

The legal principle of freedom of navigation (and overflight) has been so central that it has been a pillar of US arguments that China's positions and behavior may more broadly challenge international law of the sea norms and, thus, regional order more generally.[9] Equally tellingly, China has responded to the US's and others' concerns about possible Chinese impediments to free

---

8 On the centrality of sovereignty to Chinese conceptions of international law, see generally, XUE HANQIN, CHINESE PERSPECTIVES ON INTERNATIONAL LAW: HISTORY, CULTURE, AND INTERNATIONAL LAW (2012), pp. 68–97; Wang Tieya, *International Law in China: Historical and Contemporary Perspectives*, RECEUIL DES COURS, 221 (1990), Chapter 4. In relation to China's views on the law of the sea, see Jacques deLisle, *From Accepting to Challenging the International Law of the Sea: China and the South China Sea Disputes*, in CHANG-FA LO, NIGEL N.T. LI AND TSAI-YU LIN, (EDS.), LEGAL THOUGHTS BETWEEN THE EAST AND THE WEST IN THE MULTILEVEL LEGAL ORDER (2016), pp. 256–260.

9 See, for example, John G. Odom, *South China Sea and Freedom of Navigation*, DIPLOMAT, 9 March 2006, available at: http://thediplomat.com/2016/03/south-china-sea-and-freedom-of-navigation/; Lynn Kuok, *The U.S. FON Program in the South China Sea: A Lawful and Necessary Response to China's Strategic Ambiguity*, BROOKINGS CENTER FOR EAST ASIA POLICY STUDIES EAST ASIA POLICY PAPER NO. 9 (June 2016).

access with repeated statements that China—whatever its rights might be—would not do anything to interfere with free navigation in the region.[10]

Framing policy in terms of these legal principles has helped the US to defend its interests and assert its preferences while also portraying itself as protecting and providing international public goods, and avoiding taking sides with any of the disputants. Under the US's interpretation of the relevant international legal principles, there is especially little tension between not taking sides among the disputants and insisting on freedoms of navigation and overflight: in the US view, many of the freedoms obtain regardless of whether a particular maritime area is a high seas area, an exclusive economic zone, or (for some US Navy activities) even a territorial sea of one State or another.[11]

Here, too, the Philippines-China arbitration decision resembled preexisting US policy positions. The tribunal could not address demarcation of potentially overlapping maritime zones because China's legally permissible reservation to the provisions of UNCLOS governing dispute resolution precluded the tribunal's deciding those issues.[12] China's reservation covered maritime boundary delimitations, historic bays and titles, and military and law enforcement activities. On Beijing's view, this, too, was enough to deny the arbitration body jurisdiction over the Philippines' claims.

The tribunal, while accepting its lack of authority over demarcation, nonetheless, concluded that it had jurisdiction to decide that China did not enjoy the vast maritime rights it claimed in the SCS. By determining that China definitively lacked rights (beyond those enjoyed by States generally) under the law of the sea over almost all of the disputed SCS area, the tribunal's decision supported the US's position, and weakened China's, on the issues of navigation

10 See, for example, Peh Shing Huei, *China Will Always Ensure Freedom of Navigation in South China Sea, Xi Says*, SOUTH CHINA MORNING POST, 7 November 2015; *China Values South China Sea Navigation Freedom More than Anyone: Spokesperson*, XINHUA, 2 March 2017, available at: http://news.xinhuanet.com/english/2017-03/02/c_136097306.htm.

11 For descriptions of U.S. positions, see *Chapter 10: Air, Sea and Space Law*, OPERATIONAL LAW HANDBOOK (2015), pp. 173–177; James W. Houck and Nicole M. Anderson, *The United States, China, and Freedom of Navigation in the South China Sea*, 13(2) WASHINGTON UNIVERSITY GLOBAL STUDIES LAW REVIEW (2014), pp. 443–447; Raul (Pete) Pedrozo, *Coastal State Jurisdiction over Marine Data Collection in the Exclusive Economic Zone: U.S. Views* in PETER DUTTON, (ED.), MILITARY ACTIVITIES IN THE EEZ (2010), pp. 23–36.

12 See South China Sea Arbitration Award (Jurisdiction and Admissibility) ¶¶ 155–157; China, Declaration under Article 298, UNCLOS, 25 August 2006, http://www.un.org/depts/los/convention_agreements/convention_declarations.htm#China; United Nations Convention on the Law of the Sea, art. 298 (optional exceptions to applicability of Part XV, Section 2, concerning compulsory dispute resolution procedures).

and overflight.[13] With the judgment having rebuffed China's claims to large maritime zones, broad historic rights, and any other special rights over most of the relevant area, the US's opposition to Chinese objections to activities in the SCS area undertaken or endorsed by the US had less need to assert a strong (and not entirely uncontroversial) version of legal rights to exercise many high seas freedoms in another State's coastal zones. Conversely, if the arbitration decision is accepted as a valid ruling (a position that the US in general supports), China's claim of legal rights to reject or resist US operations must retreat to more unconventional and controversial arguments that assert significant legal restrictions on the US's (and others') exercise of high seas freedoms.[14]

The tribunal's decision rejected China's position, and lined up with the US's, on specific issues within the ambit of freedom of navigation and overflight. For example, in ruling that marine formations at which China recently had been undertaking massive land reclamation projects were mere low-tide elevations, the tribunal undercut key bases for Chinese claims of a right to exclude or limit the Philippines, the US, and others.[15] As mere LTEs, these formations could generate no territorial sea (much less, an EEZ) in which China could assert its long-standing (but dubious under international law) claim of a right to require permission or notification for innocent passage.[16] Indeed, as mere LTEs (except for those that are close enough to a larger land form that is itself the basis for a properly claimed maritime zone), such formations could generate no more than a minimal safety zone under UNCLOS—a tiny space much smaller than the area covered by China's newly constructed "islands." Similarly, the panel's controversial decision that none of the relevant landforms—not even Itu Aba/Taiping

13 South China Sea Arbitration Award (Merits) §§ V–VII.

14 For a discussion of these Chinese arguments, see Jacques deLisle, *Troubled Waters: China's Claims and the South China Sea*, 56 (4) ORBIS (2012), pp. 632–635; Jacques deLisle, *China's Territorial and Maritime Disputes in the South and East China Seas*, in JACQUES DELISLE AND AVERY GOLDSTEIN, (EDS.) CHINA'S GLOBAL ENGAGEMENT: COOPERATION, COMPETITION AND INFLUENCE IN THE 21ST CENTURY (2017), pp. 269–270; People's Republic of China Ministry of Foreign Affairs, *China Adheres to the Position of Settling through Negotiation the Relevant Disputes Between China and the Philippines in the South China Sea*, 13 July 2016, ¶ 139, http://www.fmprc.gov.cn/mfa_eng/zxxx_662805/t1380615.shtml ("when exercising freedom of navigation and overflight in the South China Sea, relevant parties shall fully respect the sovereignty and security interests of coastal States").

15 South China Sea Arbitration Award (Merits) §VI.B.

16 Law of the People's Republic of China on the Territorial Sea and the Contiguous Zone (1992), arts. 6, 12; China, *Declaration upon Ratification of UNCLOS,* 7 June 1996, available at: http://www.un.org/depts/los/convention_agreements/convention_declarations.htm#China.

Island—qualified as an island capable of generating an Exclusive Economic Zone undercut another long-standing (and questionable under international law) rights to regulate US Navy reconnaissance activities as "maritime scientific research" (which a coastal State may regulate in its EEZ), or as potentially transgressing some form of EEZ-based "security rights," or as being otherwise subject to China's regulatory authority or police powers within its EEZ.[17]

By denying China such zone-based rights (and historic rights), the panel's decision offered additional legal support for the US policy of freedom of navigation operations (FONOPs) near landforms and marine features claimed by China. FONOPs and reconnaissance missions have been a longstanding and recurring focus of relatively serious adverse encounters between the US and China, including the relatively early, and notorious, EP-3 incident of 2001 (in which a Chinese air force jet struck a US reconnaissance plane that it was shadowing) and the USNS Impeccable Incident of 2009 (in which five Chinese vessels harassed and came dangerously close to a US surveillance ship).[18] Such problematic encounters had recurred in the years since, and the US had increased high-profile FONOPs before the arbitral panel's decision and amid China's accelerated island-building program.[19] The pattern continued after the arbitration award, including when a Chinese naval vessel snagged a drone

---

17 South China Sea Arbitration Award (Merits) §VI.B; Law of the People's Republic on the Exclusive Economic Zone and Continental Shelf (1998) ("EEZ Law"), art. 11; Surveying and Mapping Law of the People's Republic of China, art. 7 (1992, 2002); *China Demands U.S. Navy End Surveillance Missions*, SINA.COM, 12 March 2009, available at: http://english.sina.com/china/2009/0311/225194.html (Defense Ministry Spokesperson Huang Xueping).

18 USNS—United States Naval Ships—are auxiliary vessels, staffed by civilians, and charged with a variety of missions, including surveillance. Raul Pedrozo, *Close Encounters at Sea: The USNS Impeccable Incident*, 62 (3) U.S. NAVAL WAR COLLEGE REVIEW (2009), pp. 101– 111; Ji Guoxing, *The Legality of the Impeccable Incident*, 5 CHINA SECURITY (2009), pp. 16–21; Eric Donnelly, *The United States- China EP-3 Incident: Legality and Realpolitik*, 9 (1) JOURNAL OF CONFLICT AND SECURITY (2004), pp. 25–42; W. Allan Edmiston III, *Showdown in the South China Sea*, 16 (2) EMORY INTERNATIONAL LAW REVIEW (2002), pp. 639–688.

19 See, for example, Remarks by US Secretary of Defense Ashton Carter, *IISS Shangrila Dialogue: A Regional Security Architecture Where Everyone Rises*, 30 May 2015, available at: http://www.defense.gov/News/Speeches/S[eech-View/Article/606676/iiss-shangri-la-dialogue-a-regional-security-architecture-where-everyone-rises; Sam LaGrone, *U.S. Destroyer Challenges More Chinese South China Sea Claims in New Freedom of Navigation Operation* USNI NEWS, 30 January 2016, available at: http://news.usni.org/2016/01/30/u-s-destroyerchallenges-more-chinese-south-china-sea-claims-in-new-freedom-of-navigation-operation%3B; *Full Statement of US Dept of Defense on USS Curtis Wilbur's FONOP Past Triton Island*, South China Sea Research, 31 January 2016, https://seasresearch.wordpress.com/2016/01/31/full-statement-of-us-dept-defence-on-uss-curtis-wilburs-fonop-past-triton-island/; Idrees Ali and Matt Spetalnick, "U.S. Warship Challenges

deployed by the USNS Bowditch (a ship that, like the Impeccable, has had more than one run-in with Chinese vessels, and that was, on this occasion, operating outside the nine-dash line that China claims as marking the extent of its SCS jurisdiction).[20]

What changed in this regard with the arbitration decision was that the panel's ruling undercut one cause for the US often to be ambiguous or muddled about the nature of some of its naval operations—that is, whether a particular operation by a US naval vessel is an innocent passage through a State's territorial sea, an exercise of the residual high seas freedoms that all States enjoy in conducting noneconomic activity in China's or some other State's EEZ, an invited presence in the EEZ or territorial sea of the Philippines (or another claimant State), an exercise of law of the sea rights on the high seas, or a generic use of navigational freedom (without specifying the particular subtype). These questions of how to characterize US activities at times had become contentious on the US side: when a US Navy ship passed near Subi reef in 2015 (one of the landforms on which China had undertaken land reclamation of the type that the Philippines challenged in its arbitration claim), the suggestion that the operation was one of innocent passage stirred considerable controversy in US legal-policy circles, drawing criticism from those who saw it as conceding that some State (or, worse yet, China) had territorial sea rights over the area.[21]

The tribunal's thoroughgoing rejection of China's positions also buttressed the US's long-articulated views on freedom of overflight and its related condemnation of any move by China to establish an Air Defense Identification Zone over the SCS. In the immediate aftermath of the ruling, concerns grew that China might respond by declaring an ADIZ in the area. If Beijing had done

---

China's Claims in South China Sea," Reuters, October 21, 2016, http://www.reuters.com/article/us-southchinasea-usa-exclusive-idUSKCN12L1O9.

20 Terri Moon Cronk, "Chinese Seize U.S. Navy Underwater Drone in South China Sea," DoD News, 16 December 2016, available at: https://www.defense.gov/News/Article/Article/1032823/chinese-seize-us-navy-underwater-drone-in-south-china-sea; Helene Cooper, *U.S. Demands Return of Drone Seized by Chinese Warship*, New York Times, 16 December 2016.

21 Bonnie S. Glaser and Peter A. Dutton, *The U.S. Navy's Freedom of Navigation Operation around Subi Reef: Deciphering U.S. Signaling*, National Interest, 6 November 2015, available at: http://nationalinterest.org/feature/theusnavy%E2%80%99sfreedomnavigationoperationaroundsubireef14272; Raul "Pete" Pedrozo and James Kraska, *Can't Anybody Play This Game? US FON Operations and Law of the Sea*, 17 November 2015, Lawfare Blog, available at: https://www.lawfareblog.com/cant-anybody-play-game-us-fon-operations-and-law-sea; Joseph Bosco, *US FONOPs Actually Conceded Maritime Rights to China*, Diplomat, 8 March 2017, available at: http://thediplomat.com/2017/03/usfonopsactuallyconcededmaritimerightstochina/.

so, or were to do so, it would have reprised China's proclamation of an ADIZ over the East China Sea during the confrontation with Japan over the Senkaku/Diaoyu Islands in 2013—a move that the US had rejected as provocative and likely unlawful.[22]

If China were to make statements or take actions that seem to challenge the US's (or other States') access to places where the Philippines-China arbitration panel has rejected China's claims of maritime rights, the decision will help the US depict its own approach as less controversial and more consistent with established principles—a point that extends beyond freedom of navigation and oversight to international legal rules more broadly.

*Third, the US has called on all parties to the SCS disputes to respect international law, including the law of the sea, which includes UNCLOS for the States that are parties to the convention and, for all States, customary international law that, in the US view, tracks the relevant substantive provisions of UNCLOS.* This is a broader and more fundamental position that parallels and underlies the US stance on freedom of navigation and overflight. The exhortation to adhere to international law has been a significant component of the US's effort to cast itself as a supporter of the existing order and a provider of international public goods in the region and beyond. Often implicitly and sometimes explicitly, the US has claimed that it is pursuing not its own parochial preferences and narrow national interests, but rather is upholding international legal norms that are widely accepted and universally binding, and that generally support the international political status quo.[23]

The US's opposition to China's expansive claims over the region partly reflect conflicting great power interests and policy preferences, but the US's position also is based in an argument that China's claims are untenable under existing international legal norms. On the US's view, to accept China's claims in the SCS is to acquiesce in China's assertion of rights (or dominance) in defiance of

---

22 *Secretary Hagel Issues Statement on East China Sea Air Defense Identification Zone*, 23 November 2013, available at: http://archive.defense.gov/news/newsarticle.aspx?id=121223; Secretary of State John Kerry, *Statement on East China Sea Air Defense Identification Zone*, 23 November 2013, available at: https://2009-2017.state.gov/secretary/remarks/2013/11/218013.htm; see also Jaemin Lee, *China's Declaration of an Air Defense Identification Zone in the East China Sea: Implications for Public International Law*, 18 (17) ASIL INSIGHTS, 19 August 2014, available at: https://www.asil.org/insights/volume/18/issue/17/china%E2%80%99s-declaration-air-defense-identification-zone-east-china-sea#_ednref2.

23 Jacques deLisle, *International Law in the Obama Administration's Pivot to Asia: The China Seas Disputes, the Trans-Pacific Partnership, Rivalry with the PRC, and Status Quo Legal Norms in U.S. Foreign Policy*, 48 (1) CASE WESTERN RESERVE JOURNAL OF INTERNATIONAL LAW (2016), pp. 143–161.

international law, or to open the door to a revisionist Chinese agenda in international law that could reach well beyond the SCS.[24]

This central law-focused element of US policy has been most fully elaborated in response to the escalation of disputes, and what the US sees as China's increasing assertiveness, in the SCS in recent years.[25] The most detailed articulation of the US view that China's positions are legally unsustainable is a document issued in 2014 in the US State Department's "Limits in the Seas" series.[26] The US's call on all parties to follow relevant international law, and specifically the law of the sea, entails disputing particular Chinese claims of rights over the SCS and on broader points of international law that are relevant to such claims.

The US's rejection of China's *physically or geographically* expansive claims has included specific doctrinal points, most notably ones that dismiss the nine-dash line as lacking a legally defensible basis because none of China's apparent arguments is consistent with established law, in that: (1) application of ordinary law of the sea rules basing maritime rights on sovereignty over landforms cannot give China rights to the entire area within the nine-dash line because (even if the landforms are all China's) they are too small and scattered to generate the zones China claims; (2) China's possible claim that the nine-dash line represents a maritime boundary fails, for some of the same reasons (that is, a lack of relevant land that might be under Chinese sovereignty), and because lawful delimitation of any potentially overlapping zones has not been undertaken (nor would a fair and lawful delimitation plausibly yield the nine-dash line); and (3) China's claim of historic rights over the area inside the line is legally insupportable because historic rights under the law of the sea are limited narrowly to coast-adjacent zones and/or must meet a high standard

---

24 See generally, deLisle, *From Accepting to Challenging the International Law of the Sea*, *supra* note 8; deLisle, *China's Territorial and Maritime Disputes*, *supra* note 14 pp. 265–272; Zachary M. Hosford and Ely Ratner, *The Challenge of Chinese Revisionism*, CENTER FOR A NEW AMERICAN SECURITY EAST AND SOUTH CHINA SEAS BULLETIN 8 (1 February 2013), available at: http://www.dragon-report.com/Dragon_Report/home/home_files/The%20Challenge%20of%20Chinese%20Revisionism.pdf.

25 For assessments of China's "new assertiveness," see Alistair Iain Johnston, *How New and Assertive is China's New Assertiveness?* 37 (1) INTERNATIONAL SECURITY (2013), pp. 7–48; Michael Yahuda, *China's New Assertiveness in the South China Sea*, 22 (81) JOURNAL OF CONTEMPORARY CHINA(2013), pp. 446–459; S. 659 South China Sea and East China Sea Sanctions Act of 2017, 115th Cong. 1st Sess. (15 March 2017), sec. 2 ("Findings").

26 UNITED STATES DEPARTMENT OF STATE, BUREAU OF OCEANS AND INTERNATIONAL ENVIRONMENTAL AND SCIENTIFIC AFFAIRS, LIMITS IN THE SEAS NO. 143, CHINA: MARITIME CLAIMS IN THE SOUTH CHINA SEA (5 December 2014), available at: http://www.state.gov/documents/organization/234936.pdf.

of historic usage akin to the requirements of adverse possession in domestic property law.[27]

The US also has rejected China's *conceptually or jurisdictionally* expansive claims of rights in maritime zones as inconsistent with existing international law. More specifically, in the US view: (1) rights of innocent passage (by the US Navy) through another State's territorial sea do not require prior notification (much less permission) from the coastal State; (2) peaceful operations (by the US Navy) in another State's EEZ are permissible because a coastal State's EEZ rights do not include "security" rights, and because surveillance or reconnaissance is not maritime scientific research subject to regulation by the EEZ State; and (3) activities (by the US Navy) to which China objects do not violate the obligations of peaceful use of the high seas, or constitute abuse of law of the sea rights, or transgress broader international legal norms restricting the use of force or the threat of force against other States. With the principles understood in this way, China's opposition to—and claims of a right to reject or regulate—various US Navy operations (as well as much civilian maritime and airborne traffic) are legally incorrect, and Chinese activities (ranging from harassment of US planes and ships, to warning off US forces that come close to Chinese-controlled—and newly expanded—marine formations, to asserting rights to require notification or permission of foreign ships and planes operating in marine and air spaces over which China claims some form of jurisdiction) lack legal basis—while also being adverse to US political and security interests.

Here, again, the Philippines-China arbitration panel's conclusions align well with established US positions. The content of relevant international law as reflected or determined in the arbitral decision is consistent with many of the understandings of specific law of the sea rules previously embraced by the US, generally and in opposition to China and its very different views. In declaring that the nine-dash line has no independent significance and entails no rights—including historic rights—beyond those that might be conferred upon China by operation of the ordinary, geography-driven rules of UNCLOS for deriving maritime rights from sovereignty over landforms, the tribunal adopted a position that is close to preexisting US legal analyses.[28] When the panel

27 For a more detailed examination of the issues discussed in this paragraph and the following paragraph, see deLisle, *From Accepting to Challenging the International Law of the Sea*, *supra* note 8, pp. 260–271; deLisle, *China's Territorial and Maritime Disputes in the South and East China Seas*, *supra* note 24, pp. 265–272; deLisle, *Troubled Waters*, *supra* note 14, pp. 620–635.

28 South China Sea Arbitration Award (Merits) §V. On US views, see, for example, *Remarks at Press Availability* (*Hillary Clinton*), *supra* note 4. ("Consistent with customary

decided on the status of disputed landforms and lesser features—declaring them mere rocks (not islands) or mere LTEs (not rocks)—and that China's actions on and near the contested formations are unlawful, its conclusions paralleled the US's long-standing assertions that China lacks authority to restrict, regulate, or require notice of US Navy activities in much of the SCS, and the US's more recent, focused challenges to China's land reclamation and related facilities-building.[29]

After the tribunal's award, the US's broad call for all the SCS disputants to respect international law morphs easily into a call on China to respect the panel's decision, as a formal, procedurally proper, and substantively authoritative decision on some of the major legal issues in the SCS disputes. The decision strengthens the US's rhetorical or political hand, relative to China's, in obvious ways. China is now not just rejecting US views (shared broadly but not universally by other States). China now is rejecting what the US can portray (and has characterized) as a legally binding decision by a neutral and authoritative tribunal (one that, to be sure, faces criticisms—likely not very persuasive ones—from Chinese sources for procedural illegitimacy and bias).[30] The more China stridently rejects the decision and the tribunal's legitimacy, and the more China acts in ways that appear to flout the tribunal's ruling or international legal rules more broadly, the more the US can align arguments of legal principle with the US's interests in opposing China's assertiveness and preserving the normative and political status quo.

There is, of course, a glaring weakness in the US position: the US has not joined UNCLOS and thus is not itself bound by treaty to the rules that it insists

---

international law, legitimate claims to maritime space in the South China Sea should be derived solely from legitimate claims to land features").

29 South China Sea Arbitration Award (Merits) §§VI, VII(D)–(E). On US views, see, for example, Ashton Carter, *Secretary of Defense Speech,* U.S. Pacific Command Change of Command, 27 May 2015, available at: http://archive.defense.gov/Speeches/Speech.aspx?SpeechID=1944.

30 Secretary of State John Kerry, *Remarks with Philippines Foreign Secretary Perfecto Yasay,* 26 July 2016, available at: https://www.state.gov/secretary/remarks/2016/07/260541.htm ("It's impossible for it to be irrelevant. It's legally binding… And it's obviously a decision of a court that's recognized under international law. It has to be part of the calculation"); John Kirby, *Press Statement,* Assistant Secretary and Department Spokesperson, Bureau of Public Affairs, 12 July 2016, available at: https://ph.usembassy.gov/statementusdepartmentstatespokespersonjohnkirbydecisionphilippineschinaarbitration/ ("the Tribunal's decision is final and legally binding on both China and the Philippines. The United States expresses its hope and expectation that both parties will comply with their obligations"). China's criticisms are discussed in a later section.

China (and others) should accept and that the Philippines-China arbitration panel interpreted. To be sure, the US has long argued—and will continue to argue in light of the arbitral decision—that the relevant rules are part of customary international law, binding on China, as well as the other rival claimants in the SCS, and the US.[31] But the US's failure to accede to UNCLOS nonetheless blunts the arbitration decision somewhat as a tool for pressing US legal views and policy goals.

There is another, more substantive aspect of the decision that is problematic for US aims and interests, and thus strains somewhat the alignment between US agendas and a tribunal-supporting "pro-legality" stance: the very high standard for UNCLOS Article 121(3) islands capable of generating EEZs that the tribunal formulated to disqualify all SCS landforms, including Taiping Island/Itu Aba. This standard is one that the US will not welcome in other contexts because its application could pose significant problems for maritime zones claimed by the US or its friends and allies.[32] Resistance by the US or others to the tribunal's interpretation of Article 121(3) will create, at least for a time, uncertainty about maritime zones derived from small landforms, and thus will muddy and complicate the otherwise clean and simple call by the US for China and others to respect the tribunal's ruling and follow international law more generally.

*Fourth, the US has emphasized all parties' obligations to address their disputes peacefully and has urged all parties to accept multilateral and/or formal dispute resolution.* Given the general international legal obligation of States to resolve disputes peacefully and to refrain from force or threats of force,[33] this point is something of a corollary to the US position of calling on all parties to respect

---

31 American Law Institute, Restatement (Third) of Foreign Relations Law of the United States, vol. 2 (1987) p. 5 "[B]y express or tacit agreement accompanied by consistent practice, the United States, and states generally, have accepted the substantive provisions of the Convention, other than those addressing deep sea-bed mining, as statements of customary law binding upon them apart from the Convention."); Hillary Clinton Statement on the South China Sea [note 3 above] ("call[ing] on all parties to clarify their claims in the South China Sea in terms consistent with customary international law, including as reflected in the Law of the Sea Convention").

32 See, for example, M. Taylor Fravel, *The Strategic Implications of the South China Sea Tribunal's Award*, National Interest, 13 July 2016, available at: http://nationalinterest.org/feature/why-the-south-china-sea-tribunals-ruling-may-backfire-16951; Alex G. Oude Elferink, *The South China Sea Arbitration's Interpretation of Article 121(3) of the LOSC: A Disquieting First*, 7 September 2016, available at: http://site.uit.no/jclos/2016/09/07/the-south-china-sea-arbitrations-interpretation-of-article-1213-of-the-losc-a-disquieting-first/.

33 United Nations Charter, arts. 2(3), 2(4).

international law. Here, too, the US legal position has suited US preferences and interests in: (1) avoiding escalation of the SCS disputes into crises, or incidents at sea, or larger-scale conflicts into which the US could be drawn and that would be harmful to US allies and other parties in the region and beyond; and (2) promoting multilateral and relatively formal modes for handling disputes (such as could be conducted under the long-promised but unachieved Code of Conduct for the SCS or through international arbitration or adjudication), which are likely to be less advantageous to China than are the informal, bilateral, less-rule-governed negotiations that China favors between itself and the weaker rival claimants.[34]

The Philippines-China arbitration case resonates with this aspect of US policy as well. The decision is, after all, the product of a highly formal dispute resolution process—one which in this case the US specifically supported. The US's relatively well-established policy of favoring multilateral and formal approaches to the SCS disputes had laid a felicitous foundation for the US to take a dim view of China's recalcitrance toward the Philippines' initiation and pursuit of arbitration. China's approach to the proceedings highlighted the procedural aspect and thus reinforces this aspect of the US position: China refused to participate even at the jurisdictional phase—a choice that was controversial among Chinese international law experts and within the Chinese government. This refusal invited unflattering comparisons to what generally has been a weak point in US claims to be a strong supporter of international law: in the case that Nicaragua brought against the US in the International Court of Justice in the 1980s, the US had refused to participate in the merits phase (and subsequently withdrew its general submission to ICJ jurisdiction), but the US at least had appeared to contest jurisdiction—an approach that some in China and elsewhere had urged Beijing to take in the SCS arbitration case.[35]

34 See, for example, Kirby, *supra* note 30. (US "support[s] efforts to resolve territorial and maritime disputes in the South China Sea peacefully, including through arbitration"); *Remarks of Susan A. Thornton*, Acting Assistant Secretary, Bureau of East Asia and Pacific Affairs, Beijing, 26 May 2017, available at: https://www.state.gov/p/eap/rls/rm/2017/05/271410.htm (expressing US support for "respect for legal processes and diplomatic processes like the arbitral tribunal" and for ongoing efforts to develop multilateral Code of Conduct); Foreign Ministry, People's Republic of China, China Adheres to the Position of Settling Through Negotiation, supra note 14.

35 *Military and Paramilitary Activities in and against Nicaragua* (Nicaragua v. United States of America), Jurisdiction and Admissibility, Judgment, I.C.J. Reports 1984, p. 392; *Military and Paramilitary Activities in and against Nicaragua* (Nicaragua v. United States of America), Merits, Judgment, I.C.J. Reports 1986, p. 14.

With the panel's judgment issued, US support for resort to a formal legal mechanism for peaceful dispute resolution could merge into calls for China to respect a decision that is the product of such a process. The US response to the decision tellingly emphasized procedure, more than substance.[36] This distinction is politically and legally significant. As just noted, China was on politically weaker ground on legal procedure than on legal substance. Rather than insist that the tribunal's decision is correct on the merits and invoking that as a basis for calling on China to accept as lawful a decision that it deemed unacceptable on the merits, US official statements primarily called on China to respect the outcome of a process to which China had, in the US view, consented (and that did not have the fatal jurisdictional flaws that China has asserted). For the US, this proceduralist approach had the perhaps-modest virtues of: deflecting slightly a confrontation with China over the substance of the ruling; avoiding a clearer US embrace of aspects of the ruling that the US might not welcome (such as the decision on Article 121(3) islands); and reducing, perhaps, the extent to which full Chinese compliance with the award would be the measure of success for US policy.

Here, too, however, the tribunal's ruling does pose some challenges for US positions and policies. Urging respect for the decision in effect calls upon China to accept an adverse outcome from a dispute resolution process to which the US will not subject itself: China's accession to the UNCLOS treaty-based dispute resolution provision provided the only basis for the tribunal's authority, given the absence of China's specific consent to the case being heard. Chinese (and other critics) have made much of the US's approach to the ICJ case that Nicaragua brought against the US, as well as the US's absence from the UNCLOS regime.[37] Legally accurate distinctions between the US's participating in the jurisdictional phase and refusing to participate in the merits phase, on the one hand, and China's refusal to participate in either phase, on the other hand, have only limited political traction. This is all the more so, given that the Philippines-China arbitration panel, unlike the ICJ in the US-Nicaragua case,

36 Kirby, *supra* note 30; Nick Wadhams, *U.S. Presses China to be Responsible Power after Sea Ruling*, (quoting State Department spokesman), BLOOMBERG, 12 July 2016, available at: https://www.bloomberg.com/news/articles/2016-07-12/u-s-presses-china-to-be-responsible-power-after-maritime-ruling.

37 See, for example, Simon Denyer, *U.S. 'Hypocrisy' and Chinese Cash Strengthen Beijing's Hand in South China Sea*, WASHINGTON POST, 19 June 2016; *Spotlight: U.S. Refusal to Honor Court Ruling in Nicaragua Case Reflects Double Standards*," XINHUA, 14 July 2016, available at: http://news.xinhuanet.com/english/2016-07/14/c_135512985.htm.

did not so clearly distinguish between the jurisdiction and merits phases and left half of the jurisdictional questions to be decided in the same opinion that addressed the merits. The weakness of such lawyerly arguments as means to undo the political damage of the US's lack of clear moral high ground mean that US policy and behavior have made it all too easy for China to invoke a narrative that great powers have been free to ignore international law and that the US's call on China to do otherwise is, therefore, hypocritical.[38]

As much of the foregoing suggests, *the US agenda and interests related to the SCS face significant challenges and uncertainty despite the arbitration decision's apparent vindication of—or, at least, alignment with—US positions*. There are several reasons for this. First, US calls upon China to obey international law as interpreted by the tribunal invite familiar charges from China of US hypocrisy or double-standards, invoking the US's failure to accede to UNCLOS, unwillingness to subject itself to binding arbitration akin to the process in the Philippines-China case, or insistence on what (in China's view) are self-serving interpretations of international law that give a principal potential adversary a seemingly free hand (particularly in military operations in the SCS) and imperil China's own core interests.

Second, the relatively close alignment between the tribunal's decision and established US positions encourages China to indulge its already-prominent suspicions (or, at least, rhetorical claims) about US behavior and goals. These include notions that: Washington is the "black hand" behind Manila's successful legal gambit (and possible imitation by other claimants), and is emboldening weaker regional powers to challenge China in China's pursuit of what it sees as its natural and proper place as the preeminent regional power; and international law and legal institutions continue to reflect the interests and preferences of the US and other status quo powers, to the detriment of China's legitimate rights and interests as a rising power.[39]

---

38 For an example of this view from an American scholar that quickly gained currency in Chinese policy intellectual circles, see Graham Allison, *Of Course China, Like All Great Powers, Will Ignore an International Legal Verdict*, DIPLOMAT, 11 July 2016, available at: http://thediplomat.com/2016/07/of-course-china-like-all-great-powers-will-ignore-an-international-legal-verdict/.

39 Yang Jiechi, *supra* note 6. ("Certain countries outside the region have attempted to deny China's sovereign rights and interests in the South China Sea through the arbitration."); *Abuse of International Law Impacts International Order*, RENMIN RIBAO, 12 July 2016, available at: http://paper.people.com.cn/rmrb/html/2016-07/12/nw.D110000renmrb_20160712_4-03.htm (blaming Western forces led by the United States for manipulation of arbitration and international law more generally); *Western Countries*

Third, the tribunal's decision—by making specific rulings that demand significant changes in China's behavior and reject long-held Chinese claims about legal rights—increases the complexity for the US of neither pushing too much nor pushing too little for China to follow international legal rules. With the tribunal's decision seemingly ineluctably part of the "international law" that Washington generally calls on Beijing to respect, and with China's acceptance and compliance not forthcoming, the US's choices become more pointed and difficult. If the US fails to press the norms of international law that the US and the tribunal share, or ostensibly presses hard but lacks the will or the ability to induce some degree of compliance by a recalcitrant China, the US could face a version of the "abandonment" problem that is a characteristic risk in alliance relationships.[40] Narrowly, the US's long-running, purportedly robust commitment to international law as a means for addressing the SCS disputes could be shown to be relatively hollow. This could deepen broader concerns about the US among its allies and partners in the region. As with critical accounts of the Obama-era "pivot" or "rebalance" to Asia, so too with the US commitment to international law: the US's formal and informal security partners in the East Asian region (including some that are not SCS claimants, most significantly Japan and Korea) may at least incrementally lose confidence in the US's resolve and commitment to their security and the international rules (both formal legal ones and less formal political ones) that help to safeguard the status quo. This, in turn, could weaken US influence and the US's ability to pursue its aims (including maintaining peace and stability) in the region.

On the other, somewhat less sharp horn of the dilemma, the tribunal's decision also may increase the risk of "entrapment" that the US faces in relations with China's rival claimants in the SCS. Although there is much posturing, or paranoia, in some Chinese sources' claims that Washington is responsible for the Philippines'—and Vietnam's—temerity in opposing China, an especially ardent (and not obviously hollow) US push to implement the terms of a panel decision—and international legal norms—that so clearly reject China's position could invite over-interpretation by China's neighbors. It could encourage regional States to become more assertive and intransigent in dealing with

---

*Should Stop Playing International Law as Political Card*, PEOPLE'S DAILY, 10 July 2016, http://en.people.cn/n3/2016/0710/c98649-9083897.html.

40 On the twin risks of abandonment and entrapment (discussed below) in alliance relationships, see generally, Glenn H. Snyder, *Alliance Theory: A Neo-Realist First Cut*, 44 (1) JOURNAL OF INTERNATIONAL AFFAIRS, 2013–123 (1990); in the East Asian context, see Victor D. Cha, *Abandonment, Entrapment and Neoclassical Realism in Asia*," 44(2) INTERNATIONAL STUDIES QUARTERLY, 261–291 (2000).

China over the SCS or other issues. Such developments, in turn, could impede the US's ability to promote a viable compromise or a relatively face-saving path for China in the aftermath of the tribunal's decision, or to pursue other priorities in US-China relations (including ones with grave implications for regional security, such as North Korea).

The behavior of regional States following the arbitral panel's ruling suggests that serious risks of entrapment are not imminent. With the Aquino government, which had brought the arbitration case, giving way to the very different Duterte government in the Philippines on the eve of the tribunal's decision, the party that had won the resounding legal victory in the Hague immediately opted for caution, endorsing restraint, sobriety, peace, stability, and peaceful resolution and management, and expressing a willingness to negotiate—alongside its initial celebration of a legal victory.[41] Shortly thereafter, Duterte announced that the decision would "take the back seat," and traveled to Beijing to engage in bilateral negotiations, which has long been China's preferred mode for addressing the SCS disputes, and which yielded modest benefits for Manila in regaining access to parts of the disputed maritime region.[42]

To some extent, the approach taken by the Philippines under Duterte may reflect differences in leaders' preferences. In the Philippines, as elsewhere, it matters who is president. But Manila's post-ruling approach, to a great extent, also may reflect a sober realism about what is possible following so sweeping a decision and in the face of China's stern rejection of that decision. Negotiation in light of the ruling (rather than simple, and in this case surely futile, insistence on implementation of the award) is an outcome that is relatively common in international practices that are shaped by the parties' political calculations and power. It is far from unusual even in systems with much more robust enforcement mechanisms than an ad hoc international arbitration tribunal constituted under the dispute resolution provisions of UNCLOS.

Other interested States, including most notably Vietnam, took a tempered approach in response to the arbitral panel's decision, generally praising the

41 *Statement of Foreign Secretary Perfecto Yasay on the West Philippine Sea arbitration case The Republic of Philippines v. The People's Republic of China,* Department of Foreign Affairs, Pasay City, 12 July 2016, available at: http://globalnation.inquirer.net/140968/full-text-dfa-foreign-affairs-perfecto-yasay-west-philippine-sea; Chris Larano, *Philippines' Duterte Asks Ex-President to Begin Talks in South China Sea Dispute,* WALL STREET JOURNAL, 15 July 2016.

42 Benjamin Kang Lim, *Philippines' Duterte Says S. China Sea Arbitration Case to Take 'Back Seat,'* REUTERS, 19 October 2016, available at: http://www.reuters.com/article/us-china-philippines-idUSKCN12J10S; Jane Perlez, *Philippines' Deal with China Pokes a Hole in US Strategy,* NEW YORK TIMES, 2 November 2016.

proceeding's outcome while showing ambivalence or hedging in calling for peaceful means and legal *and* diplomatic processes.[43] With the arbitration decision having accomplished as much as was reasonably to be hoped for in rejecting China's expansive legal claims (and arguably more), but having yielded the Philippines no more than modest real-world gains, Vietnam and other rival claimants appeared to see little to be gained by bringing additional, similar claims.

Taiwan's reaction was especially complicated and ambivalent, due to unique features of Taiwan's situation, including: its awkward partial alignment with China on some issues (including claims of broad rights rooted in Chinese historical claims to an area within a dashed line that dated to the pre-PRC era); its long-standing alignment with the US on many regional security and related legal issues; its objection to the tribunal's refusal to accept a formal submission by Taiwan (because Taiwan has been prevented from joining UNCLOS), indication that its consideration of Taiwan's materials was contingent on the parties' lack of objection, and reference to Taiwan as the "Taiwan authority of China"; and its strong objection to the tribunal's determination that the criteria for an EEZ-generating island were not met by Taiping Island / Itu Aba—the largest naturally occurring landform in the SCS and the only significant feature under Taiwan's control.[44]

Although the near-term risks of entrapment thus seem small for the US, they cannot be discounted entirely. Although the SCS disputes remained relatively quiet more than a year after the arbitration decision, the panel's ruling did purport to clarify and rearrange economically and strategically valuable legal rights in a region that has been prone to sometimes years-long—but quickly

43 *Vietnam Welcomes Tribunal Ruling on South China Sea Dispute*, ASSOCIATED PRESS, 12 July 2016; *Remarks of the Spokesperson of the Ministry of Foreign Affairs of Vietnam*, 12 July 2016; *Press Release Following the Decision of the Arbitral Tribunal on the South China Sea Issue—Statement by Malaysia*, 13 July 2016; Amy Searight, *Diplomacy and Security in the South China Sea: After the Tribunal*, Statement before the House Foreign Affairs Subcommittee on Asia and the Pacific, 22 September 2016, available at: http://docs.house.gov/meetings/FA/FA05/20160922/105354/HHRG-114-FA05-Wstate-SearightA-20160922.pdf (summarizing ASEAN States' reactions).

44 See Chinese (Taiwan) Society of International Law, In the Matter of an Arbitration under Annex VII to the 1982 United Nations Convention on the Law of the Sea on the Issue of the Feature of Taiping Island (Itu Aba) Pursuant to Article 121(1) and (3) of the 1982 Convention on the Law of the Sea, PCA Case No. 2013-19 between the Republic of the Philippines and the People's Republic of China, Amicus Curiae Submission, 23 March 2016, available at: http://csil.org.tw/home/wp-content/uploads/2016/03/SCSTF-Amicus-Curiae-Brief-final.pdf; South China Sea Arbitration Award (Merits) ¶¶ 89, 92, 139–142; Jacques deLisle, Why Taiwan President Ma Ying-jeou's Day-Trip to Taiping Island was Such a Big Deal, FPRI Enote, February 2016, available at: http://www.fpri.org/article/2016/02/why-taiwan-president-ma-ying-jeous-day-trip-taiping-island-was-such-big-deal/

shifting—phases of clam and strife. It is all too easy to envision scenarios in which serious tensions reemerge—and implicate the Philippines-China case's holdings. These could be due to actions taken by China (including moves manifesting its rejection of the tribunal's views of international legal rights and rules) or by rival claimants (who might invoke the legal conclusions reached by the arbitration panel to support their own claims and their opposition to China's moves, and who thereby would call—perhaps explicitly—on the US to make good on its often-proclaimed support for observance of international law in the SCS region). Notably, initial US reactions to the panel's decision did not seem to be free of concerns akin to entrapment: one US official told the press that the US was issuing "a blanket call for quiet, not some attempt to rally the region against China, which would play into a false narrative that the U.S. is leading a coalition to contain China."[45]

The risks of the abandonment dynamic might seem relatively remote as well. Indeed, with the Philippines under Duterte eschewing efforts to implement the award, and other claimant States showing little appetite for filing follow-on arbitration claims or adopting other similarly assertive stances, it would seem that the absence of a strong US push for China to comply with the ruling or accept the validity of its conclusions would not be characterized plausibly as "abandoning" allies or partners who were seeking a more proactive approach. Indeed, it would be problematic for the US to be more vigorous than the Philippines in asserting the Philippines' legal rights. Yet, the situation may not prove to be so simple for the US in the longer run. The US commitment to legal rules and interpretations of those rules that align with US interests, to protect the interests of regional States that are rival claimants of China's and allies or friends of the US, and to reject China's views of relevant international law, are deeper and broader than the tribunal's decision. US actions or statements that back away from prior opposition to China's land reclamation projects and exclusion of Filipino vessels from waters near Scarborough Shoal or other areas long open to the Philippines' fishing fleet, or that begin to acquiesce in Chinese forces' warning off or harassing US ships, and so on, easily could trigger law-of-the-sea-related concerns about abandonment. Indeed, the seemingly rapid decline in the arbitration decision's salience may have deprived the US of a relatively cheap and easy way of signaling "non-abandonment" by emphasizing support for the decision in principle while eschewing robust efforts in practice that all interested parties would have recognized would be dangerous and possibly counterproductive.

45 Lesley Wroughton and John Walcott, *U.S. Launches Quiet Diplomacy to Ease South China Sea Tensions*, REUTERS, 14 July 14, 2016.

These complexities and challenges would exist even in a context where the US approach remains stable, unaffected by changes akin to those that the Philippines' stance underwent with the succession from Aquino to Duterte. *Prospects for continuity in US policy on issues of international law and the SCS are uncertain, however.* At a minimum, US positions will adapt to changes in the relevant legal, political, and policy environments. Examples noted above include the Philippines-China arbitration panel's decision itself and the change of governments in Manila. Other examples, addressed in more detail below, include China's reaction to the decision and China's broader—and possibly rapidly evolving—policy choices. But the most obvious and direct cause of uncertainty in US policy is the outcome of the 2016 US presidential election. Although the US approach to SCS issues has roots in the Clinton administration, in its contemporary form, it is largely the product of the Obama administration and its response to escalating tensions and a growing number of incidents in the SCS (and the East China Sea as well). The prospect of a new president inevitably creates some unpredictability. But if Hillary Clinton had won the election, a high degree of continuity would have been likely. As Secretary of State, she was, after all, the principal framer of the Obama administration's principles concerning legal and political issues the SCS disputes, and the "pivot" or "rebalance" to Asia more generally. Notwithstanding a late-found skepticism toward the Trans-Pacific Partnership trade agreement, her policies on the SCS and broadly related legal and policy issues were expected to be in line with her predecessor's, albeit with a possible proclivity toward being somewhat "tougher" on China (although probably not as much tougher as critical PRC observers appeared to expect).

Donald Trump's electoral victory, a rocky transition period, and a tumultuous early presidency have created much uncertainty. Trump's strongly anti-China campaign rhetoric suggested that his administration might take a harder line on SCS issues. Although candidate Trump criticized China mostly for its economic behavior, a narrative that portrayed China as a bully and a scofflaw on territorial disputes and law of the sea issues seemed to be complementary. Trump's repeated pledges to "rebuild" US military strength seemed to imply a more assertive stance toward China—the most salient rival in scenarios for which a larger US Navy would be needed. President-elect Trump seemed to signal a tough line toward China on security-related matters with significant international legal aspects when he suggested that the US might not adhere to its long-standing "one China policy" concerning Taiwan, and when a Trump tweet linked continued support for that policy to China's being less recalcitrant on the SCS (with the island-building projects a particular focus) and more cooperative on economic issues. The line of confrontational tweets continued in response to the December 2017 drone seizure: "China steals US

Navy research drone in international waters—rips it out of water and takes it to China in unpresidented act." With the new administration freshly in office, a seemingly not-well-briefed Secretary of State nominee Rex Tillerson offered a short-lived embrace of a more aggressive and legally fraught policy toward China in the SCS, saying that the US might undertake a blockade to prevent China's access to disputed marine features on which it had been reclaiming land and building facilities. Other statements by Tillerson and White House spokesperson Sean Spicer seemed perhaps to cast doubt on the US's long-standing position of not taking a position on sovereignty questions in the SCS (and not challenging established patterns of control) when they spoke of not allowing China illegally to take over disputed or "international" territory.[46]

On the other hand, when candidate Trump suggested that even treaty allies such as Japan and Korea might have to rely more on themselves for their own security (amid broader talk of an "America first" foreign policy with a focus on narrowly defined national interests), he raised greater doubts about the US's future commitments to the security of other friendly or informally allied States that were claimants in the SCS disputes and, in turn, long-standing US positions on international legal issues that were generally favorable to those States' interests. Subsequent assurances by leaders of Trump's national security team partly—but only partly—assuaged those concerns. As president, Trump soon abandoned his flirtation with abandoning the one China policy and backed

46 Ros Krasny, *Trump Takes on China in Tweets on Currency, South China Sea*, BLOOMBERG, 4 December 2016, available at: https://www.bloomberg.com/news/articles/20161204/trumptakesonchinaintweetsaboutcurrencysouthchinasea ("Did China ask us if it was OK to devalue their currency (making it hard for our companies to compete), heavily tax our products going into their country (the U.S. doesn't tax them) or to build a massive military complex in the middle of the South China Sea? I don't think so!"); *Trump Slams China's Seizure of U.S. Drone in Tweet*, POLITICO, 17 December 2016, available at: http://www.politico.com/story/2016/12/trump-china-drone-seizure-232775; Transcript, Confirmation Hearing for Secretary of State Nominee Rex Tillerson, Senate Foreign Relations Committee, 14 January 2017, available at: http://edition.cnn.com/TRANSCRIPTS/1701/14/cnr.04.html ("We're going to have to send China a clear signal that, first, the island building stops and, second, your access to those islands is also not going to be allowed"); *Statement of Secretary of State Nominee Rex Tillerson,* Senate Foreign Relations Committee, 11 January 2017, available at: https://www.state.gov/secretary/remarks/2017/01/267394.htm ("We should also acknowledge the realities about China. China's island-building in the South China Sea is an illegal taking of disputed areas without regard for international norms."); Sam LaGrone, *Spicer South China Sea Comments Draw Negative Beijing Response*, USNI NEWS, 24 January 2017, available at: https://news.usni.org/2017/01/24/spicersouthchinaseacommentsdrawnegativebeijingresponse ("So it's a question of if those islands are in fact in international waters and are not part of China proper then yeah we're going to make sure we defend international territories from being taken over by one country").

away from campaign threats to label China a currency manipulator or to impose trade sanctions—thereby reducing, the likelihood of a serious deterioration in the overall US-China relationship and potentially destabilizing consequences in the SCS region. Under Trump, the US Navy for a time stopped its FONOPs near Chinese-held landforms in a move that was widely construed as reducing US pressure on China, although that was offset by continued operations of US Navy commissioned ships and USNS surveillance vessels in other parts of the SCS and by an apparent return to FONOPs in May 2017. Much of the more conciliatory tone in relations with China over the SCS and more generally, however, appeared to be in the service of seeking Beijing's cooperation in addressing North Korea's nuclear weapons and missile programs—a policy approach that raised the specter of the Trump administration subordinating, or sacrificing, traditional, China-challenging positions on the SCS and related legal issues (unless or until Trump were to grow frustrated with China over North Korea, or other issues, and, in turn, take a tougher line toward China on questions that might include the SCS).[47]

The transition from Obama to Trump included other sources of uncertainty as well. Tough words on China policy from candidates of the out-of-power party often fade—sometimes quickly—once such a candidate takes office. Trump's apparent ignorance of foreign and security policy and international law, disdain for Obama-era and establishment approaches, and very thinly staffed administration—along with conflicting signals and impulses of the campaign, transition and early incumbency—have made his administration's positions on SCS issues more difficult to assess, both generally and on more narrow and specialized questions such as the Philippines-China tribunal's decisions on doctrinal issues and implementation of the panel's award.

## III China

The arbitration panel's adverse and unanimous decision triggered a predictably negative reaction from Beijing. China's choices in addressing the challenges it

47 Javier C. Hernandez, *Trump's Mixed Signals on South China Sea Worry Asian Allies*, New York Times, 10 May 2017; *South China Sea: US Carrier Group Begins 'Routine' Patrols*, BBC, 19 February 2017, available at: http://www.bbc.com/news/world-asia-china-39018882; Idrees Ali and David Brunnstrom, *U.S. Warship Drill Meant to Defy China's Claim over Artificial Island: Officials*, Reuters, 26 May 2017, available at: http://www.reuters.com/article/ususasouthchinaseanavyidUSKBN18K353 (quoting Pentagon spokesman, "We are continuing regular FONOPS, as we have routinely done in the past and will continue to do in the future").

faces in the aftermath of the tribunal's ruling will do much to determine the longer term legal and political implications of the decision and, in turn, the trajectory of the SCS disputes. China's options can be understood as a spectrum of escalation. Beijing resorted to some of the lower-end options during the multi-year arbitration process and in response to the panel's award. Some of China's options go into effect almost by default, simply by China not abandoning positions or activities that are inconsistent with the panel's rulings. Other, more assertive alternatives, although not yet undertaken, remain possible and a potential problem for security and stability in the region.

Near the lower end of the range of possible responses are arguments that the tribunal's decision are inconsistent with a proper understanding of international law and therefore can be lawfully disregarded. In the words of China's foreign minister, the decision was "just a piece of waste paper," and was merely a "so-called award."[48] In Beijing's view, China had been justified in its "four noes" approach to the arbitration: no participation, no acceptance, no recognition, and no enforcement. Drawing in part on long-held positions and on arguments China had made at earlier phases in the arbitration, official Chinese sources launched a sweeping and multipronged denunciation.

On the Chinese account, the tribunal lacked jurisdiction, for several reasons: Deciding the issues presented by the Philippines' claims concerning rights in maritime zones inevitably implicated issues of territorial sovereignty over the disputed landforms (because sovereignty over landforms is the basis for rights over maritime areas under the principle—pervasive in UNCLOS rules—that "the land dominates the sea"), but questions of territorial sovereignty are beyond the scope of UNCLOS and thus beyond the jurisdiction of the panel as an ad hoc tribunal constituted under UNCLOS.[49] Deciding on the Philippines' claims also inescapably entailed ruling on questions of maritime zone delimitation (given the overlapping claims that the Philippines, China, and others could assert based on their purported sovereignty over disputed landforms) and Chinese military and law enforcement activities (some of which would

48 Vice Foreign Minister Liu Zhenmin at the Press Conference on the White Paper Titled China Adheres to the Position of Settling Through Negotiation the Relevant Disputes Between China and the Philippines in the South China Sea, 13 July 2016, available at: http://www.fmprc.gov.cn/mfa_eng/wjdt_665385/zyjh_665391/t1381980.shtml; Yang Jiechi, *supra* note 6.

49 China Adheres to the Position of Settling Through Negotiation, *supra* note 14, ¶125; ; Position Paper of the Government of the People's Republic of China on the Matter of Jurisdiction in the South China Sea Arbitration Initiated by the Republic of the Philippines, December 7, 2014 ¶¶ 4–29, available at: http://www.fmprc.gov.cn/mfa_eng/zxxx_662805/t1217147.shtml.

be illegal or at least less clearly legal if the tribunal accepted the Philippines' view, and rejected China's, on the issue of the status—EEZ-generating islands, lesser rocks, or mere LTEs—of contested features, and the scope of historic rights within the nine-dash line), but China's lawful reservation to the dispute resolution provisions of UNLCOS had placed such matters beyond the compulsory jurisdiction of an UNCLOS-based tribunal.[50] The tribunal lacked jurisdiction because the Philippines and China had made a binding agreement—bilaterally or on the basis of the multilateral Declaration on the Conduct of the Parties in the SCS—to address their disputes bilaterally, thus eliminating any right the Philippines might otherwise have had to seek arbitration without China's case-specific consent.[51]

On the Chinese account, the panel's procedures were flawed, in a few overlapping ways: The tribunal's handling of the decision on jurisdiction (such that the panel determined its jurisdiction over half the claims jointly with its decision on the merits) was suspect. The panel failed to fulfill its obligation to give adequate attention to China's legal arguments on key issues—a duty that the panel had notwithstanding China's refusal to participate in the proceedings, and a duty that the panel could have fulfilled, given that China provided an extensive, albeit not formally submitted, brief detailing its positions. The decision lacked adequate basis.[52]

In China's assessment, the arbitration tribunal also got the substantive law wrong when it rejected China's views—many of them long-standing—on crucial issues. These included: the existence of China's customary international law-based historic rights that survived the advent of UNLCOS;[53] the status of

50 China Adheres to the Position of Settling Through Negotiation, *supra* note 14, ¶¶ 26–31; Position Paper, *supra* note 49, ¶¶ 30–79; Statement of the Ministry of Foreign Affairs of the People's Republic of China on the Award of the Arbitral Tribunal in the South China Sea Arbitration Established at the Request of the Republic of the Philippines, 12 July 2016 ¶ 2, available at: http://www.fmprc.gov.cn/mfa_eng/zxxx_662805/t1379492.shtml.

51 China Adheres to the Position of Settling Through Negotiation, *supra* note 14, ¶¶ 5, 74–91, 115–120; Position Paper, *supra* note 49 ¶¶ 80–85; Statement of the Ministry of Foreign Affairs of the PRC on the Award, *supra* note 50, ¶ 3.

52 See, for example, Yang Jiechi, *supra* note 6, (tribunal "disregard[ed] China's staunch position,…went beyond its authority, turned a blind eye to the history and reality of the South China Sea and misinterpreted relevant stipulations of UNCLS…and overstepped and expanded its authority to render this award").

53 Zhiguo Gao and Bing Bing Jia, *The Nine- Dash Line in the South China Sea: History, Status and Implications,*" 107 (1) AMERICAN JOURNAL OF INTERNATIONAL LAW (2013), pp. 98–123; *Foreign Ministry Spokesperson Jiang Yu's Regular Press Conference,* 15 September 2011, available at: http://vancouver.china-consulate.org/eng/fyrth/t860126.htm, (asserting

the disputed landforms and features and, thus, their capacity to generate maritime zones under UNLCOS; and the lawfulness of China's activities in relevant areas of the SCS (including land reclamation and the exploitation of economic resources).[54] Also, the tribunal fundamentally misunderstood the nature of the case, seeing China as responsible for disputes that stemmed from unlawful actions by the Philippines that had infringed China's sovereignty and other international legal rights.[55]

Some statements from official and orthodox Chinese sources moved from narrowly legal responses toward the more political ones that comprise a zone farther along the spectrum of challenging or provocative responses. They suggested that the panel—although it included prominent and respected international experts—was biased and unfair to China. This was because: China had no role in selecting the members (a consequence of China's refusal to participate in any part of the proceedings); or the members were from European States that did not represent the full international legal community (or include adherents to interpretations of international law favored by China); or a "right-wing" Japanese jurist—someone from a country unfriendly to China and a party to disputes with China similar to those raised by the Philippines—had played a key role in determining the panel's composition; or the jurists were improperly influenced by the other side.[56]

Farther along the spectrum of responses and shading further from legal to political arguments, Chinese sources blamed the US for encouraging the

---

that UNCLOS "does not restrain or deny a country's right which is formed in history and abidingly upheld"); EEZ Law, art. 14 (law implementing UNCLOS EEZ provisions following China's accession "shall not affect [China's] historic rights"); Statement of the Ministry of Foreign Affairs of the PRC on the Award, *supra* note 50, ¶ 3, (tribunal "speculatively interprets and applies UNCLOS, and obviously errs in ascertaining facts and applying the law").

54 Statement of the Ministry of Foreign Affairs of the PRC on the Award, *supra* note 50, ¶ 3, (tribunal "selectively takes relevant islands and reefs out of the macro-geographic framework" of larger island groups); *Negotiation is the Only Way to Solve the South China Sea Problem*, RENMIN RIBAO, 14 July 2016, available at: http://paper.people.com.cn/rmrb/html/2016-07/14/nw.D110000renmrb_20160714_4-03.htm (criticizing "absurd" interpretation of standards for reefs and islands).

55 China Adheres to the Position of Settling through Negotiation, *supra* note 14, ¶¶ 56–61, 73, 93–114.

56 Huang Huikang, *Dao Inhabits People's Hearts," Ministry of Foreign Affairs of the People's Republic of China*, 21 July 2016, available at: http://www.fmprc.gov.cn/mfa_eng/wjb_663304/zwjg_665342/zwbd_665378/t1383350.shtml; Yang Jiechi, *supra* note 6; compare Statement of the Ministry of Foreign Affairs of the PRC on the Award, *supra* note 50, ¶ 3 (arbitral panel and its award "substantially impair the integrity and authority of UNCLOS").

Philippines to bring its arbitration claim (and perhaps emboldening Vietnam and others to contemplate doing the same or, at least, more determinedly resist China). The ostensibly bilateral arbitration, thus, was part of a broader political struggle for influence in a region where China's vital national interests were at stake and threatened by US actions and the claims of legal rights that the US used to justify its own actions and criticize China's.[57]

Moving beyond specific reactions to the arbitral decision, China can, and does, continue its familiar assertions that the Philippines, Vietnam, and other rival claimants have no right to occupy what Beijing claims is Chinese sovereign territory in the SCS area or to exercise jurisdiction or undertake various activities in the maritime areas within the nine-dash line over which China enjoys UNCLOS-based and broader historic rights. So, too, China can, and does, continue to insist on the impermissibility of US Navy activities, including FONOPS near Chinese-controlled islands and maritime features and a variety of activities by surveillance vessels and armed ships in and around the SCS.

Both before and after the decision, China often has foregone active and potentially provocative or escalatory measures. Many operations by US Navy ships and aircraft go unchallenged. Duterte's post-ruling negotiations with Beijing resulted in the Philippines maintaining and expanding access—particularly for fishing—in areas that the tribunal's decision found to be part of the Philippines' EEZ but that China sees as properly under its jurisdiction. China has only rarely sought to expel rival claimant States' forces from contested islands and maritime features. China has tolerated, and at times cooperated in, the exploitation of economic resources in what China claims to be its EEZ and continental shelf or areas over which it holds historic rights.[58] Such acquiescence and cooperation are, of course, fully consistent with China's claims of legal rights (as is the Philippines' non-pursuit of enforcement of the arbitration award). After all, legal rights are, fundamentally, options that the rights-holding State may choose not to exercise or to exercise only selectively.

On the other hand, and still farther along the spectrum of assertive actions, China has, over the years, taken status quo altering steps that enforce or implement its claimed rights, ranging from violently expelling Vietnamese forces from occupied reefs, to deploying oil exploration platforms in contested areas, to stringing a net across the entrance to Philippines-controlled

---

57 See *supra* note 39.

58 See, for example, CNOOC, Petro-Vietnam, PNOC, *Joint Statement on the Signing of a Tripartite Agreement, for Joint Marine Seismic Undertaking in the Agreement Area in the South China Sea*, 14 March 2005, available at: http://ph.china-embassy.org/eng/zt/nhwt/t187333.htm.

Scarborough Shoal, to launching large-scale land-reclamation projects on several Chinese-controlled features in 2014, to numerous incidents with US ships and planes. China persisted in some of these types of activity after the tribunal rejected many of China's claimed rights. China's construction projects on features that the tribunal declared to be mere LTEs located in the Philippines' EEZ and continental shelf have continued. So, too, has harassment of US Navy vessels in the SCS region. So, too, have actions by Chinese State ships that impede Filipino access to areas that the tribunal declared not subject to Chinese jurisdiction.

The panel's sweeping rejection of China's positions and China's sharp rejection of the decision raised concerns that Beijing might move farther along the spectrum of escalating, stability-threatening actions. China could have taken a more unyielding approach to exclude the Philippines (and others) from contested areas addressed in the tribunal's decision. China could have accelerated the already-substantial and recently-rapid island-building on formations covered by the arbitral award or in other Chinese-controlled areas. Beijing could have proceeded with a long-rumored and much-discussed declaration of an Air Defense Identification Zone over much of the SCS. Such a move would have reprised and extended a similar move in the East China Sea that had been a major step in the escalating tensions in the region, and that had prompted significant pushback from the US. Some expressed concern (with varying degrees of plausibility) that China might occupy (and perhaps begin land reclamation) on sensitive landforms that had been controlled by the Philippines, particularly Scarborough Shoal (where China's deployment of a net to block access had raised the stakes and the temperature in the Philippines-China dispute) or Second Thomas Shoal (where a handful of Filipino servicemen are stationed precariously on a long-grounded ship).[59] So far, Beijing has foregone such measures.

Although China's statements of positions and patterns of behavior since the arbitration panel's decision are, thus, not new and in some respects are very long-standing, the tribunal's ruling has altered their meaning and implications

---

59 *Experts Worry China May Soon Establish South China Sea ADIZ*, VOICE OF AMERICA, 29 July 2015, available at: www.voanews.com/content/experts-concerned-china-may-soon-establish-southern-adiz/2882795.html; Charles Clover, *Beijing Seeks New Ways to Assert South China Sea Authority*, FINANCIAL TIMES, 12 October 2016 (quoting Wu Shicun); *Manila Expects China to Build on Scarborough Shoal*, SOUTH CHINA MORNING POST, 7 February 2017; Patricia Lourdes Viray, *Think Tank: China Might Occupy Scarborough, Ayungin after UN Court Ruling*, 13 July 2016, available at: http://www.philstar.com/headlines/2016/07/13/1602433/think-tank-china-might-occupy-scarborough-ayungin-after-un-court-ruling.

and, even more so, the meaning and implications of any more assertive words or deeds that China might undertake. Even if China's approach remains relatively unchanged (and all the more so if China moves farther along the spectrum of escalation), China will have doubled down on a posture that had already spawned charges that Beijing is an international scofflaw and a revisionist in its approach to major components of the international legal and political order.[60] Where Beijing previously could claim it was taking one side in debates over the meaning and application of vague or contested principles of international law, continuation or escalation of China's prior approach now must reject an arguably and purportedly authoritative determination by a major international tribunal. Where the PRC could previously hope for a mixed verdict from a divided tribunal that could lend credence to post-decision Chinese arguments that the issues were close ones and still subject to reasoned disagreement, debate, and challenge, China now has to reject a clear and strong decision nearly in its entirety if China wishes to maintain its long-standing positions. Where China previously might have expected that its uncompromising refusal to participate in the arbitration process—even in the very limited and segregable form of appearing to contest the tribunal's jurisdiction—would undermine the legitimacy of any subsequent decision on the merits, that line of argument has to coexist with the counterargument that China is showing itself to be contemptuous of international legal procedures—to which the tribunal judged China to have consented—from soup (determining jurisdiction) to nuts (implementing or enforcing a final judgment).

China might take the outcome of the arbitration and the advent of the newly hard or risky choices it faces as reasons to forego a "double or nothing bet," and adopt a more accommodating approach. Beijing can reinvigorate efforts to seek cooperation on concrete issues (such as resource management and development) with the Philippines and with other rival claimant States.

Here, features of international law, including ones manifested in the tribunal's decision, can help facilitate a politically desired and potentially desirable solution. China could reinvigorate its long-favored position on "setting aside sovereignty" which at least implicitly recognizes that legal rights are options. A similar perspective is inherent in the Philippines' willingness to put the award in the backseat and negotiate with Beijing (although recently renewed

60 Barry Buzan, *China in International Society: Is 'Peaceful Rise' Possible?* 3 (1) CHINESE JOURNAL OF INTERNATIONAL POLITICS (2010), pp. 5–36; Alistair Iain Johnson, *Is China a Status Quo Power?*, 27 (4) INTERNATIONAL SECURITY, (2003), pp. 5–56; Kong Qingjiang, *Beyond the Love-Hate Relationship: International Law and International Institutions and the Rising China*, 15(1) CHINA: AN INTERNATIONAL JOURNAL, (2017), pp. 41–62.

bilateral friction over China's disregard for the Philippines' rights under the arbitral award caution against over-interpreting episodes of cooperation or compromise). Leaving aside the relatively small risk of extinction of rights through non-assertion (desuetude/abandonment, loss by prescription, etc.), legally recognized rights give the rights holder a bargaining chip of somewhat uncertain value. While this is a relatively ubiquitous feature of legal rights, it is particularly pronounced in the context of international law and its notoriously weak institutions and processes for implementation or enforcement of judgments. This element of uncertainty international law may give Manila—and Beijing as well—reason to negotiate and compromise after the tribunal's decision.

Other aspects of uncertainty in the post-arbitral-award environment may give China additional reasons for restraint. Other things being equal, harsher measures from China are likely to increase tensions with the Philippines and other claimant States and to prompt stronger measures from the US. But, again, this aspect of the political implications of the decision is far from definite. Except in the case of Chinese reactions at the extreme ends of the spectrum described above (and perhaps even there), there will be uncertainty (even after some of the confusion sewn by the transition to the Trump presidency abates) about the US's likely response to various moves that China, or others, might make. And, of course, moves by either side are not a one-off. China, other claimants, and the US will react iteratively to one another's moves.

## IV International Law

The Philippines-China arbitration panel's decision—by determining a clear winner (the Philippines and, prospectively, other Southeast Asian claimants) and a clear loser (China), rejecting many of China's claims and long-asserted positions on law of the sea doctrines, condemning many of China's actions in the region, ordering significant behavioral changes by China, and reaching conclusions on the many and varied claims raised by the Philippines across many doctrinal issues—is, at least on the surface, a bold proclamation of international law's reach, power, and potential utility in addressing conflict-generating controversies in international politics. This bold outcome diverged from expectations in some quarters that the panel might determine that it had no jurisdiction over especially tough or controversial claims (including some or all of the eight of the original fifteen claims on which it initially deferred a decision concerning jurisdiction), or might decide it had insufficient information to rule on some issues, or might say that China's nine-dash line claim was ambiguous in its legal nature and potentially acceptable under some but not other interpretations, or might find Taiping Island / Itu Aba to be a potentially EEZ-generating island, thus placing a significant part of the disputed sea area outside the tribunal's jurisdiction (because decisions about territorial sovereignty and maritime boundary delimitation would be necessary to determine rights over a large area around the island), or might resort to unprincipled, half-a-loaf solutions, or might simply lack the temerity to issue an award that China was likely to flout, and so on.[61]

But with such boldness come obvious and significant risks for international law and legal institutions—including ones that extend beyond those directly involved in the Philippines-China SCS arbitration. Although the panel's decision is understandably, and likely correctly, seen as an important statement on major issues in the law of the sea, there are reasons to be somewhat cautious in proclaiming that it has definitively settled some major and heretofore uncertain doctrinal issues. Under international law, the panel's decision is, of course, "final" in the sense that it cannot be appealed. But it is less than "final" in that it has only persuasive, rather than precedential, effect in other international tribunals—the International Court of Justice, the International Tribunal for the Law of the Sea, other ad hoc UNCLOS tribunals, and perhaps others—that can address law of the sea claims.[62]

To be sure, this is a vulnerability of decisions by international tribunals generally, but it may be especially prominent in this case, for several reasons. First, although the presence of leading experts on the panel gives the decision considerable stature, the status of the arbitral body—an ad hoc entity rather than the ICJ, ITLOS or the Permanent Court of Arbitration in the Hague—is a potential weakness.[63] Second, some of the panel's rulings on legal issues—such

61 See, for example, Paul Gewirtz, *Limits of Law in the South China Sea*, BROOKINGS CENTER FOR EAST ASIA POLICY STUDIES EAST ASIA POLICY PAPER NO. 8 (2016); Xu Xiaobing, *A UN Ruling against China Won't Help Resolve the South China Sea Dispute with the Philippines*, SOUTH CHINA MORNING POST, 6 July 2016; Ian Forsyth, *A Legal Sea Change in the South China Sea: Ramifications of the Philippines' ITLOS Case*, 14 (1) CHINA BRIEF (4 June 2014), available at: https://jamestown.org/program/a-legal-sea-change-in-the-south-china-sea-ramifications-of-the-philippines-itlos-case/

62 On these issues, see Stefan Talmon, *The South China Sea Arbitration and the Finality of 'Final' Awards*, 8(2) JOURNAL OF INTERNATIONAL DISPUTE SETTLEMENT, (2017) pp. 388–401.

63 Notably (and as some of the sources cited above reflect), there was some confusion in media reports and even more specialized commentary, some of which indicated that the tribunal was a panel of the Permanent Court of Arbitration in the Hague (or ITLOS or the UN), rather than an ad hoc tribunal that used some PCA resources. Some critics of the opinion emphasized the error, and the distinction, with the hope or expectation

as the high bar established for Article 121(3) EEZ-generating islands or the narrow interpretation of historic rights—are relatively controversial and, other things being equal, less likely to settle the questions. Third, the unrelenting attacks that China has launched on the tribunal's jurisdiction and legitimacy are something that most international decisions do not face and that may leave more room for those opposed to the decision's interpretations to resist their application in other contexts. Fourth, a phenomenon that can sometimes enhance the impact of a major and controversial decision—the successful pursuit of similar, follow-on claims by other interested parties—seems relatively unlikely to occur in this case. At least for a considerable period following the Philippines-China decision, Vietnam, Malaysia, and other rival claimant States showed little inclination to pursue an arbitration case against China. There was no compulsory jurisdictional mechanism, and seemingly little political inclination, for the US or China to pursue legal claims against one another. And such claims could overlap only to a limited extent with the issues addressed in the Philippines-China case.

More fundamentally, the apparent win for international law faces the challenge that the tribunal all too evidently lacks enforcement power. This obvious and brute fact is what makes China's calculus of risks and interests and the US's calibration of its commitment to supporting the decision, and the underlying process, so important and complex. If, in the end, reality on the ground (or, more precisely, on the water) comes substantially into line with the arbitration decision, that will mark at least a partial victory for international law. If an important reason for such an outcome is China's recognition of the reputational costs of openly flouting international law (and doing so in ways that deeply alarm neighboring States about China's intentions more generally), or the US's—and others'—commitment to backing the decision (because of the direct and indirect benefits that flow from adherence to international legal rules), then it will have been a more significant success for international law and the peaceful resolution of disputes by legal procedures.

If, on the other hand, China successfully resists and rejects implementation of the decision, and the US, the Philippines and others are opposed to

---

that doing so would lessen the decision's stature and impact. See, for example, *Permanent Court of Arbitration Clarifies Role in South China Sea Case*, XINHUA, 16 July 2016, available at: http://www.globaltimes.cn/content/994642.shtml; Ambassador Tian Xuejun Gives an Exclusive Interview to the Independent Media on the So-called Award by the Arbitral Tribunal for the South China Sea Arbitration, People's Republic of China Ministry of Foreign Affairs, 20 July 2016 (question 1), available at: http://www.mfa.gov.cn/zflt/eng/jlydh/sjzs/t1383074.htm.

that outcome but are unwilling or unable to do much about it (and this result occurs without Chinese arguments about the legal infirmities of the decision having persuaded international opinion), then the initial win for international law will have been very short-lived. If the tribunal's comprehensive rejection of China's long and purportedly deeply held views on so many issues exacerbates or revives hoary Chinese suspicions that existing international law is unfair and harmful to China's interests, the ruling will have diminished prospects for integrating a rising and potentially system-challenging China into the established, generally stability-supporting international legal order. The tribunal's determination to issue a "big" decision then will have been a hollow, even pyrrhic, victory for law.[64]

64 Chinese sources have stressed this argument. See *South China Sea Arbitration Abuses International Law, Threatens World Order*, PEOPLE'S DAILY, 29 June 2016; but see Tara Davenport, *Why the South China Sea Arbitration Case Matters (Even if China Ignores It)*, THE DIPLOMAT, 8 July 2016, available at: http://thediplomat.com/2016/07/why-the-south-china-sea-arbitration-case-matters-even-if-china-ignores-it/; and Roncevert Ganan Almond, "The South China Sea Ruling," THE DIPLOMAT, 16 July 2016, available at: http://thediplomat.com/2016/07/interview-the-south-china-sea-ruling/.

# The South China Sea Arbitration and Its Implications for ASEAN Centrality

*Alan H. Yang*[1]

## 1 The Obscure South China Sea Dispute

The South China Sea (SCS) dispute is not only a struggle among countries in the area for sovereignty over various land features, territorial waters, and underwater natural resources, but also the focal point of great power politics. The international dispute over the SCS has been going on for decades. The Declaration on the Conduct of Parties in the South China Sea (DOC), signed by China and the ASEAN countries, has no binding power.[2] Since the DOC was signed, the SCS has continued to be the focus of traditional and non-traditional security threats.[3] There have been intermittent conflicts and standoffs between fishing boats and government vessels, including the cutting of the cables of Vietnamese and Filipino fishing boats by Chinese coastguard vessels.[4]

The majority of the most prominent conflicts within the region involve China, on the one hand, and either Vietnam or the Philippines, as Beijing views the SCS as its "traditional sphere of influence."[5] In April 2012, there was

---

1 Associate Professor and Associate Research Fellow, Graduate Institute of East Asian Studies and Institute of International Relations, National Chengchi University, Taiwan; and Executive Director, Center for Southeast Asian Studies, National Chengchi University, Taiwan. The author would like to thank the Institute of International Relations and the Ministry of Science and Technology (R.O.C) for its support to this project.

2 CHRISTOPHER B. ROBERTS, ASEAN REGIONALISM: COOPERATION, VALUES, AND INSTITUTIONALISM (2012) 74–81.

3 David Rosenberg, *The Maritime Borderlands: Terrorism, Piracy, Pollution, and Poaching in the South China Sea*, in JAMES CLAD, SEAN M. MCDONALD, AND BRUCE VAUGHN, eds., THE BORDERLANDS OF SOUTHEAST ASIA: GEOPOLITICS, TERRORISM, AND GLOBALIZATION (2011) 107–127.

4 Jeremy Page, *Vietnam Accuses Chinese Ships*, NEW YORK TIMES, 3 December 2012, available at: https://www.wsj.com/articles/SB10001424127887323717004578157033857113510; Thu Chung, *Chinese Boats Intrude Vietnam's Waters, Cut Cables Again*, VIETNAM BREAKING NEWS, 31 January 2017, available at: https://www.vietnambreakingnews.com/2017/01/chinese-boats-intrude-vietnams-waters-cut-cables-again/.

5 Carlyle A. Thayer, *China and Southeast Asia: A Shifting Zone of Interaction*, in Clad, McDonald, and Vaughn, *supra* note 3, at 235.

a ten-week standoff between Chinese and Filipino naval vessels in the Scarborough Shoal.[6] This incident could easily have escalated, as it also affected China's relations with the United States (U.S.). In 2014, while a Chinese oil platform, the HD 981, was operating in the SCS, there was a more serious standoff between Chinese and Vietnamese naval vessels. Vietnamese coastguard vessels kept cruising around the HD 981, trying to prevent it from establishing a fixed position, while the Chinese coastguard took countermeasures, producing a crisis in Sino-Vietnamese relations.[7]

In addition to these two large-scale confrontations, China continued to strengthen its law enforcement measures in the SCS, adopting a tough stance toward fishermen from neighboring countries and carrying out land reclamation projects in the Spratly Islands. Beijing's assertive presence in these troubled waters caused a deterioration in its relations with its Southeast Asian maritime neighbors. However, more efforts are being made by Beijing to reduce confrontation in the SCS.[8]

This continuing unrest in the SCS has attracted the attention of the international community. The development of the SCS dispute has been discussed at various Track I and Track II multilateral forums. On 4 July 2016, during a special session of the IISS Shangri-La Dialogue in Singapore, on "Managing South China Sea Tensions," Adam Ward, the IISS Director of Studies, described the situation in the SCS as "a set of zero-sum territorial and sovereignty disputes, prosecuted with some vehemence." The dispute fuels nationalist impulses and militarization and has given rise to security dilemmas. Attempts to resolve it include third-party mediation and arbitration. It is true that "regional security institutions have failed, so far, to impose themsclvcs mcaningfully on the problem."[9] It is also true that the SCS dispute has not only affected the bilateral

---

6 Daniel Wagner, Edsel Tupaz, and Ira Paulo Pozon, *China, the Philippines, and the Scarborough Shoal*, THE WORLD POST, 20 May 2012, available at: http://www.huffingtonpost.com/daniel-wagner/china-the-philippines-and_b_1531623.html.

7 The oil rig was moved into the Gulf of Tonkin on 3 April 2016. See Shannon Tiezzi, *Vietnam to China: Move Your Oil Rig out of the South China Sea*, THE DIPLOMAT, 9 April 2016, available at: http://thediplomat.com/2016/04/vietnam-to-china-move-your-oil-rig-out-of-the-south-china-sea/.

8 Mingjiang Li describes China's behavior in the SCS as a "combination of non-confrontation and assertiveness." See Mingjiang Li, *China Debates the South China Sea Dispute*, in IAN STOREY AND LIN CHENG-YI, eds., THE SOUTH CHINA SEA DISPUTE: NAVIGATING DIPLOMATIC AND STRATEGIC TENSIONS (2016)67.

9 IISS, *Managing South China Sea Tensions*, THE IISS SHANGRI-LA DIALOGUE: THE ASIA SECURITY SUMMIT, 4 June 2016, available at: http://www.iiss.org/en/events/shangri%20la%20dialogue/archive/shangri-la-dialogue-2016-4a4b/special-sessions-ff25/session-5-af76.

relations of the parties concerned, but also led to further confrontation between China and the U.S., presenting a serious challenge to the ASEAN community. While ASEAN and other major powers in the Asia-Pacific region depend on the strengthening of institutionalized, multilateral dialogue channels to avoid possible conflicts, China is annoyed by the SCS claimants' efforts to internationalize the dispute.[10]

In 2010, when Vietnam held the chair of ASEAN, the internationalization and multilateralization of the disputes over territorial sovereignty and maritime resources in the SCS developed rapidly. Vietnam leveraged on the power structure of SCS politics by introducing the U.S., Japan, and neighboring major powers into the emerging confrontation, threatening China's ability to dominate the issue. However, what really bothers China is not Vietnam, but the Philippines.

For decades, China has sought to resolve the SCS dispute bilaterally, while the Southeast Asian claimants, most of which are small and medium powers, insist that it should be settled through international and multilateral channels.[11] Differences in national strength and preferred method of settlement between stakeholders complicate the SCS dispute. In January 2013, the Philippines took its dispute with China to the Permanent Court of Arbitration (PCA) in The Hague, Netherlands, with a four-thousand-page submission requesting that the court clarify the legality of China's sovereignty claims in the SCS.[12] China rejected the Philippines' claims and refused to accept that the court had jurisdiction in this case. Beijing insisted that the dispute should be resolved through bilateral channels.

The final ruling, which has important implications for the region, was released on 12 July 2016. This paper briefly discusses the strategic environment of the SCS from the perspective of ASEAN. By highlighting the influence of

10 The United States is the key to the internationalization of the SCS dispute. For example, at the 2016 G20 meeting, President Barack Obama sent a warning signal to China concerning its behavior in the SCS, *Obama Crashes G20 by Warning Beijing of 'Consequences' in the South China Sea*, SPUTNIK INTERNATIONAL, 5 September 2016, http://sputniknews.com/asia/20160905/1044997015/obama-xi-china-war-g20.html.

11 As Tran Truong Thuy has argued, it would be better to manage the dispute through ASEAN, including a Declaration of Conduct and Code of Conduct. See Tran Trong Thuy, *Recent Development in the South China Sea: From Declaration to Code of Conduct*, in TRAN TRUONG THUY, ed., THE SOUTH CHINA SEA: TOWARD A REGION OF PEACE, SECURITY, AND COOPERATION (2011) 101–115.

12 For the case submitted by the Philippines to the PCA, see SHICHUN WU AND KEYUAN ZOU, eds., ARBITRATION CONCERNING THE SOUTH CHINA SEA: PHILIPPINES VERSUS CHINA (2016).

power politics, this paper explains how ASEAN has failed to secure its centrality and unity since 2012. China continues its strategic projection in the SCS, seizing islands and building on them, and enhancing its military capability, thus demonstrating its presence in these troubled waters both substantially and symbolically. It is difficult for ASEAN to remain united on this issue since its individual member-States' interests and threat perceptions differ depending on whether they are mainland or maritime countries.

This paper argues that the final award of arbitration issued on 12 July will not put an end to the dispute. Rather, from another angle, this is to legally socialize China's behavior in SCS. The cost of this is a more divided ASEAN, a more fragmented regional community, and more dangerous maritime communications routes.

## II The SCS Dispute in the Context of Power Politics

The SCS dispute is essentially a clash over maritime territory and resources. Nevertheless, it is taking place in the context of power politics and hegemonic rivalry. This power struggle involves not only the great powers, but also the ASEAN States themselves.[13]

At a structural level, the contest among the regional powers (China, Japan, and the U.S.) simultaneously constrains and enables the dispute. It constrains it because rivalry between China and the U.S. undermines ASEAN's role in maintaining peace and stability in the disputed waters. The hegemonic rivals enable the dispute by providing individual ASEAN member-States with aid (Beijing) or funding coastguard capacity-building projects (Washington). This makes it difficult for ASEAN to present a strong united front on the SCS disputes.

ASEAN members seem to take sides whenever a dispute occurs in the SCS, despite their reluctance to get embroiled in the great power rivalry. The SCS dispute has severely damaged the unity of ASEAN and it has become a test for the ASEAN Political Security Community (APSC) *per se*.[14] The China factor is

13 For recent insightful monographs on the policy implications of power politics, see ENRICO FELS AND TRUONG-MINH VU, eds., POWER POLITICS IN ASIA'S CONTESTED WATERS: TERRITORIAL DISPUTES IN THE SOUTH CHINA SEA (2016); TRAN TRUONG THUY AND LE THUY TRANG, eds., POLITICS, LAW, AND MARITIME ORDERS IN THE SOUTH CHINA SEA (2015).

14 Hideo Tomikawa, *Southeast Asia: Forming an ASEAN Political-Security Community and Further Challenges*, in NATIONAL INSTITUTE FOR DEFENSE STUDIES, ed., EAST ASIAN STRATEGIC REVIEW 2016, (2016) 150.

the most critical concern. Those continental ASEAN countries which are not directly involved in disputes with China in the SCS have tended to acquire more room for strategic maneuvering due to their "calmness" on the issue. For instance, countries such as Cambodia, Thailand, and Laos, which are not SCS claimants and seek to keep strong economic and trade links with China, usually give tacit approval to Beijing's SCS position. In late June 2016, Prime Minister Hun Sen of Cambodia indicated that he was in favor of ASEAN supporting an arbitration award against China. Then, on 15 July, right after the announcement of the PCA award, Beijing granted Cambodia US$600 million-worth of aid.[15]

The core interest of most of the maritime ASEAN countries which are involved in the SCS dispute with China is protecting their State sovereignty. Even though they need to maintain good economic and trade relations with China, intensification of the territorial dispute means that sovereignty takes precedence over these economic interests.

Strategic maneuvering has prompted ASEAN SCS claimants, including Vietnam and the Philippines, to actively seek support from regional powers such as the U.S. and Japan in recent years. Whether they take the form of capacity-building projects such as security assistance, the training of coastguard personnel, or the upgrading of maritime governance and law enforcement, these maritime capability build-up programs are essential for the Philippines and Vietnam. For example, Manila reinforced its bilateral ties with the U.S. concerning security and legal assistance. In April 2014, Manila signed a military cooperation agreement with the U.S. which included plans for the construction of joint military bases over the next ten years. The Philippines also received patrol ships and F16 C/D aircraft from the U.S. which has helped Manila enhance its weak air and naval power as well as its island-control capability. Most importantly, the Philippines has enjoyed the full support of the U.S. during the PCA arbitration process and on issues such as fisheries enforcement missions after the PCA ruling.[16]

Vietnam has also been seeking international support in recent years. It upgraded its military capability by purchasing YAK130 trainer aircraft, Su 30 MK2 fighter jets, and submarines from Russia. It also strengthened bilateral ties with the U.S. when President Obama lifted the arms embargo on Vietnam

---

15 Sok Khemara, *China Gives $600m to Cambodia in Exchange for International Support*, VOA CAMBODIA, 15 July 2016, available at: http://www.voacambodia.com/a/china-gives-600-million-to-cambodia-in-exchange-for-international-support/3419875.html.

16 Kerry Lynn Nankivell, *South China Sea: Fishing in Troubled Waters*, THE DIPLOMAT, 18 August 2016, available at: http://thediplomat.com/2016/08/south-china-sea-fishing-in-troubled-waters/.

in May 2016.[17] On 15 July, Vietnam and Japan agreed that the parties concerned should comply with the SCS ruling that would "eventually lead to the peaceful settlement of disputes."[18]

The efforts made by Vietnam and the Philippines to encourage the engagement of the major external powers illustrate the kinds of strategies these countries are adopting to safeguard their core interests. Besides confronting China directly, they need to devise countermeasures, and their best course of action is to develop strategic ties with the U.S., Japan, and India.

When the result of the PCA arbitration was announced, the positions adopted by the ASEAN member-States were equivocal and diverse. First, for ASEAN, there is no consensus right after the announcement of award. Second, Laos and Cambodia were more sympathetic to China, Indonesia's and Malaysia's attitudes were unclear but mention the importance of UNCLOS, while Vietnam and the Philippines welcome the results with cautious attitudes of evaluating its political and security implications.[19] Obviously, the question whether the SCS dispute is a core interest or not is the key factor in determining whether an individual ASEAN State is "for" or "against" China. The final award announced on 12 July highlights the fact that the SCS dispute is essentially a zero-sum game and part of the power struggle among the claimants and their great power allies.

## III The Erosion of ASEAN Centrality

It is inevitable that the SCS dispute and the award of arbitration will challenge ASEAN unity and centrality.[20] Since the late 1990s, ASEAN had been striving to develop an ASEAN Community, a solid and united regional grouping.

17 Alan H. Yang, *Prioritizing National Interests in the South China Sea: Policy Continuities and Changes in Key ASEAN Countries*, in K.H. Wang and S.S. Ho, eds., A Bridge over Troubled Waters: Prospects for Peace in the South and East China Seas (2015)161.

18 *Japan, Vietnam Agree South China Sea Ruling Must Be Observed as China Digs in Heels*, Straits Times,15 July 2016, available at: http://www.straitstimes.com/asia/east-asia/japan-pm-abe-meets-china-counterpart-li-keqiang-as-south-china-sea-tensions-flare.

19 Termsak Chalermpalanupap, *No ASEAN Consensus on the South China Sea*, The Diplomat, 21 July 2016, available at: http://thediplomat.com/2016/07/no-asean-consensus-on-the-south-china-sea/.

20 At the time of writing, a collection of the latest studies on the impact of the territorial disputes on ASEAN centrality was due to be released in December 2016. See Alfred Gerstl and Maria Strakova, eds., Unresolved Border, Land, and Maritime

On 31 December 2015, this community was establish on three "pillars": a political pillar (the ASEAN Political Security Community, APSC), an economic pillar (the ASEAN Economic Community, AEC), and a social pillar (the ASEAN Socio-Cultural Community, ASCC). The purpose of this community is to put ASEAN and its members securely in the "driving seat" as far as regional settings and processes are concerned.

In recent years, almost all the regional processes led by ASEAN have emphasized the importance of ASEAN Centrality. The underlying rationale is that most of the individual ASEAN countries are small, and so must rely on a "regional grouping" or "community" to increase their regional resilience and to prevent them from being marginalized in global power politics or manipulated by the major powers. Discussions and debates regarding the core values of ASEAN Centrality have taken place both in academia and among the policy-making community.[21]

There are at least three aspects of ASEAN Centrality. First, it means that ASEAN should hold a central position in Southeast Asian integration, with ASEAN representing the common interests, common position, and common identity of the Southeast Asian countries. That is, the unity and cohesiveness of regional community.[22] As ASEAN strengthens regional integration, the core value of the ASEAN Community will be recognized and fully supported by its members. Realizing ASEAN Centrality will facilitate closer integration of the collective interests of the ASEAN Community and the interests of individual ASEAN members, putting ASEAN at the heart of regional and national development.

A second aspect of ASEAN Centrality is the consolidation of ASEAN as a hub in the context of international power politics and "the core of regionalism in

---

DISPUTES IN SOUTHEAST ASIA: BI- AND MULTILATERAL CONFLICT RESOLUTION APPROACHES AND ASEAN'S CENTRALITY (2016).

21 For recent contributions to the centrality and unity debates, see Evan A. Laksmana, *Can There be ASEAN Centrality without Unity?*, JAKARTA POST, 6 September 2016, available at: http://www.thejakartapost.com/news/2016/09/06/can-there-be-asean-centrality-without-unity.html; Mathew Davies, *ASEAN Centrality Losing Ground*, EAST ASIA FORUM, 4 September 2016, available at: http://www.eastasiaforum.org/2016/09/04/asean-centrality-losing-ground/; Robert A. Manning, *Time to Rethink ASEAN*, NIKKEI ASIAN REVIEW, 6 September 2016, http://asia.nikkei.com/Viewpoints/Viewpoints/Robert-A.-Manning-Time-to-rethink-ASEAN?page=2.

22 Sihasak Phuangketkeow, *Special Session: ASEAN and the Emerging Regional Security Order*, THE IISS SHANGRI-LA DIALOGUE, 31 May 2014, available at: https://www.iiss.org/en/events/shangri%20la%20dialogue/archive/2014-c20c/special-sessions-b0a1/session-4-948e.

East Asia and the Asia Pacific".[23] As ASEAN and its community-building project develops, its members will be able to rely on ASEAN's good offices in the political struggles among the regional powers. ASEAN Centrality is closely connected to how ASEAN maintains balance in Asia-Pacific power politics through ASEAN Plus Three (APT), the East Asia Summit (EAS), and other ASEAN-led networking efforts. Over the past decade, the regional powers have, for the most part, respected and valued ASEAN Centrality, enabling ASEAN to calm potential political rivalries among the regional powers which could have negative implications for ASEAN members. Practicing ASEAN Centrality in ASEAN-led processes is also essential if ASEAN is to be able to consolidate the regional and individual interests of the Southeast Asian countries and prevent those interests from being marginalized.

Last but not least, ASEAN Centrality is particularly important if ASEAN is to maintain its agenda-setting and bargaining capability in ASEAN-led processes. If ASEAN can consolidate its unity and cohesion, collective regional interests will be secure.

In recent years, however, confrontations in the SCS have eroded ASEAN centrality. First, the ASEAN members have had difficulty finding common ground on the SCS dispute, and this has caused problems regarding the wording of joint statements. This is important evidence that ASEAN's core position is under challenge. One example is what happened in 2012, when the Cambodian chair of the 45th ASEAN Foreign Ministerial Meeting (AMM) in Phnom Penh failed to get the member-States to reach a consensus on the SCS dispute, resulting in this AMM being the first to end without a joint communique.[24] In November 2015, delegates at the expanded ASEAN Defense Ministerial Meeting (ADMM Plus) again took different positions on the SCS dispute and on China's land reclamation project in the disputed waters, thus failing to reach a consensus and once again concluding without a joint statement. In June 2016, a joint communique drawn up at the Special China-ASEAN Foreign Minister's Meeting in Nanning, China, which highlighted ASEAN's "serious concerns" about the SCS dispute, was withdrawn.[25]

---

23 Simon Tay and Cheryl Tan, *ASEAN Centrality in the Regional Architecture*, SIIA POLICY BRIEF, January 2015, 2.

24 Bridget Welsh, *Divided or Together? Southeast Asia in 2012*, in OOI KEE BENG ET AL., eds., THE 3RD ASEAN READER (2015), 290–293.

25 Roy Mabasa, *China-ASEAN Communique Retreated*, MANILA BULLETIN, 16 June 2016, available at: http://www.mb.com.ph/china-asean-communique-retracted/#JBByUZy5BrYVBdof.99.

More recently, ASEAN, under Laotian chairmanship, failed to issue a joint statement on the PCA's ruling. According to media reports, it was Laos that announced that "ASEAN would not be issuing a joint statement due to a lack of consensus."[26]

This is all evidence of a crisis within ASEAN caused by a fragmentation of interests in the SCS disputes. ASEAN Centrality will be undermined still further by great power rivalry following on the PCA ruling. With China seeking support from non-claimants among the ASEAN members, it will be extremely difficult for the regional grouping to stand firm and reach a unanimous position of its own. The position taken by Laos of not issuing any ASEAN statement on PCA ruling reduces the legitimate and normative influence of the Association, as the ASEAN Community is about to lose its moral authority and capacity to set the agenda on the SCS dispute. Worse still, the erosion of ASEAN Centrality will likely endanger ASEAN control over regional processes.

## IV A Tougher China as a Disintegrating Factor?

In the week before the PCA's ruling was announced, Beijing used various channels to assert its position and its tough stance. For example, the spokesman for China's Foreign Ministry, Hong Lei, argued that the tribunal had no jurisdiction over the case and "the arbitration and any award are obviously unpopular."[27] On 5 July, a former Chinese State councilor, Dai Bingguo, criticized the PCA at the China-US Dialogue on SCS between Chinese and US Think Tanks. He argued that the tribunal should stop its hearings and dismissed the arbitration award as "nothing more than a piece of paper."[28] Dai's statement was consistent with that of Hong Lei, who emphasized that the tribunal had no jurisdiction over the SCS case and was trying to expand its power by making a political decision.

---

26 *ASEAN 'Abandons' Joint Statement on Ruling*, BANGKOK POST, 14 July 14, 2016, available at: http://www.bangkokpost.com/news/asean/1035694/asean-abandons-joint-statement-on-ruling.

27 Hannah Beech, *China's Global Reputation Hinges on Upcoming South China Sea Court Decision*, TIME, 11 July 2016, available at: http://time.com/4400671/philippines-south-china-sea-arbitration-case/.

28 Ministry of Foreign Affairs of the People's Republic of China, "Speech by Dai Bingguo at China-US Dialogue on South China Sea Between Chinese and US Think Tanks," Ministry of Foreign Affairs of the People's Republic of China, 5 July 2016, available at: http://www.fmprc.gov.cn/mfa_eng/zxxx_662805/t1377747.shtml.

Despite China insisting that the U.S. is not a party to the SCS dispute, the Chinese have admitted that Washington has a key role to play. On 6 July, China's foreign minister, Wang Yi, and the US Secretary of State, John Kerry, discussed the dispute through their hotline. Wang emphasized that China would never change its position concerning sovereignty over the SCS, and he urged the U.S. to stick to its policy of neutrality and non-involvement.[29]

In addition to its diplomatic communications, on 5 July, China launched a week-long military exercise in the SCS during which more than one hundred ships and jet fighters were mobilized. Beijing's decision to proceed with the military exercise right before the release of the arbitration award sent a strong signal of its intention to protect its sovereignty in these troubled waters.

The release of the PCA ruling on 12 July sharpened the difference between China and the Philippines and highlighted the gap between the pro-Philippines and pro-China groups. The former argues that "a rules-based international order must be respected," while China argues that the "illegal ruling is nothing but a piece of paper" and insists that outside powers should stop interfering in the issue.[30] The PCA ruling disadvantages China's legal status in the SCS and it is likely to result in China taking a tougher stance in the future. So far, Beijing has responded with "relative restraint" with regard to maintaining the regional status quo.[31] However, China is expected to secure its perceived legal rights and enhance its presence in the area by declaring an air defense information zone (ADIZ) and an exclusive economic zone (EEZ), expanding militarization initiatives and pushing forward bilateral cooperation with Taiwan on SCS issues in a more assertive manner.

## V Conclusion: An Uncertain Future or Back to Normal?

The arbitration award by no means marks the resolution of the SCS dispute. First, China has made its disapproval clear, refusing to recognize the PCA's jurisdiction. However, the jurisdiction made Chinese policy communities aware

29 David Brunnstrom and Ben Blanchard, *Beijing Warns U.S. on Sovereignty ahead of South China Sea Ruling*, REUTERS, 7 July 2016, available at: http://www.reuters.com/article/us-southchinasea-china-kerry-idUSKCN0ZM2GU.

30 *Japan, Vietnam Agree South China Sea Ruling Must Be Observed as China Digs in Heels*, STRAITS TIMES, 15 July 2016, available at: http://www.straitstimes.com/asia/east-asia/japan-pm-abe-meets-china-counterpart-li-keqiang-as-south-china-sea-tensions-flare.

31 Tuan N. Pham, *The South China Sea Ruling: 1 Month Later*, THE DIPLOMAT, 12 August 2016, thttp://thediplomat.com/2016/08/the-south-china-sea-ruling-1-month-later/.

of the importance of international law and norms in any policy making relevant to SCS. Nonetheless, it is important to note that China's domestic political reform and anti-corruption movement have created strong pressure from within, and this is may lead Beijing to respond more assertively to external challenges. As China learns from the PCA jurisdiction, Beijing is likely to unilaterally engage in proactive and assertive military projection in the SCS in the future, but more likely to enhance itself in internationally legitimatizing sovereignty claims in the troubled waters.

Second, even though the PCA ruled in favor of the Philippines, it would be difficult for Manila to act on the ruling because of its limited law enforcement and military capability. At the same time, the Philippines' newly elected president, Rodrigo Duterte, expressed willingness to start a dialogue with China on the SCS dispute. In late 2016, Duterte paid the State visit to Beijing for the purpose of improving bilateral relations between both countries. There were 13 agreements and Memorandum of Understanding (MOU) signed during his visit, including one on the Establishment of a Joint Coastal Guard Committee on Maritime Cooperation, which may ease the tension between the two parties.[32] Beijing is more confident that a less proactive Philippines will do no harm to its presence nor governance in SCS.

Overall, the arbitration award will not do ASEAN much good in the short run. This is mainly because it will not help the SCS claimant countries "solve" the dispute any time soon, although one positive effect for the Philippines is that Duterte was able to use the award to help in negotiations with China and gain economic benefits from Beijing. A recent development is China has committed to provide \$6 billion in soft loans and a \$3 billion credit line to the Philippines to fulfill its need in the development of national infrastructure projects.[33]

However, one thing is certain, the already eroded ASEAN Centrality will continue to deteriorate due to the differing national interests of the individual ASEAN members. The ASEAN Summit in Vientiane still kept its silence in not mentioning the PCA award in any statements and declarations. ASEAN Centrality can only exist if the major powers respect its importance and value ASEAN's influence. ASEAN will no longer occupy a central position without the support

32 Jane Perlezoct, *Rodrigo Duterte and Xi Jinping Agree to Reopen South China Sea Talks*, NEW YORK TIMES, 20 October 2016, available at: https://www.nytimes.com/2016/10/21/world/asia/rodrigo-duterte-philippines-china-xi-jinping.html.

33 ABC-CBN News, *China Promises "Corruption-free" Infrastructure Aid to Philippines*, ABC-CBN NEWS, 10 February2017, available at: http://news.abs-cbn.com/news/02/10/17/china-promises-corruption-free-infrastructure-aid-to-philippines.

of the major powers. Regional security may either become more uncertain or it may, on the contrary, go back on track. This will depend on the following developments.

First, the differing positions and interests of the ASEAN members will make ASEAN Centrality more vulnerable, threatening the unity and further integration of the ASEAN Community, especially the APSC. Undeniably, the Asia-Pacific region needs a more all-embracing and united ASEAN. This is particularly significant in 2017, when ASEAN is celebrating its fiftieth anniversary. In 2017, the Philippines takes over the chairmanship of ASEAN. This will give Manila more strategic opportunities to enhance its influence in the SCS through various ASEAN-led processes, although resistance from non-claimants within ASEAN may be expected. If the new government in the Philippines makes use of the arbitration award in a strategic manner while at the same time moving against China by leaning toward the U.S. and Japan, Vietnam and Malaysia may be encouraged to follow suit. In response to such a newly reinforced anti-China coalition, Beijing will inevitably invest more resources into the countries of Indochina. This will divide ASEAN still further.

Second, it is worth considering what President Duterte's attitude will be, faced with an uncompromising China. Duterte's position was inconsistent in the two months after the PCA ruling. On 15 July, he delegated former president Fidel Ramos to enter into a dialogue regarding the arbitration in Hong Kong. Although this was seen as no more than a gesture designed to demonstrate Duterte's friendliness toward China, on 23 July, just a week after Ramos' visit to Hong Kong, Duterte openly criticized China's "nine dash line" claim as a greedy scheme to plunder the entire SCS. On 29 July 29, as the quarrel intensified, Duterte yet again changed his tone, saying that the Philippines would avoid extreme standpoints in its dialogues with China in the future. On 17 August, he offered the Chinese leaders direct talks, saying, "We maintain good relations with China. Let's create an environment where we can sit down and talk." Duterte's main purpose is to avoid war by means of under-the-table bilateral diplomacy. However, on 24 August, he again toughened up, threatening that "if China invades the Philippines' territorial water in SCS, there will be an irrevocable bloody confrontation."

Duterte has adopted a carrot and stick strategy, under which he has made multiple offers of dialogue within the space of a single year while also issuing belligerent statements about safeguarding the sovereignty of the Philippines. The belligerence is likely to be a response to domestic public opinion. In other words, the two new elements in the SCS dispute—and the problem of ASEAN Centrality—are the president of the Philippines and public opinion in the Philippines.

Third, the militarization of the SCS is likely to develop still further as the claimants seek to protect their sovereignty. Security assistance programs and arms sales between the ASEAN claimants (Vietnam, the Philippines, and Indonesia) and the external powers (Japan and the U.S.) will be reinforced. A *de facto* naval and coastguard partnership between the U.S. and Japan on the one hand and the ASEAN States on the other will be targeted at China's presence (military and law enforcement) in the SCS.

Increasing the scale of military exchanges and cooperation with other stakeholders is a clear sign of major power intervention in the SCS issue. Military engagement by the U.S., Japan, and other regional powers may serve to heighten the tension in the region still further. The future development of the dispute depends on whether the major powers intervene constructively and work to facilitate stability in the SCS.

Finally, China is likely to intensify its presence in the SCS and become more assertive. Although Beijing usually prefers a bilateral framework, it is still calling for dialogue with ASEAN foreign ministers or senior officials as part of a multilateral arrangement, in the hope that the DOC can be implemented and a code of conduct agreed as soon as possible. Meanwhile, Beijing continues to communicate bilaterally with the Philippines. Ongoing Chinese projects include linking up the artificial islands they have created and installing civilian facilities. This will tighten China's control over the remote Spratly Islands.

It may be a long time before ASEAN can achieve a satisfactory resolution to this complicated dispute. But ASEAN should not be too pessimistic. A crisis can also be a turning point. The international community is likely to expect more from this most important regional organization, which is celebrating its fiftieth anniversary, in terms of ensuring a more harmonious and stable regional environment. Despite the fact that ASEAN unity and centrality have been challenged by the current SCS dispute, the PCA ruling should mark a new starting point for ASEAN in its efforts to strengthen its member-States' understanding of what it means to be a "community."

# Caught in the Middle: South Korea and the South China Sea Arbitration Decision

*Terence Roehrig*[1]

## 1 Introduction

The July 2016 decision handed down by the Permanent Court of Arbitration (PCA) at The Hague provided a ruling that went far beyond what many expected concerning the scope of the case. The United States celebrated the ruling receiving a far more decisive verdict than most had expected. Though the Philippines filed the suit, its response has been surprising and confusing. President Rodrigo Duterte, who assumed power in June 2016, initially indicated he would "strongly affirm and respect" the decision.[2] However, in October, Duterte visited China and since has appeared to back away, willing to "set aside the arbitration ruling."[3]

Others have weighed in with a variety of positions ranging from positive support to simply acknowledging the decision to opposing the result.[4] Of course, China was bitterly disappointed with the outcome and vowed to ignore the PCA judgment. Foreign Minister Wang Yi declared the ruling "completely a political farce staged under legal pretext,"[5] and President Xi Jinping vowed that "China will not accept nor recognize the decision, while the country's territorial sovereignty and maritime interests in the South China Sea will not be affected under any circumstance."[6]

---

1 U.S. Naval War College. The views expressed here are the author's alone and do not represent the official position of the Navy, the U.S. Department of Defense or the U.S. government.

2 *Duterte says to 'affirm' PH arbitration win vs China*, ABS-CBN NEWS, 25 July 2016, available at: http://news.abs-cbn.com/news/07/25/16/duterte-says-to-affirm-ph-arbitration-win-vs-china.

3 Alexis Romero and Edith Regalado, *Rody ready to set aside ruling on sea dispute*, PHILIPPINE STAR, 18 December 2016, available at: http://news.abs-cbn.com/news/07/25/16/duterte-says-to-affirm-ph-arbitration-win-vs-china.

4 *What countries are taking sides after the South China ruling?* ASIA MARITIME TRANSPARENCY INITIATIVE, available at: https://amti.csis.org/sides-in-south-china-sea/.

5 *Chinese foreign minister says South China Sea arbitration a political farce*, XINHUA NEWS, 12 July 2016, available at: http://news.xinhuanet.com/english/2016-07/13/c_135508275.htm.

6 Hannah Beech, *China Slams the South China Sea Decision as a 'Political Farce'*, TIME, 13 July 2016, available at: http://time.com/4404084/reaction-south-china-sea-ruling/.

DOI 10.1163/9789004344556_007

Prior to the PCA decision, South Korea (Republic of Korea – ROK) had only recently and reluctantly taken a public position where it called for respect of international norms, freedom of navigation, and the peaceful resolution of disputes, in large part, resulting from urging by the Obama administration. The decision was a stark reminder for South Korea of the difficult position it can find itself in when an issue puts it between the policies of Beijing and Washington. While the South Korean economy and its future prosperity is closely tied to China, and China remains a key player for dealing with North Korea, the United States has long been a close ally and central to maintaining ROK security. In addition, the PCA decision came soon after South Korea's announcement to allow the United States to deploy a Terminal High-Altitude Area Defense (THAAD) battery to the peninsula, another decision that hurt ROK relations with Beijing.

The South China Sea (SCS) dispute and the PCA decision may not have a direct impact on South Korean interests but it does raise the possibility South Korea will increasingly be called upon to support the position of one side or the other with the chance of economic retaliation and Chinese intransigence in dealing with North Korea, or continued pressure from Washington. In addition, though South Korea did not have a direct stake in the PCA ruling, it does have an interest in upholding international law, regional peace and stability, and the free flow of commerce. There is also a possibility of follow-on ramifications that could affect South Korea's maritime disputes with China (Ieodo, illegal fishing, EEZ delimitation), Japan (Dokdo/Takeshima), and North Korea (Northern Limit Line – NLL). Though it is not yet clear if the PCA ruling will affect these disputes, ROK authorities are likely giving this careful consideration in case the PCA decision stirs the waters in any of these issues.

This article will examine the ROK stance on the South China Sea dispute along with the uncomfortable position it finds itself in between two countries important to ROK interests. In addition, it will assess the possible impact of the PCA decision on South Korea's maritime disputes and interests. For South Korea, the SCS dispute and the PCA ruling is a classic case of an issue that involves several competing interests with varying stakes. The South Korean government has worked to navigate a complex interest set and done a relatively good job of balancing the competing interests it has at stake. However, depending on how the dispute evolves, and more importantly, the future of Sino-U.S. relations, South Korea may have some increasingly difficult choices to make concerning international law, maritime security and its relations with China and the United States.

## II South Korea's Interests in the South China Sea Dispute

The dispute in the SCS is a classic case of an issue that involves a host of cross-cutting interests with different stakes and priorities. One of the most direct connections South Korea has is its economic interests and commercial ties to the region.[7] The ROK economy is heavily dependent on international trade including markets for its exports and the importation of raw materials, especially energy imports on which South Korea is almost totally dependent. According to the World Bank, in 2015, ROK total trade as a percent of GDP was 85 percent.[8] South Korea is ranked as the world's 7th largest trading State. A large share of ROK energy imports come from Saudi Arabia and the United Arab Emirates which must pass through the South China Sea. South Korea also imports various ores and metals from China and Australia to feed its industrial sectors.[9]

South Korea has important and growing economic ties with the countries of Southeast Asia. In 2015, ROK trade with Vietnam reached $37.6 billion followed by Singapore ($22.95 billion), Indonesia ($16.72 billion), Malaysia ($16.35 billion), and the Philippines ($11.57 billion).[10] ROK companies also have expanding investments in the region to take advantage of lower labor costs and to expand its market presence in a region projected to have significant economic growth in the years ahead.[11] Southeast Asia is also an important destination for ROK foreign aid with six of its top fifteen recipients in the region including Cambodia, Indonesia, Laos, Myanmar, the Philippines, and Vietnam.[12] In 2006, the ROK government concluded a free trade agreement with ASEAN and has designated the organization a strategic partner. South Korea hosts the ASEAN-Korea Centre founded in 2009 with the intention to "strengthen mutual cooperation and deepen friendship among the ASEAN Member States and Korea

---

7 Lee Jaehyon, *South Korea and the South China Sea: A Domestic and International Balancing Act*, ASIA POLICY 21, National Bureau of Asian Research (January 2016): 36–40.

8 World Bank, *Trade (% of GDP)*, 2016, available at: http://data.worldbank.org/indicator/NE.TRD.GNFS.ZS?end=2015&start=1960&view=chart.

9 ING, ING INTERNATIONAL TRADE STUDY – DEVELOPMENTS IN GLOBAL TRADE: FROM 1995 TO 2017 – SOUTH KOREA (2017).

10 Korea Customs Service, *Export/Import by Country, 2015*, available at: http://www.customs.go.kr/kcshome/trade/TradeCountryList.do?layoutMenuNo=21031.

11 Uk HEO AND TERENCE ROEHRIG, SOUTH KOREA'S RISE: ECONOMIC DEVELOPMENT, POWER, AND FOREIGN RELATIONS (2014), 162–165.

12 Organization for Economic Co-operation and Development, *DAC member profile: Korea*, 2016, available at: http://www.oecd.org/dac/korea.htm.

through increasing trade volume, accelerating investment flow, invigorating tourism and enriching cultural and people-to-people exchange."[13]

South Korea has important interests in play in the South China Sea and the stakes are high. Should instability and conflict disrupt or block trade routes through the South China Sea, the ROK economy would be affected in numerous, negative ways. The free flow of commerce is central to South Korea's economy and maintaining stability to facilitate these commercial flows is crucial. Moreover, when disputes arise within the region, it is equally important for South Korea's interests that they be settled peacefully while upholding the rule of law along with international norms and commitments.

## III ROK Maritime Disputes

While South Korea is not a direct participant in the SCS dispute, it does have its own maritime disputes with China, Japan, and North Korea that could be affected by the ruling. All of the disputes are different though there are some common issues present such as fishing rights. We now turn to a brief review of each set of disputes.

### *China*

First, Seoul and Beijing have overlapping claims for their respective Exclusive Economic Zones (EEZ) in the Yellow or West Sea. The Yellow Sea is approximately 378 nautical miles (nm) at its widest point so that their 200 nm EEZS have considerable overlap. When States have overlapping EEZ claims, the United Nations Convention on the Law of the Sea (UNCLOS) calls on States to arrive at a negotiated settlement, and South Korea and China have held numerous meetings to try to resolve their competing claims but have been unable to reach agreement. South Korea has called for the issue to be settled through the "median line" principle which draws the line equidistant from ROK and Chinese baselines while China has insisted the line be drawn proportionally taking into account the extent of its coastline and population.[14]

13 ASEAN-Korea Centre, *Vision – Activities*, available at: http://www.aseankorea.org/eng/AKC/introduction.asp.

14 *S. Korea, China to hold EEZ talks Friday*, KOREA TIMES, 21 April 2016, available at: http://koreatimes.co.kr/www/news/nation/2016/04/113_203102.html.

A second and related issue is that of illegal fishing by Chinese boats in South Korean waters.[15] As the Chinese population has grown along with the demand for food, Chinese fishing fleets have overfished waters adjacent to the mainland requiring boats to venture farther out to sea to maintain the size of their catches. This problem has been compounded by pollution in Chinese coastal waters that has also depleted fishing stocks pushing Chinese boats to fish elsewhere. Seoul and Beijing have concluded agreements to manage the fishing problem but enforcement concerns continue, particularly regarding Chinese vessels in ROK waters. Violence has been a regular occurrence between the ROK Coast Guard and Chinese fishing boats. In December 2010, two Chinese fishermen died from a collision with a ROK Coast Guard vessel and in December 2011, a crewmember on a ROK Coast Guard cutter was killed and another wounded when a Chinese ship captain stabbed him with a piece of glass during a boarding operation. Though Chinese enforcement has improved, ROK authorities deem it insufficient as illegal fishing continues to be a serious problem. In 2015, South Korea seized over 600 Chinese ships for illegal fishing, and ROK naval vessels have now joined the maritime police and coast guard to patrol for Chinese fishing boats.[16]

Finally, South Korea and China have a dispute over a reef in the East China Sea that Koreans call Ieodo and the Chinese call Suyan Rock. Both parties agree that this is not a territorial dispute as defined by UNCLOS since the reef remains submerged up to four to five meters at low tide. The reef's location is approximately 80 nm from the island of Marado, the closest ROK territory and 155 nm from the nearest Chinese island of Tongdao. In 1952, President Syngman Rhee drew his maritime "Peace Line" that included Ieodo under ROK administrative control and during the next several decades, little was made of the issue. In 2003, South Korea built the Ieodo Ocean Research Station on the reef to collect data on ocean currents, fishing, weather, and climate change. South Korea has argued that it was permissible to build the research facility under Articles 60 and 80 of UNCLOS that allow for the construction of installations, artificial islands, and structures on the continental shelf or within the EEZ.[17]

---

15 Terence Roehrig, *Republic of Korea Navy and China's Rise: Balancing Competing Priorities*, in Michael A. McDevitt and Catherine K. Lea, CNA Maritime Asia Project, Workshop Two: Naval Developments in Asia, August 2012, available at: http://belfercenter.ksg.harvard.edu/files/rok-navy-chinas-rise-roehrig.pdf.

16 *South Korea Cracks Down on Illegal Chinese Fishing*, Wall Street Journal, 10 June 2016, available at: http://www.wsj.com/articles/south-korea-cracks-down-on-illegal-chinese-fishing-1465550310.

17 *No territorial dispute*, Korea Herald, 13 March 2012, available at: http://www.koreaherald.com/view.php?ud=20120313000457&cpv=0.

Chinese authorities were very displeased with the Ieodo facility and filed regular protests expressing their opposition. Beijing has also periodically challenged South Korea's claim to the region. In July 2011, China sent three patrol ships to the reef to stop a ROK salvage operation of a commercial vessel, and in December 2011, sent a monitoring ship to the area to support its jurisdictional claim.[18] Sparks flew again in March 2012 when Liu Xiqui, the head of China's State Oceanic Administration, maintained Suyan Rock was in China's "jurisdictional waters," requiring it to increase patrols and law enforcement of the area.[19] Further exacerbating the issue, in November 2013, China declared an air defense identification zone (ADIZ) in the East China Sea that included Ieodo.[20] The following month, South Korea responded by expanding its ADIZ southward to include the reef after notifying Japan, China, and the United States.[21]

In December 2015, Chinese officials again raised the issue that the reef fell within China's EEZ and hence, Suyan Rock was under Chinese jurisdiction. South Korea has been adamant the reef falls under its administration and settling the EEZ claims would resolve this dispute as well. One analyst noted, "Until now, Seoul has avoided taking sides in territorial disputes involving China and other countries in the region. Now that it faces its own territorial tug of war with China [over Ieodo], South Korea may find it difficult to remain neutral in such disputes in order to counteract China's growing assertiveness in claiming territories in the region."[22]

### *Japan*

The maritime dispute with Japan concerns a cluster of islets in the East Sea known as Dokdo to Koreans and Takeshima to Japanese. Dokdo consists of two small islands and several surrounding reefs that are located approximately halfway between Korea and Japan. The islands are important largely for fishing

---

18 *China renews territorial … claim to Ieodo waters*, KOREA HERALD, 11 March 2012, available at: http://www.koreaherald.com/view.php?ud=20120311000369&cpv=0.

19 Jeremy Page, *China, South Korea in Row Over Submerged Rock*, WALL STREET JOURNAL, 13 March 2012, available at: http://blogs.wsj.com/korearealtime/2012/03/14/china-south-korea-in-row-over-submerged-rock/.

20 Chung Min-uck, *Seoul protests China's air defense zone*, KOREA TIMES, 25 November 2013, available at: http://www.koreatimes.co.kr/www/news/dr/120_146830.html.

21 Jack Kim and Jane Chung, *South Korea expands its air defense zone to partially overlap China's*, REUTERS, 8 December 2013, available at: http://www.reuters.com/article/us-korea-china-air-idUSBRE9B703M20131208.

22 Rahul Raj, *China's Claim on Ieodo*, KOREA TIMES, 19 January 2016, http://www.koreatimes.co.kr/www/news/opinon/2016/03/162_195794.html.

and the possibility of oil and gas deposits. South Korea occupied the islands in 1954 and gradually established a presence including a lighthouse, wharf, and facilities for approximately 50 to 60 government and Coast Guard personnel. Despite ROK possession of the islands, sovereignty remains a bone of contention between South Korea and Japan with arguments drawing on evidence from centuries ago.[23] The dispute is also grounded in the period of Japanese occupation from 1910–1945 and the five years prior when Korea was a protectorate. In February 1905, Japan incorporated the islands maintaining they were unoccupied and *terra nullius*, belong to no one. Japan argues its acquisition occurred before the November 1905 protectorate and 1910 annexation treaties so that when these were nullified after World War II, Tokyo retained possession.

South Korea sees these events differently contending that Korean sovereignty had been established over the islands prior to 1905 and cite Japanese documents and maps from the late 1800s and 1950s that demonstrate Korean ownership.[24] Consequently, the islands were not *terra nullius* and were returned to South Korea after World War II. At the end of the war, Japanese and South Korean authorities lobbied U.S. occupation officials hard for possession of the islands and initially, Washington sided with Japan where Assistant Secretary of State Dean Rusk noted "the island does not appear ever before to have been claimed by Korea."[25] The U.S. position may have had more to do with the success of Japan's lobbying efforts than the strength of the evidence. It was not long after, however, that the U.S. position evolved to its current policy of not taking a position on sovereignty and accepting whatever diplomatic settlement could be reached between Seoul and Tokyo.[26]

The dispute remains a flashpoint in ROK-Japan relations and periodically flares up as a bone of contention. Both countries regularly assert their claim through a variety of routes including government documents, teaching materials, visits, and expressions by their respective publics regarding the sovereignty

---

23 Sean Fern, *Tokdo or Takeshima?: the International Law of Territorial Acquisition in Japan-Korea Island Dispute*, 5(1) STANFORD JOURNAL OF EAST ASIAN AFFAIRS (Winter 2005) 86 and Jon Van Dyke, *Legal Issues Related to Sovereignty over Dokdo and Its Maritime Boundary*, 38 OCEAN DEVELOPMENT & INTERNATIONAL LAW (2007) 183–184.

24 *Japan Must Give Up False Claims to Dokdo*, CHOSUN ILBO, 5 January 2009, available at: http://english.chosun.com/site/data/html_dir/2009/01/05/2009010561031.html, and *More Maps Weaken Japan's Claim to Dokdo*, CHOSUN ILBO, 18 February 2010, available at: http://english.chosun.com/site/data/html_dir/2010/02/18/2010021800465.html.

25 Dean Rusk, *1951 Aug 10 – Sec. of State Dean Rusk Letter to S. Korean Ambassador*, available at: http://dokdo-or-takeshima.blogspot.com/2008/08/1951-august-rusks-letter.html.

26 Terence Roehrig, *Caught Between Two Allies: The United States and the Dokdo/Takeshima Dispute*, unpublished conference paper, April 2016.

claims. South Korea maintains there is no dispute and thus, nothing to settle, but Japan has threatened on several occasions to take the matter to the International Court of Justice, the most recent in 2012. South Korea has refused to participate in any arbitration process, but the PCA ruling could have an impact on the dispute.

### *North Korea*

Finally, the North–south maritime dispute concerns the NLL, a maritime demarcation line believed to have been promulgated on August 30, 1953 shortly after the Korean War.[27] During the armistice talks, negotiators were unable to reach agreement on a maritime border in the West Sea and were unwilling to delay the armistice over this issue. Soon after, it became clear to United Nations Command (UNC) authorities that a maritime boundary was needed. The armistice had designated five islands known today as the Northwest Islands (NWI) in the West Sea as under UNC control and the line was drawn approximately mid-channel between the North Korean shore and these islands. The line was largely intended to keep ROK fishing vessels from straying north, and though North Korea was never notified of the line, it was not long before it deciphered the location of the NLL.

In December 1973, North Korea lodged its first formal protest of the NLL maintaining the five NWI were in its territorial waters and access to islands would require Pyongyang's permission. At the time, U.S. officials understood that the NLL rested on shaky legal ground. A 1974 U.S. State Department cable noted "reservations" regarding South Korea's claim to the NLL and that "we would be in an extremely vulnerable position of charging [North Korea] with penetrations beyond a line they have never accepted or acknowledged."[28] In 1999 following the first large scale naval clash along the NLL, North Korea proclaimed the line null and void while drawing their own version of a maritime boundary that was approximately the median line between the North and South Korean coasts but allowing two corridors of two nm each to access the

27 See Terence Roehrig, *Korean Dispute over the Northern Limit Line: Security, Economics, or International Law?*, 3 MARYLAND SERIES IN CONTEMPORARY ASIAN STUDIES (2008), available at: http://digitalcommons.law.umaryland.edu/mscas/vol2008/iss3/1/, and Jon M. Van Dyke, Mark J. Valencia, and Jenny Miller Garmendia, *The North/South Korea Boundary Dispute in the Yellow (West Sea)*, 27 MARINE POLICY (2003).

28 U.S. Department of State, *ROKG Legal Memorandum on Northwest Coastal Incidents*, 22 December 1973, National Archives, available at: http://aad.archives.gov/aad/createpdf?rid=107420&dt=2472&dl=1345. See also *Summary Public Affairs Aspects of North Korea*, 28 February 1975, National Archives, http://aad.archives.gov/aad/createpdf?rid=25832&dt=2476&dl=1345.

NWI. The use of a median line to settle overlapping claims of adjacent coastal States is outlined in Article 15 of UNCLOS.[29]

South Korea has been adamant in maintaining the current NLL as the de facto maritime boundary. Given the hostile relations, the line is essential for ROK security, especially for the NWI which would be near impossible to defend without the current NLL. Moreover, many ROK analysts maintain that at various times, North Korea has indicated acceptance of the line. As demonstrated in 2007 when President Roh Moo-hyun sought to broach the issue with the North during his summit meeting with Kim Jong-il, any ROK leader who attempted to shift the line south would face stiff opposition at home. Without a significant improvement in the overall security situation, South Korea will not accept any adjustment to the line.

## IV Caught in the Middle

Another element of the dispute for South Korea is the indirect aspect of being caught between two important players in the SCS dispute – China and the United States. Both countries are important to South Korea's future but for different reasons. Moreover, both countries would be delighted to have South Korea provide vocal support for their position in the dispute. Debate continues in South Korea over the interests, stakes, and direction of ROK policy as it navigates between these two powers. Much will depend on the future of Sino-U.S. relations that might force South Korea's hand and make any type of hedging strategy increasingly difficult.

### *ROK-China Relations*

Korea's ties to China are extensive and rooted in centuries of history as neighbors through geographic proximity, trade, and cultural exchange along with years of the Kingdom of Korea existing under the suzerainty of the Chinese Empire. After the division of Korea in 1945 and the Korean War, South Korea and China were squarely on opposite sides of the Cold War as Beijing first rescued North Korea early in the Korean War and then supported the chief threat to South Korean security with military aid and subsidized trade.[30] China has been a central player in Korean affairs throughout history and its role will always be important in determining the future of the peninsula.

29 Article 15, UNCLOS.

30 Min-Hyung Kim, *South Korea's Strategy toward a Rising China, Security Dynamics in East Asia, and International Relations Theory*, 56 ASIAN SURVEY (July/August 2016) 707–730.

For South Korea, there are two chief elements in its relations with China. First, economic ties with China are crucial for the continued prosperity of the ROK economy. China is South Korea's top trading partner with total trade in 2015 over $227 billion and a trade surplus of close to $47 billion. South Korea's trade with China is more than the combined total of its next two trade partners, the United States ($113.85 billion) and Japan ($71.43 billion).[31] Trade with China represents approximately 25 percent of total ROK trade.[32] South Korea and China also have extensive economic ties through foreign direct investment (FDI).

On 1 June 2015, Seoul and Beijing signed a free trade agreement (FTA) that went into effect on 20 December 2015. Negotiations began in 2012 and it took twelve rounds of talks to conclude the deal. The agreement will remove tariffs on over 90 percent of their trade within 20 years and initial estimates indicate that trade volume will likely increase by more than 20 percent.[33] However one study noted that the agreement was disappointing in its efforts to liberalize trade and "both sides incorporated extensive exceptions to basic tariff reforms and deferred important market access negotiations on services and investment for several years."[34] Seoul has also been part of the early rounds of negotiations to conclude the Chinese-sponsored Regional Comprehensive Economic Partnership and has joined China's Asian Infrastructure Investment Bank, one of several U.S. allies to do so despite Washington's opposition.

South Korea's ties to the Chinese economy are extensive and a significant opportunity for growth. However, they are also a vulnerability providing China leverage with which to influence South Korean policy. For example, in the wake of the decision to deploy the THAAD missile defense battery, China has retaliated against ROK companies that do business in and with China, imposed restrictions on travel and tourism to South Korea, and cancelled K-Pop

---

31 *Korea Customs Service, 2016,* available at: http://www.customs.go.kr/kcshome/trade/TradeCountryList.do?layoutMenuNo=21031.

32 *South Korea: Trade Statistics, 2014*, available at: http://globaledge.msu.edu/countries/south-korea/tradestats.

33 Ram Garikipati, *Dynamics of Korea-China economic relations*, KOREA HERALD, 9 March 2013, available at: http://www.koreaherald.com/view.php?ud=20150309001221.

34 Jeffrey J. Schott, Euijin Jung, and Cathleen Cimino-Isaacs, *An Assessment of the Korea-China Free Trade Agreement*, Peterson Institute, December 2015, available at: https://piie.com/sites/default/files/publications/pb/pb15-24.pdf.

concerts.[35] Thus, the economic stakes are high for South Korea in its relationship with China.

Second, South Korea recognizes that Chinese assistance is essential for dealing with the problem of North Korea's nuclear weapons. China is the North's main trading partner and economic life line as well as political protector. Beijing is the only country that appears to have any power and influence over Pyongyang, and without Chinese support, managing the North Korea problem becomes infinitely more difficult. As a result, President Park sought to build a close relationship with China and President Xi Jinping. The two leaders met on numerous occasions after Park took office in February 2013, either through bilateral summits or on the sidelines of other multilateral meetings such as ASEAN or the Asia-Pacific Economic Cooperation forum. In September 2015, Park travelled to Beijing for the parade through Tiananmen Square that commemorated the end of World War II and the victory over Japan. Park's attendance, her third trip to China, was controversial and she took a considerable risk attending since few other democratic leaders chose to do so. During the trip, Park met with Xi where the two cautioned North Korea to refrain from taking any actions that might raise regional tensions. Regarding denuclearization, they "shared the view that meaningful six-way talks should be quickly resumed," citing the success of the Iran nuclear deal.[36] A Chinese press report noted that both leaders expressed a willingness to cooperate in achieving denuclearization on the Korean Peninsula along with communicating and coordinating on regional and international affairs.[37]

Despite Park's efforts, when North Korea conducted its fourth nuclear weapon test in January 2016 and followed up in February with another satellite launch, China's response was far less than she had hoped. All of the ground work and risk Park had taken in building up a close relationship with Xi seemed to be for naught given the tepid Chinese response. Subsequently, the ROK government reversed its position on the possibility of deploying the THAAD system to South

35 Jonathan Cheng, *Chinese Retaliation Over Antimissile System Has South Korea Worried*, Wall Street Journal, 3 March 2017, available at: https://www.wsj.com/articles/in-south-korea-jitters-grow-that-china-is-punishing-it-1488519202.

36 Kim Kwang-tae, *Park, Xi warn N. Korea against any provocations*, Yonhap News, 2 September 2015, available at: http://english.yonhapnews.co.kr/national/2015/09/01/52/0301000000AEN20150901010454315F.html.

37 *China, ROK vow to boost cooperation*, Xinhua News, 2 September 2015, available at: http://news.xinhuanet.com/english/2015-09/02/c_134581381.htm.

Korea. ROK leaders had been hesitant based on China's strong opposition to U.S. missile defense efforts in the region. While the government held off, China's objections struck some in South Korea as bullying over an issue that was important to ROK security. After China's lukewarm response to the nuclear test and satellite launch, THAAD was back on the table, despite Chinese objections. As talks proceeded, Qiu Guohong, the Chinese ambassador to South Korea warned that Sino-ROK relations could be "destroyed in an instant" if the THAAD system were deployed to Korea.[38] But a Park Administration spokesman fired back: "This is a matter we will decide upon according to our own security and national interests. The Chinese had better recognize this point."[39] A senior official at the ROK Foreign Ministry who wanted anonymity chimed in further that China should "look into the root of the problem [North Korea's nuclear weapon and ballistic missile programs] if it really wants to raise an issue with it."[40]

On July 8, 2016, the ROK Defense Ministry announced an agreement with Washington to deploy the system and Chinese anger was quick to follow. Chinese Foreign Minister Wang Yi remarked, "The recent move by the South Korean side has harmed the foundation of mutual trust between the two countries. THAAD is most certainly not a simple technical issue, but an out-and-out strategic one."[41]

The decision has also been contentious in South Korea with vocal opposition in some quarters over the location of the THAAD battery, the possible negative effects on ROK-Sino relations, and the potential health effects of the radar system. However, the ROK government remained committed to its decision. After announcing the THAAD decision, Park argued: "Growing nuclear and missile threats are a very critical issue where the future of the Republic of Korea and the lives of our people are at stake. As president, I have the obligation to protect our people and nation." Moreover, Park declared "THAAD will not target any country other than North Korea,

38 Choe Sang-han, *South Korea Tells China Not to Intervene in Missile-Defense System Talks*, NEW YORK TIMES, 24 February 2016, available at: http://www.nytimes.com/2016/02/25/world/asia/south–north-korea-us-missile-defense-thaad-china.html.

39 *Ibid.*

40 *Ibid.*

41 *China says South Korea's THAAD anti-missile decision harms foundation of trust*, REUTERS, 25 July 2016, http://www.reuters.com/article/us-southkorea-thaad-china-defence-id USKCN1050Y7. See also *China, Russia voice serious concern over THAAD deployment in South Korea*, XINHUA, 28 July 2016, available at: http://news.xinhuanet.com/english/2016-07/29/c_135547912.htm.

and will not encroach upon the security interests of any third country. (We) have no reason to do so."[42] Chinese objections were also undercut by North Korea's fifth nuclear detonation in September and continued ballistic missile tests.

During the 2016 G-20 meeting in China, Park and Xi held a bilateral session where Xi reiterated China's opposition to the deployment but also appeared to craft a more conciliatory tone by noting "China and South Korea should make efforts to get their bilateral ties back on track toward stable development" and that "close neighbors with common interests … should hold dear the foundation of their political cooperation and get over difficulties and challenges."[43] Some ROK analysts speculated that China would adopt a two-track approach to THAAD that opposed its deployment but would work to grow political and economic ties with South Korea. ROK Finance Minister Yoo Il-ho argued: "There will be no large-scale retaliation from China. We speculate that [the Chinese government] will separate economics with politics. Although we are concerned, it is unlikely that economic relations between South Korea and China will see a sudden decline. We will try to convince China that this is a political issue and not an economic one."[44] Given China's economic retaliation, these assessments appear to have been overly optimistic.

Though ROK leaders recognize the crucial role China plays in dealing with North Korea, this has been tempered by the realization that there are limits to what Beijing will do to control the North, no matter how close ROK-Sino relations become. Yet, while South Korea's hopes that China was willing to exert more pressure on North Korea to moderate its behavior have been dampened, economics remains a central factor in South Korea maintaining a hedging strategy regarding its relations with China.[45]

---

42 Song Sang-ho, *Park strongly defends THAAD deployment decision*, YONHAP NEWS, 11 July 2016, available at: http://english.yonhapnews.co.kr/news/2016/07/11/0200000000AEN20160711004700315.html.

43 Kang Seung-woo, *Xi softens tone over THAAD*, KOREA TIMES, 5 September 2016, available at: http://www.koreatimes.co.kr/www/news/nation/2016/09/116_213480.html.

44 *Finance minister: China retaliation over THAAD unlikely*, JOONGANG DAILY, 13 July 2016, available at: http://koreajoongangdaily.joins.com/news/article/article.aspx?aid=3021219.

45 Park Jin, *Korea Between the United States and China: How Does Hedging Work?*, 26 JOINT U.S.-KOREA ACADEMIC STUDIES (2015) 59–73.

### *ROK-U.S. Relations*

Since the end of World War II, South Korea's security has been closely linked to ties with the United States. When the Korean War ended, Washington and Seoul concluded a formal alliance that included a mutual security treaty, U.S. ground forces stationed close to the demilitarized zone acting as a trip wire to ensure a U.S. response should North Korea invade, over $5.7 billion in economic and military aid, and the inclusion of South Korea under the U.S. nuclear umbrella along with the deployment of U.S. tactical nuclear weapons to the peninsula.[46] The ROK-U.S. alliance has grown from its initial founding as a patron-client relationship where Washington provided security for a poor, war-torn country to one that now is more of a partnership. In 2009, Presidents Barack Obama and Lee Myung-bak concluded a joint vision statement that conceived of a relationship where "we will build a comprehensive strategic alliance of bilateral, regional and global scope, based on common values and mutual trust" to address a variety of problems and common interests beyond only regional concerns.[47] A crucial element of the changing relationship has been South Korea's economic growth and political development that has led to a broader set of interests and tools to pursue these goals either independently or as part of the alliance.[48] Though support for the alliance in South Korea has ebbed and flowed over the years and there have been periods of serious anti-Americanism,[49] overall support for the alliance and its role in preserving ROK security remains strong. In surveys done by the Asan Institute, it found that from 2010 to 2014, public support for the alliance and a belief that the alliance is a necessity for ROK security has been over 85 percent.[50]

Over the years, alliance planning and strategy have evolved into a close and effective deterrence posture. For example, in 1978, South Korea and the United States formed the Combined Forces Command (CFC). The new arrangement created a highly integrated command structure that reinforced the U.S. defense commitment while improving the alliance's ability to fight should deterrence fail.

---

46 Terence Roehrig, From Deterrence to Engagement: The U.S. Defense Commitment to South Korea (2001) 164–193.

47 White House Office of the Press Secretary, *Joint Vision for the alliance of the United States of America and the Republic of Korea*, 16 June 2009, available at: http://www.cfr.org/proliferation/joint-vision-alliance-united-states-america-republic-korea/p19643.

48 Heo and Roehrig, *supra* note 11.

49 See David Straub, Anti-Americanism in Democratizing South Korea (2015).

50 Choi Kang, Kim Jiyoon, Karl Friedhoff, Kang Chungku, and Lee Euicheol, *South Korean Attitudes on the Korea-US Alliance and Northeast Asia*, Asan Institute, 24 April 2014.

The past decade, Washington and Seoul have taken other measures to bolster the alliance and deterrence in the face of a growing North Korean nuclear and ballistic missile capability. In October 2013, the alliance announced a new "Tailored Deterrence Strategy" (TDS) to counteract North Korea's nuclear, chemical, and biological weapon capabilities.[51] Though the details are classified, the TDS contains plans for further integration of US and ROK forces for a joint response to DPRK threats, including the possibility of preemptive strikes should a North Korean attack appear imminent. Alliance planning has also included a new operations plan – OPLAN 5015 that, according to press reports, contains contingency plans for conducting rapid counterstrikes on North Korean leadership and military targets after an attack.[52]

To rehearse these plans as well as to send a message of U.S. determination to defend South Korea, each year the alliance conducts a series of joint exercises, Ulchi Freedom Guardian (UFG) in the fall, and Key Resolve (KR) and Foal Eagle (FE) in the spring. UFG and KR are computer-simulated, command post exercises that work on intelligence, logistics, and operations challenges to enhance readiness by working through a series of possible North Korea scenarios. Both of these exercises last approximately two weeks. FE takes place in spring and is a large, combined forces field training exercise to flow U.S. forces to the peninsula and conduct joint combat operations to defend South Korea. In addition to ground combat units, FE also includes naval and air components, special forces, and at times, high profile displays of U.S. strategic assets such as a B-52 or ballistic missile submarine. The 2016 exercise simulated a new pre-emptive strike plan labelled "4D" (detect, disrupt, destroy, and defend) that rehearsed operations to destroy and secure DPRK chemical and nuclear weapon assets during a conflict so that these stockpiles remain secure and do not fall into the hands of other States or terrorist organizations.[53]

Deterrence at the strategic level has been relatively stable for over six decades with the likelihood of North Korea conducting another invasion of the South very low. Many analysts have instead been raising concerns for increases in North Korea's lower level provocations. Borrowing the Cold War concept

---

51 Department of Defense, Joint *Communique – the 45st ROK-U.S. Security Consultative Meeting*, 2 October 2, 2013, available at: http://archive.defense.gov/pubs/Joint%20Communique,%2045th%20ROK-U.S.%20Security%20Consultative%20Meeting.pdf.

52 Global Security.org, *OPLAN 5015 [Operational Plans]*, 7 March 2016, available at: http://www.globalsecurity.org/military/ops/oplan-5015.htm.

53 Anna Fifield, *In drills, U.S., South Korea practice striking North's nuclear plants, leaders*, WASHINGTON POST, 7 March 2016, available at: https://www.washingtonpost.com/world/in-drills-us-south-korea-practice-striking-norths-nuclear-plants/2016/03/06/46e6019d-5f04-4277-9b41-e02fc1c2e801_story.html?utm_term=.b783258e1f44.

of a stability-instability paradox, Pyongyang might undertake more provocative behavior as it did in 2010 with the sinking of the *Cheonan* and shelling *Yeonpyeong* Island knowing it had a nuclear capability as a shield. Though North Korea has not displayed the type of behavior predicted by the paradox, to counter any potential problems in this area, Seoul and Washington agreed to a Combined Counter-Provocation Plan (CCP). Details are classified but reports of the plan point to South Korea being in the lead for responding to DPRK provocations but can request assistance from Washington. The CCP is intended to enhance joint planning and consultation to improve readiness while providing a determined and rapid response to North Korean actions.[54]

These examples, among many others, of alliance planning and preparation demonstrate the extensive integration of the alliance and the determined commitment of the United States to defend South Korea if attacked. There is little doubt the United States and the alliance plays a crucial role in ROK security. While the focus of the alliance has been deterrence and defense against North Korea, there is also some apprehension and wariness tied to China's rise and the possibility that China will seek to dominate the region in ways that hurt ROK interests. The United States and the alliance remain essential for South Korea's security, not only for the defense of South Korea against another DPRK invasion but also to support South Korea in the face of lower level provocations perpetrated by the North.[55]

ROK-U.S. relations also have an important economic component though not as large as economic ties with China. In 2015, South Korea and the United States had bilateral trade worth $113.85 billion.[56] The United States is South Korea's 2nd largest trading partner while South Korea is the 8th largest for the United States. In 2007, South Korea and the United States signed a free trade agreement (KORUS FTA) and after considerable political wrangling, both legislatures finally passed the deal in 2011, entering into force the following year. The KORUS FTA ends approximately 95 percent of tariffs during the first five years with the remaining duties eliminated over the next ten years. The agreement has opened markets in automobiles, tires, and motion pictures, as well as

---

54 Ashley Rowland, *US, South Korea agree on a response plan if North Korea attacks*, STARS AND STRIPES, 24 March 2013, available at: http://www.stripes.com/news/us-south-korea-agree-on-response-plan-if-north-korea-attacks-1.213210#.WNBGZ2_yuUk.

55 Terence Roehrig, *Reinforcing Deterrence: The U.S. Military Response to North Korean Provocations*, 26 JOINT U.S.-KOREA ACADEMIC STUDIES, (2016), available at: http://www.keia.org/sites/default/files/publications/reinforcing_deterrence_the_u.s._military_response_to_north_koren_provocations.pdf.

56 Korea Customs Service, *Export/Import By Country, 2015*, available at: http://www.customs.go.kr/kcshome/trade/TradeCountryList.do?layoutMenuNo=21031.

service sectors in health, education, and finance. The deal is the largest FTA for the United States since the 1994 North American Free Trade Agreement and is South Korea's second largest FTA surpassed only by the one with the European Union.[57]

## V South Korea's Position on the South China Sea

Though South Korea is not a direct participant in the SCS dispute and the PCA ruling, it does have some important interests in the issue with relatively high stakes. Freedom of navigation, regional peace and stability, and the peaceful settling of disputes are very important for ROK economic and strategic interests. These issues, as well as others raised here, also tie South Korea to the future of Sino-U.S. relations. Should ties between Beijing and Washington continue to deteriorate, South Korea could potentially be squeezed between these powers in both the economic and security spheres. However, it is important to note that the SCS dispute is not, at its core, a China-U.S. issue but rather a dispute over international law and norms, along with numerous disagreements over sovereignty. Thus, South Korea's position on these issues is part of a complex, geopolitical context but also involves its position on international law and the peaceful settlement of disputes.

For a number of years, South Korea has been fairly quiet on the SCS providing little public clarification of its position. In 2015, the United States began to exert pressure on the Park administration to speak out against Chinese actions in the SCS. In October 2015, President Park traveled to Washington DC for a summit meeting with Obama. The meeting had been scheduled for June but was postponed due to the outbreak of the MERS virus and Park's need to remain at home to coordinate the government response. During their discussions, Obama brought up the SCS and when answering a question at the summit press conference remarked:

> So there's no contradiction between the Republic of Korea having good relations with us, being a central part of our alliance, and having a good relationship – good relations with China.
>
> I think as I communicated to President Park, the only thing that we're going to continue to insist on is that we want China to abide by international norms and rules. And where they fail to do so, we expect the Republic of Korea to speak out on that, just as we do, because we think

57 HEO AND ROEHRIG, *supra* note 11, at 63–66.

> that both of our countries have benefitted from the international norms and rules that have been in place since the end of World War II. And we don't want to see those rules of the road weakening, or some countries taking advantage because they're larger. That's not good for anybody – including South Korea.[58]

Soon after, ROK officials began to present more precise statements of the ROK position. At the November 2015 ASEAN Defense Ministers' Meeting-Plus (ADMM-Plus), ROK Defense Minister Han Min-koo offered South Korea's first pronouncement by a high ranking official: "The stance of the Republic of Korea is that a peaceful resolution of the South China Sea dispute and the freedom of navigation and flight should be guaranteed. The dispute should be settled peacefully through an agreement among related parties and in accordance with international standards."[59] Later in the month at the 2015 East Asian Summit, President Park called the South China Sea dispute a "grave concern" and that "Korea has consistently stressed that the dispute must be peacefully resolved according to international agreements and code of conduct. China must guarantee the right of free navigation and flight."[60] The Philippines had initiated the case in January 2013, and the tribunal ruled in October 2015 that it had jurisdiction in the matter. With the final ruling expected in summer 2016, it was likely South Korea would have to further clarify its position.

## VI PCA Ruling: ROK Reaction and Implications

The ruling by the PCA was announced on July 12, 2016 and was far more favorable to the Philippine side of the case than many had expected. The decision had four key elements. First, the Court rejected China's claims to the area of the South China Sea enclosed by the nine-dash line. According to the tribunal, China never established exclusive control over the region and any historic

58 White House Press Secretary, *Remarks by President Obama and President Park of the Republic of Korea in Joint Press Conference*, 16 October 2015, available at: https://www.whitehouse.gov/the-press-office/2015/10/16/remarks-president-obama-and-president-park-republic-korea-joint-press.

59 *Freedom of navigation should be guaranteed in disputed South China Sea: S. Korean defense minister*, YONHAP NEWS, 4 November 2015, available at: http://english.yonhapnews.co.kr/news/2015/11/04/0200000000AEN20151104008751315.html.

60 Shin Yong-ho, *Park Appeals to Beijing on South China Sea*, JOONGANG DAILY, 24 November 2015, available at: http://koreajoongangdaily.joins.com/news/article/Article.aspx?aid=3011908.

claims were extinguished by UNCLOS. Second, the Spratly Islands, including Itu Aba that is currently occupied by Taiwan, are, according to UNCLOS "[r]ocks which cannot sustain human habitation or economic life of their own [and as a result] shall have no exclusive economic zone or continental shelf." Third, Chinese actions that prevent Philippine fishing, the exploration of oil and gas, and the construction of islands in the Philippine EEZ are illegal. Finally, Chinese construction of islands begun after the start of the arbitration case aggravated the dispute and caused permanent damage to the marine environment.[61]

South Korea responded to the ruling the next day with a brief, two paragraph statement from the Ministry of Foreign Affairs:

1. The Government of the Republic of Korea has consistently held the position that the peace and stability, and the freedom of navigation and overflight should be safeguarded in the South China Sea, one of the world's major sea lines of communication, and that disputes in the South China Sea should be resolved in accordance with relevant agreements, non-militarization commitments, as well as internationally established norms of conduct.
2. The Government of the Republic of Korea takes note of the arbitration award issued on July 12, and hopes, following the award, that the South China Sea disputes will be resolved through peaceful and creative diplomatic efforts.[62]

The first paragraph is essentially a restatement of the ROK government position that supports international law and the peaceful settlement of disputes. The ROK statement acknowledges the importance of "peace and stability" along with the need to protect freedom of navigation and overflight in the SCS, a position that is largely in line with Washington and many others in the international community. Resolving the dispute based on "relevant agreements" is an acknowledgement of the importance of UNCLOS and other elements of

61 Permanent Court of Arbitration, *Press Release: The South China Sea Arbitration*, 12 July 2016, available at: https://pca-cpa.org/wp-content/uploads/sites/175/2016/07/PH-CN-20160712-Press-Release-No-11-English.pdf.

62 Ministry of Foreign Affairs, *Statement by the Spokesperson of the Ministry of Foreign Affairs of the Republic of Korea on the South China Sea Arbitration Award*,13 July 2016, available at: http://www.mofa.go.kr/ENG/press/pressreleases/index.jsp?menu=m_10_20&sp=/webmodule/htsboard/template/read/engreadboard.jsp%3FtypeID=12%26boardid=302%26seqno=316765.

international law. Finally, the reference to "non-militarization commitments" is a reminder of the assurance Xi Jinping gave to Obama during his August 2016 trip to the White House regarding the Spratlys/Nansha where Xi said, "China does not intend to pursue militarization."[63] Thus, the first paragraph provided no substantive concession to China on the key issues involved in the PCA ruling and showed no indication of moving in Beijing's direction on these points. This paragraph was a strong affirmation of the importance of international law in this matter and consistent with the U.S. position.

However, after giving no substantive ground, in paragraph 2, South Korea was also careful to avoid language that would antagonize China by simply acknowledging the ruling.[64] Yet, the last clause of paragraph two was also a practical recognition that despite the ruling, both sides were at an impasse and the matter was far from being resolved. China was not going to follow the legal ruling and any effort to use force to solve the problem would be catastrophic. As a result, the ROK government called for "peaceful and creative diplomatic efforts" that might find an alternative diplomatic path to resolving the problem. Thus, the ROK government sought to walk a fine line that balanced the competing interests it has at stake in this issue.

The South China Sea dispute and the PCA decision may have several important implications for South Korea. First, the ruling may further complicate ROK relations between China and the United States. Following the ruling, one ROK official who wished to remain anonymous lamented: "The diplomatic situations for us have become very tough."[65] In the wake of the PCA ruling, there may be increased pressure on South Korea to speak out in support of the decision and to support the U.S. position on the South China Sea. The Trump administration has had tough words for China and its actions in the South China Sea, indicating it will push back against Chinese actions in the region. However, the United States does not appear to be placing greater pressure on South Korea to support its position, at least for the moment.

---

63 David E. Sanger and Rick Gladstone, *New Photos Cast Doubt on China's Vow Not to Militarize Disputed Islands*, NEW YORK TIMES, 8 August 2016, available at: http://www.nytimes.com/2016/08/09/world/asia/china-spratly-islands-south-china-sea.html?_r=0.

64 Lee Je-hun, *Response on South China Sea ruling shows S. Korea's fragile position*, HANKYOREH, 14 July 2016, available at: http://english.hani.co.kr/arti/english_edition/e_international/752372.html.

65 Koh Bung-joon and Lee Haye-ah, *South China Sea ruling poses diplomatic conundrum for S. Korea*, YONHAP NEWS, 13 July 2016, available at: http://english.yonhapnews.co.kr/national/2016/07/13/58/0301000000AEN20160713006600315F.html.

In addition, there may be reputational costs internationally if South Korea provides only lukewarm support for a decision that is grounded in international law and the peaceful settlement of disputes. Conversely, while China does not appear to have placed a great deal of public pressure on South Korea to support its side of the SCS dispute and the PCA ruling, Chinese officials have likely expressed their views quietly and reminded Seoul that a strong ROK position that is counter to China's would damage their relations. These issues are further complicated by Chinese opposition to THAAD and the difficulties of dealing with North Korea.

While both sides exert pressure on South Korea, in different ways and both formally and informally, there are also limits to how far Washington and Beijing can and should go in seeking South Korean support for their position. Should either side push too hard, it risks causing problems on other bilateral and regional issues and creating a backlash in South Korea that would be counterproductive. For example, China could exert economic pressure in ways that punish South Korea for supporting the PCA decision similar to actions taken in response to the THAAD decision. Yet too much Chinese pressure could be counterproductive. Chinese efforts to pressure South Korea in the past including the row over Koguryo in the 2000s,[66] illegal Chinese fishing, Ieodo, and the response to the THAAD decision have worsened bilateral ties. Over the past few years, Chinese President Xi has made a concerted effort to court South Korea in hopes of pulling Seoul more in its direction and away from the United States. A harsh Chinese response to any of these disagreements risks negating work Xi has done to improve Sino-ROK relations and would likely push South Korea closer to the United States and Japan.

Washington would like to see South Korea be a more vocal supporter of its positions on the South China Sea and will continue to ask Seoul to do so. Yet, should the United States push too hard, it also risks a backlash from ROK leaders and the public. South Korea is an important ally in the region and pushing too hard would risk alienating Seoul while straining ROK-U.S. ties. A level of anti-Americanism remains below the surface in some quarters of South Korea and U.S. pressure that is perceived to be bullying could stir up strong opposition that would be reminiscent of the difficult days of the 2000s for the alliance.

As a result, while South Korea may be caught in the middle of these two powers as they struggle over various issues, China and the United States cannot

66 Terence Roehrig, *History as a Strategic Weapon: The Korean and Chinese Struggle over Koguryo*, 45(1) JOURNAL OF ASIAN AND AFRICAN STUDIES (2010) 5–28.

overplay their hands and have their actions backfire in ways that drive South Korea to the other side. Thus, while South Korea may lack the power these two countries have, it is not powerless. With deft handling and leadership, South Korea may be able to handle the fallout of being caught in the middle of the South China Sea dispute and minimize any negative impact. Moreover, it is important to note that South Korea's decision should be guided as much by its support for international law and norms as it is by geopolitics.

One element of Sino-ROK relations that may be affected by the PCA ruling is the settling of their maritime disputes. In June 2016, South Korea and China made another attempt to solve their differences concerning overlapping EEZ claims. From 1996 to 2008, Seoul and Beijing have held over a dozen rounds of talks to delimit their EEZs but to avail. During their 2014 summit, Park and Xi agreed to restart talks and elevate the dialogue from director-level to vice minister-level meetings, a signal of the increased importance of the issue to both governments.[67] However, the talks made no substantive progress but both agreed to meet again the following year. In addition to delimiting the EEZ, the talks will also settle the fate of Ieodo/Suyan. South Korea's argument for a median line would place Ieodo in its EEZ while China's proposal of a proportional settlement would include the reef under Chinese administration. Though Beijing and Seoul have concluded several agreements to manage fishing in their zones, this remains another point of friction that could be aided by a resolution of the EEZ overlap. South Korea continues to report numerous cases of illegal fishing by Chinese vessels maintaining the Chinese government needs to do more to rein in their activities.[68] On the one hand, it is possible that China's negotiating position on these issues may become more firm in the wake of the PCA decision and South Korea's stance on the ruling. On the other hand, China may have been pleased with ROK efforts to craft a nuanced response. Moreover, the ruling may prompt Beijing to be more forthcoming in resolving its maritime concerns with Seoul in a renewed effort to woo South Korea and show that it does support international law and the peaceful settlement of disputes. In the end, it is unclear how Chinese leaders have viewed South Korea's careful response to the ruling and there could also be no difference in China's negotiating position.

---

67 Jun Ji-hye, *Seoul-Beijing EEZ talks face tough road ahead*, KOREA TIMES, 22 December 2015, available at: http://www.koreatimes.co.kr/www/news/nation/2015/12/116_193794.html.

68 *S. Korea to toughen punishment against illegal fishing*, KOREA TIMES, 11 July 2016, available at: http://www.koreatimes.co.kr/www/news/nation/2016/07/116_209069.html.

A second possible outcome is that the PCA decision may encourage other States to pursue arbitration, even if one side in the dispute refuses to participate. South Korea has some vulnerability on this since Japan has threatened on a few occasions to take the Dokdo/Takeshima case to the International Court of Justice. Indeed, ROK Foreign Ministry spokesman Cho June-hyuck commented after the PCA decision: "the contents of the ruling and the legal implications [and the relevance of the ruling to the Dokdo issue] will be scrupulously examined by the government."[69] In addition, though China has not threatened to do so, might it challenge South Korea's administration of Ieodo and the building of the research station on the reef in some form of arbitration?

South Korea is likely safe on all accounts, despite the PCA ruling, because these states are all involved in disputes whose own claims are either based on tenuous legal grounds or have little to gain by seeking arbitration creating a circumstance of "mutual assured arbitration." Akin to the Cold War nuclear weapons concept of mutual assured destruction, most of the players in the region have vulnerabilities regarding their maritime claims that make it unlikely one will pursue legal action against the other. For example, China will likely not pursue an arbitration case against either South Korea or Japan anytime soon because it would undercut its efforts to delegitimize the PCA ruling and the jurisdiction claimed by the tribunal. To ignore the PCA case and then pursue one of its own would be self-defeating for China and will not happen.

Though Japan has suggested it might pursue arbitration over Dokdo/Takeshima, it is vulnerable over its claims to Okinotori. The area is an atoll with only two small boulders exposed above the water. Japan has built up the area spending $250 million to construct concrete casings to protect the outcroppings from further deterioration. Japan claims sovereignty over Okinotori along with a 200 nm EEZ that would entitle it to a 116,474 square nm EEZ and control of the fish and mineral resources within the zone.[70] However, these "islands" do not qualify as such under UNCLOS and according to maritime scholar Jon Van Dyke, "you simply can't make a plausible claim that Okinotori should be able to generate a 200 [nautical]-mile zone."[71] Moreover, if Japan filed a

69 Lee Je-hun, *Response on South China Sea ruling shows S. Korea's fragile position*, HANKYOREH, 14 July 2016, available at: http://english.hani.co.kr/arti/english_edition/e_international/752372.html.

70 June Teufel Dreyer, *The curious case of Okinotori: reef, rock, or island?* PACNET #59, Pacific Forum CSIS, 18 July 2016, available at: https://www.csis.org/analysis/pacnet-59-curious-case-okinotori-reef-rock-or-island.

71 Martin Fackler, *A Reef or a Rock? Question Puts Japan In a Hard Place*, WALL STREET JOURNAL, 16 February 2005, available at: http://www.wsj.com/articles/SB110849423897755487.

case concerning Dokdo/Takeshima, it is not at all certain that Japan has a sufficiently strong case to win. While this might give the Japanese government the political cover to abandon its claim, a defeat would be embarrassing and might open Japan up to similar suits over other claims. Japan can tolerate the status quo and will likely not follow through on an arbitration case. Finally, the status quo is essentially in South Korea's favor. It occupies Dokdo and maintains administrative control over Ieodo with no incentive to submit either of these two disputes to arbitration. Though South Korea appears to have a stronger case, it is not airtight; Seoul has a lot to lose but little to gain by pursuing arbitration over Dokdo. As a result of all of these factors, China, Japan, and South Korea have mutual vulnerabilities that make it unlikely they will test the waters with more arbitration cases despite the PCA ruling.

Another issue arising from the PCA ruling that will likely have an effect on the future of Dokdo/Takeshima is the determination that the Spratly islands, including Itu Aba, are, according to UNCLOS article 121, para. 3 rocks, not islands and "Rocks which cannot sustain human habitation or economic life of their own shall have no exclusive economic zone or continental shelf."[72] Though South Korea maintains a contingent of police and coast guard personnel on Dokdo and in the past, an elderly couple resided on the islands, under the interpretation of article 121 para. 3 as noted in the PCA ruling, Dokdo is more accurately characterized as "rocks" and would likely be granted only a 12 nm territorial sea and not a 200 nm EEZ. As a result, the value of possessing Dokdo/Takeshima would be reduced but would continue to be substantial, especially for South Korea as Dokdo's value goes well beyond economics.

Finally, is it possible the PCA ruling could have some type of impact on the North–south dispute over the NLL? North Korea has signed but not ratified UNCLOS, and as a result, has an obligation to support the "objectives and purpose of the treaty." However, its status does not allow it to bring a case for arbitration under the agreement. Yet, is it possible that Pyongyang might feel further emboldened to challenge the NLL either through military provocations or politically with more vehement protests forcing South Korea to defend its position that is not fully supported by international law? It is certainly possible, but it is unclear whether North Korea's behavior will be affected in any way by the PCA ruling. In any case, the NLL will remain as it is, at least until the security situation improves.

72 Article 121(3), UNCLOS.

## VII Conclusion

Despite the PCA ruling, the disputes and claims in the SCS are a long way from being settled, if they ever will be. Yet the importance of international law and the cases that clarify that law are essential for helping to maintain peace and stability, not only in the maritime domain but in others as well. South Korea's position in these disputes is part of a complicated array of competing interests with different stakes that require careful management. In part, these issues concern South Korea's interests and role in building and supporting the development of international law to help maintain regional as well as global peace and stability. South Korea has been an active participate and leader in numerous international forums dealing with economics and nuclear security and its potential role in maintaining international maritime law can be another important contribution. Indeed, given South Korea's geography as a peninsula surrounded on three sides by the ocean and its commercial interests and dependence on trade means that South Korea has a great deal at stake in these issues.

Yet, as is usually the case, legal issues are often bound up in geopolitical and security matters that further complicate decision making and often trump the role of international law. South Korean leaders have sought to strike a delicate balance that supports its interests in international law that aligns with the position of the United States while not being overly blunt and direct in its challenge to Chinese actions. So far South Korea has been able to maintain the balance of its competing interests in the legal, geopolitical, and economic spheres, and the initial reactions of Beijing and Washington in the wake of the PCA ruling seem to indicate South Korea was relatively successful in this balancing act. Moreover, South Korea is not completely powerless in its dilemma of being caught between two powers because its economic, political, and military clout gives it some degree of leverage in its relations with China and the United States.

The crucial variable will be Sino-U.S. relations. It does no one any good if these ties deteriorate and it is crucial that Beijing and Washington work to improve their relationship. However, should relations worsen and tensions increase, South Korea could find itself in an increasingly difficult spot concerning the SCS and other issues. For example, might pressure grow for the ROK Navy to conduct freedom of navigation operations in the SCS with other States? It is incumbent on all parties to find methods that can lower tension levels and seek to find permanent solutions that solve these disputes based on international law and norms. For all concerned, the stakes are too high to fail.

# Law and *Realpolitik*: The Arbitral Tribunal's Ruling and the South China Sea

*Leszek Buszynski*[1]

## I Introduction

In the positivist understanding, international law is a product of accumulated State practice. It is what States have recognized as accepted practice forming customary international law, which may be codified into a convention governing State interaction. International law reflects State practice over a range of functional issues including trade, investment, the environment and also maritime rights and territorial claims. International law is desirable because it brings predictability and stability in relations between States, facilitating co-operation and removing sources of friction and conflict. It is in the interest of States to align their activities with international law because of the benefits which accrue from a cooperative and predictable order. Policy, however, represents the intentions and objectives of a State and is not law. The distinction between law and policy is important as international law builds on accumulated State practice while policy expresses the transient interests of a political leadership or State, which may not provide a stable basis for State interaction. International law may change and adjust to changes in State practice, particularly as new issues arise that require regulation. However, changes cannot be imposed by any one State, no matter how powerful, which attempts to shape the direction of law in a way favourable to its interests. International law cannot be rewritten because of the political desires of a particular leadership or ruling party, or because it is opposed by a particular country. When a State attempts to impose its policy upon law it is resorting to realpolitik, or the forceful if not violent pursuit of its own interests in complete disregard of the interests of others.

## II Reputation and International Law

Compliance with international law is a matter of State interest without the need for punitive or enforcement mechanisms of the kind associated with

1 Visiting Fellow, Strategic and Defence Studies Centre, Australian National University.

DOI 10.1163/9789004344556_008

domestic law. A reputation for compliance will enhance a State's status making possible cooperative arrangements from which other States will benefit. Through compliance with law, a State can demonstrate a reputation for cooperation which can further its goals in international relations and commerce, and obtain the cooperation of others. More can be achieved through cooperative arrangements than by unilateralism, which would clash with the interests of other States and stimulate enmity and antagonism. The concern with reputation ensures that States will comply with agreements whereas unreliability will damage that reputation undermining cooperative relationships while creating an unwillingness on the part of other States to enter into future agreements. A reputation for compliance has value in international affairs as a means of furthering a State's interests through cooperation. Long-term relationships with other cooperative States are possible leading to the smooth running of international transactions without monitoring and verification.[2] Not every agreement has the force of law and the status of law is a way of ensuring compliance from governments that would be concerned about the loss of reputation if they reneged or failed to comply.[3] Law specifies acceptable behavior in particular circumstance and in relation to a particular issue and is indicative of the seriousness and solemnity of the commitment and the willingness to undertake it. International law may be created by UN organs and conventions as subject to the ratification process of States, and also by international judicial and arbitration bodies such as the International Court of Justice, the International Criminal Court and the Law of the Sea Tribunal.

States may develop "multiple or segmented reputations" complying with some regimes and treaties while resisting and even opposing others. This may contradict the notion of a unitary reputation which is valid for all agreements.[4] The notion of segmented reputation depends upon the function and the area covered by law as compliance is expected and normal with trade and commercial agreements even for regimes that may have a poor reputation in other areas. A State may comply with trade or commercial agreements which are in its interest but not necessarily with legal judgements which affect its security. A reputation for compliance in commerce is not

2 Andrew T. Guzman, *A Compliance-Based Theory of International Law*,90 (6) CALIFORNIA LAW REVIEW (2002).

3 Beth A. Simmons, *International Law and State Behavior: Commitment and Compliance in International Monetary Affairs*, 94 AMERICAN POLITICAL SCIENCE REVIEW (2000).

4 George W. Downs and Michael A. Jones, *Reputation, Compliance, and International Law*, 31 JOURNAL OF LEGAL STUDIES (2002).

necessarily transferable to other areas such as security where a State may reveal a poor reputation for compliance, the Soviet Union was such a case. The liberal theory of international law claims that compliance with international law is a product of regime type and the domestic structure of a country. Domestic regime type may be a guide to compliance with international law as governments that are committed to the rule of law are more likely to take their legal obligations seriously. Liberal democracies with independent judiciaries and a vibrant legal culture are likely to be compliant with international law and are unlikely to jeopardize their reputation by non-compliance. Outcaste States such as North Korea may not be constrained by these considerations as they pursue their own interests such as nuclear weapons programs but they are few in number, and their future viability is dubious. Larger States with economic and military power may be tempted to ignore international law for reasons related to immediate and pressing security interests or domestic politics. The reputational costs of non-compliance, however, cannot be avoided.

Non-compliance comes with costs even for powerful states that may place themselves above law. The Reagan Administration ignored the International Court of Justice's decision of 1986 in the case of *Nicaragua v. United States* over the mining of Nicaraguan ports, the US trade embargo, and support and financing of the Contra rebels against the Sandinista regime.[5] This has been a blot on America's reputation ever since and has often been cited by regimes that justify their own non-compliance with law. The Bush Administration's lurch towards *realpolitik* was a more significant departure from law when it promulgated the doctrine of pre-emption in the "National Security Strategy for the United States" of September 2002. Since 1945 the US promoted the international rule of law and a liberal world order based on institutions and democratic values, but the Bush Administration acted in way to undermine those institutions and values.[6] The US invasion of Iraq in March 2003 was justified by the doctrine of pre-emption as an act of self-defence under Article 51 of the UN charter. It was supposedly a response to the claim that Saddam Hussein had amassed a huge arsenal of weapons of mass destruction, a claim which was not vindicated subsequently. UN Secretary General at the time Kofi Annan publicly declared that the US-led war on Iraq was illegal because it did

5 International Court of Justice, *Case concerning the Military and Paramilitary activities in and against Nicaragua* (Nicaragua v. United States of America) 1986 I.C.J. 4 27 June 1986.

6 Shirley V. Scott, *Is There Room for International Law in Realpolitik?: Accounting for the US 'Attitude' Towards International Law*, 30 REVIEW OF INTERNATIONAL STUDIES (2004).

not receive the sanction of the UN Security Council or any of its resolutions.[7] The Bush Administration suffered the consequences of this unilateral action as it lost the trust of its allies and faced constant attacks on its reputation. This action divided NATO as France was unwilling to cooperate with US policies and public opinion in Britain later turned against America. Russia's seizure of Crimea in March 2014 was an even more blatant disregard of international law because it involved a territorial revision and overtly challenged the territorial integrity of a sovereign State – the Ukraine. Russia has similarly suffered reputational costs which have cast it in the role of an aggressor serving to facilitate NATO cooperation and triggering international sanctions against it. The EU strongly opposed Russia's action and its efforts to support the rebels in the Eastern Ukraine which were regarded as an attempt to dismember the State. The EU imposed ever widening sanctions on Russia beginning in March, July and September 2014 and March 2015 which later included sanctions imposed by the US. Russia's positive relationship with Germany was undermined as the Germans joined the EU consensus against what was perceived as the actions of a predatory State.

Big powers may indeed ignore law at times, but this has consequences for their reputation that they may not have foreseen. *Realpolitik* may seem to be licence for a great power to do what it wants and to employ any means it may deem necessary to achieve its objectives. This remains a popular view today. However, a persistent disregard of law stimulates resentment and brings about opposition against the State concerned. When a judicial or arbitration body has ruled over a particular issue, the effect is one of clarification of the rights and wrongs of behaviour. What previously may have been a complicated issue that could be justified from different points of view becomes clearer and subject to quick judgement and even condemnation. The deliberate disregard of law in such circumstances creates a counter alignment of international opinion which then facilitates cooperation and the formation of coalitions against the State concerned. Indeed, in this situation the pursuit of *realpolitik* does have its costs. What may have been more easily achieved through cooperative policies which bring together interested States excite antipathy and counteraction from those who otherwise may have been receptive to cooperation.

---

7 *Iraq war was illegal and breached UN charter, says Annan*, THE GUARDIAN, 16 September 2004 available at: https://www.theguardian.com/world/2004/sep/16/iraq.iraq.

## III The Philippine Arbitration Case

The Philippine decision to appeal to legal arbitration was the result of much frustration in dealing with China which had encroached upon its claim area and Exclusive Economic Zone (EEZ). In 1994 China occupied Mischief Reef in the Philippine claim zone and built structures on the reef to support fishing activities. The Philippines appealed to ASEAN and the ASEAN Regional Forum for support but members were uninterested and wary of antagonising China. In April 2012 China squeezed out the Philippines from Scarborough Shoal when the Chinese coast guard orchestrated a fleet of fishing vessels which moved into the surrounding waters and prevented Philippine vessels from entering the area. Negotiations with the Chinese who were bent on retaining control of the features they had occupied had lead nowhere and the Philippines was left with no other option except an appeal to legal arbitration. The proposal to go to law was credited to Supreme Court Senior Associate Justice Antonio Carpio, and was promoted by the Philippine Department of Foreign Affairs under Minister Alberto Del Rosario. President Benigno Aquino then adopted the proposal and gave the green light to go ahead.[8] When the Department of Foreign Affairs launched the appeal it issued a statement on 22 January 2013 saying that it had exhausted "almost all political and diplomatic avenues for a peaceful negotiated settlement of its maritime dispute with China."[9]

The case was heard by a tribunal under Annex VII of the UN Convention of the Law of the Sea (UNCLOS) with the Permanent Court of Arbitration (PCA) acting as registry. The Arbitral Tribunal finally made its ruling public on 12 July 2016 and accepted 14 out of the 15 points raised by the Philippines. Two main points are of relevance here. First, it decided that China may have had historic rights to the resources of the South China Sea, but "such rights were extinguished to the extent they were incompatible with the exclusive economic zones provided for in the Convention." The Tribunal sidestepped the sovereignty issue which was not within its remit by deciding that China's historical claim had been superseded by UNCLOS in the negotiations for which China participated. China had signed the convention on 10 December 1982, and ratified it on 7 June 1996 and therefore should have accepted its provisions accordingly. The Tribunal also noted that there was no evidence that China had actually exercised exclusive control over the South China Sea or the resources

8 *Communication with Jay Batongbacal*, 26 August 2016.

9 Department of Foreign Affairs Republic of the Philippines, *SFA statement on the UNCLOS Arbitral proceedings against China*, 22 January 2013,available at: http://www.dfa.gov.ph/newsroom/unclos.

there. Secondly, the Tribunal found that none of the features in the Spratly Islands is capable of generating extended maritime zones, including those occupied and artificially reclaimed by China. The Tribunal clarified the meaning of Article 121 of the Convention and the definition of an island by saying that "this provision depends upon the objective capacity of a feature, in its natural condition, to sustain either a stable community of people or economic activity that is not dependent on outside resources." The Tribunal also found that Chinese activities had "violated the Philippines' sovereign rights in its exclusive economic zone" and that China had "inflicted irreparable harm to the marine environment" because of its reclamation projects.[10]

The Chinese claimed that the ruling had no legal significance because China was not a party to the action and could not be bound by the decision, that the Tribunal had overstepped the mark by dealing with issues of sovereignty, and that China had opted out of compulsory third party adjudication in its declaration of 25 August 2006 by invoking Article 298 of UNCLOS. In response to China's argument that an UNCLOS Tribunal did not have jurisdiction over sovereign claims, the Tribunal held that this was an issue of maritime rights under UNCLOS, and that this dispute did not concern maritime boundary delimitation. In response to the claim that China was not a party to the dispute and would not be bound by the outcome the Tribunal decided that being a party to the Convention bound China to the arbitration provisions. Once China had acceded to UNCLOS, it had accepted third party arbitration in regard to the maritime rights which fall under its provisions. The Tribunal referred to Article 9 of Annex VII to the effect that the absence of a party or failure of a party to defend its case "shall not constitute a bar to the proceedings." In addition, Article 287 (3) states that a party, "which is a party to a dispute not covered by a declaration in force, shall be deemed to have accepted arbitration in accordance with Annex VII." In response to China's claim that in its declaration of 25 August 2006 it had opted out of compulsory arbitration, the Tribunal noted that this declaration concerned sea boundary delimitation. The Tribunal was not constituted to deal with sea boundary disputes but it could deal issues arising from the Convention so it decided it could proceed, and that China would indeed be bound by the outcome.

China also contested the legitimacy of the ruling when it claimed that the Tribunal was unrepresentative and biased. A *People's Daily* article claimed that the Japanese Judge who was former president of the International Tribunal of

10 Permanent Court of Arbitration, *The South China Sea Arbitration*, Press Release, The Hague, 12 July 2016, available at: https://pca-cpa.org/wp-content/uploads/sites/175/2016/07/PH-CN-20160712-Press-Release-No-11-English.pdf.

the Law of the Sea, Shunji Yanai, was the "manipulator" behind the ruling since he appointed four of the five judges leaving the Philippines to appoint one.[11] The article averred that the judges were biased from the start because they had been appointed by a Japanese. However, had China joined the proceedings as a party, it would have had the right to nominate four arbitrators under Article 2 of Annex VII. China lost this right because of its refusal to join the proceedings and then attempted to defend itself by making accusations of bias. Indeed, some Chinese scholars have said that not to participate was a major error since China lost the opportunity not only to nominate arbitrators but to present its case more persuasively before the Tribunal.

The Tribunal's ruling was final and binding on the parties to the dispute. Article 296 states that "any such decision shall have no binding force except between the parties and in respect of that particular dispute" which formally limited its application to the parties concerned. However, despite this formal restriction, the ruling creates a precedent that would be applied or referenced in other maritime disputes, particularly those involving historical claims and overlapping maritime zones. In this case the Tribunal has clarified the relationship between China's historical claims, the nine dash line, and UNCLOS and ruled that the Law of the Sea has priority. Since this is the first time that five eminent justices in a legal Tribunal have dealt with the issue of the South China Sea the ruling has legal effect in terms of illuminating a complicated situation and identifying who has the law on their side and who does not. The Tribunal's contribution is clarification of a complex legal situation in the South China Sea, one that will not be expunged by the defamatory criticisms of aggrieved governments.

The Tribunal's ruling will have repercussions for other claimants and not just China. In its position paper dated 21 March 2016 Taiwan claimed similar historical rights to those of Beijing and argued that its government has exercised high-level jurisdiction over the islands since the end of World War II. Taiwan also occupies the largest island in the Spratly Islands called Itu Aba or Taiping Island with 600 military and coast guard personnel and a runway of 1,100 meters capable of taking STOL aircraft. Taiwan's position paper claimed that Taiping Island meets the requirements for an island according to Article 121 of UNCLOS. To the extent that Taiwan shares Beijing's claim it has been legally undermined on both counts, in regard to historical claims and the status of "islands." Vietnam has similarly been affected in that the Tribunal's ruling did not mention the Paracel Islands which are claimed by Vietnam but occupied

11 "People's Daily unmasks manipulator behind South China Sea arbitration" People's Daily 18 July 2016 http://www.globaltimes.cn/content/995003.shtml.

by China. Vietnam has also based its claim to the South China Sea on history but it has been attempting to bring that claim into conformity with UNCLOS by clarifying the outer limits of its maritime zones.[12] Vietnam's Law of the Sea declaration of 2012 desists from labelling the features in the South China Sea either as islands or rocks implying that they have no maritime zones. Moreover, Vietnam's Law on Sea and Island Natural resources and Environment of 2015 incorporated UNCLOS provisions on the EEZ, continental shelves and territorial sea into domestic law.[13] Significantly, under international law Vietnam has incumbency rights to the 21 features it occupies in the Spratly Islands. Its effort to bring its claims into line with international law can be seen as a measure to defend these incumbency rights.

## IV China's Response

China's Ministry of Foreign Affairs declared that the ruling is "null and void and has no binding force and China neither accepts nor recognizes it." The Ministry also said that "the Chinese government will continue to abide by international law and basic norms governing international relations" which means that Beijing will selectively decide what it will accept and what it will reject.[14] Beijing has orchestrated an international campaign to vilify the Tribunal, which sometimes reached a rather crude level. The Chinese ambassador to the Netherlands Wu Ken called the Philippine case a "legal monstrosity" which "reeks of hegemony from Washington."[15] The Chinese Ambassador to the United Kingdom, Liu Xiaoming, called the Tribunal's ruling a "political farce under the cloak of law" and declared that "by not accepting or recognizing the ruling, China is not violating but upholding the authority and dignity of international

12 Do Thanh Hai, *Vietnam's evolving claims in the South China Sea*, National Security College, The Australian National University, 2014, available at: http://nsc.anu.edu.au/documents/occasional-5-brief-5.pdf.

13 Nguyen Thai Giang, *Implementation of the United Nations Law of the Sea Convention in Vietnam*, in SEOKWOO LEE AND WARWICK GULLETT (Editors) ASIA-PACIFIC AND THE IMPLEMENTATION OF THE LAW OF THE SEA: REGIONAL LEGISLATIVE AND POLICY APPROACHES TO THE LAW OF THE SEA CONVENTION, 134 (2016).

14 *Full text of statement of China's Foreign Ministry on award of South China Sea arbitration initiated by Philippines*, XINHUA, 12 July 2016, available at: http://news.xinhuanet.com/english/2016-07/12/c_135507754.htm.

15 *Arbitration on South China Sea a legal monstrosity: Chinese Diplomat*, XINHUA, 28 May 2016

law."[16] China's Ambassador to Australia, Cheng Jingye, called the ruling "fatally flawed" and that the arbitration initiated by the Philippines was "completely politically motivated." The Ambassador also claimed that by rejecting the ruling, China was safeguarding "the integrity and authority of UNCLOS."[17] It is difficult to imagine that the integrity and authority of law can be safeguarded by its deliberate transgression.

Official Chinese representatives have made the public claim that the Declaration of Conduct (DOC) which China concluded with ASEAN in November 2002 bound the Philippines to negotiate with China. This obligation precluded the Philippines from resorting to the Arbitral Tribunal. However, the Philippines had in fact attempted to negotiate with China but the Chinese simply stonewalled and the appeal to an Arbitral Tribunal was a reaction to Chinese stalling tactics. Moreover, the DOC was not conceived as a legally binding treaty and though ASEAN had attempted to interest the Chinese in a legally binding Code of Conduct they remained steadfastly opposed. The result was a non legal Declaration of Conduct which was conceived as a stepping stone to a fully-fledged Code of Conduct. In any case there is no provision in the DOC which prevents an aggrieved party from resorting to law. Article 4 of the DOC mentions that the parties "undertake" to resolve their disputes through "friendly consultations and negotiations." The Philippines had attempted this but to no avail. Moreover, Article 5 says that the parties will "refrain from activities" which would "complicate or escalate disputes" including "inhabiting on the presently uninhabited islands, reefs, shoals, cays, and other features." China's reclamation activities in the South China would fall under this Article and if China now regards the DOC as having legal effect, which it did not in the past, then it would be bound by Article 5.[18] Arguments raised by the Chinese Ambassadors, and also Chinese scholars, that claim that the Philippines was prevented from appealing to law by some kind of estoppel are overtly contradictory.

---

16 *South China Sea arbitration is a political farce*, THE TELEGRAPH, 23 July 2016, available at: http://www.telegraph.co.uk/news/2016/07/23/south-china-sea-arbitration-is-a-political-farce/.

17 Cheng Jingye, *Arbitration on the South China Sea dispute is fatally flawed*, THE AUSTRALIAN 14 July 2016, available at: http://www.theaustralian.com.au/opinion/arbitration-on-the-south-china-sea-dispute-is-fatally-flawed/news-story/399a838be578d26ecda1a44a411b4ba2.

18 *Declaration on the Conduct of Parties in the South China Sea,* available at: http://asean.org/?static_post=declaration-on-the-conduct-of-parties-in-the-south-china-sea-2.

## V The Domestic Impact and China's Notion of Law

The unpleasant rhetoric which flooded the international news agencies from Beijing and the attacks on the integrity and composition of the Tribunal have been beyond the pale and reveal a fundamental disrespect for law in Chinese society. This is the first time that China has been subject to a claim for arbitration over a maritime territorial dispute which for Beijing is intolerable. Moreover, traditional Chinese hierarchy recoils at the notion that law could put a small country such as the Philippines on the same level as an ancient civilisation and powerful State such as China, or that it could be allowed to bring a legal action against it. Traditionally, legality has not been part of Chinese political culture and though China has made progress in adopting legal forms from the outside, the idea of law restraining the political leadership conflicts with that culture and the role of the Communist Party politically and socially.[19] Since Deng Xiaoping proclaimed the "open door policy" in 1978, China has been importing law and related institutions to regulate the economy and to cope with the social effects of high economic growth. Around 2010, however, the Chinese leadership drew back from the legal reforms they had previously supported as it was understood that they could lead to political liberalisation undermining the role of the party. They reverted to the notion of the "socialist rule of law" which was set against Western concepts of the rule-of-law, considered inappropriate for China, to preserve "social stability".[20]

The key feature of the "socialist rule of law" is the importance given to mediation and dispute resolution by non-legal means which in many respects relies on traditional notions of justice in China. Mediation or dispute resolution can be conducted by local party officials with lawyers and court officials in attendance together with the parties and their families, and invokes popular notions of justice. Mediation in this sense may bring social stability as aggrieved parties are obliged to accept a resolution based on the power hierarchy but whether or not it accords with the principles of justice is something else. What is acceptable socially by local officials would be imposed on all the parties as a resolution and may depart significantly from those legal principles.[21] A family that has had its land confiscated by local officials would be obliged to accept a settlement meted out by those officials. In this approach there is

19 On the role of law in China see Chuan Feng, Leyton P. Nelson, and Thomas W. Simon, China's changing legal System: Lawyers & Judges on Civil & Criminal Law (2016); Pitman B. Potter, China's Legal System (2013).

20 Carl F. Minzner, 1, 59 (4) American Journal of Comparative Law (2011).

21 Benjamin L. Liebman, *China's Law and Stability Paradox*, in Jacques deLisle and Avery Goldstein (editors) China's Challenges, 2015.

little room for the supremacy of law or its abstract principles, or indeed for autonomous legal institutions or an independent judiciary. In the Chinese view of international law, a ruling by an international tribunal should be a product of mediation in which all views particularly those of the most powerful should be taken into account.[22] The idea that a tribunal that has no stake in the issue could impose abstract principles of justice upon this maritime dispute flies in the face of the Chinese understanding of how justice is implemented. If Chinese notions of dispute resolution were applied to the South China Sea there would be no invocation of abstract principles but an effort to settle the dispute based on mediation that acknowledges the rights of the power hierarchy, in this case China. From this perspective the tribunal should have enjoined the Philippines and the other ASEAN claimants to negotiate with China and accept whatever terms Beijing would have to offer. In this scenario, stability could be ensured not by abstract notions of justice but by recognition of the power hierarchy in this dispute.

The impact of the ruling upon Chinese domestic politics should not be overlooked. Xi Jinping was elevated to the presidency with the promise that he would preside over the "great dream of the renewal of the Chinese nation" and would demonstrate "the superiority of China's socialist system."[23] He has strengthened his position in Chinese politics by removing rivals in the anti-corruption campaign, particularly those associated with former president Jiang Zemin. In this context the Arbitral Tribunal's ruling entailed a loss of face for Xi Jinping because of his failure to obtain a decision favourable or at least neutral to China. A second failure has been China's inability to prevent South Korea from deploying Terminal High Altitude Area Defences (THAAD) with the US as a missile defence against North Korean missiles. Xi Jinping has come under attack for these failures which are regarded as humiliations for China and the vitriolic outbursts against the Arbitral Tribunal's ruling can be partly explained as an attack on the Xi Jinping leadership in this context. Moreover, there are reports of dissatisfaction with Xi Jinping's leadership amongst the economic ministries and the supporters of Premier Li Keqiang who are concerned about excessive controls over the economy and the unwillingness of the Party to follow through with economic and financial reform. To protect himself and his appointees from a purge unleashed by his successor, Xi Jinping had himself declared as "core leader" of the Chinese Communist Party by the party's Central Committee in October 2016. This elevated his status to the level of Mao and Deng Xiaoping strengthening his position for the 19th Party

22 Minzner, *supra* note 19.

23 *Profile: Xi Jinping: Pursuing dream for 1.3 billion Chinese*, XINHUA.NET, 17 March 2013, available at: http://news.xinhuanet.com/english/china/2013-03/17/c_124467411.htm.

Congress due to be held in 2017.[24] No doubt, opposition and cleavages in the ruling party will be exacerbated by the ruling and related events.

The ruling has become controversial amongst Chinese scholars. Some have adopted an attitude of righteous anger calling for China's withdrawal from UNCLOS. Others have suggested that failure to participate in the Tribunal's proceedings was a mistake and China missed an opportunity to obtain a more favourable ruling. Yet others have claimed that once a State has ratified UNCLOS it has an obligation to implement it effectively in "good faith" and that "any abuse or omission is impermissible." They have argued that the "pick and choose" mentality towards international norms will not promote and realize rule of law and justice in the international community.[25] However, Chinese officials have publicly adopted the "pick and choose" approach when they deny the validity and legality of the Tribunal's ruling yet proclaim that China would nonetheless abide by UNCLOS and international law.

## VI The Impact of the Ruling on the Western Pacific

What would be the impact of the ruling on the Western Pacific? China may become more belligerent internationally as the political leadership attempts to boost its credibility before its domestic critics. Beijing will attempt to compensate for loss of legality over this issue by resorting to bellicose language and threatening behaviour. Ambassador to the US Cui Tiankai declared that the ruling will "intensify conflict and even confrontation."[26] The Chinese cast the South China Sea dispute not as an issue involving the legal rights of the ASEAN claimants but as a strategic contest between China and the US. They claim that the ruling will allow the US to strengthen its alliances to confront China and will deepen this strategic rivalry.[27] In the first instance, a deterioration of

24 Chris Buckley, *China's Communist Party declares Xi Jinping "core" leader*, THE NEW YORK TIMES, 27 October 2016.

25 Zou Keyuan, *Implementation of the United Nations Law of the Sea Convention in China*, in SEOKWOO LEE AND WARWICK GULLETT (Editors) ASIA-PACIFIC AND THE IMPLEMENTATION OF THE LAW OF THE SEA : REGIONAL LEGISLATIVE AND POLICY APPROACHES TO THE LAW OF THE SEA CONVENTION (2016) 31–33.

26 *South China Sea ruling will 'intensify conflict': Chinese envoy*, REUTERS, 12 July 2016, available at: http://www.reuters.com/article/us-southchinasea-ruling-stakes-idUSKCN0ZS02U.

27 Michael Swaine, *Chinese views of the Arbitration case between the People's Republic of China and the Philippines*, CHINA LEADERSHIP MONITOR, 24 August 2016, available at: http://carnegieendowment.org/2016/08/24/chinese-views-on-south-china-sea arbitration case-between-people-s-republic-of-china-and-philippines-pub-64397.

security can be expected, not only in the South China Sea but in the East China Sea and the Korean Peninsula. Outrage and anger may well be raised to new levels by the Chinese media in a way reminiscent of the Maoist era.

China's increased assertiveness has become apparent elsewhere as the political leadership has felt the need to compensate for loss of face, and to demonstrate its power and resolution before domestic audiences. On the Korean Peninsula Beijing has been ambivalent about the sanctions that the UN Security council imposed upon North Korea on 2 March 2016 after its fourth nuclear test. China's desire to retain the North as an ally has conflicted with its intention to denuclearise the regime and its enforcement of UN sanctions has been half hearted. After the South's decision in July 2016 to deploy THAAD against the North's missile threat, China has eased up on those sanctions that have been applied, and has reached out to the regime. North Korea is for China its only means of bargaining with the South and a counter to the US-South Korean alliance. Increased Chinese assertiveness has been reported around the Senkaku/Diaoyu islands where the Japanese have recorded increased intrusions by Chinese coast guard and fishing vessels in the wake of the Tribunal's ruling. Tokyo fears that the Chinese are resorting to the same tactics they used to push out the Philippines from Scarborough Shoal in 2012 when they blocked access to the area to Philippine vessels and imposed a *fait accompli* upon Manila. Needless to say, the Japanese have demanded that China respect the Tribunal's ruling.

China will not only ignore the ruling but will use its dominant position in the South China Sea to press the ASEAN claimants into bilateral negotiations to set it aside. Beijing has persuaded the Chinese population that the South China Sea was always "ancient" Chinese territory despite the absence of convincing historical evidence, and with a controlled press it has whipped up popular nationalism over the issue. It has produced passports which show the area as Chinese territory and has directed nationalist fervour against the US for supposedly interfering into the dispute and inciting ASEAN resistance. China has attained a dominant position there as the result of its reclamation projects which have been promoted by bureaucratic interests and supported by a rising nationalism. The State Oceanic Administration (SOA) under the Ministry of Land and Resources has pushed for the expansion of China's interests in the maritime domain, not only in the South China Sea but in the Senkaku/Diaoyu Islands.[28] Since August 2014, the Chinese have been dredging sand from the

28 Robert S. Ross and Mingjiang Li, *Xi Jinping and the Challenges to Chinese Security*, in ROBERT S. ROSS, AND JO INGE BEKKEVOLD (editors), CHINA IN THE ERA OF XI JINPING: DOMESTIC AND FOREIGN POLICY CHALLENGES (2016).

ocean floor and extending the size of Fiery Cross, Johnson South, Subi, Quaterton, Gaven, Mischief, and Hughes reefs. China has constructed 3,000 meter airfields on Fiery Cross and Subi Reef and a 2,600 runway on Mischief Reef. As a result of these activities, China will have three airfields on reclaimed features, with berthing facilities for transport vessels and radar and signals monitoring facilities which will enhance its ability to track the movement of shipping and aircraft in the area. China will be able to deploy front line air superiority fighters, bombers and heavy lift transport aircraft to these airfields strengthening its position there. The Chinese claim that these moves are defensive and are intended to protect their claim but they have political consequences for the ASEAN claimants.

With this strengthened position in the South China Sea and its renewed belligerence, China hopes to deprive the ASEAN claimants of any hope that they could gain any support from the Tribunal's ruling. Beijing will apply dispute resolution techniques to push for negotiations that will confirm its sovereignty over the South China Sea while disregarding the Tribunal's ruling. The outcome will then be presented to the world as a negotiated regional agreement in conformity with international law, which China professes to uphold. China may offer access to the area to the fishing vessels of the ASEAN claimants as an incentive but acknowledgement of China's sovereignty would be a necessary condition. In this way, Beijing would nullify the Tribunal's ruling and its relevance for the South China Sea. To demonstrate defiance, China has stepped up military exercises in the South China to intimidate the ASEAN claimants and convince them of the irrelevance of the ruling to their situation. Prior to the ruling China launched a series of naval exercises in the area involving two guided missile destroyers and a missile frigate. After the ruling was made public, China's air force in early August conducted a combat air patrol over disputed areas of the South China Sea. This may become a regular practice. At the same time China's navy conducted live firing drills in the East China Sea in a similar demonstration of power. In September 2016 China also conducted a military exercise with Russia called "Joint Sea 2016" to demonstrate joint defiance of the ruling and opposition to the international legal system which both claim is dominated by the West.

ASEAN has been divided over the South China Sea. The Philippines and Vietnam regularly pressed for a united ASEAN stand which Cambodia and Laos, both effective allies of China, rejected. Other members such as Thailand and Myanmar have been uninterested in the dispute while Malaysia has acted to preserve what it regards as its special relationship with China. Cambodia in particular has been China's close ally and when it was chair of ASEAN in 2012, Foreign Minister Hor Namhong ensured that the regional body would avoid the issue. When ASEAN Foreign Ministers met in July 2012 they failed to issue a communiqué for the first time in their history, which was the result of Chinese pressure exercised through Cambodia. ASEAN inaction could be seen during the Foreign Ministers' meeting in Vientiane on 24 July 2016, the first after the Tribunal's ruling was made public. The communiqué from this meeting avoided mention of the ruling, which was regarded as a "diplomatic victory" for China. Once again, Cambodia, which had received a promise of a $600 million loan package from China, and Laos both worked on behalf of Beijing to prevent the emergence of a consensus over the issue.[29] Reports from the meeting indicated that Laos was prepared to accept a diluted statement on the South China Sea and was not inclined to prevent mention of the issue. However, Cambodia adopted a hard-line position opposing even statements that had appeared in previous ASEAN communiqués in relation to the dispute. ASEAN Foreign Ministers at least referred to the communiqué of the ASEAN Regional Forum where ministers were "seriously concerned" over the land reclamations and "escalation of activities in the area" and reaffirmed freedom of navigation in and over flight above the South China Sea.[30]

In view of ASEAN's paralysis over the issue, some members have been moved to accept bilateral negotiations with China to reduce tensions as it becomes more bellicose. Chinese Foreign Minister Wang Yi called for bilateral negotiations without reference to the Tribunal's ruling to resolve the issue and resorted to aggressive language when he warned that the Philippines risked possible "confrontation" with China if it insisted on the ruling.[31] ASEAN claimants hope that by professing friendship and good relations, Beijing would respond magnanimously and respect their positions in the South China Sea, without the need to invoke the Tribunal's ruling. Within ASEAN, the use and profession of friendship to create an obligation for reciprocity is often referred to as the "Asian way" of dealing with disputes. Newly elected Philippine President

29 Vijay Joshi and Daniel Malloy, *China scores diplomatic victory, avoids criticism from ASEAN*, YAHOO NEWS, 26 July 2016, available at:https://sg.news.yahoo.com/china-scores-diplomatic-victory-avoids-060946776.html; Vijay Joshi, *Analysis: China emerges more muscular after ASEAN meetings*, WASHINGTON POST, 28 July 2016, available at: https://www.washingtonpost.com/world/asia_pacific/analysis-china-emerges-more-muscular-after-asean-meetings/2016/07/27/81a153bc-53cd-11e6-b652-315ae5d4d4dd story.html.

30 *Joint Communiqué of the 49th ASEAN Foreign Ministers' Meeting Vientiane*, 24 July 2016, ASEAN.org, available at: http://asean.org/storage/2016/07/Joint-Communique-of-the-49th-AMM-ADOPTED.pdf.

31 Patricia Lourdes, *Philippines rejects talks not based on arbitral ruling; China warns of confrontation,* PHILSTAR.COM, 19 July 2016, available at: http://www.philstar.com/headlines/2016/07/19/1604466/philippines-talks-hague-verdict-confrontation-china.

Rodrigo Duterte espoused this approach when he tilted towards China in a deliberate snub to the US which had criticized his promotion of extra judicial killings of drug offenders. Duterte visited Beijing in October 2016 and declared that he had "realigned" himself with China and Russia and announced a "separation" from the US.[32] Duterte said that he would review the Enhanced Defence Cooperation Agreement concluded with the US when President Obama visited Manila in 2014, and that military exercises with the US would be terminated. However, when Defense Secretary Delfin Lorenzana said that joint patrols and naval exercises with the US in the disputed South China Sea were put on hold, he did not say terminated.[33] When he returned to the Philippines, Duterte said that he had no intention of cutting ties with the US and that by "separation" he meant charting "another way" in foreign policy. Indeed Presidential spokesperson Ernesto Abella issued a public statement that the Philippines would not break any established alliances, particularly with the United States.[34] It is no wonder that Duterte's critics called him "incoherent."[35]

Duterte claimed that he had obtained a Chinese agreement to let Filipino fishing vessels return to Scarborough Shoal from which they had been evicted by the Chinese Coast Guard in 2012. By the end of October 2016 the Chinese Coast Guard had withdrawn from the area and some Philippine fishing vessels moved in. The Philippine President regarded this as a triumph and a vindication of his visit to Beijing but Philippine commentators were aware that China had "permitted" the return of the fishing vessels in a temporary concession in return for Duterte's shift against the US. However, China was not softening its claim of "indisputable sovereignty" over the area.[36] The concession could

32 Gabriel Dominguez, *Philippine leader announces 'separation' from US*, JANE'S DEFENCE WEEKLY, 21 October 2016.

33 Lorenzana also said that 107 U.S. troops involved in operating surveillance drones against Muslim militants would be asked to leave the southern part of the country once the Philippines acquires those intelligence-gathering capabilities in the near future. Jim Gomez, *Philippines, US halt plans on joint South China Sea patrols*, PHILSTAR.COM, 7 October 2016, available at: http://www.philstar.com/headlines/2016/10/07/1631266/philippines-us-halt-plans-joint-south-china-sea-patrols.

34 Elena L. Aben, *PH allays US fears, says treaties will remain in place*, MANILA BULLETIN, 25 October 2016, available at http://www.mb.com.ph/ph-allays-us-fears-says-treaties-will-remain-in-place/.

35 Ana Marie Pamintuan, *Incoherent*, THE PHILIPPINE STAR, 24 October 2016, available at: http://www.philstar.com/opinion/2016/10/24/1636759/incoherent.

36 Manuel Mogato, *Philippines says Chinese vessels have left disputed shoal*, REUTERS, 28 October 2016, available at: http://www.reuters.com/article/us-philippines-southchinasea-china-idUSKCN12S18B.

always be withdrawn in which case the President would be obliged to offer more in return to satisfy the demands of the Chinese and to maintain his popularity with his supporters. In this way the Philippines may slide into a dependent relationship with Beijing, which would effectively sideline the ruling. Before Duterte visited Beijing, Filipinos had attempted to place the ruling at the centre of any negotiations that would be conducted with the Chinese. Ernesto Abella affirmed this and said that talks with China had to abide by the Constitution and international law, and that The Philippines aimed to realize rights to its EEZ as granted by the Arbitration Court.[37] Foreign Minister Perfecto Yasay reiterated that bilateral talks with China cannot proceed while Beijing insists on negotiations "outside of the framework of the arbitral tribunal's decision."[38] Subsequently, however, the Foreign Minister changed his view when he declared that dialogue with China based on the ruling "may not happen in our lifetime." The ruling, he said, would be placed on the "backburner." Yasay said it was more important to develop other areas of the relationship including trade, investment, commerce, infrastructure development, people-to-people contact and cultural exchanges.[39]

Malaysia's Prime Minister Najib Razak also visited Beijing in November 2016 though the South China Sea was not publicly discussed. Najib hoped that business with China would generate much publicity and overshadow the scandal that had erupted over the misappropriation of funds from 1Malaysia Development Berhad (1MDB) which went into the Prime Minister's private accounts. Malaysia had claimed a special relationship with China since Najib Razak's father Tun Razak had established diplomatic relations with China in 1974, the first ASEAN country to do so. Malaysian leaders expected this relationship to give them special treatment from Beijing and were prepared to tolerate Chinese incursions in their claim area in the South China Sea for this reason. However, Malaysian concerns over intrusions by Chinese fishing vessels increased and it seemed that the special relationship was having little effect. Malaysian Navy Chief Admiral Abdul Aziz Jaafar said that intrusions by Chinese vessels had

37 Genalyn D. Kabiling and Ben R. Rosario, *Malacanang Economic rights non-negotiable*, MANILA BULLETIN, 20 July 2016, available at: http://www.mb.com.ph/malacanang-economic-rights-non-negotiable/.

38 Patricia Lourdes Viray, *Yasay: Philippines not ready for bilateral talks with China*, PHILSTAR.COM, 16 September 2016, available at: http://www.philstar.com/headlines/2016/09/16/1624399/yasay-philippines-not-ready-bilateral-talks-china.

39 Patricia Lourdes Viray, *Yasay: Philippines-China talks based on tribunal's decision may not happen in our lifetime*, PHILSTAR.COM, 2 December 2016, available at: http://www.philstar.com/headlines/2016/12/02/1649621/yasay-philippines-china-talks-based-tribunals-decision-may-not-happen.

been occurring daily since 2014.[40] In June 2016, Chinese coast guard vessels pushed out Malaysian patrol boats from Luconia Shoal in Malaysia's EEZ and escorted about 100 Chinese fishing vessels into the area.[41] In Beijing, Najib agreed to purchase four Chinese naval vessels for inshore patrols, two of which were to be manufactured in China and two in Malaysia.[42] Najib had hoped to return in triumph from Beijing but for some within the ruling UMNO party stronger ties with China are disturbing. Former Prime Minister Mahathir accused Najib of surrendering Malaysia's claims in the South China Sea to China and threatening Malaysia's position there.[43] Though it was intended to restrain Chinese behaviour in the Malaysian claim area, the special relationship may have the opposite effect of silencing Malaysia's complaints in relation to Chinese claims and incursions into that area.

International legal scholars have declared that the ruling cannot be imposed on the parties and should be regarded as an opportunity and a stimulus to negotiation.[44] Both the Philippines and Malaysia have reacted to the Arbitral Tribunal's ruling by seeking negotiations with China in the expectation that this would obligate the Chinese to moderate their behaviour in the South China Sea. The ruling supports their efforts and gives them confidence but their concern to avoid all public controversy with China may lead them into the situation where they may be obliged to disavow it. Some in ASEAN have been embarrassed by the ruling since from their perspective it introduces new difficulties in the relationship with China and stimulates Chinese ire which they would prefer to avoid. However, what could happen in this situation is that in their effort to be assured of China's good behaviour, the ASEAN claimants may accept a settlement that would acknowledge the Chinese claim and

40 Raul Dancel, *China's intrusion into Malaysia more extensive than reported: Analyst*, THE STRAITS TIMES, 20 June 2015, available at: http://www.straitstimes.com/asia/se-asia/chinas-intrusion-into-malaysia-more-extensive-than-reported-analyst; Jenifer Laeng, *China Coast Guard vessel found at Luconia Shoals*, THE BORNEO POST, 3 June 2015, available at: http://www.theborneopost.com/2015/06/03/china-coast-guard-vessel-found-at-luconia-shoals/.

41 *Malaysia eyes stronger response to Chinese maritime incursions*, STRAITS TIMES 2 June 2016, available at: http://www.straitstimes.com/asia/east-asia/kl-eyes-stronger-response-to-chinese-maritime-incursions.

42 Sue-Lin Wong, *China and Malaysia sign deals on navy vessels*, REUTERS, 1 November 2016, available at: http://www.reuters.com/article/us-china-malaysia-idUSKBN12W3WF.

43 *Najib has hurt Malaysia's sovereignty: Mahathir*, THE STRAITS TIMES, 3 November 2016.

44 Donald R. Rothwell, *Could law save the South China Sea from disaster*, THE NATIONAL INTEREST, 26 July 2016, available at: http://nationalinterest.org/blog/the-buzz/could-law-save-the-south-china-sea-disaster-17123.

its superiority over UNCLOS. This may remove the sense of insecurity that the claimants feel in relation to the Chinese presence in the South China Sea. It may bring other benefits such as access to the area by their fishing vessels and agreements for joint development of the hydrocarbon reserves there. A resolution of this nature would be in line with Chinese notions of justice but it would be a significant departure from the Tribunal's ruling and would demonstrate the irrelevance of UNCLOS to this issue. With its irrelevance demonstrated in this way UNCLOS would be significantly weakened and made subject to power and the *realpolitik* of powerful States.

## VII The Future

Realists regard international law as an epiphenomenon to the *realpolitik* that governs relations between States, and somewhat unrelated to their interests and behaviour. Hans J. Morgenthau has argued that international law and international politics are separate from one another and operate in different spheres. Graham Allison wrote that in ignoring the Tribunal's ruling China will be doing just what the other great powers have repeatedly done for decades and this was "normal behaviour" for great powers.[45] However, noncompliance with international law has consequences at various levels and in ways that may not be immediately apparent. The great powers may ignore international law but the result will be the stimulation of suspicions and counter activities that would work against their interests. The slide into *realpolitik* may seem normal to realists but it brings with it insecurity and a potentially destructive competition which could otherwise be mitigated through cooperative efforts. In this case non-compliance with the ruling entails a loss of opportunity for China to resolve the South China Sea dispute though cooperative measures such as a maritime regime, which would take into account the legal claims of all. As China resorts to unilateral efforts to secure its position there it stimulates a damaging action-reaction cycle with external powers such as the US and Japan to the detriment of all concerned.

In international history there are seemingly minor events that precipitate unexpected and extensive changes in global affairs. The Arbitral Tribunal's ruling may be one such event in the Asia Pacific region as it concerns China's behaviour and whether it will act to uphold regional order or disrupt it. China has

45 Graham Allison, *Of Course China, Like All Great Powers, Will Ignore an International Legal Verdict*, THE DIPLOMAT, 11 July 2016, available at: http://thediplomat.com/2016/07/of-course-china-like-all-great-powers-will-ignore-an-international-legal-verdict/.

reacted belligerently to the ruling by unleashing an extensive and oftentimes offensive public relations campaign to deny its legality. The Chinese leadership has acted to demonstrate power before domestic audiences and to silence those who have criticised it for weakness. In ignoring the ruling, Beijing has attempted to deny reputational loss by claiming political and legal exceptionalism and demanding that as the second largest global economy and a rising military power the world should accept China's position on the South China Sea, and work around it. The Chinese expect that international law will be revised to accommodate China's historical claims and its special interests and their refusal to accept the Tribunal's ruling will be the first step in the revision of international law and UNCLOS. In this way China's leaders want to make it clear that their reputation is not at stake, but that of the Tribunal and the judges who issued the ruling. In so doing, Beijing would decide the law of the sea and how it is applied in which case law would be shaped by the policy and interests of Chinese political leadership.

China's reaction to the Arbitral Tribunal's ruling demonstrates clashing interpretations of law and how it may be implemented. The overriding importance of abstract principles of justice is very Western, as is the effort to ensure their literal interpretation and implementation. A significant departure from these principles in actual practice is cause for condemnation or an accusation of hypocrisy, saying one thing and doing something else. However, abstract principles carry little weight in the Chinese notion of law as imposed mediation, which recognizes the power hierarchy and takes into account its interests. Abstract legal principles are understood by the Chinese as guidelines or aspirations and not as hindrances or restrictions upon negotiating possibilities. What is most important is a settlement which brings stability even if this entails a departure from those legal principles. The difficulty is that as Chinese notion of law divests itself of these principles it offers no regulatory framework for the resolution of disputes, no precedents that could bring predictability to State interaction and add to the corpus of law other than the recognition of power. The resort to *realpolitik* is inherent in this approach. International law cannot be devised or constructed without these legal principles and the regulatory framework they support which the Chinese in this instance reject. By repudiating the Arbitral Tribunal's ruling China is creating greater uncertainty in maritime affairs when the resort to force to settle disputes will become more likely. As a major trading country with a strong interest in the security of maritime trade, China would be the first to face the consequences of a deterioration in maritime security. Rather than acting like an aggrieved victim, Beijing should assume the responsibilities commensurate with its economic weight and support a maritime order based on law and the legal principles that sustain it.

# China's Three Distinctive Assertions under the 'Nine-dash-line' Claims and the Annex VII Arbitral Tribunal's Interpretation of Article 121 Regarding an Island and Rocks under the 1982 UN Convention on the Law of the Sea

*Eiichi Usuki*[1]

## 1 The Historical Background of the South China Sea

As depicted in the 'Map of Southern Sea' published in 1940 in Japan (MAP 8.1, see below at the end of this article),[2] Japan's 'New Southern Islands' ['shin-nan-gunto'] might be said to be the prototype of China's 'nine-dash-line', although the former claimed area was limited to the Spratly Islands only (Nánshā Qúndǎo). Japan's Cabinet, on 23 December 1939, decided to incorporate the southern part of the South China Sea and made an attempt to assert its sovereignty over all the islands and rocks, including their territorial waters, not only giving Japanese names to several major islands (e.g. 'Nagashima' to the largest one, at the present moment Taiwan's 'Tàipíng Dǎo' or 'Itu Aba Island') but also making use of 'seven straight lines' so as to encompass those maritime features by a heptangular zone.[3] Indeed, from the very start, France and the United

1 Ph.D (Cantab.), LL.M (Hitotsubashi Univ.), B.L and B.L.A (Univ. of Tokyo), Professor of International Law, Department of Asian Area Studies, Graduate School of Daito Bunka University, Japan.

2 ran-in (nanyo) oyobi futsuin zenzu [Complete map of Dutch India (Southern Sea) and French India] (kinreisha, 15 December 1940).

3 [extending from 7 degrees to 12 degrees North (latitude) and between 111 degrees 30 minutes and 117 degrees East (longitude)] Japan's Cabinet, on 23 December 1939, decided to incorporate the southern part of the South China Sea [hereinafter SCS]. Japan's Cabinet decision, 23 December 1938; Decree No.3, Government-General, Taiwan, 30 March 1939, and Notification No.122, Government-General, Taiwan, 30 March 1939.kanpo [Government Bulletin] (18 April 1939). It would seem that this incorporation of the New Southern Islands relied on the occupation of no man's land on the basis of an attempt to exploit *guano* by a Japanese company.

DOI 10.1163/9789004344556_009

States staged diplomatic protests against Japan's incorporation of 'shin-nan-gunto' (the Spratly Islands) into its colony, Taiwan.[4]

Japan's measure of incorporation appears to have been motivated by the 1938 French *note verbale* conveyed to Japan, informing the French intention to appropriate another group of islands, the Paracel Islands (Xīshā Qúndǎo), as France regarded them as *res nullius* or no man's land, although Imperial China (qīng; Ch'ing dynasty) had already, in 1909, intended to appropriate them as islands under its sovereignty, and this Chinese position had been recognized by Japan, and such a status was confirmed by Japan in its *note verbale* to France (12 July 1938). In December 1938, indeed, Japan's Cabinet decided to incorporate the Paracel Islands, too, but it was not implemented in law (presumably because it would be an action repugnant to Japan's prior confirmation of July 1938 for the Chinese position), while there were the mineral-phosphate mining activities continued by a Japanese company on those Islands, and Japan, as a matter of fact, utilized them for military purposes later in spite of French continual *demarches*.[5]

In passing, as far as the Pratas Islands (Dōngshā Qúndǎo) were concerned, they were already recognized by Japan as islands remaining under Imperial China through the 1909 Japan- Ch'ing Agreement for Handing Over Pratas Island (11 Oct. 1909).

Accordingly, it appears that, even before the Second World War, the status or the sovereignty of the islands in the South China Sea (SCS) was unsettled in law, except for the Pratas Islands.

When the Japanese Forces surrendered to the Allied Powers after the Second World War, the islands in the SCS, all of sudden, became virtually no man's land (*terra nullius*). Soon after that, the Republic of China, French Vietnam, the Philippines, British Colony of Sarawak (which became Malaysia) and Indonesia began to compete with one another for recovery or appropriation of territories. Then, Article 2 (f) of the 1951 Treaty of Peace with Japan only provided that Japan shall renounce all rights, titles and claims to the New Southern Islands (Spratly Islands) and to the Paracel Islands.[6] It means that

4 nihon no kokusaiho jirei kenkyu (3), ryodo [Digest of Japanese Practice in International Law (3), Territory] (Keio Tsushin Co. Ltd., 1990) 65.

5 *Ibid.* at 66–67.

6 On 15 August 1951, the People's Republic of China (Zhōu Ēnlái, Minister of Foreign Affairs) published statements denouncing the draft treaty as a whole, stating that it was illegal and should not be recognized. Besides, the People's Republic of China claimed that it did not refer to the return of the sovereignty over Paracel Islands, Spratly Islands, in particular 'Spratly Island' in the SCS, and that they were all part of China. nihon gaiko shuyo bunsho/nenpyo (1) [Main Documents/Chronological Table on the Japanese Diplomacy (1)] 406–411.

the allocation of territories in this region remained unsettled, and on the other hand, that the paragraph of the 1943 Cairo Declaration to the effect 'that all the territories Japan has stolen from the Chinese, such as Manchuria, Formosa, and the Pescadores, shall be restored to the Republic of China' was only incompletely implemented.[7]

Thus, the sovereignty dispute over the islets in the Spratly Islands and the Paracel Islands remains in limbo, as we witness today. When it comes to sovereignty, the SCS area is regarded as territories which remain unsettled under the post-war deals regarding the allocation or recovery of former occupied territories.

When the People's Republic of China (PRC) was established in 1949 and participated in this competition for territorial recovery, it found that major land territories in the SCS had already been occupied by the other States concerned, and so it felt that it was destined to assert an ideological or historic sovereignty over its intrinsic territory by the use of China's traditional 'Nine-dash-line' claims as the successor State of China, a modified version of the similar 'Eleven-dash-line' claims made by the former Government, and the PRC has continually made an attempt to effectively control the rest of mostly untouched features such as low tide elevations, underwater shallow reef (or shoal) through dredging and reclamation, and it has actually occupied some features in the Paracel Islands and the Spratly Islands by the use of force in 1979 and 1988, although, as a matter of principle, it is impossible in law to appropriate or incorporate underwater maritime features (except for islands or high-tide rocks).

It is true that, from the 18th century to the 19th century, hǎinán fishermen engaged in traditional fisheries in the adjacent waters of the Spratly Islands and left a series of log books (entitled gēnglùbù) registering sea routes and fisheries, which the Arbitral Tribunal considered as evidence for the Chinese fishermen's traditional but non-exclusive right in the territorial waters of a rock, while the Tribunal recognized the similar traditional non-exclusive rights of the Filipino fishermen and others as well.

It appears that, in its history, China has made a vague distinction between the coastal sea and the offshore sea, but their scope and demarcation were not clear. In the 1930s, the Republic of China issued a decree on three-mile territorial sea. It is said that a U-shaped lines had appeared in a non-official map around 1933. After the Second World War, in 1948, the Ministry of Interior of the Republic of China published the 'Eleven-dash-line' map produced

7 The Cairo Declaration, 27 November 1943, Department of State [USA], The Department of State Bulletin, No.232, at 393. 1 Japan's Foreign Relations-Basic Documents 55–56.

in December 1947. This was the direct origin of the 'nine-dash-line' map and claims for islands as well as related waters. After that, in 1949 the PRC Government was established, and it adopted that map and claims, and since 1953 two dash-lines were deleted in the Gulf of Tonkin (Dōngjīng Wān), or Northern Gulf (Běibù Wān).[8]

In 1958 the PRC made a declaration on 12-mile territorial sea, allowing for straight lines between the mainland and the coastal islands and requiring not only foreign airplanes but also foreign military vessels to procure the permission from the Chinese authorities for their passage through the territorial waters. While it was stipulated that these rules also apply in the Spratly Islands, it was unknown whether they meant to apply the straight baselines or to require foreign military vessels to seek and get passage permits from the authorities. In 1992 the PRC enacted the Law on Territorial Sea and Contiguous Zone, which formally introduced 12-mile territorial sea and straight baselines without any geomorphological restriction, and it clarified that China's territory includes the Spratly Islands, the Paracel Islands and the Pratas Islands in the SCS.[9] In 1996 it issued a Declaration on Territorial Sea Baselines, and in the same year the PRC ratified the UN Convention on the Law of the Sea (UNCLOS), and it issued a Declaration on Exclusive Economic Zone (EEZ) but therein did not mention any historic right yet. Then, in 1998 it enacted the EEZ law, in Article 14 of which, for the first time, the preservation of a historic right was mentioned as 'the rights that the People's Republic of China has been enjoying ever since the days of the past'.[10] However, it was in 2009 that the PRC officially gave an international law formula to the so-called 'Nine-dash-line' claims.

In that year, Malaysia and Vietnam jointly submitted to the Commission on the Limits of the Continental Shelf (the CLCS) an application for extending the continental shelf over 200 miles, and in the *notes verbales* conveyed to the UN Secretary-General in response to this joint submission, China stated as follows:

> China has indisputable sovereignty over the islands in the South China Sea and the adjacent waters, and enjoys sovereign rights and jurisdiction

8 For the recent deals, *see* COALTER G. LATHROP, INTERNATIONAL MARITIME BOUNDARIES, VOLUME VII, Report No.5–25 (Add.1), (2016) 4842–4846.

9 As well as the Pinnacle Islands (Diàoyúdǎo; Senkaku) in the East China Sea.

10 In the Matter of the South China Sea Arbitration (Philippines v. PRC), An Arbitral Tribunal Constituted under Annex VII to the 1982 UN Convention on the Law of the Sea, Award of 12 July 2016 para. para.179, PCA Case No.2013–19 (Registry: Permanent Court of Arbitration), https://pcacases.com/web/sendAttach/2086 [hereinafter Tribunal's Award (merits)].

> over the relevant waters as well as the seabed and subsoil thereof (see attached map). The above position is consistently held by the Chinese Government, and is widely known by the international community.[11]

It is to be noted that the Arbitral Tribunal regards this statement as a definitive answer to the question of the 'Nine-dash-line' claims. And a well-known map depicting the 'nine-dash-line' was appended to those, the PRC's *notes verbales*. Malaysia and Vietnam as well as the Philippines lodged their protests against the statement. And, in its rebuttal to these protests, the PRC repeated the same statement as above (regarding a series of log books entitled gēnglùbù registering sea routes and fisheries) and said that 'China's sovereignty and related rights and jurisdiction in the South China Sea are supported by abundant historical and legal evidence.' What it mentioned as such evidence, however, is the publicised geographical scope and Chinese names of the maritime features in the SCS; the 'relevant provisions of the 1982 UNCLOS' as well as the domestic laws of the PRC on the Territorial Sea and Contiguous Zone (1992) and on the EEZ and the Continental Shelf (1998), under which the PRC asserted that 'China's Nansha Islands (Spratly Islands) is (*sic*) fully entitled to Territorial Sea, Exclusive Economic Zone (EEZ) and Continental Shelf.'[12] In China's formal statement released after the Tribunal's Award on Jurisdiction (29 October 2015), it was said that 'China's sovereignty and relevant rights in the South China Sea' had been 'formed in the long historical course', and that they were reaffirmed by China's domestic laws and 'protected under international law *including the UN Convention on the Law of the Sea*' [emphasis added].[13]

## II The Arbitral Tribunal's Characterisation of the 'Nine-Dash-Line' Claims: (I) Historic Sovereignty, (Ii) Historic Waters, And (Iii) Historic Rights, and the Tribunal's Definitive Reasoning

Partly in accordance with the Philippines' quite sophisticated submissions and partly relying on its own former jurisprudence,[14] the Arbitral Tribunal has, in

11 *Notes verbales* from the Permanent Mission of the PRC to the UN to the Secretary-General of the UN, no.CML/17/2009 (7 May 2009); no.CML/18/2009 (7 May 2009).

12 Tribunal's Award (merits) para. 185.

13 Ministry of Foreign Affairs, PRC, Statement of 30 October 2015. Tribunal's Award (merits) para. 187.

14 In the Matter of the Chagos Maritime Protected Area Arbitration the majority of the Tribunal considered that, so long as the core of a submission by the plaintiff is not primarily

the preliminary phase, already concluded that the question of existence or source of entitlements has no direct relevance with the question of sovereignty over the islands or rocks in the SCS, and that it has no direct relevance to the delimitation of the maritime zones, either. The question of delimitation would not occur unless there is any overlapped area to which the Parties have laid claim. So, the Tribunal has, in principle, considered that it has jurisdiction over the issue of the 'Nine-dash-line' claims in general terms. Besides that, the reason the Tribunal decided to judge on the claims, combining the question of jurisdiction with the merits of the case, is that the Tribunal considered it necessary to characterise what the PRC claimed as 'the [historic] rights that the People's Republic of China has been enjoying ever since the days of the past' (1998) or what it claimed as sovereign rights or jurisdiction in the official statement on the 'Nine-dash-line' claims, *i.e.* the *notes verbales* to the UN Secretary-General (2009). That is because the Tribunal considered that the final judgment on jurisdiction depends on (a) the nature of the 'historic rights' the PRC claimed and (b) whether those 'historic rights' fall under the matters of 'historic bay or titles' excluded from the Tribunal's jurisdiction (Article 298, UNCLOS).

The Arbitral Tribunal, as mentioned above, noted China's formula in law for the 'Nine-dash-line' claims in the 2009 *notes verbales*. The formula in the PRC's statements consists of two parts: the former part of the sentence 'indisputable sovereignty over the islands in the South China Sea and the adjacent waters', which corresponds to the assertion for *sovereignty* itself (*dominium*) over the landmass of the maritime features and their territorial waters; and the latter part of the sentence 'sovereign rights and jurisdiction over the relevant waters as well as the seabed and subsoil thereof ', which correspond to *historic rights* (*imperium*) for preferential treatment similar to the EEZ/continental shelf in the maritime area within the 'nine-dash-line' but beyond the entitlements or

---

aimed at the argument of sovereignty over disputed islands, although the dispute itself involves some sovereignty matters but only supplementarily, the legal issue, in its core, amounts to the interpretation of the UNCLOS (evaluating where the relative weight of the dispute lies). *The Chagos Marine Protected Area Arbitration* (Mauritius v. UK), Award of 18 March 2015, An Arbitral Tribunal Constituted under Annex VII of the UN Convention on the Law of the Sea,. paras. 211–212, PCA Case No.2011–03 (Registry: Permanent Court of Arbitration), available at: http://www.pcacases.com/pcadocs/MU-UK%2020150318%20Award.pdf.

For whether or not the UK is the 'coastal State' concerned, *see* also the Dissenting and Concurring Opinion by Judges J. Kateka and R. Wolfrum (18 March 2015) paras. 3–17, available at: https://pcacases.com/web/sendAttach/1570.

the scope of the UNCLOS. It is *prima facie* not known whether this formula also means to indicate the assertion for *historic titles to waters*, which would make the whole maritime area within the 'nine-dash-line' integral part of China's internal waters or pseudo-archipelagic waters (although this kind of adamant assertion is repugnant to the UNCLOS).

The Philippines made against it the submissions (a) that the rights which the PRC has asserted beyond those recognized under the UNCLOS have all been relinquished and disappeared by China's accession to the UNCLOS (*i.e.* in the Filipino view, territorial waters around the high-tide maritime features are only acceptable.); and (b) that such historic rights claimed by the PRC have never been established.

Judging from China's statements, conduct and State practice,[15] the Tribunal eventually characterised one aspect of China's 'Nine-dash-line' claims as claims formed in the long, historical process, namely its sovereign rights or jurisdiction far beyond the adjacent water of the maritime features within the 'nine-dash-line', which would be beyond the entitlements to territorial waters, EEZs or continental shelves normally recognized under the UNCLOS.

Accordingly, the Arbitral Tribunal limited its scope of examination to one aspect of the 'Nine-dash-line' claims related to the 'historic rights to the living resources and non-living resources', the legal basis of which is not the UNCLOS but 'a constellation of historic rights' that do not amount to the title to the related waters.[16] And the Tribunal interpreted the relevant articles of the UNCLOS and concluded that (i) the UNCLOS, in particular the articles for the EEZ regime, neither preserve nor protect such rights to the living or non-living resources as established by a unilateral act, independently of the UNCLOS, while such rights within the territorial waters might be taken for consideration [the Tribunal's definitive reasoning]; (ii) in addition, if that is not the case, China's asserted historic rights have never fulfilled any of three requirements in law for them: (a) actual exercise of authority in the waters concerned; (b) the continuity of the exercise of authority; and (c) other States'

15 *e.g.* The Tribunal referred to the China's bit to unilaterally establish zones for exploiting the seabed oil resources near the Vietnamese coast far beyond over 200 miles from its claimed islets in the Spratly Islands; the exchange of objections between the PRC and the Philippines regarding the act of obstructing the Filipino research activities for gas and oil in sunken Reed Bank; the PRC's 2012 decree forbidding the fisheries all over the Spratly Islands in a season of summer; and China's policing activity in the area of Scarborough Shoal on the basis of that decree.

16 Tribunal's Award (merits) para. 229.

attitude such as recognition, acquiescence or the historic consolidation of a title, *etc.*[17]

The PRC neither had nor exercised such historic rights or jurisdiction as a State for the period of years until the UNCLOS was made into force. As per the Chinese traditional fisheries within the territorial waters of the maritime features like rocks, it is true, the Chinese fishermen enjoyed such fisheries but they were not of exclusive nature, and the Filipino and other countries' traditional fisheries coexisted with the Chinese. And the Chinese authorities in any period of time had never provided fishery permits for those fishermen. Furthermore, as per the asserted jurisdiction on the seabed oil or gas fields, the PRC has just recently claimed them after it ratified the UNCLOS, and so it is unacceptable. In the Tribunal's view, it is considered that, by acceding to the Convention in 1996, the PRC renounced or relinquished the assertion for such rights remaining in other States' EEZs, newly allocated under the UNCLOS; and (iii) after its entry into the UNCLOS, the PRC mentioned its preserved historic rights in a vague manner, but other States could not judge on the nature and scope of such rights for considering whether they should raise objections to them. This does not amount to any acquiescence on the part of other Parties. On the other hand, there is no doubt that the PRC's assertions in law which have been developed since 2009 met the other Parties' diplomatic protests. Consequently, the Tribunal did not consider that such rights had any way been established, after or since the UNCLOS came into force. They are repugnant to the EEZ/continental shelf regimes under the Convention.

By acceding to the UNCLOS, in the Tribunal's view, the PRC did not make its historic rights relinquished, but rather it gave up the rights enjoyed under the freedom of sea in the high seas area which was newly allocated to other States' EEZs by the international community.[18]

After all, the Tribunal admitted the submissions made by the Philippines regarding the unlawfulness of China's 'Nine-dash-line' claims. It considered that the legal issue in the Philippines' assertion is concerned only with one of the 'Nine-dash-line' claims related to the maritime rights and entitlements in the SCS; the scope of such entitlements is not allowed to be beyond that allocated by the UNCLOS; the historic rights, or other sovereign rights or jurisdiction, which the PRC claimed, has no legal effect, as far as they are, in geographical

17 UN, Juridical Regime of Historic Waters, including Historic Bays, UN Doc.A/CN.4/143, para.185 (9 March 1962).

18 Tribunal's Award (merits) paras. 222; 255; 271.

or substantive limit, beyond the entitlements under the UNCLOS; and any of China's historic rights, sovereign rights or jurisdiction, beyond the Convention's limit is regarded as relinquished.[19]

## III The Evaluation of the 'Nine-Dash-Line' Claims

By way of a conclusion, the Arbitral Tribunal characterised the meanings of the 'nine-dash-line' under international law. Leaving aside the relevance to the naval command or national security, China asserted 'nine-dash-line' as the demarcation line of its maritime zone under its jurisdiction based on the historic rights. However, that is not historic waters, *i.e.* neither internal waters nor archipelagic waters.

It is to be noted that the substantive claims consist of several legal issues (i) firstly, asserting the sovereignty over the land territory and territorial waters within the nine-dash-line with a full-fledged jurisdiction (just like Japan's claims for New Southern Islands were so intended in 1939); (ii) secondly, asserting sovereign rights and jurisdiction over the relevant waters as well as the seabed and subsoil thereof within the nine-dash-line; but (iii) thirdly, allowing all foreign States to enjoy freedoms of overflight, navigation and laying the submarine cables and pipelines; (iv) fourth, asserting the competence to authorise foreign and domestic companies to engage in exploring and exploiting the living and non-living resources within the nine-dash-line in the SCS; (v) fifth, the traditional maritime borders are demarcated by the 'nine-dash-line' as between the PRC and ASEAN coastal countries (although the more practical lines are *sine qua non* for practical negotiations); (vi) sixth, the status or entitlements of islands, seabed or upper waters thereof should be interpreted in accordance with the sovereign rights and jurisdiction in the territorial waters, EEZ and continental shelf regimes under the UNCLOS; however, (vii) lastly, the rules of distance on 200-mile EEZs/continental shelves or outer continental shelves beyond 200 miles under the UNCLOS do not apply.[20]

---

19 Tribunal's Award (merits) para. 278.

20 *Cf.* Yasuyuki Yoshida, *minami shina kai ni okeru chugoku no "kyudansen" to kokusaiho* [China's "nine-dash-line" in the SCS and international law], 5–1 kaijo jieitai kanbu gakko senryaku kenkyu [Strategic Studies, Maritime Self-defense Forces Senior Officers College] 9 (June 2015); *Agora: The South China Sea*, 107 AMERICAN JOURNAL OF INTERNATIONAL LAW 95 et seq. (2013); D.R. ROTHWELL, ET AL, (EDS.) THE OXFORD HANDBOOK OF THE LAW OF THE SEA 629–630 (2015).

## IV Some Implications for the PRC and ASEAN

It appears that the PRC still has some alternative courses of action available. The first alternative in law might be to retreat simply into the prototype of the 'New Southern Islands', a pre-war position asserting the sovereignty over the maritime features above water only, on the basis of historic title or occupation, whereas I know the PRC leadership could not follow it in terms of its domestic politics. In any case, the Tribunal's Award preserves this aspect of the 'Nine-dash -line' claims. The Tribunal stated as follows: 'because the Tribunal considers the question of historic rights with respect to maritime areas to be entirely distinct from that of *historic rights to land*, the Tribunal considers it opportune to note that certain claims remain unaffected by this decision.'[21][emphasis added] As far as the sovereignty over the landmass above water is concerned, there is a possibility for the PRC to contend for the occupation of part of territory in the SCS, invoking historical records of actual control or acquiescence on the part of other States (for instance, by *historical consolidation of a title*).[22] As far as the military or policing activities by the naval forces are concerned, they are outside of the Tribunal's jurisdiction (Article 289 1(b)).

The second alternative might be to denounce the UNCLOS straightforwardly by notifying its withdrawal from the Convention itself, invoking Article 317 of the UNCLOS, although such withdrawal does not affect the binding force of the SCS Award itself. However, should it follow this alternative course, the PRC would only stand in the same position as that the United States has held ever since the UNCLOS came into force. The US is still outside of the UNCLOS, holding a virtually free hand in the Pacific without any possibility of being sued in unilateral legal action. In the United States practice, in fact, the US Government also has established a 200-mile EEZ extending from the baseline of both 'Johnston Atoll' with no inhabitant, hundreds miles southwest from the Hawaii Islands and 'Kingman Atoll' in the American Samoa.[23]

---

21 Tribunal's Award (merits), para. 272.

22 Z. Gao and B.B. Jia, *The Nine-Dash-Line in the South China Sea: History, Status and Implications*, 107 AMERICAN JOURNAL OF INTERNATIONAL LAW 98–123 (2013).

23 The Ministry of Foreign Affairs (MOFA), Japan, also follows the US practice despite the fact that Japan is a party to the UNCLOS, unlike the US. In the case of a rock in the offshore sea like the Pacific Ocean, the issue is related to whether the 200-mile continental shelf concerned or any outer continental shelf beyond 200 miles affects the Common Heritage of Mankind or the object and purpose of the Deep Seabed regime. Japan still relies on a dubious position in law concerning Douglas Atoll (Okinotorishima). *Infra* note 59, *cf.* Tribunal's Award (merits) para. 623.

For example, the PRC might evade the very restrictive tests of an island and rocks which could have their own EEZs and continental shelves (which would be completely limited to a small number of rocks being capable of sustaining a 'local community of people and livelihood of coastal fishermen and ethnic inhabitants in their natural conditions'[24]), if it were outside of the Convention. In other words, only if it would manage to withdraw from the UNCLOS in the future, the PRC might, as a matter of policy, continue asserting that every rock above the water not only has territorial waters but also is entitled to both an EEZ and a continental shelf in the SCS (as a whole), irrespective of brand new tests on the maritime features in question devised by the Tribunal.[25]

Presumably the third and practical alternative for the PRC and ASEAN coastal States would be to open 'parliamentary' negotiations, including bilateral ones, again and seek a *compromise* agreement among them for the purpose of establishing a 'new local maritime regime'. Article 311, paragraph 3, provides that the Parties, as between them, may conclude agreements modifying or suspending the operation of the UNCLOS, provided that those agreements not affect the object and purpose of the Convention or other Parties' rights and obligations. Accordingly, only if the PRC and other States concerned in the South China Sea would succeed in working out such agreements, then those States, including the PRC, might be capable of applying some exceptional straight baselines for their territorial waters between high-tide features and low-tide elevations without objections.[26] Or, that compromise may be based on a totally innovative measure like a basic treaty on the complete freezing or moratorium of further territorial claims with the establishment of a provisional common

24 This is a test, quite novel to not a few lawyers, devised by this Award for sustaining the object and purpose of the EEZ regime: *i.e.* supporting the livelihood of coastal fishermen and ethnic inhabitants.

25 *Infra* Section 5.

26 The Tribunal, however, indicated that the use of such a straight baseline might be repugnant to the UNCLOS with respect to an offshore archipelago. Tribunal's Award (merits) paras. 573, 575, and 576. Nevertheless, such State practice has been partly witnessed, in spite of the Tribunal's interpretation of Articles 7 and 47. *See, e.g.* too freely drawn straight baselines of Myanmar's more than 222-mile long line across the Gulf of Martaban, Vietnam's more than 161-mile long line between its islets, and Japan's straight baselines off the North-Western coast of Shimane and Yamaguchi Prefectures, Chugoku Region. Y. TANAKA, THE INTERNATIONAL LAW OF THE SEA (2012) 49; A.V. LOWE AND R.R. CHURCHILL, THE LAW OF THE SEA (1999) 57. Apart from its 'Nine-dash-line' claims, it is to be noted that China is not clearly claiming an EEZ or continental shelf from any of these particular maritime features in question, just as the other claimants like Philippines, Malaysia and Vietnam have not done so.

zone for sharing resources, like a draft treaty on the Spratly Islands proposed by M.J. Valencia in 1992 Jogjakarta unofficial consultation.[27] Mr Rodrigo Duterte, new President of the Philippines, appears to have intended to put it behind the Parties after the Award was delivered and 'is moving toward a more neutral stance'.[28] However, a mere pandering to a *modus vivendi* on rules of conduct such as the lowest common denominator amongst the States concerned would no way help.

## V The Arbitral Tribunal's Tests of an Island and Rocks[29]

When it comes to the Award's impact on the UNCLOS and the law of the sea regime, it is to be noted that in that Award the Arbitral Tribunal has elaborated thoroughly the definition of an island and rocks and adopted a correlative interpretation of Article 121 regarding the regime of islands as a whole. In its operative conclusions the Tribunal stated that all the maritime features in the SCS are rocks or low-tide elevations, indicating that there is no islands in law and, on the basis of assistance by specialists or experts of oceanographic geomorphology or geology, recognizing six features as rocks and four as low-tide elevations amongst the maritime features of which the Philippines has made an issue. Moreover, the Tribunal discussed the status of the largest island in the SCS, *i.e.* 'Tàipíng Dǎo' or 'Itu Aba Island', in the course of reasoning, enquiring whether it could be entitled to have an EEZ or continental shelf. That is because it is unavoidable for the Tribunal to do so in order to ascertain whether they were part of EEZs to be delimited from the mainland of the Philippines (Palawan Island); and whether the Tribunal would be entitled to have competence or admissibility for deliberation on the jurisdiction issue. If

27 M.J. Valencia, J.M. Van Dyke and N.A. Ludwig, Sharing the Resources of the South China Sea, (1997) Chapter 3.

28 Mark J. Valencia, *Perilous South China Sea plan*, Japan Times, 18 January 2017 (This piece first appeared in the ipp Review).

29 As regards Article 121 (3), *see* D.R. Rothwell, et al. eds., The Oxford Handbook of the Law of the Sea (2015) 262–263, 272–274; Yoshifumi Tanaka, the International Law of the Sea (2012) 64–68, 402; D. Freesone, et al., eds.The Law of the Sea (2016) 89–90; Sookyeon Huh, *kokusaiho jo no shima no teigi to kokunaiho seido* [the definition of an island and domestic law regime], 19 ronkyu jurisuto [Exhaustive Discussion, Jurists] 14 (autumn 2016, yuhikaku); Naoki Iwatsuki, *minami shinakai chusai saiban to kokusai funso no heiwateki kaiketsu* [the SCS arbitration and the peaceful settlement of an international dispute], 435 hogaku kyoshitsu [Jurisprudence Classroom] 48, 52–54 (December 2016, yuhikaku); D.R. Rothwell and Tim Stephens, The International Law of the Sea (2016) 89–90.

the defendant State has made such a declaration for exception as the PRC did, the UNCLOS does not allow arbitral tribunals to deal with disputes concerning the delimitation of the overlapping EEZs or continental shelves between States with opposite coasts.

As per the regime of islands and rocks, Article 121 states as follows:

1. An island is a naturally formed area of land, surrounded by water, which is above water at high tide.
2. Except as provided for in paragraph 3, the territorial sea, the contiguous zone, the exclusive economic zone and the continental shelf of an island are determined in accordance with the provisions of this Convention applicable to other land territory.
3. *Rocks which cannot sustain human habitation or economic life of their own shall have no exclusive economic zone or continental shelf.* [emphasis added]

The Tribunal considers that, so far as the maritime features concerned indicate no 'capacities' of their own in the natural conditions, they have no relevance even if there was real habitation or economic life in the certain period of time. And the wording of '*sustain*' means the elements of time and quality. It matters whether there is a certain length of time for habitation and what the yardstick for its quality is. Furthermore, the Tribunal considers that the maritime features have entitlements to the EEZ and continental shelf, *either* if it is possible to dwell on *or* if there exists the economic life of their own by the *local community of people*. That is because, given the object and purpose of the regime, it is understood that such entitlements to those maritime zones ought to help and ensure that such communities could be sustained or developed. It does not matter if only a few families settled there, so far as they are not intentionally settled by the outer authorities. They may move from the adjacent islands to live and lead an ordinary life on the features concerned. However, the Tribunal further goes on to restrict the conditions. It considers that, although it is difficult to draw a distinction between economic 'life' and economic 'activities', the wording of 'life of their own' is very important, and that the activities such as (a) those based on the resources from the outside completely; (b) those making use of the features as the object of 'extractive activity' only, without any participation by the local people; and (c) those using the adjacent waters only, like fisheries conducted by the companies from the outside, do not fall within the realm of 'economic life of their own'.[30] In passing, the Tribunal classified the maritime features into (a) islands [landmass] and rocks [rocks

30 Tribunal's Award (merits) para. 505.

above water], (b) low-tide elevations, rocks, sandbanks and sandbars, (c) underwater features (underwater shoals, reefs, banks, sunken rocks, submarine elevations).[31] The status of rocks may vary with the methods of measurement and topographical survey either in accordance with the average tide level or the lowest tide level during years.

In the course of preparatory works of the UNCLOS, it was pointed out by Singapore that it would be necessary to restrict the scope of EEZs somehow so that they might encroach the new regime of Deep Seabed based on the idea of common heritage of mankind, while France was all against it and Mexico proposed for an exception on the basis of equitable principles. However, this issue was moved to deliberation by the unofficial committee, which finally produced a draft article leading to the present Article 121. Then, Japan, Greece and the UK still resisted with attempts to remove Paragraph 3, but the draft was at last adopted as consensus after much complicated negotiation. It was a result of package deal for ensuring EEZs interests on the part of coastal people and the preservation of the common heritage of mankind.[32]

The Tribunal has drew attention to the facts that (a) Article 121, para.3, is a restrictive clause; (b) in the course of negotiations it was discussed with reference to other aspects or questions of the UNCLOS, such as ensuring the interests of people of the coastal States, the question of an island under foreign control or colonial governments, the introduction of the Deep Seabed regime and the idea of common heritage of mankind, the protection of interests of archipelagic States, the role of an island in the maritime delimitation, residual concerns about the possibility of an artificial structures generating maritime zones, etc.; (c) the diversity of maritime features unfortunately makes a unitary, clear test unacceptable.[33] In particular, such diversity makes it of no practical use to draw a distinction by yardsticks concerning size and gross area, so long as there is, on one hand, a vast, large uninhabited island or there is, on the other hand, a tiny island where the population leads a normal life, depending on the maritime resources.[34] The Tribunal considers that, although the size of a maritime feature has correlation with the availability of food, water, space for living and resources for economic life, the size for itself is not conclusive with respect to determination on the status of the maritime feature, whether it is an island or a rock. The size of a feature has no important relevance in law.[35]

31 Tribunal's Award (merits) para.507.

32 Tribunal's Award (merits) paras.529–533.

33 Tribunal's Award (merits) paras. 536–537.

34 Tribunal's Award (merits) para. 538.

35 *Territorial and Maritime Dispute* (Nicaragua v. Colombia), Judgment, 2012 I.C.J. 624, para. 37 (19 November).

Interpreting Article 121, paragraph 3, the Tribunal, by way of a conclusion, stated as follows:

(i) 'rocks' are not limited to solid rocks in geology or geomorphology.

(ii) The status of rocks is determined on the basis of their 'natural capacity'.

(iii) 'human habitation' must not be a temporary dwelling but must be said to constitute the natural population of the maritime feature. In brief, it must be able to sustain a 'stable community of people' who can remain there and consider it as their home. Such a community does not necessarily need to be large, and in the case of remote, offshore atolls, a small number of people ('a few individuals and family groups') may well suffice. Migrating nomadic people's periodic, habitual residence falls within the realm of 'human habitation'. That includes the dwelling and livelihoods of not only indigenous people in the sense of anthropology but also non-indigenous people, so long as the latter really intend to reside in and make their lives on the features.

(iv) 'Economic life of their own' is closely related to the requirement of human habitation, but it does not mean economic value the maritime feature contains. It means sustaining economic life. It normally means that people make their home, lead everyday life and livelihoods there on the island or group of islands, or on maritime feature or features. The wording of economic life 'of their own' means such a life oriented to the maritime feature or its adjacent zones around it. It does not mean such economic life as oriented exclusively to the waters or seabed of the surrounding territorial sea. It does not mean activities such as (a) those entirely dependent on the external resources completely; (b) those making use of the features as an object for 'extractive activities' only, without any participation or involvement of local people; and (c) it is rational to consider that, although extractive economic activity to harvest the natural resources of an island or rocks (in particular, by the companies for the benefit of stakeholders elsewhere) might be the development or exploitation of resources for gaining economic profit but would not reasonably constitute the economic life 'of their own'.

(v) 'human habitation' under Article 121, paragraph 3, is one thing, and 'economic life of their own' another. They are to be disjunctively read. Indeed, high-tide features which could sustain either of them may have entitlements to the EEZ and continental shelf. However, as a practical matter, such features where a stable community of people inhabits will ordinarily be able to sustain economic life of their own.

There will be one exception where there are people sustaining themselves through a network of related islands and rocks. In that case, the existence of human habitation would not be denied even if they do not dwell on a single island. Similarly, even in the case that local people's economic life or livelihood straddles a number of islands, the element of human habitation or economic life of their own will not be denied.

(vi) Article 121, paragraph 3, concerns the 'capacity' of maritime features to sustain human habitation or economic life of their own.[36] So, it does not necessarily mean that people do live at the moment, have lived ever since or once lived there, or that they do lead at the moment, have led ever since or once led economic life. The 'capacity' itself is the objective test. And the issue of sovereignty with respect to the maritime features has no relevance. Accordingly, the Tribunal considers that it would not be precluded from evaluating the maritime features concerned.

(vii) The capacity of a feature must be assessed on a case-by-case basis. The Tribunal considers that it would be possible to identify the principal factors for the 'natural capacity' of a feature: *i.e.* the presence of (a) water, (b) food and (c) shelter in sufficient quantities. Moreover, such factors also include (d) the prevailing climate, (e) the proximity of the feature to other inhabited areas and populations, and (f) the potential for livelihoods on and around the feature. Although minute, barren features may be obviously uninhabitable and large, heavily populated features obviously capable of sustaining human habitation, the Tribunal considers, an abstract test of the objective requirements for human habitation or economic life could or should not be formulated. On the other hand, it is true that human habitation must entail more than the mere survival of humans on a feature, while economic life must entail more than the presence of resources.

(viii) The capacity of a feature should be assessed with due regard to the potential for a group of small island features. The requirement for human habitation or economic life in Article 121, paragraph 3, excludes a dependence on external supply. Likewise, (a) economic activity that remains entirely dependent on external resources or (b) economic activity that makes use of a feature as an object for extractive activities, without the involvement of local people does not constitute economic life 'of their own'. However, it is comprehensible that remote island

36 Tribunal's Award (merits) para. 545.

populations often make use of a number of islands, spread over significant distances, for sustenance and livelihoods. The Tribunal does not equate the role of multiple islands as a network with the continued supplies from outside, provided that such islands collectively form part of a network of islands. Likewise, it does not equate the local use of nearby resources as part of the livelihood of the community with the use by distant economic interests aimed at extracting natural resources.[37]

(ix) By way of a conclusion on the interpretation of Article 121, paragraph 3, evidence of the objective, physical conditions on a particular feature could be guidelines for classification. In particular, evidence of physical conditions will ordinarily suffice to classify features into one category or the other. If a feature is (a) entirely barren of vegetation and (b) lacks drinkable water and (c) the foodstuffs necessary even for basic survival, it lacks the capacity to sustain human habitation. The opposite conclusion will be reached where the physical size of a large feature makes it definitively habitable. The evidence of physical conditions, nevertheless, is insufficient in borderline cases of features. It is difficult to determine, from the physical characteristics of a feature alone, where the capacity merely to keep people alive ends and the capacity to sustain habitation by a human community begins. The threshold may differ from one feature to another.[38]

(x) In such circumstances, the most reliable evidence of the capacity of a feature will be the evidence of the 'historical use'. If the historical record of a feature indicates that nothing resembling a stable community of people has ever developed there, the reasonable conclusion would be that the natural conditions are too difficult for such a community to form and that the feature is not capable of sustaining human habitation. In such circumstances, however, it is to be ascertained whether human habitation has been prevented by natural or artificial forces from outside that are separate from the intrinsic capacity of the feature, such as war, pollution, environmental destruction or harm, etc., which could lead to the depopulation of a feature, although it is capable of sustaining human habitation in its natural state. In the absence of such natural or artificial intervening forces, however, a feature that has never historically sustained a human community lacks the capacity to sustain human habitation.[39]

37 Tribunal's Award (merits) para. 547.
38 Tribunal's Award (merits) para. 548.
39 Tribunal's Award (merits) para. 549.

(xi) Conversely, if a feature is inhabited or has historically been inhabited, it is to be ascertained whether there is evidence to indicate that habitation was only possible through outside support. So far as they are conducted to improve the quality of life of its inhabitants, trade and links with the outside world do not disqualify the status of a feature or its entitlements to maritime zones. However, where outside support is so important that it constitutes a necessary condition for the inhabitation of a feature, then it is no longer the feature itself that sustains human habitation. In this respect, a purely official or military population, serviced form the outside, does not constitute evidence for human habitation. It is to be noted that the purpose of Article 121, paragraph 3, is to place limits on excessive and unfair claims by States. That purpose would be undermined if people were sent on to an inhabitable feature in order to stake a claim to the territory and the maritime zones. Consequently, historical evidence of human habitation that existed before the creation of EEZs may be more significant than contemporary evidence, if the latter is motivated by no more than an apparent attempt to claim maritime zones.[40]

(xii) The same method of analysis would apply likewise to the past or current existence of economic life. With respect to economic life, in the first place, it is necessary to consider evidence of the use of a feature in historical record, and then go on to consider whether that historical record does not fully reflect the economic life the feature could have sustained in its natural condition.[41]

On the basis of the jurisprudence of the ICJ and other cases, the Tribunal concludes that there is no evidence for an agreement based on subsequent State practice (in the sense of Article 31, paragraph 3, of the 1969 Vienna Convention on the Law of Treaties) on the interpretation of Article 121, paragraph 3, which differs from the Tribunal's above interpretation.[42]

As the preceding summary of the Tribunal's interpretation shows, apparently, the new, restrictive definition of a feature which would be entitled to have the EEZ and continental shelf does not draw a distinction between an island and rocks, and it might undermine stability in law in that it would disqualify still not a few maritime States' practice that has unilaterally established not only territorial waters but also other maritime zones around uninhabitable rocks. It might also undermine an ordinary perception about the idea of

40 Tribunal's Award (merits) para. 550.

41 Tribunal's Award (merits) para. 551.

42 Tribunal's Award (merits) paras. 552–553.

an island on the part of the general public. The Tribunal interprets 'human habitation' as constituting a 'stable community of people' on a feature in the anthropological or sociological sense of the word. Moreover, in this respect, it considers that it is necessary to see not factual habitation but the capacity of a feature in its natural conditions, regardless of basic, technological development, such as an underground water dam system.[43] It also considers that the Tribunal could assess such capacity of a feature in its natural state on a case-by-case basis, with the assistance or advice from specialists or experts. It remains to be seen whether this could ever become a practical and equitable test.

In any case, the Tribunal invoked this test comprehensively in assessing not only the maritime features which the Philippines requested the Tribunal to assess but also Itu Aba Island (at the present moment Taiwan's 'Tàipíng Dǎo') and other features in the SCS, and it concluded that all the maritime features in the SCS, including Itu Aba Island, are 'rocks' or low-tide elevations which have no entitlements to the EEZ or continental shelf of their own. And, because, without such judgement, the proceedings would have become a dispute on the maritime delimitation of overlapping EEZs between States with opposite coasts, the Tribunal could not have had jurisdiction over this case in accordance with Article 298 (a), UNCLOS. Likewise, the Tribunal in the merits, too, invoking the same reasoning, concluded that Mischief Reef and Second Thomas Shoal are not even 'rocks' but low-tide elevations, and that they are part of the 200-mile EEZ delimited from the mainland Philippines (Palawan Island). However, so long as the PRC, the absent defendant Party to the case, might keep the position that even rocks can have EEZs, it might have been necessary to ascertain exactly what position it keeps.

The Tribunal's Award did not discuss how to distinguish the 1993 case on maritime boundary in the area between Greenland and Jan Mayen, in which the International Court of Justice recognized that Jan Mayen Island (Norway) could have 200-mile fisheries zone in accordance with the former regime of the law of the sea, although it was a rock whose population only constituted governmental officials. Moreover, although the legal issue concerned delimitation on the maritime zones, the Tribunal did not in detail discuss the 2009 case

43 An underground water dam system has traditionally been built for islanders' habitation and economic life of agriculture, for example it is to be seen in Fukusato, Miyako Jima Island, one of the southernmost Ryukyo Islets of Japan, which sustains a population of over 54,000. miyako jima ni okeru chikadamu kaihatsu chosa no gaiyo [The general outlines of the research and development of underground dams in Miyako Jima Island] (Japan's Ministry of Agriculture and Fisheries, October, 1981).

on the Black Sea maritime delimitation,[44] in which the International Court of Justice (ICJ) dealt with the role of Serpents' Island, an uninhabited Ukrainian island in the Black Sea off the borders between Rumania and Ukraine, and the ICJ was faced with the interpretation of Article 121, paragraph 3. It does not appear that the Tribunal in the SCS judgement elaborated sufficient reasoning for relying on or distinguishing from it, nor that it indicated sufficient correlation with the former principal jurisprudence. In the Black Sea delimitation case, although the ICJ intentionally avoided a direct interpretation of Article 121, paragraph 3, it only took into consideration the territorial sea around Serpents' Island in delimitation, ignoring Ukraine's claim for the EEZ of the Island itself by enclaving it. That corresponds with the consequences of the SCS Award.[45]

Amongst the dispositive conclusions of the Award, there is statements that 'none of high-tide features in the Spratly Islands, in their natural condition, are capable of sustaining human habitation or economic life of their own', and that 'none of the high-tide features in the Spratly Islands generate entitlements to an exclusive economic zone or continental shelf'.[46] In the body of the Award, the Tribunal discussed the status of Itu Aba Island.[47] However, these might be a logical consequence of *ratio decidendi* for the Tribunal's jurisdiction or admissibility, not *ratio decidendi* for the Tribunal's judgement on the merits (although it considered that, for the same reason, some low-tide elevations are part of the EEZ of the Philippines). It appears that these statements only constitute *obiter dictum*, and that such indication by the Tribunal neither binds the Philippines nor the PRC as a matter of *res judicata*, and much less Taiwan, which is neither Party to the contentious case nor Party to the UNCLOS, or even Japan. This is a logical reasoning for judging on Tribunal's jurisdiction to deal with the status of a rock. In the Dispositif of the Award, no name of other islands in the SCS is mentioned except for those of the features the Philippines raised as objects of issue. The definitive conclusions of the Award bind China and the Philippines only.

For all that, it is to be doubted whether it is well-advised for the Prime Minister Abe and his Cabinet Office of Japan to politically urge the PRC for observing the Tribunal's Award which contains such new tests of an island and rocks.

44 The Tribunal briefly mentioned the 2009 case on the Black Sea maritime delimitation, *e.g.* with connection to the Philippines' submission on the proposed tests of rocks. Tribunal's Award (merits) para. 420.

45 *See, e.g. Maritime Delimitation in the Black Sea* (Romania v. Ukraine), Judgment, 2009 ICJ para.180 (3 February).

46 Tribunal's Award (merits), X. Despositif, para.1203, B. (7) a. and b (at 474).

47 Tribunal's Award paras. 580–584.

It would produce a backlash against or at least make a reciprocal impact on Japan's position regarding Okinotorishima, or the Douglas Atoll.[48] While, generally speaking, the international cases do not have *stare decisis*, the Tribunal's interpretation or definition of 'rocks' in Article 121, Paragraph 3, would exert a critical influence on the jurisprudence of the international courts in future as well as on the position or policy of States Parties to the UNCLOS.

Provided that the detailed tests of the Award should be applied, you see little possibilities that, apart from the coastal islands, an oceanic, offshore remote island like Okinotorishima (the Douglas Atoll), would be regarded as an exception, even if there was a (failed) attempt to build a lighthouse on it in 1940 or the former practice establishing a 200-mile fisheries zone around it for the period of 1977–1996. Not only the outer continental shelf beyond 200 miles but also the inner (200-mile) continental shelf of Okinotorishima has come to be questioned as a matter of compatibility with the common heritage of mankind or the Deep Seabed regime. It is only too important for policy makers on maritime matters to take note of the changing trend of jurisprudence in international law. The alternatives for Japan would be either to transform its maritime claim and laws so as to contribute furthermore to the Deep Seabed regime, or otherwise to relinquish all except for territorial waters.

The Tribunal's tests of an island and rocks has made it impossible to claim the EEZ or continental shelf even if there have been traditional fisheries or exploitation of *guano* as extractive economic activity in historical record, which does not qualify as economic life of their own. Those activities would not constitute evidence for historic rights. This is the case with respect to the capacity of Douglas Atoll (Okinotorishima) and Itu Aba Island (Tàipíng Dǎo) in the natural state. The gist of the SCS Award by the Arbitral Tribunal consists in that, so long as they remain Parties to the UNCLOS, the States which have in fact controlled a maritime feature ought to establish no maritime zones around it or to exercise no jurisdiction over them in such a manner as undermining the object and purpose of any particular article of the UNCLOS.

## VI Conclusions: A Japanese Perspective

After all, the nine-dash-line is an outer delimitation line of self-proclaimed maritime zones based on China's historic rights in the SCS. However, it is

48 Cf. Ryota Kaji, *okinotorishima wo meguru shomondai to nishitaiheiyo no kaiyo anzen hosho* [the questions regarding the Douglas Atoll (Okinotorishima) and the maritime security in the Western Pacific], 321 rippo to chosa [Legislation and Research] (October 2011).

neither historic waters nor internal waters. This has been only a goal of the PRC's maritime policy, so long as no domestic law was enacted, in particular relating to the SCS, or no attempt was made to exercise actual control over the features or reclaim land from underwater reefs.

As for the tests of an island and rocks, if it had been applied in the Jan Mayen case, Norway's Jan Mayen Island, which did not have any local community of people except for governmental officials, would not have the capacity for human habitation or economic life of their own, and so it would have had no entitlement to the EEZ or continental shelf. However, the 1993 classic judgement of the ICJ on the maritime delimitation between Greenland and Jan Mayen fully recognized the status of an island and the entitlements to the 200-mile fisheries zone (part of the current EEZ), dividing the interstitial zone into three subzones on the basis of a median line in favour of Denmark, given the comparative assessment of the mutual length of coastal lines and the distribution range of fishery resources in accordance with the law of the sea at that time.[49] However, the jurisprudence of the international courts or tribunals has evolved and gradually transformed itself since the coming into force of the UNCLOS. In the 2009 judgement on the maritime delimitation of the Black Sea, finally, although avoiding the direct interpretation of 'rocks' in Article 121, paragraph 3, the ICJ considered that it would be able to restrict or ignore the effect or role of a minute islet, provided that it creates a grossly 'inequitable effect' to the purpose of achieving an equitable solution. The ICJ in fact ignored the existence of an islet which remained beyond Ukraine's 12-mile territorial waters but within the 200 miles from the Ukrainian mainland coast (a possible EEZ around the islet) and on which there was only a lighthouse.[50]

As examined above, the Tribunal's Award directly and in details interpreted Article 121, paragraph 3, and suggested an unprecedented tests of an island and rocks (without distinguishing high-tide maritime features). Unfavourably to States Parties to the UNCLOS retaining a rather conservative approach, it appears that the jurisprudence of international courts or tribunals has already begun to make a complete, definite transition to such restrictive approach with respect to Paragraph 3. And what is worse, from the Japanese perspective, it would be impossible to emulate the US practice on this issue, for the

49 *Maritime Delimitation in the Area between Greenland and Jan Mayen* (Denmark v. Norway), Judgment, 1993 ICJ 38 (14 June).

50 *Maritime Delimitation in the Black Sea* (Romania v. Ukraine), Judgment, 3 February 2009 ICJ, paras.185–186 (3 February), and *see* ROTHWELL AND STEPHENS, *supra* note 33 at 437–439.

US is not a party to the UNCLOS. Indeed, the US Government could maintain a 200-mile EEZ around the Johnston Atoll several hundred miles away from Hawaii, where even military officials no longer inhabit there because of conspicuous environmental damages, or around the Kingman Atoll at far northeastern sea of the American Samoa, in accordance with the former international conventions and customs. Japan, however, might not be able to maintain such maritime zones unless it will contend for exception on the appropriate grounds under general law or persuade the adjacent, coastal States involved to reach a new agreement and establish a 'new local maritime regime' with due regard to the Deep Seabed regime and the common heritage of mankind,[51] partially modifying or suspending part of the UNCLOS so that they could co-operate in creating a new local order of law of the sea amongst them in accordance with Article 311, paragraph 3, of the UNCLOS.

Japan's claims for the southern part of the *outer* continental shelf beyond 200 miles around the Douglas Atoll (Okinotorishima) might infringe on the common heritage of mankind,[52] while, in any case, it could be bound by Article 82 on the payments and contributions in kind in respect of exploitation. As per the 200-mile *inner* continental shelf of the Douglas Atoll, it remains to see whether a more sophisticated attempt will be made in the jurisprudence of the international courts to find a well-balanced and more practical test of the continental shelf for achieving an equitable solution. Taiwan was only the victim of the Tribunal's Award, so to speak, and it would have been ill-advised for the PRC to continue absence and did not assert its position at courtroom even after the Tribunal's unfavourable judgement on jurisdiction and admissibility (29 Oct. 2015),[53] save for a dire statement such as 'waste paper'.[54]

On the other hand, despite the aforesaid trend of change in case law, Japan's MOFA position or interpretation of Article 121 is without doubt extraordinarily singular. It has not changed ever since 30 years ago, and unfortunately it would

51 It is to be noted that the Parties to the UNCLOS shall not derogate from the *basic* principle (or the object and purpose) relating to the common heritage of mankind (Article 311, paragraph 6).

52 Tribunal's Award (merits) para. 419 and para. 624.

53 In the Matter of an Arbitration (Philippines v. PRC), Award of 29 October 2015, An Arbitral Tribunal Constituted under Annex VII to the 1982 UN Convention on the Law of the Sea (Registry: Permanent Court of Arbitration, PCA Case No. 2013–19).

54 In a tough speech in Washington last week, a former senior Chinese official, Dai Bingguo, said that the findings would amount to no more than 'waste paper.' Jane Perlez, *Tribunal Rejects Beijing's Claims in South China Sea*, NEW YORK TIMES, 12 July 2016.

rather be illogical or no longer helpful than has gone out of date.[55] Meanwhile, Japan has never invoked even historic-rights-type grounds as the basis of its entitlements to the continental shelf around Okinotorishima (the Douglas Atoll). As already mentioned, Japan could not emulate the US practice with respect to that Atoll, provided that it remains the State Party to the UNCLOS. The two high-tide minute rocks on the Atoll, indeed, were literally named 'North Rock' and 'South Rock' respectively for a long time, while they are now figuratively named 'North Island' and 'South Island' in an official hydrographic chart. It is to be noted that it would take much more time for Japan to navigate its way to a new position. About time, too.

55 Japan's Ministry of Foreign Affairs, twelve years ago, explained as follows: Status of Okinotorishima island(Japan's MOFA, Press Conference, 18 February 2005): '... The island, under the Tokyo Municipal Government, has been known as an island under Japanese jurisdiction since 1931, long before the United Nations Convention on the Law of the Sea came into existence. Having ratified the Convention in 1996, Japan registered its domestic laws concerning its territorial waters, in which Okinotorishima is included as an island, to the Secretary-General of the UN in 1997. Seven years passed without a single claim. As recently as in 2004, a research vessel of a certain country, having violated Japan's Exclusive Economic Zone (EEZ) by ignoring necessary procedures, was asked why it took the liberty to do so. It justified its trespassing on grounds that they construed Okinotorishima as a rock. *Article 121 of the United Nations Convention on the Law of the Sea defines that "an island is a naturally formed area of land, surrounded by water, which is above water at high tide." This is exactly what Okinotorishima is. In the same Article, there is a paragraph stating that "rocks which cannot sustain human habitation or economic life of their own shall have no EEZ or continental shelf." This paragraph talks about a rock which is [un]inhabitable and does not define what an island is. The definition of an island is spelled out in Paragraph 1, and there is no room for lay interpretation* and this does not serve as a pretext for arbitrary intrusion. Vessels of a single country have been repeatedly trespassing, 18 times in the Pacific and as often as nine times around Okinotorishima alone, by defining the nature of foreign soil at their discretion. [emphasis added]'
[available at: http://www.mofa.go.jp/announce/press/2005/2/0218.html#3].

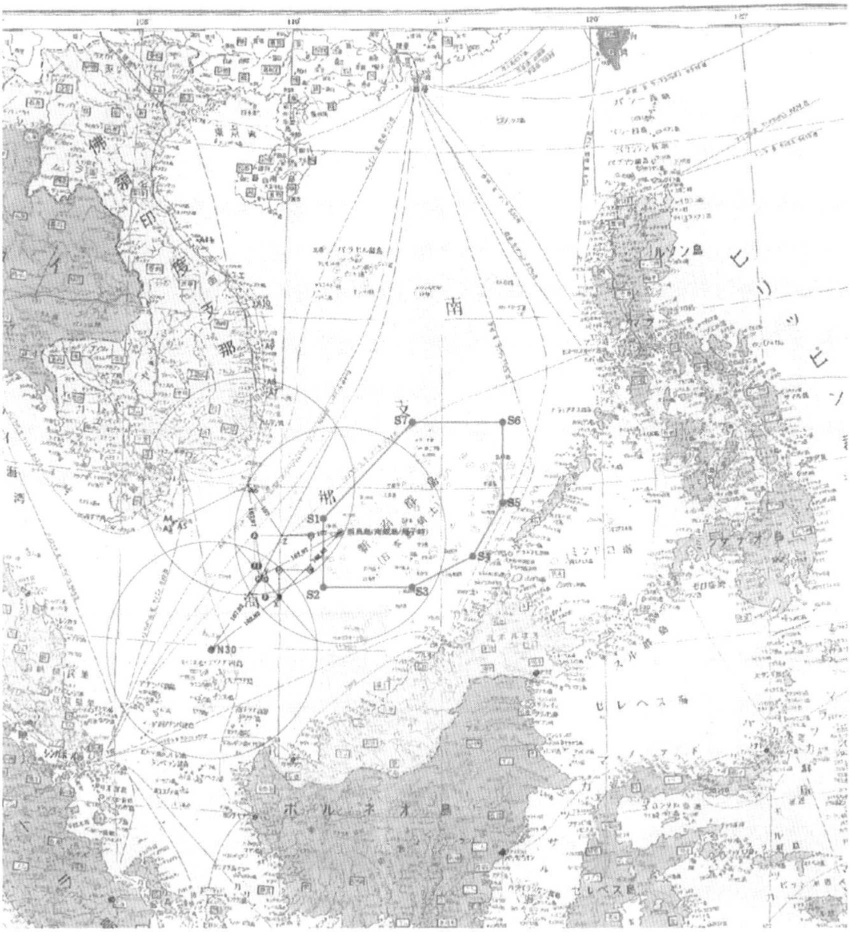


MAP 8.1 *Japan's 'New Southern Islands' (1939)* [*Spratly Islands*] (©KINREISHA, 15 DEC. 1940) RAN-IN (NANYO) OYOBI FUTSUIN ZENZU [COMPLETE MAP OF DUTCH INDIA (SOUTHERN SEA) AND FRENCH INDIA]

Notification No.122, Government-General, Taiwan (Japan), 30 March 1939

S1 9 degrees Latitude (North)/111 degrees 30 minutes Longitude (East)
S2 7 degrees North/111 degrees 30 minutes East
S3 7 degrees North/114 degrees East
S4 8 degrees North/116 degrees East
S5 9 degrees 30 minutes North/117 degrees East
S6 12 degrees North/117 degrees East
S7 12 degrees North/114 degrees East

# South China Sea Arbitration and the Protection of the Marine Environment: Evolution of UNCLOS Part XII Through Interpretation and the Duty to Cooperate

*Chie Kojima*[1]

## I Introduction

The Arbitral Award of 12 July 2016 in the *South China Sea Arbitration*[2] is progressive not only in the sense that it contributed to clarify the definition of an island in international law, but also in the sense that it confirmed that Part XII (Protection and Preservation of the Marine Environment) of the United Nations Convention on the Law of the Sea[3] (UNCLOS) can evolve through interpretation and the duty to cooperate. The Award touches upon fundamental questions regarding to what extent Part XII of UNCLOS can interact with other environmental treaty regimes and whether such interaction through interpretation can be seen as an evolution of Part XII of UNCLOS to adapt to new challenges without creating an implementation agreement or amending to UNCLOS. The Award is also illuminating because the Tribunal confirmed that the duty to communicate the results of an environmental impact assessment (EIA) is absolute, regardless of different capacities of States. The Tribunal further alluded to a link between the duty to communicate results of an EIA and the duty to cooperate, which is recognized as a fundamental principle in the protection of the marine environment in international jurisprudence.

This article first provides an overview of the Arbitral Award regarding the protection and preservation of the marine environment. It then analyses the

---

1 Associate Professor, Faculty of Law, Musashino University, Tokyo, Japan; Ph.D. (Chuo), LL.M. (Yale) and J.S.D. (Yale). The author would like to thank Ms. Katherine Cherry D. Bandanwal for her assistance in research.

2 *South China Sea Arbitration* (*Republic of the Philippines v. People's Republic of China*), PCA Case No 2013–19, Judgment, 12 July 2016.

3 United Nations Convention on the Law of the Sea, opened for signature 10 December 1982, 1833 UNTS 3 (entered into force 16 November 1994) (UNCLOS).

 | DOI 10.1163/9789004344556_010

Tribunal's references to the 1992 Convention on Biological Diversity (CBD)[4] and the 1973 Convention on International Trade in Endangered Species of Wild Fauna and Flora (CITES)[5] in interpreting Article 192 and 194(5) of UNCLOS. It discusses reasons why the Arbitral Tribunal's application of Article 31(3)(c) of the Vienna Convention on the Law of Treaties[6] was limited to the clarification of general terminologies such as "ecosystem" and "depleted, threatened or endangered species." The article then examines the Arbitral Tribunal's interpretation of Article 206 of UNCLOS on EIA and the duty to communicate the results of an EIA in the context of the duty to cooperate enshrined as a fundamental principle under Part XII of UNCLOS. Finally, it assesses to what extent the *South China Sea Arbitration* contributed to advance international marine environmental law and whether it will have impacts on future decision-making.

## II The Background

The Philippines made 15 submissions in the *South China Sea Arbitration*.[7] Submissions No. 11 and No. 12 (b) were related to the protection of the marine environment in two categories of conduct: fishing practices and construction activities. In Submission No. 11, the Philippines claimed that China had violated its obligations to protect and preserve the marine environment under UNCLOS at Scarborough Shoal, Second Thomas Shoal, Cuarteron Reef, Fiery Cross Reef, Gaven Reef, Johnson Reef, Hughes Reef and Subi Reef, by tolerating and actively supporting environmentally harmful fishing practices undertaken by Chinese fishing vessels at these features.[8] Submission No. 12(b) was related to the Philippines' claim that China's construction activities on Mischief Reef, including constructing artificial islands, installations, and structures, violated China's duties under UNCLOS to protect and preserve the marine

4 Convention on Biological Diversity, opened for signature 5 June 1992, 1760 UNTS 79, (entered into force 29 December 1993) (CBD).

5 Convention on International Trade in Endangered Species of Wild Fauna and Flora, opened for signature 3 March 1973, 993 UNTS 243 (entered into force 1 July 1975) (CITES).

6 Vienna Convention on the Law of Treaties, opened for signature 23 May 1969, 1155 UNTS 331 (entered into force 27 January 1980).

7 *South China Sea Arbitration, supra* note 2, at para. 112.

8 *Ibid.* The original Philippines' Submission No. 11 was related only to Scarborough Shoal and Second Thomas Shoal, but the Tribunal granted the Philippines to amend its Submissions upon its request because the proposed amendment to add six other reefs was "related to or incidental to the Philippines' original Submissions and did not involve the introduction of a new dispute between the Parties" (paras 818–820).

environment.[9] The Arbitral Tribunal found that it had jurisdiction for both Submissions 11 and 12(b).[10]

With regard to Submission No. 11, the Arbitral Tribunal found that Chinese fishing vessels had engaged in the harvesting of endangered species "on a significant scale", that Chinese fishing vessels had engaged in the harvesting of giant clams "in a manner that was severely destructive of the coral reef ecosystem," and that China was aware of, tolerated, protected and failed to prevent the harmful fishing activities.[11] The evidence indicated that the China Marine Surveillance (CMS) vessels not only accompanied, escorted and protected the Chinese fishing vessels, but also organized and coordinated their harmful fishing activities.[12] It was therefore concluded that the activities conducted by these Chinese fishing vessels were attributable to the Chinese Government.[13] The Tribunal accordingly declared that China breached its obligations to protect and preserve the marine environment under Article 192 and to take all measures to protect and preserve rare or fragile ecosystems and the habitat of depleted, threatened or endangered species and other forms of marine life under Article 194(5) of UNCLOS.[14]

In examining Submission No. 12(b), the Arbitral Tribunal appointed three independent experts, in accordance with Article 24 of the Rules of Procedure, in order to test the reliability of the expert reports submitted by the Philippines ("Carpenter Reports") in the light of China's non-participation in the proceedings.[15] The experts appointed by the Tribunal jointly submitted their "Assessment of the Potential Environmental Consequences of Construction Activities on Seven Reefs in the Spratly Islands in the South China Sea" (the "Ferse Report"). The Ferse Report concluded that China's construction activities had caused and would cause environmental harm to coral reefs at the seven reefs in the Spratly Island,[16] which largely confirmed the

9 *Ibid.* The Philippine filed an expert report by a reef ecologist in support of its Submission (para. 818).

10 *Ibid.* at para. 938.

11 *Ibid.* Dispositif, para. 1203, B(12).

12 *Ibid.* at paras. 746, 749 and 755.

13 *Ibid.* at para. 755.

14 *Ibid.* Dispositif, para. 1203, B(12).

15 *Ibid.* at para. 136. Three experts were appointed: Dr. Sebastian C.A. Ferse of the Leibniz Center for Tropical Marine Ecology in Bremen, Germany, Professor Peter J. Mumby and Dr. Selina Ward of the School of Biological Sciences at the University of Queensland, Australia.

16 Cuarteron Reef, Fiery Cross Reef, Gaven Reef, Johnson Reef, Hughes Reef, Mischief Reef, and Subi Reef.

conclusions reached in the Carpenter Reports.[17] Furthermore, despite China's assertion that its land reclamation activities were based on "thorough studies and scientific proof,"[18] only a 500-word statement made by the State Oceanic Administration of China (SOA) and a slightly longer report prepared by researchers of SOA were identified during the proceedings. China failed to respond to the Tribunal's request to provide a copy of an EIA. Consequently, the Arbitral Tribunal found that China's reclamation and construction of artificial islands, installations, and structures at the above seven reefs had caused "severe, irreparable harm to the coral reef system," that China had not cooperated or coordinated with the neighboring States in the South China Sea concerning the protection and preservation of the marine environment in relation to its construction activities, and that China had failed to communicate an assessment of the potential effects of such activities on the marine environment.[19] The Tribunal therefore held that China breached its obligations to cooperate with States bordering an enclosed or semi-enclosed sea under Article 123 of UNCLOS, to protect and preserve the marine environment under Article 192 of UNCLOS, to take all measures necessary to prevent, reduce and control marine pollution under Article 194(1) of UNCLOS, to take all measures to protect and preserve rare or fragile eco-systems and the habitat of depleted, threatened or endangered species and other forms of marine life under Article 194(5) of UNCLOS, to cooperate on a global or regional basis for the protection and preservation of the marine environment under Article 197 of UNCLOS, and to conduct environmental impact assessments and communicate reports of the results of such assessments under Article 206 of UNCLOS.[20]

Although much attention has been paid to what the Arbitral Award said with regard to interpretation of Article 121 of UNCLOS concerning the regime of islands and rocks, the above conclusion of the Tribunal regarding the protection of the marine environment should not be underestimated for the development of international marine environmental law. The following sections examine the reasoning of the Arbitral Tribunal in finding that China had violated its obligation to protect the marine environment under UNCLOS.

## III Evolutionary Interpretation of UNCLOS Part XII

In examining the Philippines' claim that China violated its obligations to protect and preserve the marine environment under UNCLOS by tolerating and

17 *South China Sea Arbitration, supra* note 2, at paras. 979–980.

18 *Ibid.* at para. 920.

19 *Ibid.* Dispositif, para. 1203, B(13).

20 *Ibid.*

actively supporting environmentally harmful fishing practices undertaken by Chinese fishing vessels, it was necessary for the Arbitral Tribunal to interpret the meaning of framework provisions such as Articles 192 and 194(5) of UNCLOS in the light of other treaty regimes, namely, the CBD and CITES. This section analyses the implications of importing outside norms into Part XII of UNCLOS through the principle of "systematic integration"[21] expressed under Article 31(3)(c) of the Vienna Convention on the Law of Treaties.

The interaction of UNCLOS with other treaty regimes indicates the unique character of UNCLOS as a "living" instrument. It must be reminded that, while UNCLOS is considered to be the "Constitution of the Oceans,"[22] it is a widely held view that its interpretation and application are considered flexible and responsive to emerging problems.[23] UNCLOS codified a number of customary rules on the one hand, but it also provides "umbrella or framework provisions [...] capable of being implemented at a later date" on the other hand.[24] Therefore, the *South China Sea Arbitration* is only an example where UNCLOS continues to evolve through various techniques, which include references to "international rules and standards established through competent international organizations" in its provisions,[25] the adoption of an implementing agreement,[26] and the evolutionary interpretation/application of norms

21 International Law Commission, *Fragmentation on International Law: Difficulties Arising from the Diversification and Expansion of International Law*, Report of the Study Group of the International Law Commission Finalized by Martti Koskenniemi, UN Doc. A/CN.4/L.682 (13 April 2006), available at: legal.un.org/ilc/documentation/english/a_cn4_l682.pdf , paras 410–423.

22 United Nations, *A Constitution for the Oceans: Remarks by Tommy T.B. Koh, of Singapore, President of the Third United Nations Conference on the Law of the Sea*, 6 and 11 December 1982, available at: www.un.org/depts/los/convention_agreements/texts/koh_english.pdf.

23 Alan Boyle, *Further Development of the Law of the Sea Convention: Mechanisms for Change* 54 INTERNATIONAL AND COMPARATIVE LAW QUARTERLY, 563–584 (2005). See also, JILL BARRETT AND RICHARD BARNES, LAW OF THE SEA: UNCLOS AS A LIVING TREATY (2016).

24 CAMERON JEFFERIES, MARINE MAMMAL CONSERVATION AND THE LAW OF THE SEA (2016), at 37.

25 *E.g.*, Articles 211, 213, 214, 216, 217, 218, 222 of UNCLOS.

26 Agreement Relating to the Implementation of Part XI of the United Nations Convention on the Law of the Sea of 10 December 1982 (with annex), opened for signature 28 July 1994, 1836 UNTS 3 (entered into force (provisionally) 16 November 1992, (definitively) 28 July 1996); Agreement for the Implementation of the Provisions of the United Nations Convention on the Law of the Sea of 10 December 1982 relating to the Conservation and Management of Straddling Fish Stocks and Highly Migratory Fish Stocks, opened for signature 4 August 1995, 2167 UNTS 3 (entered into force 11 December 2001).

through the principle of systematic integration.[27] How UNCLOS can evolve through interpretation is exemplified in the *South China Sea Arbitration* as discussed below.

### 1 *Article 192 and Other Applicable Rules of International Law*

The Arbitral Award indicated the relationship between Part XII of UNCLOS and other applicable rules of international law in order to state the specific content of Article 192 of UNCLOS. Article 192 provides the most general obligation in Part XII of UNCLOS; it reads, "States have the obligation to protect and preserve the marine environment."

When considering the Philippines' claims that China failed to protect and preserve the marine environment through harmful fishing practices and construction activities, the Arbitral Tribunal noted that the content of Article 192 was informed by other provisions of Part XII including Article 194 and "other applicable rules of international law."[28] The Tribunal emphasized that a State could violate Article 192 not only by harming the marine environment but also by failing to take active measures to protect and preserve the marine environment.[29] As stated in the Advisory Opinion in *Legality of the Threat of Use of Nuclear Weapons*,[30] the Arbitral Tribunal reiterated a due diligence obligation that States must ensure that activities within their jurisdiction and control respect the environment of other States or of areas beyond national control.[31] This obligation originates from the *Trail Smelter* case[32] and predates UNCLOS as a customary international rule.[33] The Tribunal further pointed to more recent cases such as the *Iron Rhine Arbitration*[34] and reiterated that States have a "positive" duty to prevent or mitigate significant harm to the environment when engaging in large-scale construction activities, as opposed to a "negative" duty not to degrade the environment.[35] This positive

27 Boyle, *supra* note 23, at 566. Boyle wrote, "UNCLOS is a treaty which functions within a larger legal system."

28 *South China Sea Arbitration, supra* note 2, at para. 941.

29 *Ibid.*

30 *Legality of the Threat of Use of Nuclear Weapons* (Request for Advisory Opinion), Advisory Opinion of 8 July 1996, ICJ Reports 1996, para. 29.

31 *South China Sea Arbitration, supra* note 2, at para. 941.

32 *Trail Smelter Arbitration* (United States v. Canada), Award of 11 March 1941, III RIAA 1905.

33 PHILIPPE SANDS, PRINCIPLES OF INTERNATIONAL ENVIRONMENTAL LAW (2003), at 242.

34 *Iron Rhine Arbitration* (Belgium v. Netherlands), Award of 24 May 2005, XXVII RIAA 35, para. 59.

35 *South China Sea Arbitration, supra* note 2, at para. 941.

duty was declared as a principle of general international law in the *Iron Rhine Arbitration*, i.e., a customary rule that was crystalized after the adoption of UNCLOS. Accordingly, the phrase "other applicable rules of international law" is interpreted to encompass both treaties and customary international law. Customary international law comprises a customary rule established after the adoption of UNCLOS in 1982 within and beyond the context of the law of the sea.

In determining the content of Article 192, the Arbitral Tribunal referred to Article 237 of UNCLOS, having implied that specific obligations included in other international agreements that were concluded previously or later than UNCLOS would also fall under the scope of Part XII including Article 192.[36] Article 237 of UNCLOS is generally construed as a provision harmonizing conflict between treaties as generally envisaged in Article 30 of the Vienna Convention on the Law of Treaties. A general interpretation of Article 237 is that "all future agreements that are compatible with UNCLOS are allowed and in the case of incompatibility, the obligations stemming from UNCLOS prevail."[37] It appears, however, that the Tribunal went one step further and considered Article 237 as a provision positively linking the general obligations of Part XII of UNCLOS and specific obligations under other international agreements that are previously or subsequently concluded. The reference to Article 237 by the Arbitral Tribunal indicates the Tribunal's positive attitude towards the principle of systematic integration in interpreting UNCLOS.[38]

### 2 *UNCLOS Art 194(5), CBD, and CITES*

Article 194(5) of UNCLOS provides that measures to protect and preserve the marine environment include "those necessary to protect and preserve rare or fragile ecosystems as well as the habitat of depleted, threatened or endangered species and other forms of marine life." The Tribunal considered that the conservation of marine living resources forms a part of the protection and preservation of the marine environment and that Article 192 includes "a due

---

36 *Ibid.* at para. 942.

37 MALGOSIA FITZMAURICE AND OLUFEMI ELIAS, CONTEMPORARY ISSUES IN THE LAW OF TREATIES (2005) at 335.

38 Further question might arise as to whether any later agreement, concluded by some or all of the parties to UNCLOS for the purpose of adapting its general rules to a specific region or a specific topic, can be considered as an agreement implementing a framework provision of UNCLOS. For a discussion on this broad understanding of an implementation agreement to UNCLOS, see, Chie Kojima and V.S. Vereschchetin, *Implementation Agreements*, in RÜDIGER WOLFRUM (ED), MAX PLANCK ENCYCLOPEDIA OF PUBLIC INTERNATIONAL LAW, VOL. V (2012) 110–116.

diligence obligation to prevent the harvesting of endangered species that are recognized internationally as being at risk of extinction and requiring international protection."[39]

There is no definition provided in UNCLOS of an "ecosystem" or what species are included in "rare and fragile ecosystems," but the Tribunal stated that Article 2 of the CBD, which defines an ecosystem as "a dynamic complex of plant, animal and micro-organism communities and their non-living environment interacting as a functional unit", is an internationally accepted definition.[40] The Tribunal stated that the marine environments where China's harmful activities took place constituted "rare and fragile ecosystems" under Article 194(5) and were habitats of "depleted, threatened or endangered species" which included the giant clam, the hawksbill turtle and certain species of coral and fish, as supported by the scientific evidence presented by both the Carpenter Reports and Ferse Report.[41]

In examining Submission No. 11 concerning China's failure to control harmful fishing practices by its nationals, the Arbitral Tribunal considered Appendixes of CITES to identify whether the species such as sea turtles (*Cheloniidae*) and giant clams (*Tridacnidae*) harvested by Chinese fishing vessels were indeed threatened or endangered.[42] The Arbitral Tribunal emphasized that CITES was the "subject of nearly universal adherence" and informed the content of Articles 192 and 194(5) of UNCLOS.[43] Although sea turtles and giant clams were under different levels of international protection under the Appendixes to CITES, the Tribunal concluded that not only sea turtles listed under Appendix I to CITES but also giant clams harvested from Scarborough Shoal, the Spratly Islands and many of the corals found in the Spratly Islands, as listed under Appendix II to CITES, were unequivocally threatened.[44] It must be noted that species under Appendix I and II to CITES are updated through adding, removing, or moving species between Appendix I and II by the Conference of the Parties to CITES, either at its regular meetings or by postal procedures. Therefore, the Arbitral Tribunal's references to CITES indicate an example whereby the content of UNCLOS can be updated or revised over time by interacting with other treaty regimes existing at the time.

39 *South China Sea Arbitration, supra* note 2, at para. 956.

40 *Ibid.* at para. 945.

41 *Ibid.* at para. 945.

42 *Ibid.* at paras. 956–957.

43 *Ibid.* at para. 956.

44 *Ibid.* at para. 957.

The universal character of CBD and CITES is an important element for assessing whether updating the content of UNCLOS by an international decision can be widely supported by the international community, or at least by all States parties to UNCLOS. In other words, the interpretation should be acceptable for both China and the Philippines at least,[45] both of which were parties to the CBD and CITES at the time, but it should also reflect expectations of the international community. While UNCLOS has an "innovative, complex yet flexible system of dispute settlement" in order to address new challenges that were not foreseen or addressed during its drafting process,[46] an act of clarifying the meaning of UNCLOS provisions through interpretation should be satisfactory to all States parties to UNCLOS in order to maintain the integrity and universality of UNCLOS.[47]

With regard to measuring and assessing universality of these instruments, CBD had 196 Parties and CITES 183 Parties when the Tribunal rendered the Award. In the Award, the Tribunal explicitly stated that CITES formed part of the "general corpus of international law" with "universal adherence" that informs the content of certain obligations under UNCLOS.[48] The Tribunal similarly emphasized the general character of CBD by expressing the definition of ecosystem under CBD as the "internationally accepted definition."[49] These references to the universality of CBD and CITES would set certain standards for future decisions by international courts and tribunals.

By referring to other international agreements, the Arbitral Tribunal relied on the principle of systematic integration provided under Article 31(3)(c) of the Vienna Convention on the Law of Treaties. Article 31(3)(c) of the Vienna Convention provides that "any relevant rules of international law applicable in the relations between the parties" must be taken into account together with the context in interpreting a treaty. The Tribunal, at the same time, followed international jurisprudence concerning the application of Article 31(3)(c) with caution.

As Alan Boyle writes, the jurisprudence on Article 31(3)(c) has been "narrowly circumscribed."[50] An example is the *Shrimp-Turtle* case before the WTO

---

45 Boyle argued that when another treaty is referred in interpreting UNCLOS, the "level of participation in that treaty cannot be ignored" as it proves that the treaty has "the consensus support of all the parties, or there is no objection." Boyle, *supra* note 23, at 571.

46 Shunji Yanai, *Can the UNCLOS Address Challenges of the 21st Century?* 57 GERMAN YEARBOOK OF INTERNATIONAL LAW 43–62 (2014) at 45.

47 Boyle, *supra* note 23, at 569.

48 *South China Sea Arbitration, supra* note 2, at para. 956.

49 *Ibid.* at para. 945.

50 Boyle, *supra* note 23, at 567.

Appellate Body in which UNCLOS, Agenda 21, CBD, and Resolution on Assistance to Developing Countries, adopted in conjunction with the Convention on Conservation of Migratory Species were referred to in determining whether living natural resources can be included in the meaning of "exhaustible natural resources" under Article XX(g) of the GATT 1994.[51] It was remarkable that the Appellate Body stated that the generic term "natural resources" in Article XX(g) was "by definition, evolutionary."[52] Boyle observed that such references are not general revision or re-interpretation of a treaty, but rather an incorporation of the existing general international law.[53] The *South China Sea Arbitration* indicated that generic terms included in UNCLOS can similarly have an active interaction with general international law and evolve through interpretation.

## IV Environmental Impact Assessment (EIA) and the Duty to Cooperate under UNCLOS

In examining Submission No. 12(b) related to China's construction activities, the Arbitral Tribunal extensively relied on the Ferse Report in order to judge its environmental impact. The Tribunal accepted the conclusion of the Ferse Report that "China's recent construction activities [had] and [would] cause environmental harm to coral reefs" at the Reefs where the island-building activities took place.[54] The Tribunal found that China violated Articles 192, 194(1), 194(5), 197, 123, and 206 of UNCLOS. This section highlights the reasoning of the Tribunal concerning the interpretation of Articles 197, 123 and 206 and discusses whether the duty to communicate the results of an EIA can be related to the duty to cooperate enshrined as a fundamental principle under Part XII of UNCLOS.

### 1 *EIA under Article 206 of UNCLOS*

Although the history of EIA started as a domestic rule only in 1969,[55] a number of multilateral environmental agreements since the early 1980s stipulate the obligation to conduct an EIA. It is a widely supported view that the duty to

51 For more analysis, see *ibid.* at 567–568. *Import Prohibition of Certain Shrimp and Shrimp Products*, WTO Appellate Body (1998) WT/DS58/AB/R, at paras 130–131.

52 *Ibid.* at para. 130.

53 Boyle, *supra* note 23, at 568.

54 *South China Sea Arbitration, supra* note 2, para. 979.

55 The United States' National Environmental Policy Act of 1969. See generally, Astrid Epiney, *Environmental Impact Assessment*, in RÜDIGER WOLFRUM (ED), MAX PLANCK ENCYCLOPEDIA OF PUBLIC INTERNATIONAL LAW, VOL. III (2012), 580–592, at para.3.

carry out an EIA is customary international law.[56] The obligation to assess the potential effects of planned activities on the marine environment is stipulated under Article 206 of UNCLOS as follows:

> When States have reasonable grounds for believing that planned activities under their jurisdiction or control may cause substantial pollution of or significant and harmful changes to the marine environment, they shall, as far as practicable, assess the potential effects of such activities on the marine environment and shall communicate reports of the results of such assessments in the manner provided in Article 205.

Article 206 does not indicate the specific meaning of "substantial pollution of or significant and harmful changes to the marine environment" or what is required in an EIA or the manner in which an EIA should be conducted. Furthermore, there is no reference to "international rules and standards established through competent international organizations" unlike some other framework provisions in Part XII.[57] The only procedure stipulated under UNCLOS is that States must publish reports of the results of an EIA to the competent international organizations, which will be disclosed to all States, under Article 205 of UNCLOS.

In the *South China Sea Arbitration*, the Arbitral Tribunal reiterated that the obligation to conduct an EIA was a direct obligation under the UNCLOS and a general obligation under customary international law as confirmed in the Advisory Opinion on the *Responsibilities and Obligations of States with respect to Activities in the Area* by the International Tribunal for the Law of the Sea (ITLOS) in 2011.[58] The customary nature of the obligation to conduct an EIA was also confirmed in *Pulp Mills on the River Uruguay* in 2010, in which the International Court of Justice described EIA as "a practice, which in recent years has gained so much acceptance among States that it may now be considered a requirement under general international law."[59]

Although Article 206 of UNCLOS contains an element of discretion for States as expressed in the terms "reasonable" and "as far as practicable," the Arbitral Tribunal opined that the obligation to communicate reports of the

56 *Ibid.* at paras. 49 and 64.

57 See *supra* note 25.

58 *South China Sea Arbitration, supra* note 2, at para. 948; *Responsibilities and Obligations of States with respect to Activities in the Area,* Advisory Opinion of 1 February 2011, ITLOS Reports 2011, at para. 145.

59 *Pulp Mills on the River Uruguay* (Argentina v. Uruguay), Judgment of 20 April 2010, ICJ Reports 2010, at para. 204.

results of the assessments was "absolute."[60] This remark highlights the importance of Article 206 in connection to the due diligence obligation under Article 194(2).[61] In further clarifying the meaning of the obligation to communicate under Article 206, the Tribunal stated that simple assertions produce no proof of actual conduct.[62] The Tribunal insisted that China's repeated assertions that it had undertaken thorough environmental studies were not sufficient to meet the obligation not only to conduct an EIA, but also to communicate it, under Article 206.[63] The Chinese Delegation at the 25th Meeting of States Parties to the UNCLOS held in June 2014 only stated that China's construction activities followed "a high standard of environmental protection" although the Tribunal did not find any written assessment submitted to the meeting or any other international body. Furthermore, China did not respond to the Tribunal's request to submit a copy of any EIA.

The Tribunal went a step further and evaluated whether China acted in compliance with its own domestic law, the EIA Law of 2002, and whether what was argued by China met the standards of the international jurisprudence. The Tribunal concluded that the SOA statement and SOA report fell short of China's own legislative standards and were "far less comprehensive" than EIAs reviewed by other international courts and tribunals or EIAs filed in the foreign construction projects which were referred in the SOA report.[64] Although these examinations were unnecessary to find a breach of Article 206 in the present case, it is remarkable that the Tribunal alluded to the existence of a certain international standard that an EIA should meet under international law, despite the absence of explicit requirements in Article 206 of UNCLOS. This may be regarded as another example of evolutionary interpretation of UNCLOS.

### 2 *Duty to Cooperate and Duty to Communicate*

The Award in the *South China Sea Arbitration* is significant in the sense that the Tribunal underlined the importance of the duty to cooperate.[65] The Arbitral Tribunal reiterated that the duty to cooperate is "a fundamental principle in

60 *South China Sea Arbitration, supra* note 2, at para. 948.

61 *Ibid.*

62 *Ibid.* at para. 989.

63 *Ibid.* at para. 991.

64 *Ibid.* para. 990. The Tribunal cited *Pulp Mills on the River Uruguay* (Argentina v. Uruguay) and Australia's Final Environmental Impact Statement for the proposed Abbot Point Growth Gateway Project (footnote 1189).

65 See generally, Rüdiger Wolfrum, *Cooperation, International Law of*, in RÜDIGER WOLFRUM (ED.) MAX PLANCK ENCYCLOPEDIA OF PUBLIC INTERNATIONAL LAW VOL. II (2012) 783–792.

the prevention of pollution of the marine environment under Part XII of the Convention and general international law" as repeatedly confirmed in the jurisprudence of ITLOS.[66] China had a duty to cooperate under Articles 197 and the duty to coordinate under Article 123.[67] Article 197 stipulates the duty to cooperate, on a global or regional basis, directly or through competent international organizations in developing international rules, standards and recommended practices and procedures. The duty to cooperate under Article 123 is stipulated weakly, stating that States bordering an enclosed or semi-enclosed sea "should" cooperate and they "shall" endeavor to coordinate.

The origin of the duty to cooperate derives from Principle 7 of the Rio Declaration on Environment and Development, which reads: "States shall co-operate in a spirit of global partnership to conserve, protect and restore the health and integrity of the Earth's ecosystem." The duty to cooperate is an evolving norm, but functions actively in some fields of international law. Rüdiger Wolfrum, therefore, distinguished a general obligation to cooperate as integrated in the Charter of the United Nations from the obligation to cooperate in specific areas of international law, such as spaces beyond national jurisdiction, international environmental law, the protection of human rights and international economic law.[68] In the context of international environmental law, the duty to cooperate serves as "the driving force for the progressive development" of universal environmental agreements having the character of framework agreements, which develops "through additional instruments such as protocols or measures."[69]

UNCLOS is not a so-called framework agreement that requires the adoption of protocols for its implementation, but a number of provisions in Part XII of UNCLOS can are of the character of framework provisions to be developed progressively and to be implemented through a separate agreement. For example, Part XII envisages the development of international rules and standards through competent international organizations or general diplomatic conference as stipulated for example in Article 211(1) concerning vessel-source marine pollution. It is reasonable to consider that the duty to cooperate is similarly the driving force for the progressive development of Part XII UNCLOS. In addition to the positive role of the duty to cooperate in international law-making, the

66 *South China Sea Arbitration, supra* note 2, at para. 946. *Mox Plant* (Ireland v. United Kingdom), Provisional Measures, Order of 3 December 2001, ITLOS Reports 2001, para. 82.

67 *Ibid.* at paras. 946, 984–986.

68 Wolfrum, *supra* note 65.

69 *Ibid.* at para. 31.

duty also plays a role in the prevention of future environmental harm in cases of provisional measures before international courts.[70]

How does the duty to cooperate play a role in the operation of procedural rules of international law? What is the relationship between the duty to communicate the result of an EIA and the duty to cooperate? The Tribunal did not find any convincing evidence that China attempted to coordinate or cooperate with other States bordering the South China Sea.[71] The Arbitral Tribunal then clearly stated that "[t]his lack of coordination [was] not unrelated to China's lack of communication."[72] In this statement, the Tribunal seemed to avoid referring to "cooperation" weakly formulated in Article 123 with "should." Rather, it emphasized that China failed to endeavor to coordinate with other States directly or through a regional organization in a manner consistent with the "shall" text of Article 123. It can also be observed that China's failure to communicate with any of the Tribunal, Meeting of States Parties to the UNCLOS, or any other international organization, undermined the fundamental principle of cooperation enshrined not only in Article 123 but also in Part XII of UNCLOS. China's breach of the duty to cooperate is further duplicated by its non-participation in the proceedings, as parties to a dispute are under a general obligation to cooperate before and during the proceedings with the body to which a dispute has been submitted.[73]

## V Conclusion

The implications of the *South China Sea Arbitration* to international marine environmental law are twofold: first, the Award provides an example whereby Part XII of UNCLOS can be linked to other environmental treaty regimes through interpretation; second, the Award gives a part of the picture of how the duty to cooperate emerges and operates in relation to other duties under Part XII of UNCLOS; in other words, how Part XII evolves through the duty to cooperate.

The first implication is related to the unique character of UNCLOS considered to be a "Constitution of the Oceans" but flexible and responsive to

70 Alan Boyle, '*The Environmental Jurisprudence of the International Tribunal for the Law of the Sea*,' 22 INTERNATIONAL JOURNAL OF MARINE AND COASTAL LAW, 369–381 (2007), at 378.

71 *South China Sea Arbitration, supra* note 2, at para. 986.

72 *Ibid.*

73 Wolfrum, *supra* note 65, at para. 38.

emerging problems as a living instrument. Potentially, a number of conventions could be similarly taken into account in clarifying the numerous generic terms under UNCLOS that are not defined. Even if UNCLOS provides a definition such as in the case of the term "marine pollution", its meaning needs to be updated as time passes to address new challenges. For instance, the protection of the marine environment from global climate change cannot be solved without interpreting the UNCLOS provisions in accordance with the Montreal Protocol on Substances that Deplete the Ozone Layer,[74] the United Nations Framework Convention on Climate Change (UNFCCC)[75] and its associated international agreements.

Does the *South China Sea Arbitration* demonstrate a way for Article 192 of UNCLOS to become a weapon against every threat to the marine environment? At least, it clearly indicated that the content of Article 192 is informed by the provisions of Part XII and other applicable rules of international law. Accordingly, in the Award, a due diligence obligation to prevent the harvesting of endangered species including giant clams and sea turtles was deduced from Articles 192 and 194(5) in the light of CBD and CITES. There is no doubt that Article 192 is a framework provision that requires living interpretation in the light of the developments in international law.

The second implication is related to an evolution of UNCLOS Part XII through the duty to cooperate. The importance of the duty to cooperate has been recognized especially in the field of international environmental law where rules and principles continue to develop and where compliance with these rules and principles is brought by cooperation rather than liability. The Arbitral Tribunal's emphasis on the importance of cooperation, coordination and communication endorses the existence of this duty to cooperate as a fundamental principle of Part XII as well as a principle under general international law, whose scope of application is wider than the explicit formulation of the duty to cooperate under Articles 123 and 197 of UNCLOS.

---

74 Montreal Protocol on Substances that Deplete the Ozone Layer, opened for signature 16 September 1987, as amended, 1522 UNTS 3 (entered into force 1 January 1989).

75 United Nations Framework Convention on Climate Change, opened for signature 9 May 1992, 31 ILM 849 (entered into force 21 March 1994) (UNFCCC).

# *Notes and Commentaries*

# China's Deep Seabed Law: Towards "Reasonably Appropriate" Environmental Legislation for Exploration and Exploitation of Deep Sea Minerals in the Area

*Xiangxin Xu, Guobin Zhang and Guifang (Julia) Xue*[1]

## 1 Introduction

Due to the rising demand for minerals or metals and the decline of land-based mineral resources, there has been an emerging surge of interest in exploration and exploitation of deep-sea mineral resources.[2] Existing marine scientific research shows that a large number of mineral resources can be found in the international deep seabed area.[3] The United Nations Convention on the Law of the Sea (hereafter "UNCLOS or the Convention")[4] gives legal effect

1 Xiangxin Xu, PhD Candidate, Kiel University, Germany; Guobin Zhang, Post-doc, Center for Polar and Deep Ocean Development & Research Base on National Marine Rights and Strategy, Shanghai Jiao Tong University, China; Guifang Xue, Chair Professor, KoGuan Law School, Shanghai Jiao Tong University, 1954 Huashan Road, Xuhui District, Shanghai, 200030, China. This article is part of research project sponsored by Shanghai University Think-Tank Research Base on National Marine Strategy and Rights (Project No.BV-COLP2016001). Some parts of this article are drawn from Xiangxin Xu's conference paper "China's Deep Seabed Law: An Effective Tool for Environmental Protection?" Corresponding author Email: juliaxue@sjtu.edu.cn.

2 For discussions on this account, see P.A.J. Lusty and A.G. Gunn, *Challenges to global mineral resource security and options for future supply*, 393 GEOLOGICAL SOCIETY 265–276 (2015); STUDY TO INVESTIGATE THE STATE OF KNOWLEDGE OF DEEP-SEA MINING' (Final Report under FWC MARE/2012/06 - SC E1/2013/04).

3 There are commonly four categories of mineral resources in the Area, which include: (1) liquid and gaseous substances, such as petroleum, gas, condensate, helium, nitrogen, and carbon dioxide; (2) minerals which occur under the seabed at depths greater than three meters; (3) ore-bearing silts and brines containing iron, zinc and copper; and (4) useful minerals occurring on the surface of the seabed or at depths of less than three meters, which include calcareous and siliceous oozes, and phosphorite and manganese nodules. See Victor Prescott, *The Deep Sea Bed*, in R.P. BARSTON, PATRICIA BIRNIE (EDS.), THE MARITIME DIMENSION (1980), pp. 54–55.

4 United Nations Convention on the Law of the Sea, opened for signature 10 December 1982, entered into force on 16 November 1994, 1833 UNTS 397.

 | DOI 10.1163/9789004344556_011

to the notion that "the Area" and its resources are the "common heritage of mankind",[5] which entitles all States to explore and exploit minerals in the International Seabed Area (hereafter "the Area") with the permission of International Seabed Authority (ISA),[6] potentially provides an exciting opportunity for those States to seek ways to address economic vulnerability and to expand a narrow resource base.

Currently, increasing numbers of exploration activities are taking place in the Area.[7] There is no doubt that China is one of the most active States that are interested in deep seabed activities.[8] This interest of China can be dated back to 1984. In this year, China initially established a strategic plan, in which China intended to apply for an exploration area regarding polymetallic nodules in the Area no later than 1990.[9] To this end, China Ocean Mineral Resources R & D Association (COMRA) was established[10] in 1990 and then registered as an international seabed pioneer investor in the United Nations in August 1991.[11] As of now, COMRA has become the contractor conducting exploration activities in the Area with all three mineral deposit types.[12] Moreover, China Minmetals

5 UNCLOS, Art. 136.

6 The ISA has its headquarters in Kingston, Jamaica, functioning as a representative of mankind as a whole for the management of deep seabed mining. The ISA is an autonomous international organization under the UNCLOS, and the 1994 Agreement relating to the Implementation of Part XI of the United Nations Convention on the Law of the Sea of 10 December 1982 [hereinafter "1994 Implementing Agreement"].

7 As of 27 April 2016, 24 contracts for exploration had entered into force: 15 for exploration for polymetallic nodules; 5 for exploration for polymetallic sulphides and 4 for exploration for cobalt-rich ferromanganese crusts. See *Status of contractors for exploration in the Area* (ISBA/22/C/5, 10 May 2016), para. 2.

8 J Qiu, *China Outlines Deep-Sea Ambitions* 466 NATURE 166 (2010).

9 See China Ocean Mineral Resources R&D Association, earnestly study and implement the Deep Seabed Law, promote the new development of China's deep seabed industry, available at: http://www.comra.org/2016-03/16/content_8638524.htm.

10 China Ocean Mineral Resources R & D Association, referred to as "COMRA", was established on 9 April 1990 approved by the state council, its purpose was: through international seabed resources research and development activities, opened up new sources of resources in our country, promoted the formation and development of seabed high and new technology industry in China, safeguarded the rights and interests of China's developing international seabed resources, and made great contribution to human development and utilization of international seabed resources.

11 See China Ocean Mineral Resources R&D Association, Brief Introduction, available at: http://www.comra.org/2013-09/23/content_6322477.htm.

12 Contract for polymetallic nodules in Clarion-Clipperton Fracture Zone (22 May 2001–21 May 2016); Contract for polymetallic sulphides in South-west Indian Ridge (18 November

Corporation (CMC) submitted a new plan of work for exploration for polymetallic nodules in 2014[13] and was approved in 2015.[14] Consequently, China becomes one of the few States who sponsored more than one contractor. It is conceivable to imagine how difficult and complex for China as a sponsoring State to regulate its sponsored contractors to ensure their compliance of international environmental obligations arising from UNCLOS and related international instruments in the process of deep seabed exploration or even exploitation activities in the Area. In doing so, China has made quite a few legislative efforts.[15] The People's Republic of China's (PRC) recent Deep Seabed Area Resource Exploration and Exploitation Law (China's Deep Seabed Law) is a significant action in this field.

The present article examines whether China's Deep Seabed Law is a "reasonably appropriate" environmental legislation for exploration and exploitation of deep sea minerals in the Area pending any Chinese Contractors

2011–17 November 2026); Contract for cobalt-rich ferromanganese crusts in Western Pacific Ocean (29 April 2014–28 April 2029), see 'Status of contractors for exploration in the Area' (ISBA/22/C/5, 10 May 2016). It should be noted that the contract for polymetallic nodules which expired on 21 May 2016, has been approved to extend another 5 years since 22 May 2016, see *Draft decision of the Council of the International Seabed Authority relating to an application by the China Ocean Mineral Resources Research and Development Association for extension of a contract for exploration for polymetallic nodules between the China Ocean Mineral Resources Research and Development Association and the Authority*(ISBA/22/C/L.7, 14 July 2016).

13 *Application for approval of a plan of work for exploration for polymetallic nodules in the Area by China Minmetals Corporation* (ISBA/21/LTC/5, 19 January 2015).

14 *Decision of the Council relating to an application for the approval of a plan of work for exploration for polymetallic nodules submitted by China Minmetals Corporation* (ISBA/21/C/17, 20 July 2015).

15 Since 1992, China has promulgated a series of laws and regulations concerning mining activities and environmental protection. However, they are applicable either to onshore mineral resources mining or to offshore oil and gas resources, rather than exploration and exploitation for international deep seabed mineral resources. Those laws are as follows: Law of the People's Republic of China on Safety in Mines (adopted 7 November 1992); Mineral Resources Law of the People's Republic of China (adopted 19 March 1986 and amended 29 August 1996); Rules for the Implementation of the Mineral Resources Law of the People's Republic of China (adopted 26 March 1994); Marine Environmental Protection Law of the People's Republic of China (adopted 25 December 1999 and amended 1 April 2000); Decision of the State Administration of Work Safety on Amending the Provisions on the Safety Training of Production and Operation Entities and Other Ten Regulations(adopted 29 August 2013); Administrative Regulation on the Prevention and Treatment of the Pollution and Damage to the Marine Environment by Marine Engineering Construction Projects(adopted 9 September 2006).

conducting deep seabed mining in the Area. It begins with an overview of China's Deep Seabed Law to present its legislative background, preliminary issues as well as main contents of this law. Next, the Seabed Disputes Chamber (hereinafter "the Chamber") of the International Tribunal for the Law of the Sea's (ITLOS) advisory opinion *Responsibilities and Obligations of States Sponsoring Persons and Entities with Respect to Activities in the Area* (hereinafter "ITLOS Advisory Opinion") that clarifies the contents of sponsoring States' international environmental obligations and the scope of sponsoring States' liabilities when sponsored persons and entities cause damages during the process of mining in the Area,[16] provides quite a few indicating hints and suggestions and thus needs closely studying. Based on above research, merits and major problems of China's Deep Seabed Law can be figured out. Finally, proposals for improvement of China's Deep Seabed Law will be put up in the last section.

## II Overview of China's Deep Seabed Law

### 1 *The Legislative Background of China's Deep Seabed Law*

#### a Legal Background

Pursuant to UNCLOS, States Parties "have the responsibility to ensure that activities in the Area, whether carried out by States Parties, or state enterprises or natural or juridical persons which possess the nationality of States Parties or are effectively controlled by them or their nationals, shall be carried out in conformity with the Convention".[17] UNCLOS requests the State Parties to carry out this obligation by way of adopting laws and regulations and taking administrative measures within the framework of its legal system.[18] Thus, laying down national deep seabed mining legal instruments means sponsoring States carry out their international responsibilities and obligations under the UNCLOS. Also, it is a reflection of the principle of *pacta sunt servanda*.[19] Otherwise, national legislation for deep seabed mining in the Area also has

16 *Responsibilities and Obligations of States Sponsoring Persons and Entities with Respect to Activities in the Area*, Case No. 17, Advisory Opinion (ITLOS Seabed Disputes Chamber 1 February 2011), 50 ILM 458 (2011).

17 UNCLOS, Art. 139 (1).

18 UNCLOS, Art. 139(1); Annex III, Art. 4(4).

19 With regard to details of this principle, see A. Aust, *Pacta Sunt Servanda*, in MAX PLANCK ENCYCLOPEDIA OF PUBLIC INTERNATIONAL LAW [MPEPIL].

the function of exempting the sponsoring State from liability deriving from damage caused by the sponsored Contractors. According to the UNCLOS, State Parties shall bear joint and several liabilities once damage arising from their failure to carry out responsibilities. But it further provides that sponsoring States who has adopted necessary and appropriate measures shall not be liable for the damage caused by contractors. However, with regard to necessary and appropriate measures, the Convention refers to Article 153, paragraph 4 and Annex III, Article 4, paragraph 4, instead of explicit explanation. Those two provisions do not give, nevertheless in fact contain, an explanation of "necessary and appropriate measures", which at least includes laws and regulations and administrative measures as to activities in the Area adopted by sponsoring States and those legal instruments should be "reasonably appropriate". Thus, in order to carry out international obligations and exempt from unnecessary liability, China has to adopt a "reasonably appropriate" legislation for regulating its sponsored Contractors' exploration and exploitation activities in the Area. That is the legal causation of China's Deep Seabed Law. The explanation of "reasonably appropriate" which could make reference to ITLOS Advisory Opinion will be provided in Section 3 of this paper.

### b Process of Legislation

Preparing work for China's deep seabed legislation substantively started in 2013. In April 2013, Environment and Resources Committee of the National People's Congress (ERC)[20] held a symposium regarding ocean legislation, exploring legislative work of deep seabed mining in the Area. Then, the plan for deep seabed legislation was included in the secondary-class legislation plan of the NPC standing committee in October 2013.[21] In December 2013, ERC set up a drafting leading group and working group (hereinafter "the legislative drafting group") specializing in deep seabed legislative work, which made deep seabed legislative work step into substantive stage. The legislative drafting group spent at least one year conducting legislative research and investigation at

---

20 Environment and Resources Protection Committee of National People's Congress (NPC), is one of the special committees of the NPC, led by the council of NPC; when the NPC is not in session, it is under the leadership of the standing committee of the NPC. Environment and Resources Protection Committee of NPC is composed of one chairman of committee, several vice-chairman of committee and several committee members.

21 See *State Oceanic Administration honors the personnel standing out in legislative work of the Deep Seabed Law*, CHINA OCEAN NEWS, 1766th edition, available at: http://epaper.oceanol.com/shtml/zghyb/20160415/.

home and abroad. Members of the legislative drafting group visited quite a few domestic prestigious research institutes in this regard and many practitioners located in coastal cities such as Guangzhou, Xiamen and Qingdao for high-frequency investigation and discussion. Moreover, in September 2014, the legislative drafting group respectively visits ITLOS headquartered in Hamburg and ISA headquartered in Kingston, asking for their opinions.[22] After more then two years' prepartory work, the First Draft of China's Deep Seabed Law came out in June 2015, which seeked the views and opinions on the content and structure of the draft from stakeholder base in the following one month. Afterwards, after twice review, the Standing Committee of the NPC adopted China's Deep Seabed Law by vote on 26 February 2016, which came into force on 1 May 2016.[23]

## 2 *Preliminary Issues of China's Deep Seabed Law*

### a Legal Framework

China's Deep Seabed Law contains 29 articles in 7 chapters (See Table 10.1 below). The first chapter provides general provisions, including legislative objective, legislative principles, applicable scope, administrative authority, etc; supplementary provisions are given in Chapter 7, incorporating terminologies mentioned in this law and their definitions, tax matters and date of entry into force of the law. The main body of China's Deep Seabed Law consists of contents as to Exploration and Exploitation (Chapter 2), Environmental Protection (Chapter 3) and Scientific Research and Resource Survey (Chapter 4), followed by provisions of Supervision (Chapter 5) and Liability (Chapter 6), which will be introduced in following sections.

### b Legislative Objective and Applicable Scope

China's Deep Seabed Law has two main objectives. The first objective aims to safeguard China's national interests, i.e. regulating the exploration and exploitation of resources in deep seabed areas conducted by China-sponsored Contractors as well as promoting deep sea scientific and technologicial research and resource investigation. Second objective focuses on maintaining

22 See Permanent Mission of the People's Republic of China to the International Seabed Authority, China oceanic legislative study group's access to international seabed management, available at: http://china-isa.jm.china-embassy.org/chn/xwdt/t1191407.htm.

23 The NPC is responsible for legislating and amending of the constitution law, civil law, criminal law, national institutional law and other basic laws, while the NPC's Standing Committee is responsible for legislating and amending of all the other national laws. *See* Legislation Law of the People's Republic of China (adopted on 15 March 2000 and amended on 15 March 2015), Art. 7.

TABLE 10.1 *The structure of the China's deep seabed law*

| General Provisions (Chap. 1) | | Supplementary Provisions (Chap. 7) | |
|---|---|---|---|
| legislative objective | art. 1 | terms and definitions | art. 27 |
| legislative principles | art. 3 | tax issues | art. 28 |
| applicable scope | art. 2 | date of entry into force | art. 29 |
| supporting policies | arts. 4 & 6 | – | – |
| administrative authorities | art. 5 | – | – |

| Explorations & Exploitations (Chap. 2) | | Environmental Protection (Chap. 3) | | Scientific Research & Resource Survey (Chap. 4) | |
|---|---|---|---|---|---|
| application & review procedure | arts. 7, 8 & 10 | pollution & hazard prevention | art. 12 | DSPP operation | art. 16 |
| contractor's rights & obligations | art. 9 | marine environment monitoring | art. 13 | data & sample management | art. 18 |
| contingency management | art. 11 | ecological sustainable development | art. 14 | incentive policies | arts. 15 & 17 |

| Supervision & Inspection (Chap. 5) | |
|---|---|
| supervision authority | art. 19 |
| contractor's periodical reports & other obligations | arts. 20 & 22 |
| contents of inspection | art. 21 |

| Legal Liability (Chap. 6) | |
|---|---|
| licence revocation & liability of compensation | art. 23 |
| fines & confiscation of illegal gains | arts. 24, 25 & 26 |
| criminal responsibility | art. 26 |

SOURCE: G. ZHANG AND P. ZHENG, *A NEW STEP FORWARD: REVIEW OF CHINA'S 2016 LEGISLATION ON INTERNATIONAL SEABED AREA EXPLORATION AND EXPLOITATION*, 73 MARINE POLICY, PP. 244–255, (2016).

the benefit of all mankind by means of protecting the marine environment and promoting the sustainable utilization of resources in the Area.[24]

The applicable scope of China's Deep Seabed Law can be divided into three aspects: eligible subjects, applicable activities and applicable area. The eligible subjects of the China's Deep Seabed Law refer to citizens, juridical person or other organizations of the PRC.[25] At present, there are two Chinese subjects signing the exploration contract with ISA, respectively COMRA and CMC, both of which are state-owned entities. In the future, there will be more business enterprises and individuals to participate in the deep seabed activities. The China's Deep Seabed Law was enacted to regulate investigation, exploration and exploitation of deep-sea resource and also intends to boost marine scientific research and marine environmental protection.[26] The applicable area is depicted as "deep seabed area". It is further explained as seabed, ocean floor and subsoil beyond the jurisdiction of the PRC and other countries.[27]

Three interesting observations are found in this part. First, this law uses "resource investigation" rather than "prospecting" although they have almost identical explaination. Second, the term "resources" is mentioned in the law. However, there is no explaination as to what constitutes "resources". It is speculated that "resources" in this law not only refer to mineral resources but also other resources such as genetic resouces. Third, in this law, the term "deep seabed area" is used instead of the term "the Area" enshrined in UNCLOS. It is still obscure whether there exists any difference between the two.[28]

## 3 *The Main Contents of China's Deep Seabed Law*

### a Exploration and Exploitation

There are four main points in the chapter. First, China's Deep Seabed Law sets up a dual-track system for application of exploration and exploitation in the Area, namely, licensing in China and granting a contract in the ISA. The former procedure is the prerequisite of the latter. Moreover, licensing can also be seen as China's procedure of assessment regarding provide sponsorship. To apply for engaging in resources exploration or exploitation activities in the Area,

24 China's Deep Seabed Law, Art. 1.

25 China's Deep Seabed Law, Art. 2 (1).

26 China's Deep Seabed Law, Art. 2 (1).

27 China's Deep Seabed Law, Art. 2 (2).

28 Pursuant to China's Deep Seabed Law, Art. 2 (2), "For the purpose of this Law, 'deep seabed areas' means seabed, ocean floor and their subsoil outside the jurisdiction of the People's Republic of China and other countries." Literally, the two terms should be identical. This article will use "the Area" referring both of two.

applicants must submit materials which the Marine Administrative Department under the State Council (MAD) identifies. The MAD shall examine the materials submitted by the applicant. If the application is in national interest and the applicant has sufficient funds, technologies, equipment and other capabilities and conditions, the MAD shall grant a license to the applicant within 60 working days.[29]

Second, the Contractor enjoys the corresponding exclusive rights of exploration or exploitation for specific resources in contract area. China's Deep Seabed Law also specifies obligations of Contractors. Specifically, the contractors shall fulfill the contractual obligations of exploration or exploitation contracts. Otherwise, they must guarantee personal safety and protect marine environment. Importantly, Contractors engaging in exploration and exploitation activities in the Area shall protect objects of an archaeological or historical natre as well as submarine cables, etc. Finally, Contractors engaging in exploration and exploitation activities also shall abide by the PRC's laws and administrative regulations in relation to production safety and labor protection.[30]

Third, the contractor may transfer the rights and obligations of exploration and exploitation contract, or change contract, but shall report to the MAD for approval.[31]

Fourth, the Deep Seabed Law stipulates the emergency system. The contractor, in the process of exploring or exploiting international seabed resources, if happen or may happen accidents seriously damaging marine environment, the contractor shall immediately start emergency plans, and take effective measures.[32]

### b Marine Environmental Protection

China's Deep Seabed Law attaches great importance to protection of the marine environment, which can be seen from setting up the special chapter of

29 China's Deep Seabed Law, Art. 7 & 8. The following materials should be submitted: (1) Basic information on the applicant; (2) An explanation on the location, size and categories of minerals that the applicant intends to explore and exploit; (3) Certificates of financial status and investment abilities as well as an explanation on technical capabilities; (4) An exploration and exploitation plan, including the materials on the possible impact of exploration and exploitation activities on the marine environment, and an emergency response plan for serious damage to marine environment; (5) Other materials required by the MAD.

30 China's Deep Seabed Law, Art. 9.

31 China's Deep Seabed Law, Art.10.

32 China's Deep Seabed Law, Art. 11.

environmental protection. This part draws lessons from the international customary law and relevant regulations of the ISA on environmental protection, aiming to reach the international standards and requirements.[33] It requires the contractors, within the reasonable and feasible scope, utilize available advanced technologies and take the necessary measures to prevent, reduce and control pollution and other hazards on the marine environment.[34] In particular, the contractor shall, in accordance with the provisions of the exploration and exploitation contract and requirements, and regulations of MAD, investigate and study the ocean conditions in exploration and exploitation area, collect environmental baseline data, evaluate exploration and exploitation activities' impact on the marine environment; formulate and implement environmental monitoring plan on exploration and exploitation activities. Morever, the normal operation of monitoring equipment should be garateed to keep original monitoring record.[35] Contractors engaged in exploration and exploitation activities shall take necessary measures, protect and preserve rare or fragile ecosystems, as well as exhausted, threatened or endangered species and other marine creatures' living environment, protect the marine biodiversity, maintain the sustainable utilization of marine resources.[36]

### c Scientific Research and Resources Investigation

Chapter 4 of China's Deep Seabed Law on scientific and technological issues sets out provisions to facilitate deep seabed research and resources investigation. China supports training of professional talents and encourages research cooperation between relevant industries. Specifically, China supports enterprises to conduct deep sea scientific and technological research as well as R&D of technical equipment.[37] The Deep Seabed Law stresses on the construction and operation of the deep sea public platform, providing professional services for deep sea scientific and technological research and resource investigation activities, and promoting deep sea scientific and technological exchange, cooperation and result sharing.[38] Furthermore, the duplicates of relevant materials, and physical samples or catalogue of investigation of resources shall be submitted to the MAD and other relevant departments for public utilization.[39]

33 See Jia Yu, Deep Seabed Law laying the cornerstone of our country's Deep Seabed legal system, available at http://www.comra.org/2016-03/08/content_8620847.htm.

34 China's Deep Seabed Law, Art. 12.

35 China's Deep Seabed Law, Art. 13.

36 China's Deep Seabed Law, Art. 14.

37 China's Deep Seabed Law, Art. 15.

38 China's Deep Seabed Law, Art. 16.

39 China's Deep Seabed Law, Art. 18.

Last but not least, scientific publicity in deep seabed mining, such as opening vessels for scientific investigation, laboratories, exhibition rooms and other places and facilities, holding seminars and providing consulting services, are encouraged.[40]

#### d Supervision and Legal Responsibility

The State organ, which is responsible to supervise and inspect contractors' exploration and exploitation activities is the MAD.[41] The MAD can inspect the contractor's ships, facilities, equipment used for exploration and exploitation activities as well as logbooks, records, data.[42] The contractors shall provide assistance and cooperation for supervision and inspection by the MAD.[43]

The Deep Seabed Law also stipulates the liability borne by the contractor in violation of the law. If contractors submit false materials to obtain the license, or fail to perform its contractual obligations, or transfer the rights and obligations of exploration and exploitation contract without approval of the MAD, or make significant changes to exploration and exploitation contract, the MAD may revoke the license.[44]

If the contractor (1) fails to file a copy of the contract to the MAD for the record; (2) fails to file on record to the MAD for reference in case of assignment, modification, or termination of the contract; (3) fails to submit data copies, material object samples or the catalogue coming from resource survey, exploration and exploitation to the MAD; (4) fails to report the contract performance status to the MAD; or (5) rejection of supervision and inspection or fail to coordinate with the MAD's supervision and inspection, the MAD shall order it to correct its action and impose a fine of CNY 20,000 to 100,000.[45]

If the contractor engages in deep seabed area resources exploration and exploitation activities, without permission, or failing to conclude a contract for the exploration and exploitation, the MAD shall order it to cease the illegal activities and impose a fine CNY 100,000 to 500,000. If illegal income exists, it shall be confiscated.[46] If the contractor causes pollution or damage to the marine environment or damage to objects of an archaeological or historical nature as well as submarine cables, the MAD shall order to stop illegal activities

40 China's Deep Seabed Law, Art. 17.
41 China's Deep Seabed Law, Art. 19.
42 China's Deep Seabed Law, Art. 21.
43 China's Deep Seabed Law, Art. 22.
44 China's Deep Seabed Law, Art. 23.
45 China's Deep Seabed Law, Art. 24.
46 China's Deep Seabed Law, Art. 25.

and impose a fine CNY 500,000 to 1,000,000. If any crime is constituted, it shall subject to criminal liability according to relevant law.[47]

## III Implications from ITLOS Advisory Opinion

It is impossible to judge whether a law is "reasonably appropriate" without a benchmark. The ITLOS Advisory Opinion provides a reference to China. It elucidates the responsibilities and obligations of the sponsoring States through three interrelated questions put up by ISA Council.[48] The first part provides two categories of obligations a State Party to UNCLOS shall carry out for deep seabed mining activities, i.e. "primary obligations" and "direct obligations"; the second part explains the extent of liability of a State Party for any failure to carry out its obligations elucidated in Part 1. It should be noted that if the State has taken all "necessary and appropriate measures" to ensure its sponsored Contractors' effective compliance of environmental obligations within the framework of its legal system, the State should be not liable even damage happens in the process of deep seabed mining. Part 3 gives some suggestions with regard to "necessary and appropriate measures". The three parts of the ITLOS Advisory Opinion are interrelated to guide sponsoring States by adopting domestic legislation. Following that, sponsoring States may avoid unpredictable liability arising from Contractor's negligence. Although advisory opinion is not a legally binding instrument, seeking an advisory opinion is a routine to assist in the consideration of the legal aspect of a tricky problem.[49] In this respect,

47 China's Deep Seabed Law, Art. 26.

48 The three questions are as follows: a. What are the legal responsibilities and obligations of States Parties to the LOS Contention with respect to the sponsorship of activities in the Area in accordance with the LOS Convention, in particular Part XI, and the 1994 Agreement relating to the Implementation of Part XI of the United Nations Convention on the Law of the Sea of 10 December 1982? b. What is the extent of liability of a State Party for any failure to comply with the provisions of the LOS Contention, in particular Part XI, and the 1994 Agreement, by an entity whom it has sponsored under article 153, para 2(b), of the LOS Convention? c. What are the necessary and appropriate measures that a sponsoring State must take in order to fulfill its responsibility under the LOS Convention, in particular art 139 and Annex III, and the 1994 Agreement? See Decision of the Council of the International Seabed Authority Requesting an Advisory Opinion Pursuant to Article 191 of the United Nations Convention on the Law of the Sea (ISBA/16/C/ 13, 6 May 2010).

49 See H. Thirlway, *Advisory Opinions*, in MAX PLANCK ENCYCLOPEDIA OF PUBLIC INTERNATIONAL LAW [MPEPIL].

ITLOS Advisory Opinion is worthy of closely reading and give reference to a sponsoring State's national legislation.

### 1 *Sponsoring State's International Environmental Obligations*

#### a The Primary Obligations

In the Advisory Opinion, the primary legal responsibility and obligation of a State sponsoring is so called "Responsibility to ensure", which can be revealed in Art. 139, para. 1; Art. 153, para. 4; and Annex III, Art. 4, para. 4. The first provision reveals directly "Responsibility to ensure", it reads:

> States Parties shall have the responsibility to ensure that activities in the Area, whether carried out by States Parties, or state enterprises or natural or juridical persons which possess the nationality of States Parties or are effectively controlled by them or their nationals, shall be carried out in conformity with this Part.

Otherwise, sponsoring States shall assist the ISA to ensure such compliance is in accordance with Article 139. Further, under Annex III, Article 4, paragraph 4, sponsoring States are obliged to take laws and regulations and administrative measures within their systems, to ensure their sponsored contractors' compliance pursuant to Article 139.

Having recognized "Responsibility to ensure" of UNCLOS, the Advisory Opinion clarified the constituent elements of this concept, pointing out that it is an obligation of conduct rather than result. It is an obligation of due diligence and of conduct.[50] With regard to the content of "due diligence", as the ITLOS Advisory Opinion said, "the sponsoring States are not requested to achieve the result in each and every case, rather, they should deploy adequate means to exercise best possible efforts, to do the utmost, to obtain this result".[51] Here, two points should be emphasized. First, the concept, due diligence, "is variable, which means measures are considered as sufficiently diligent at a certain moment but as oppositely at another moment, or measures taken in exploration phase are considered sufficiently diligent but not diligent enough in exploitation phase".[52] Second, "due diligence" requires the sponsoring States to take measures within its legal system and that the measures must be "reasonably appropriate".

50 ITLOS Advisory Opinion, paras. 110–112.

51 ITLOS Advisory Opinion, para. 110.

52 ITLOS Advisory Opinion, para. 117.

### b Direct Obligations

In addition to the Primary Obligations, the Chamber identified further "Direct Obligations" incumbent on sponsoring States under UNCLOS and the related Regulations,[53] including to:

i) The obligation to assist ISA. This obligation is a direct obligation but will be met through compliance with the due diligence obligation.
ii) Apply a precautionary approach. In the Advisory Opinion, precautionary approach is a binding obligation of sponsoring States, which means they must take all appropriate measures to prevent damage that might result from the activities of contractors that they sponsor, in situations where scientific evidence concerning the scope and potential negative impact of the activity in question is insufficient but where there are plausible indications of potential risks. That is an integral part of sponsoring States' due diligence obligations. Moreover, the Chamber noted that under Principle 15 of the 1992 Rio Declaration on Environment and Development, States are to apply precaution "according to their capabilities", which might indicate a less strict standard for developing States.
iii) Apply best environmental practices. "Best environmental practices" certainly appear to be a much higher and broader concept than best technology used in the Nodules Regulations. It should be looked as a specific obligation of precautionary approach.
iv) Ensure the sponsored contractor to provide guarantees in the event of an emergency order by ISA for the protection of the marine environment. This obligation only arises if the sponsored entity or person has not provided ISA with a guarantee of its financial and technical capability to comply with emergency orders.
v) Availability of recourse for compensation. That requires the sponsoring States to adopt laws and regulations to ensure that recourse is available in the sponsoring State's legal system for prompt and adequate compensation or other relief in respect of damage to the marine environment caused by pollution.

---

53 *Regulations on Prospecting and Exploration for Polymetallic Nodules in the Area* (adopted 13 July 2000 and updated 25 July 2013); the *Regulations on Prospecting and Exploration for Polymetallic Sulphides in the Area* (adopted 7 May 2010) and the *Regulations on Prospecting and Exploration for Cobalt-Rich Crusts* (adopted 27 July 2012), (hereafter "Nodules Regulation", "Sulphides Regulation" and "Cobalt-Rich Crusts Regulation" respectively).

vi) Conduct environmental impact assessments (EIA). The Chamber recognizes that the sponsoring State is under a due diligence obligation to ensure a potential contractor undertakes such an assessment prior to the submission of an application for a plan of work to ISA. ISA has indicated that some exploration activities, such as dredging or testing of collection systems, require prior EIA and an environmental monitoring program needed during and after the specific activity. Importantly, the Chamber indicated that the obligation to conduct an EIA is a general obligation under customary international law.

## 2 *Suggestions to Sponsoring State's National Legislation*

According to UNCLOS, the sponsoring States are required to adopt laws and regulations and to take administrative measures[54] and thus those "laws and regulations and to take administrative measures" are "necessary".[55] However, the specific scope and content of the relevant legislation depends on the legal system of each State, and the sponsoring States have the rights to decide independently. Nevertheless, such legislation should include at least a monitoring mechanism for the effective monitoring of contractor activities and a coordination mechanism to coordinate the activities of the sponsoring State and those of the ISA in order to exclude avoidable duplication of work.[56]

The abovementioned laws and regulations and to take administrative measures shall remain in force after the period of validity of the exploration contract signed between the Contractor and the ISA. Although this is not a prerequisite for a Contractor to enter into a contract with the ISA, "it is a necessary requirement for compliance with the obligation of due diligence of the sponsoring State and for its exemption from liability".[57] After completion of the exploration phase, the contractor shall continue to be liable for any damage caused by its misconduct during the course of the operation, in particular to the marine environment.[58] The laws, regulations and administrative measures of the sponsoring State should be kept under review and kept in order to ensure that they meet the prevailing standards.[59]

---

54 UNCLOS, Annex III, Art. 4, para. 4.

55 Advisory Opinion, Paragraph 218.

56 *Ibid.*

57 Advisory Opinion, Paragraph 219.

58 Advisory Opinion, Paragraph 221.

59 Advisory Opinion, Paragraph 222.

The contractual obligations in the sponsoring agreement between the sponsoring State and the contractor cannot replace the legal, regulatory and administrative measures. There is only a contractual obligation and cannot be considered as fulfilling its obligations under the Convention.[60] The sponsoring State does not enjoy the absolute discretion of its domestic laws and regulations, and the sponsoring State must be based on the principle of good faith and take reasonable, relevant and conductive manner taking into account of benefit mankind as a whole.[61] The provisions as to environmental protection in the sponsoring State's national legislation shall take ISA regulations as minimum standards and the domestic legislation of the sponsoring State shall be more stringent than that of the ISA.[62]

The necessary measures to be incorporated into the legislation by the sponsoring State include the following: the applicant's financial and technical capacity, the conditions for granting the guarantee and the penalties for the contractor not to comply with the requirements.[63] Finally, the ITLOS Advisory Opinion is specifically mentioned, and the decisions of the Chamber shall be enforced in the territory of the State party in the same manner as the Supreme Court's decision or order.[64]

## IV Proposals for Improvements of China's Deep Seabed Law

A "reasonably appropriate" environmental legislation for exploration and exploitation of deep sea minerals in the Area shall assume both "primary obligations" and "direct obligations", together with adopting ITLOS Advisory Opinion's suggestions especially reflected in Question 3. China's Deep Seabed Law basically covers the "direct obligations" in ITLOS Advisory Opinion. Furthermore, it makes efforts to fulfill its primary obligation, *inter alia*, through setting up chapters regarding supervision and liability. In particular, China's Deep Seabed Law attaches great importance to the spirit of marine environmental protection, as it sets up a special chapter as to marine environmental protection. In addition, marine scientific research and resource survey activities are encouraged and emphasis is also given on collection and sharing of information. Otherwise, the importance of the protection of seafloor relics. They

60 Advisory Opinion, Paragraph 223.
61 Advisory Opinion, Paragraph 230.
62 Advisory Opinion, Paragraph 240.
63 Advisory Opinion, Paragraph 234.
64 Advisory Opinion, Paragraph 235.

all reflects the provisions of the UNCLOS and the 1994 Implementing Agreement, the ISA regulations and the ITLOS Advisory Opinion. Nevertheless, there is still room in the future to go further.

### 1 *Providing Operationalizing Details of EIA*

Although it is applauded that there is one chapter as to environmental protection in China's Deep Seabed Law, relevant provisions are quite vague and general, which is difficult to operationalize in practice if no further elaboration of details. For instance, it is noted that there are no specific rules regulating environment impact assessment (EIA) in deep seabed mining. In Chinese legal system, there is the EIA Law of the PRC, but it only applies to mining activities within China's jurisdiction.[65] Unfortunately, the China's Deep Seabed Law does not provide more detailed stipulations on EIA and its procedures. Also, other issues, such as collection of baseline data, best environmental practice and details for granting a licence, lack details for operationalization. Those parts which lack details of operationalization need complementary regulations and guidelines to provide more information.

### 2 *Amending the Law to Add Missing Components*

Admittedly, China's Deep Seabed Law is a good starting point to protect marine environment in the process of mining in the Area. Nevertheless, certain crucial components are missing in China's Deep Seabed Law. It does not provide provisions as to rights of a contractor and right relief issues. Contractors' significant rights, e.g. extension and reservation of a contractor's license, cannot be found in China's Deep Seabed Law. Also, there is no any provisions regarding right relief if a contractor's right is infringed. Besides, there is no provisions in relation to fiscal arrangement. Notwithstanding that commercial exploitation has not yet begun, with the development of science and technology and the temptation of a large number of deep seabed minerals, it is likely to be mined in the future.[66] Before exploitation activities commence, regime as to fiscal issues should be in place.

Under the framework of China's Deep Seabed Law, complementary regulations and guidelines will make sense to provide details, dealing with the problem of lacking operationalizing details. However, in response to missing components of China's Deep Seabed Law, the approach of lodging complementary regulations and guidelines doesn't make sense as they can only confine the

65 Art. 33, Environmental Impact Assessment Law of the People's Republic of China (adopted on 28 October 2002 and amended on 2 July 2016).

66 C.L. Van Dover, *Tighten Regulations on Deep-sea Mining*, 470 NATURE, No.7332, (2011), 32.

law under the framework of law, rather than stipulating new components that doesn't exist in the law. Against this background, there are no other ways but amending the law in order to add new component to China's Deep Seabed Law.

### 3 *Institutional Improvements*

It is not adequate to achieve the desired result of ensuring Contractor's compliance of its international environmental obligations only by creating relevant legislation by sponsoring States. Besides, implementation and enforcement of the regimes are also paramount. Strong institutional structure is of significance to implement legal, fiscal and environmental matters and to oversee deep seabed mining activity in the Area. Accordingly, a "reasonably appropriate" national legislation needs a necessary ponderation of the institutional arrangement. Ideally, the institutional structure as least includes: legislative body, regulatory agency, monitoring body and oversight body of decision-making. The ideal model is that each body is standalone with crystal clear functions and duties to ensure its operationalization and independence. Alternatively, some bodies could be merged according to sponsoring States' actual conditions and administrative capacities. Whatever model is followed, the institutional system should be complete with each body performing its duties.

That is no doubt that there is a clear legislative system in China.[67] With regard to Chinas' deep seabed legislation, the National People's Congress (NPC) and its Standing Committee are the legislative bodies of "Law". Several other bodies are qualified to issue "national administrative regulations and orders" to complement China's Deep Seabed Law in details with lower hierarchy. Consequently, there is nothing to worry about in legislative issues. Regarding regulatory agency, there is a MAD in China's Deep Seabed Law and its function is presented in Article 5, it stipulated:

> The MAD shall be responsible for the supervision and administration of the exploration, development and investigation of resources in deep seabed areas. Other relevant departments of the State Council shall be responsible for the relevant administration according to the functions prescribed by the State Council.

It can be concluded that the MAD is both regulatory agency and monitoring body for China's mining activities in the Area. However, there is no any

67 With regards to China's legal system, see J. Wang *China: Legal Reform in an Emerging Socialist Market Economy*, in E.A. BLACK, G.F. BELL (EDS.), LAW AND LEGAL INSTITUTIONS OF ASIA: TRADITIONS, ADAPTATIONS AND INNOVATIONS (2011), pp. 33–41.

description of oversight of decision-making. Consequently, procedural fairness will not be guaranteed.

## V Conclusion

China's Deep Seabed Law is the first piece of specific national legislation for deep seabed mining activities in the Area, which is of significance for China to gradually pave the way towards law-based governance and effective participation to international affairs of the resource-related activities in the Area. However, the law is mere a framework, under which numerous issues should be further considered and a series of supplemented instruments are needed. Prudent attention should be generated to take "necessary and appropriate measures" to ensure the sponsored contractors' compliance of obligations promulgated in the UNCLOS and related legal instruments so as to avoid State's liability. The ITLOS Advisory Opinion specifies the responsibilities and obligations of States sponsoring persons and entities with respect to activities in the Area. It also provides specific advice for sponsoring States to cover relevant issues in their national legislations. By following these rules, China may be able set up a "reasonably appropriate" environmental legislation for exploration and exploitation of deep sea minerals in the Area.

# Further Developments in Fukushima and Other New Movements for Implementing International Human Rights Law in Japan

*Kanami Ishibashi*[1]

## 1 Introduction

This note describes the notable improvements in human rights practices in Japan in 2015 (including early 2016). One is related to personal rights: the court judgements which ordered the suspension of two nuclear reactors based on personal rights. It is the first time for a Japanese court to suspend nuclear reactors which passed the new safety standards designated after the March 2011 Fukushima Daiichi Nuclear Power Plant Accident. The others are related to improvements of the status of children and women. In 2015, Japan revised the law to lower the voting age from 20 to 18, considering Article 1 of the Convention on the Rights of the Child, although the definition of child in Japan provided in Article 4 of the Civil Code remains unchanged. Then, on 16 December 2015, Japan had the Supreme Court judgment to hold the partial unconstitutionality of Article 733 of the Civil Code and therefore revised that part of Article 733 to allow women to remarry after 100 days periods (shorter than six months) and to remarry even within 100 days from her divorce if medical certificates prove that they were not pregnant at the time of divorce.

However, it might be appropriate to address the abovementioned cases just as on the way to improve the situation of human rights in Japan. As proof of this, on the very same day, 16 December 2015, the Supreme Court held that Article 750 of the Civil Code requiring that married people share a common family name do not violate the Constitution. It is widely recognized that Japan has been criticized to hold the system of same surname against the Article 23 of the ICCPR, Article 16(1) of the Convention on the Elimination of All Forms of Discrimination against Women accompanied with several recommendation such as: "On 16 December 2015, the Supreme Court upheld the constitutionality of Article 750 of the Civil Code that requires married couples to use the same

1 Associate Professor, Tokyo University of Foreign Studies, Japan.

surname, which in practice often compels women to adopt their husbands' surnames."[2]

## II Personal Rights Invoked for Prohibition of Reactivation of Nuclear Power Plants

On 11 March 2011, at 2:46 pm, Japan was hit by a 9.0 magnitude earthquake, causing a huge tsunami which devastated the coastal areas of northeast Japan and led to the loss of 19,000 lives in those areas. To make matters worse, this natural disaster triggered the nuclear power plant accident in Fukushima and has had adverse effects to human health and on the environment.

Especially in 2015, there were significant leakages of radiation from the facilities of the Fukushima Nuclear Power Plants. Those accidental leakages shocked many people who believe and expect that the Japanese government well managed to control the operation of Tokyo Electric Power Co (TEPCO), to proceed with the decommissioning of the Fukushima power plants and to recover the environment of the area.

The first leakage happened on 22 February 2015.[3] According to the report of TEPCO to the Nuclear Regulation Authority (NRA), there was contaminated water detected in the drainage which leads to the port outside of the controlled area.[4] The second leakage was reported to the NRA on 15 September 2015, such as leakages of water from the dikes outside of the tanks in which the contaminated water was stored.[5] Although there seemed to be no leakage from the tank, rainfall water accumulated in the dike showed a certain level of contamination. However, the contamination did not affect the ocean.

These incidents remind people of horrible radioactive affects. Moreover, leaks render decommissioning more difficult. Yuichi Okamura, general

---

2 CEDAW/C/JPN/CO/7–8, Concluding observations on the combined seventh and eighth periodic reports of Japan, available at: http://www.nichibenren.or.jp/library/ja/kokusai/humanrights_library/treaty/data/woman_report_sokatsu_en.pdf.

3 *Fresh leak of highly radioactive water detected at Fukushima nuclear power plant*, THE ABC NEWS, available at: http://www.abc.net.au/news/2015-02-22/fresh-nuclear-leak-detected-at-fukushima-plant/6200746.

4 NRA, *Possible Flow of Contaminated Water to the Outside of the Controlled Area of Fukushima Daiichi NPS*, available at: https://www.nsr.go.jp/data/000098312.pdf.

5 NRA, *Leakages of water from the dikes in tank areas storing contaminated water at Fukushima Daiichi NPS*, available at: https://www.nsr.go.jp/data/000122104.pdf.

manager of TEPCO, said that "Contaminated water floating around and posing a constant risk of leaks disturbs the steady progress toward decommissioning."[6]

Under such circumstances, the movement towards reactivation of the other nuclear power plants was questioned. Although the other nuclear power plants have been suspended since 2011, the government promotes to reactivate the nuclear power plants which passed the new strict regulation of examination. It did not necessarily refer to those incidents, but there were remarkable judgements which followed such incidents which clarified the importance of personal rights, noting that we should not forget such disaster and accident.

The first judicial order was given on 14 April 2015, as a provisional injunction.[7] The Fukui District Court issued the injunction for the No. 3 and No. 4 reactors at the Takahama plant, holding as follows:

> reasonableness to be required for new regulation should be strict to the extent that it would never cause any significant disaster as far as the facilities of the nuclear power plants clear its review. However, the new regulation is too soft and therefore, it never ensures the safety of the nuclear power plants. It is no doubt that the new regulation lacks the reasonableness. Consequently, there are concrete risks of infringement of personal rights.[8]

However, the Fukui Court lifted the injunction on Takahama reactor on 24 December 2015.[9] Therefore, the No. 3 and No. 4 reactors at the Takahama plant were reactivated on January and February 2016.

It is notable that, the other district court, the Otu District Court again ordered to halt such reactivation. Based on personal rights, the court questioned

6 *Fukushima nuclear plant 'will leak radioactive water for four more years,'* THE TELEGRAPH, available at: http://www.telegraph.co.uk/news/worldnews/asia/japan/12189613/Fukushima-nuclear-plant-will-leak-radioactive-water-for-four-more-years.html.

7 Available at: http://www.courts.go.jp/app/files/hanrei_jp/038/085038_hanrei.pdf (in Japanese).

8 *Ibid.*

9 Judgement, available at: http://www.courts.go.jp/app/files/hanrei_jp/566/085566_hanrei.pdf (in Japanese). *Fukui court lifts injunction on Takahama reactor restarts*, JAPAN TIMES, available at: http://www.japantimes.co.jp/news/2015/12/24/national/japan-court-lifts-injunction-restart-takahama-nuclear-plant/#.WQX4UsGweVQ. KEPCO, available at: http://www.kepco.co.jp/ir/brief/disclosure/pdf/kaiji20151224_1.pdf (in Japanese).

the credibility of safety standards adopted after March 2011 and it ordered the suspension of the two reactors on 9 March 2016.[10] It was the first injunction order to be issued by a Japanese court for nuclear reactors that were reactivated after passing what the Nuclear Regulation Authority (NRA) calls the "world's strictest" safety standards[11] adopted after the Fukushima nuclear disaster.

## III Other State Practice of Human Rights in 2015

In 2015, there were some remarkable developments in the Japanese State practice to implement international human rights law related to the rights of children and women, although, as described above, there are still things which need to be done.

### 1 *Lowering Voting Age to 18 from 20*

In Japan, the voting age had been 20 for public election. Article 4 of the Civil Code provides that "The age of majority is reached when a person has reached the age of 20" and therefore, the Public Offices Election Act also provides that the voting age should be 20.However, nowadays in over 80 percent of the 198 countries and regions, the voting age is set forth as 18. Article 1 of the Convention on the Rights of the Child also provides as follows: "For the purposes of the present Convention, a child means every human being below the age of eighteen years unless under the law applicable to the child, majority is attained earlier."

On 17 June 2015, the amendment to the Public Offices Election Act was adopted in the Diet as one of the main purpose is to encourage younger people to be more politically active. Although this attempt proceeded prior to the reform of the Civil Code and therefore does not touch upon the issue of "adults and children," it might become a driving force to change the relationship of "adults and children" fundamentally and to enhance the reform of the Civil Code itself. It has been discussed how to match the voting age of 18 with the age of majority of 20 provided in the Civil Code. However, in 2017, Article 4 of the Civil Code is still active and it seems difficult to change the age of majority from 20 to 18.

---

10 Order, available at: http://www.news-pj.net/diary/38643.

11 Available at: https://www.nsr.go.jp/data/000070101.pdf (in Japanese).

## 2 *Elimination of Unnecessary Ban of Women's Remarriage; The Supreme Court's Judgement and Amendment of Article 733 of the Civil Code*

### a Supreme Court's Judgement[12]

In Japan, women could not remarry within six months after their divorce. This prohibition is introduced to protect possible children born after such a divorce. While this prohibition is helpful to discern who is the father of a child it has been criticized to impose undue restriction of remarriage only on women.

The old Article 733 of the Civil Code related to the ban of women's remarriage and Article 772 of the Civil Code related to the presumption of paternity of a child provides as follows:[13]

Article 733

(1) A woman may not remarry unless six months have passed since the day of dissolution or rescission of her previous marriage.

(2) In the case where a woman had conceived a child before the cancellation or dissolution of her previous marriage, the provision of the preceding paragraph shall not apply.

Article 772

(1) A child conceived by a wife during marriage shall be presumed to be a child of her husband.

(2) A child born after 200 days from the formation of marriage or within 300 days of the day of the dissolution or rescission of marriage shall be presumed to have been conceived during marriage.

The appellant suffered from domestic violence of her previous husband and applied for divorced. She divorced her husband in 2008 and gave birth to a daughter on the 221st day after the divorce. Since she could not remarry with

12 Judgment concerning whether the part of the provision of Article 733, paragraph (1) of the Civil Code, which prescribes the 100-days period of prohibition of remarriage violates Article 14, paragraph (1) and Article 24, paragraph (2) of the Constitution, 16 December 2015, 2013 (O) 1079, Minshu Vol. 69, No. 8, available at: http://www.courts.go.jp/app/hanrei_en/detail?id=1418.

13 Civil Code, available at: http://www.japaneselawtranslation.go.jp/law/detail/?id=2252&vm=04&re=02.

the current husband during six months from the divorce, her daughter born in 221 days from her divorce is presumed to be a child in wedlock of the previous husband and could not be registered as a child in wedlock of the current husband. She tried to register her as a child in wedlock of the current husband, but found that her child has to be registered as a child in wedlock of the previous husband, nevertheless the reason of divorce is domestic violence of the previous husband and damages was sought under the State Redress Act, alleging that Article 733 (1) of the Civil Code violates Article 14(1) and Article 24(2) of the Constitution and mental distress accumulated from the six month prohibition of remarriage should be compensated. The appellant also argued there is legislative inaction.

Article 14(1) provides that "(1) All of the people are equal under the law and there shall be no discrimination in political, economic or social relations because of race, creed, sex, social status or family origin" and Article 24(2) provides that "With regard to choose of spouse, property rights, inheritance, choice of domicile, divorce and other matters pertaining to marriage and the family, laws shall be enacted from the standpoint of individual dignity and the essential equality of the sexes."[14]

Article 772(2) of the Civil Code expects that it is possible to avoid confusion over paternity if a child will be born within 300 days from the death or divorce of the previous marriage and after 200 days from the formation of the current marriage. That is, a child who is born within 300 days from the death of the partner or divorce with the partner, is presumed to be a child of the previous partner. On the other hand, a child who is born after 200 days from the formation of the current marriage is presumed to be a child of the current partner. Therefore, according to Article 772(2), if women divorced and remarry at the same time and her child is born, for example, in 250 days, the father of a child is presumed to be both the previous partner and the current partner.

Therefore, in order to avoid such confusion, Article 733 of the Civil Code provides the ban to remarry for six months. In that case, a child who is born in 250 days from divorce is presumed to be a child only of the previous partner, since based on Article 733, women are forced to wait to remarry for six months and only after 70 days have passed from the date of remarriage if a child is born in 250 days from the divorce. Then such a child never meets the other criteria which Article 733 provides: after 200 days from the formation of the current

14 The Constitution of Japan, available at: http://www.japaneselawtranslation.go.jp/law/detail/?id=174.

marriage. Even a child is born at the time of 300 days form the divorce, the father of a child is presumed again to be the previous partner, since it does not meet the criteria in that it just passed 120 days from the formation of the current marriage if a woman remarried in wait for ending six-month ban. There is no case to be presumed in an overlapped way, based upon Articles 733 and 772. However, it is criticized to have six-month remarriage ban, since there is just 100-day interval between the presumption of the previous husband and current husband. Such criticism has pointed out the remarriage ban should be invoked only to fill in such 100 days' interval.

Therefore, the Supreme Court decided it is unnecessary prohibition of remarry for women and concluded that it violates if prohibition is beyond 100 days. However, it did determine the constitutionality of prohibition of 100 days nevertheless of the high possibility to discern the father of a child by scientific means such as examination of DNAs.

One of the main reasons is to stabilize the paternity of a child. If a child is born between a married couple, such child automatically can acquire the status of a legitimate child. If a child is born among non-married couple, he/she is treated as a child out of wedlock and should get affiliation from the father. While a child out of wedlock gets affiliation from his/her father, he/she will have a right of inheritance from the father, a child who is not acknowledged cannot have a right of inheritance.

While the Court fully admits the usefulness of scientific methods to identify the paternity of a child, the Court was concerned and pointed out the unstable status of a child who are forced to wait for the result of scientific examination and the judicial procedure to know his/her legal father.

In conclusion, the Supreme Court held that "the part of the Provision prescribing the 100-day period of prohibition of remarriage does not violate Article 14, paragraph (1) of the Constitution nor Article 24, paragraph (2) of the Constitution. On the other hand, the remaining part of the Provision prescribing the prohibition of remarriage for a period exceeding 100 days cannot be justified as setting a period necessary for avoiding confusion over paternity, as provided in Article 772 of the Civil Code."

As the Court examined, (1) in the past, the drafters of the Former Civil Code should not be accused, since, at that time, it might be reasonable to have six-month prohibition of remarriage. It is expected that people can easily recognize appearance of pregnancy within six month. They feel 100 days' length is not enough to know pregnancy, (2) Foreign countries, which have also provisions on the prohibition of remarriage have abolished such a system, (3) Nowadays, it is not entirely the case that there might occur a confusion in respect of the paternity of a child. It is not rare for women to give a birth to a child less than 200 days from the time of marriage. Nevertheless, to impose the restriction more than 100 days only in the case of remarriage is deemed to be excessive.

This judgment is a landmark ruling in that it clarified the partial unconditionality of Article 733. On the other hand, the court did deny the application of State Redress Act to compensate the appellant, based on the examination that there had been and are discretion of the Diet to address the reasonable length of prohibition.

### b Amendment to the Civil Code

After this judgement, the Diet decided to revise Article 733 of the Civil Code and enact the new provision,[15] considering also that the UN Committee on the Elimination of Discrimination against Women has repeatedly called on Japan to drop the ban. The New provision of Article 733 is as follows:

(1) A woman may not remarry unless six months have passed since the day of dissolution or rescission of her previous marriage.
(2) The provision of the preceding paragraph shall not apply.
  (i) In case where a woman did not conceive a child at the time of cancellation or dissolution of her previous marriage.
  (ii) In case where a woman gave birth a child after cancellation or dissolution of her previous marriage.[16]

Accordingly, women are subject to shorter remarriage prohibition period (100 days), minimizing "the interval" where the father of a child may be redundantly presumed to be either the previous husband (within 300 days from the divorce) or the current husband (200 days after the marriage) at the time of birth of a child.

More importantly, the revised law allows women who are able to prove by using medical certificates, not to be conceived of a child at the time of divorce, to remarry even right after the divorce.

15 Tomohiro Ōsaki, "Diet scraps dated marriage-ban law as session wraps up," THE JAPAN TIMES, available at: http://www.japantimes.co.jp/news/2016/06/01/national/politics-diplomacy/diet-scraps-dated-marriage-ban-law-as-session-wraps-up.

16 Translation by the Author: available at: http://www.moj.go.jp/content/001184601.pdf (Only in Japanese).

## IV Conclusion

This note described significant developments in the State practice of Japan in the area of international human rights law. The reactivation of the nuclear power plant reactors, where "personal rights" were invoked to issue an injunction and the increasing protection accorded to children and women.

However, it is not yet sufficient in some areas. As mentioned above, on 16 December 2015, the Japanese Supreme court ruled that Article 750 of the Civil Code forcing married couples to use the same surname does not violate the Constitution. Oguni and four other women sought damages for the emotional distress and practical inconvenience of having to take their husband's name. Oguni, one of the appellant, said that "By losing your surname … you're being made light of, you're not respected … It's as if part of yourself vanishes," and "If changing surnames is so easy, why don't more men do it? The system is one that says, basically, if you're not willing to change, you shouldn't be getting married."[17]

While the law does not designate which name married couples should adopt, in practice in almost all cases, or about 96 per cent, women take their husband's surname.

Japan has certainly improved its human rights situation to meet the international standard provided under numerous international human rights agreements, starting from the ICCPR. However, Japan should continue its effort to fulfil its human rights obligation much more seriously.

---

17 *Japan upholds rule that married couples must have same surname*, THE GUARDIAN, available at: https://www.theguardian.com/world/2015/dec/16/japanese-court-rules-married-women-cannot-keep-their-surnames.

# Status and International Cooperation Aspects of Air Quality Control Laws and Policies in Korea

*Taegil Kim and Eonkyung Park*[1]

## I Introduction

### 1 *Purpose and Object*

The note focuses on the State practice of Korea with regard to air quality control, especially from 2015 to 2016, and some pieces of information before 2015. The main focus are Korean domestic laws and administrative policies, and their implications upon the State practice. The relevant domestic laws are 'Clean Air Conservation Act,' 'Framework Act on Low Carbon, Green Growth,' and 'Act on the Allocation and Trading of Greenhouse-gas Emission Permits.' The administrative practices are collected mainly from 'The 2nd Comprehensive Plans to Improve the Atmospheric Environment (2016–2025)' (2nd Comprehensive Plans), which were unveiled by the Ministry of Environment, the supervisory body of the atmospheric environment, on 31 December 2015. Assembly resolutions, in addition, are introduced.

### 2 *Structure of Korean Air Quality Control Laws and Policies*

Korean polices of air quality control include two pillars: one is 'air pollutants control' and the other is 'greenhouse gas (GHG) mitigation.' The former mainly relates to domestic vehicle policies and transboundary pollutants from China. The latter relates to internal regulations, incentives and investment and relating to international cooperation and international market mechanism.

A clear structure is drawn in the 2nd Comprehensive Plans, which demonstrates that the Korean government is trying to integrate and manage the two pillars for better efficiency. The Plans have an abundance of domestic policies which strengthen regulations, on the one hand, and support eco-friendly industries, on the other hand. It states international efforts heading for the conclusion of regional agreements among the Northeast Asian countries.

---

1 Kyung Hee University, Korea.

 | DOI 10.1163/9789004344556_013

## II Domestic Laws

### 1 *Clean Air Conservation Act*

#### a Introduction

The Clean Air Conservation Act[2] functions as a framework act managing air quality and atmospheric condition. The purpose of the Act is to enable all people to live in a healthy and comfortable environment by preventing air pollution which causes harm to people and atmospheric condition and by managing and preserving the atmospheric environment in a proper and sustainable manner.[3] The Act identifies 22 terms such as air pollutant, air pollutants subject to watch for hazard, climate/ecosystem-changing substances, greenhouse gases, gas, granular matter, dust, exhaust fumes, soot, specified hazardous air pollutant, volatile organic compound, air pollutant-emitting facilities, air pollution prevention facilities, among others,[4] which have direct and indirect effects on interpreting the other air quality control regulations. The Act mandates the Minister of Environment to establish and implement Comprehensive Plans every ten years in order to improve the atmospheric environment by reducing air pollutants and GHG.[5] The act provides the legal basis that ensures the Comprehensive Plans works.

The current inclination of the Act, in accordance with recent amendments, shows two features. First, the amendments to the Act relate to damage prevention of long-range transboundary air pollutants and international cooperation for prevention. Second, articles on certain industries, especially vehicle industries, which produce specified hazardous air pollutants, are progressively tightened via amendments of the Enforcement Ordinance of the Act.

#### b Recent Amendment upon Long-Range Transboundary Air Pollutant

The amendment on 1 December 2015 implies the changing stance of the government toward transboundary pollution, which seems to mirror the public perception, that there is a more serious problem than "yellow sand." The definition of 'long-range transboundary air pollutant' is newly introduced in the amendment. The term, strictly speaking, is replaced with the 'yellow sand' which is wind-brown dust from China to the Korean Peninsula. The article before the amendment regulated upon the operation of A Yellow Dust

2 Act No. 13874, Partially amended on 27 January 2016.

3 *Ibid.* art. 1.

4 *Ibid.* art. 2.

5 *Ibid.* art. 11.

Prevention Committee and the prevention of yellow dust,[6] but the revised one expands the object of regulation to the air pollutants over the yellow dust and the Committee also changed into A Long-Range Transboundary Air Pollutant Committee.

The amendment is more detailed than before. The original text put endeavors to cooperate with relevant nations to the government. The amendment, however, enumerates seven specific means that elaborate the endeavors to co-operate: (i) holding, supporting and participating in various events, such as international conferences and academic conferences; (ii) exchanges of technology and human resources, and cooperation, between relevant countries and with international organizations; (iii) supporting research on long-range transboundary air pollutants, and disseminating findings of the research; (iv) education and public relations on long-range transboundary air pollutants in the international community; (v) raising financial resources to prevent damage caused by long-range transboundary air pollutants; (vi) establishing an air pollution monitoring system and implementing environmental cooperation and conservation projects in Northeast Asia; (vii) any other matters necessary for international cooperation.[7]

### c Strengthened Restrictions upon a Certain Industry

The amendment on 27 January 2016 focused on legal restrictions on the domestic vehicle industry. According to the amended Article 46(4) and Article 89.6-2, prohibits motor vehicle manufacturers from intentionally altering or manipulating the design of components related to exhaust gases differently from the details of certification obtained under relative provisions, and a wrongdoer shall be punished by imprisonment for not more than seven years or by a fine not exceeding 100 million KRW, or about 90,000 USD. In addition, the wrongdoers who manufacture and sell motor vehicles without obtaining certification and/or motor vehicles different from the details of certification obtained may be imposed a penalty surcharge of up to 10 billion KRW, or about 9 million USD.[8] The amount decupled, or increased by ten times from one billion KRW to 10 billion KRW.

The amendment, in the meantime, promotes and incentives eco-friendly technologies in the industries. The newly inserted provisions allows the Minister of Environment to build the charging information network to manage the information of car charging, to install and operate charging facilities for

6 Art. 13, 14, and 15, Act No. 13034, Partially amended 20 January 2015.

7 Art. 1, *supra* note 2.

8 *Ibid.* art. 56.

electric motor vehicles, and to evaluate the performance of electric vehicles to determine persons eligible for subsidies or loans.[9]

#### d Comment

The amendment on 1 December 2015 introduced new regulations upon damage prevention caused by the long range transboundary air pollutant and revised related articles on the Act. The amendment on 16 January 2016 fortified the restriction on the vehicle industries and simultaneously tried to activate new eco-technologies. The amendment mirrored the perception of Korea that domestic air pollution has been resulting not only from national causes but also from foreign ones. However, any restriction against countries or foreign industries attributable is not found in the Act. The Act relies only upon such soft means as civil communications (especially, international academic exchange), international cooperation, research support and dissemination, education and public relations activities. Meanwhile, effluent gases from vehicle pipes are dealt with as objects of tough sanctions. And the goal and purpose of the sanctions is clearly declared to protect national health and to prevent aggravation of air pollution.

This may be interpreted that the government prefers a political approach to a legal approach that appeals to international settlement. Our opinion is that the approach is a good choice for Korea. International environmental laws have been perceived in the way that the enforcement of these laws is still weak since they are operated on the basis of reciprocity. In such an international atmosphere, Korea fortifies and implements strong regulations at the level of international environment agreements or over the level, which can be a bedrock to push other countries for fortified standards.

### 2 *Framework Act on Low Carbon, Green Growth*

#### a Introduction

The 'Framework Act on Low Carbon, Green Growth'('Framework Act'),[10] adopted at the 8th Cabinet Meeting held under the superintendence of the President on 25 February 2008 and enacted on 14 April 2010, highlights two aspects: the environment('low carbon') and the economy ('green growth'). The Framework Act pushes the government to build up a comprehensive national development strategy, and to vitalize market functions initiated by the private sector, at the same time. In other words, the Framework Act propels the maximal role of private markets to help the air quality better by minimizing

9 *Ibid.* art. 58(15)~(17).

10 Act No. 13874, Partially amended on 27 January 2016.

nuisance restrictions to the economy. Article 1 envisages and underlines that its purpose is economic growth and the take-off to a mature, top-class, advanced country via the realization of a low-carbon society. The definitions of the terms in Article 2 focus mostly on such economics-related words such as growth, technology, industry, product, management, and so on.

### b Governance of Climate Change Mitigation

The Framework Act proposes the legal frame of the climate change governance.[11] The Cooperation and interdependence of each economic shaft such as the central government, local governments, business entities, and citizens is underlined.[12] Article 38 envisages the understanding of gravity of the climate change caused by global warming and the need to cover-all countermeasures by the whole nation. Simultaneously, the provision orders that mid-term and long-term goal of national GHG mitigation shall be be set up. The specific roadmap is entrusted to the lower legislation such as Presidential Decrees and/or Enforcement Ordinances, but still it signposts the ways underlining the development and utilization of cutting-edge technologies and converging technologies.[13] And the market mechanism is adopted with provisions to provide for international carbon market.

The Chapter 2 of the Act provides that 'National Strategy for Low Carbon, Green Growth' shall be established and implemented by the government, and the National Strategy may be under the control of the Prime Minister. Action Plans implementing the National Strategy, furthermore, shall be established by the central government and each local government respectively. The realization of green economic system, green technology and green industries, policies for coping with climate change, policies on energy and policies on sustainable development, and matters concerning negotiations and cooperation in relation to low carbon, green growth including climate change are included in the National Strategy. They are deliberated by the Presidential Committee on Green Growth, which is the core deliberation agency upon low carbon and green growth policies, and then brought to the State Council.

The amendment on 24 May 2016 includes transfer of jurisdiction over the Integrated Information Center for Greenhouse Gases to the Office for Government Coordination from the Ministry of Environment, which means that the Center came under the jurisdiction of the Prime Minister, in order to peak

11 *Ibid.* art. 4(1).

12 *Ibid.* art. 5(1) and 6.

13 *Ibid.* art. 38(3).

efficiency.[14] The role of the Center is deeply relating to the establishment of specific targets via studies and research. After the evaluation of its status, the Ministers of many relating agencies shall cooperate with the Center upon the work of it.

### c Implementation of the Paris Agreement

The Framework Act implies that the target mitigation shall be regulated by the lower legislation, and the Enforcement Decree of the Framework Act stipulates the national reduction target. The Article 25 of the Enforcement Decree provides, "The target for the reduction of greenhouse gases ... shall be to reduce total nationwide emissions of GHG in 2030 to 37/100 of the estimated emissions of GHG in 2020." The provision incorporates the Paris Agreement, signed on 22 April 2016 and entered into force 3 December 2016, and, interestingly, it was amended on 24 May 2016 even before the entry into force of the Agreement. The 36% (compared to BAU) is the same numerical value with the figure of the INDC which Korea voluntarily announced in June 2015.

The Framework Act provides establishment of the med- and long-term targets and the goals attached to each particular phase, and measures necessary for accomplishing the targets by the government.[15] And the government may require appropriate 'central administrative agencies, local governments, and public institutions' to set up targets for energy saving and targets for the reduction of greenhouse gases.[16] Furthermore, a measurable, reportable and verifiable manner is required so as to hit the targets for such sectors as industry, traffic, transportation, household, and commerce, which established and managed by the government.[17]

### d Comment

The title of the Framework Act consists of two key words; low carbon and green growth. The provisions, however, seem to give weight to green growth rather than environmental protection. Thus, some criticize that the Act puts economic growth before the environment. Some provisions of the Framework Act, in addition, are inconsistent with the Paris Agreement unlike the purpose of the Act and the announcement of the government. However, two ideas require concern. First, it should be considered that a change of a formed system may cost quit expenses, especially when the system had been formed without

14 Art. 36(1) of Enforcement Decree of the Framework Act on Low Carbon, Green Growth. Enforced on 1 June 2016, Presidential Decree No. 27180, amended on 24 May 2016.

15 *Supra* note 10, art. 42(1)1.

16 *Ibid.* art. 42(1)3.

17 *Ibid.* art. 42(5).

economic consideration. The system designed to cost can be sophisticated and refined. Second, swift amendments of the Framework Act can help prevent "race to the bottom," on which each country would alleviate their environmental standard to accelerate capital attraction.

### 3 *Act on the Allocation and Trading of Greenhouse-Gas Emission Permits*

#### a Introduction

'Act on Allocation and Trading of Greenhous-gas Emission Permits' ('Emission Permits Act') aims at the realization of the market mechanism enshrined in the Framework Act. In other words, the Emission Permits Act is a legal ground for the market system to allocate and transact emission permits so as to achieve the mitigation goal established in accordance with the Framework Act, and its lower legislations.

#### b Amendment Relating to the Paris Agreement

The Enforcement Decree[18] was amended on 24 May 2016, which the amendment was almost about the change of jurisdiction over the GHG allocation and trading. The general controller was changed to the Deputy Prime Minister for Economic Affairs. National emission allowances, emission trade exchange, Emissions Certificate Committee, and other tasks in general are placed under the agency. Allocation plans, emission permits in reserve, designation of emission trade exchange, measures for market stabilization, the organization and operation of the Certificate Committee, and the designation of recognition agencies became under the control of the Minister of Strategy and Finance, which is held concurrently by the Deputy Prime Minister for Economic Affairs.[19] Such executive tasks as permits allocation, adjustment of permits allocation, report-authentication, and penalty surcharging were transferred from the Minister of Environment to the Minister of Agriculture, Food and Rural Affairs, Minister of Trade, Industry and Energy, Minister of Environment, Minister of Land, Infrastructure and Transport, and/or Minister of Maritime Affairs and Fisheries, respectively.[20]

#### c Comment

Empowerment into various government branches, which looks like an effort to connect domestic transaction to the international carbon exchanges, is the highlight of the amendment of the Emission Permits Act. In spite of some

18 Presidential Decree No. 27181, partially amended on 24 May 2016.

19 *Ibid.* art. 3, 4, 5 and 32.

20 *Ibid.* art. 6(1)2 and 26(3).

criticisms that such empowerment may result in the absence of coherence of the policy, it may produce positive results. First, it may enhance flexibility and responsibility for the system of the controllers. Second, such an effort to active carbon exchanges may boost autonomous technical development by private industries and lower GHG emissions. This seems important because the relative new comer, Korea, in carbon exchanges has not been equipped with a complete market to enter the international market system. The effort of the government policy, however, should be rated 'positive' because the Korean exchange continues to grow and, simultaneously, the flow of permits is also slightly growing.

## III Administrative Measures

### 1 *Background*

In accordance with the specifics of the 1st Comprehensive Plans, which is the first package of nationwide 10-year-plans in the atmosphere-climate sector by a planning law, or Article 11 of Clean Air Conservative Act. The Plans affirms such schemes as GHG mitigation, integrated climate-atmosphere systems, climate change adaptation, establishment on management system for greenhouse gas emission, establishment on implementation process for Kyoto mechanism, technical development for support businesses, incentives to induce reduction, and international cooperation. For forcing the plans, the government drafted and the Assembly enacted 'Framework Act of Low Carbon, Green Growth' in April 2010, and 'Act on the Allocation and Trading of Greenhouse-gas Emission Permits' in May 2012 and the domestic emission trading system has been operating from 2015. The government, furthermore, invited Green Climate Fund and has been enhancing its negotiating leverage at international bargaining tables.

The 2nd Comprehensive Plans, meanwhile, focuses on integrated response to climate change and lowing damage caused by certain air pollutants. The change is attributable to the fact: While climate change has been resulting in increasing damage due to extreme weather in Korean Peninsula,[21] increasing damage seems to be cumulating owing to growing consumption of natural resources by both Korea and China recently. The 2nd Plans shows explicit numerical numbers that back up such an assumption that domestic find dust,

21 Yeora Chae, *et al.* Economic Analysis of Climate Change in Korea, Research Report, 2012.

Nitrogen ($NO_2$), Ozone ($O_3$), and other Hazardous Air Pollutants (HAPs) has been resulting in serious air pollution.[22] The Plans also anticipates the increasing risk factors, or transboundary air pollutants, from the growing economy.[23]

### 2 *Cores of the 2nd Comprehensive Plans*

#### a Air Quality Improvement

The current state and prospect of air pollutants, targets and measures to decrease air pollutant including HAPs, and atmosphere management system integrating air pollutants with GHGs are dealt with in the 2nd Comprehensive Plans.[24] Air quality improvement includes six major objectives: establishment of atmosphere management system, advancement emission management of workplaces, reduction in all steps of vehicle operation, eradication of hidden pollutants in the daily living, safe atmospheric environment from HAPs, and promoting technological foundation. While the 5 metropolitan cities and the cities with populations of 500 thousand or more were under management by the 1st Comprehensive Plans, the 2nd Plans administers the nationwide area taking into comprehensive consideration of regional statue of pollution and environmental risk. The objects to be managed by priority are the level of fine dust under PM10/PM25, Ozone and Nitrogen, emission quantity of Nitrogen and volatile organic compounds (VOCs), and the risk of HAPs.

The 2nd Comprehensive Plans included detailed solutions upon certain vehicle industries. The solutions, so called 'mobile pollution sources measures', deals with production cars, moving cars, two wheels motors, and non-road mobile pollution sources. This may be regarded as stepped-up emission management over the conventional vehicles. Meanwhile, the Plans provides for various ideas to expand eco-vehicle consumption. It presents a specific numerical value and eco-cars over 3,300,000 goes to road in 2025. In order to get to the goal, enlargement of consumer benefit such as consumer subsidies and eco-incentives are laid out.

#### b Climate Change Response Plans

Climate mitigation response establishes long-term carbon reduction plans, adaptation, and international cooperation. Following the Paris Agreement and the ratification by Korea, first of all, the government is to increase in the

---

22 The 2nd Comprehensive Plans to Improve the Atmospheric Environment (2016–2025), announced by the Ministry of Environment on 31 January 2015, at. 35–36.

23 *Ibid.* at. 32.

24 *Ibid.* at. 1.

BAU reductions in comparison with the reductions of the 1st Comprehensive Plan. Four sections to propel are GHG reductions in industrial department, the leading country for low-carbon life, reinforcement of adaptation capacity in the whole society, a win-win approach between climate and economy.

The 2nd Comprehensive Plans in the industrial department help advance carbon exchanges, support the business participating the exchanges, activate emissions offsetting in non-industrial sectors, and give efforts to join in international carbon markets. For the leading country for low-carbon life, in addition, the Plans propel the climate change response capacity of local governments, expansion of GHG reduction in the transportation sector, management of GHGs like freon gas, development of programs for green life, enlargement of low-carbon production and consumption. And reinforcement of adaptation capacity in the whole society includes the adaptation governance, observation-forecast-analysis capacity, fosterage of adaptation industries taking advantage of climate change, and social security system from the climate change. Lastly, for a win-win approach between climate and economy, the Plans devise schemes such as climate-energy ties, increased investment in R&Ds, neo-climate regime negotiations and international cooperation, and enhanced operation for exhaust statistics.

### c Comment

The air quality improvement covers a reinforced restriction over a certain vehicle industry and activation of new eco-industries, and international trade dispute may arise in terms of the WTO regime. Though the specific figures and policies seem to be induced because of the gravity and severity of national air environment, the point may be seen is the prohibited protection of a national industry in conjunction with the WTO Regime which prohibits discriminatory protection of home industries. However, WTO cases such as US-Gasoline, US-Shrimp, and EC-Asbestos recognized the need of environment protection, which is not the disguised restriction benefiting to national industry. The plans to low-carbon vehicles will enlarge the portion of high efficient and low-carbon cars and result in significant carbon reduction in the transportation sector and the plans does not distinguish Korea from foreign countries.

The climate change response is to hit the INDC goal in a manner of the total participation of central government-local government-(juristic/natural) person and international cooperation. In the meantime, the 2nd Comprehensive Plans anticipate the national side effects of mitigation, especially economic ones, and emphasize economic growth making the best use of carbon mitigation. The integrated effort may help secure the sustainability of climate change response.

## IV National Assembly Resolutions

The last meaningful action is the recursive announcement of Assembly Resolutions. Almost every year, the assembly or some members of the assembly calls for substantial reduction of the domestic fine dust and support for it, and substantial cooperation with neighboring States. A Resolution in 2014 starts with the mention, "For years to come, more frequent breakouts are expected, and repeating yellow sand may result in national disaster."[25] And it states, "A benchmark of the 'UNECE Convention on Long Range Transboundary Air Pollution' is in need … we strongly insist that Korea-China-Japan Convention on Long Range Transboundary Air Pollution' to set up the unified standard of air pollutant emission and enforce the standard." The resolution in 2015 starts with a prod for instant and active measures to reduce fine dust. It shows well the perception of Korean nationals upon the fine dust. It states "… to be free from fear of fine dust …" and "Korean government must give efforts to strengthen cooperation with China and neighboring countries … and support internal industries relating to lowering fine dust."[26]

### 1 *Comment*

The Assembly Resolution, as a way to represent the will of people, offers a navigation of further legislation. Even though the serious wordings and grave nuance of the sentences, the law-makers appeal to cooperation not to international liability for damage in international relations. And internally, they are looking to alleviate the air pollution by the promotion and support for new technology. This is similar to the stance of the government.

## V Conclusion

Scratching the surface of the practices, a few tendencies can be found. First, the stance of Korea is to appeal not to international responsibility but to international cooperation, especially between/among East Asian counties. Second, Korea responds quickly to meet the obligations under international agreements such as the IPCC recommendation. Third, Korea is eager to make certain industries developed, or to become eco-vehicle industries.

---

25 Assembly Resolution Insisting Conclusion of Korea-China-Japan Convention on Long Range Transboundary Air Pollution, submitted on 28 February 2014.

26 Assembly Resolution Insisting Measures to Protect the National Health from Fine Dust, announced on 30 April 2015.

This approach seems to be induced, on the surface, because fine dust from Korea and China are getting more and more serious and air pollution threatens Korean nationals. Climate change will have a substantial effect on the Korean Peninsula. One other reason for the approach is reciprocity. International law on the environment are still under development and imperfect. So Korea seems hard to meet her expectation in the way of an appeal to the international environmental laws. However, Korean implementation of the international standards such as IPCC recommendation can be a basis to urge other State with stronger implementation on the basis of reciprocity. A very good example of normalization of reciprocity are the Articles upon Harmonization under the SPS Agreement, and Mutual Recognition under TBT Agreement which became normalized in the WTO legal system. In the same manner, many elements of the environmental sphere may be normalized in the form of mutual recognition and reciprocity. The 2nd Comprehensive Pans expressly declare that Korea will make efforts to take a lead in the field of environment protection. This declaration may be based on the philosophy and principle of philosophy.

On investments made to the car industry, some WTO-related problems may be raised. The international economic sector, however, is also changing to consider environment protection. And formal WTO cases such as US-Gasoline, US-Shrimp, and EC-Asbestos showed that regulations for the purpose of environmental protection can be recognized. As long as Korea avoids to operate its policies without disguised trade restrictions, there may be no need for future settlement of disputes.

# The Waste You Left Behind: Polluter Liability as Tort Korean Supreme Court Decision (2009 Da 66549)

*Kyu Rang Kim and Seong Won Lee*[1]

## 1 Introduction

Traditionally in Korea, environmental rights under the Constitution and environmental laws form the basis of an individual's public obligation to prevent environmental pollution. Thus, environmental pollution has not, until now, been considered the subject of private law. This is reflected in the Supreme Court Decision of 2002, where a buyer of land (Plaintiff) sued the seller (Defendant) who had polluted the land, for the cost of purification in the form of damages under tort. In this particular case, the Supreme Court held that a tort could not be found because the Defendant had not harmed anyone other than himself, since at the time of pollution, the land belonged to the Defendant. Therefore, since the Supreme Court found that there was no damage to another, it held that an award in tort for damages was inappropriate. The importance of environmental awareness is growing all over the world, shaping every discipline. This trend is also reflected in the change in stance of the Supreme Court. The 2016 Supreme Court dramatically changed its position after fourteen years and stated that the current landowner had the right to impose liability on the former owner, (the polluter), for committing tort against the current owner, by infringing the current owner's right to enjoy ownership of untainted land. In effect, the Supreme Court's holding allows for a current landowner to hold a former landowner liable for costs incurred for the purification of polluted land where there were no other contractual or legal relations whatsoever between the two, other than the fact that both parties owned the same piece of land at different times. Many are concerned that the changed decision of the Supreme Court exceeds the bounds of civil regulations for the sake of promoting environmental conservation.

Whether environmental rights can be based on civil liability is still the subject of controversy among legal scholars in Korea. At the very least, it is notable

1 Kyu Rang Kim and Seong Won Lee are both JD Candidates, Inha University Law School, Korea. This article has been edited by Hana Shoji, Research Fellow, The Development of International Law in Asia-Korea (DILA-Korea), Korea.

DOI 10.1163/9789004344556_014

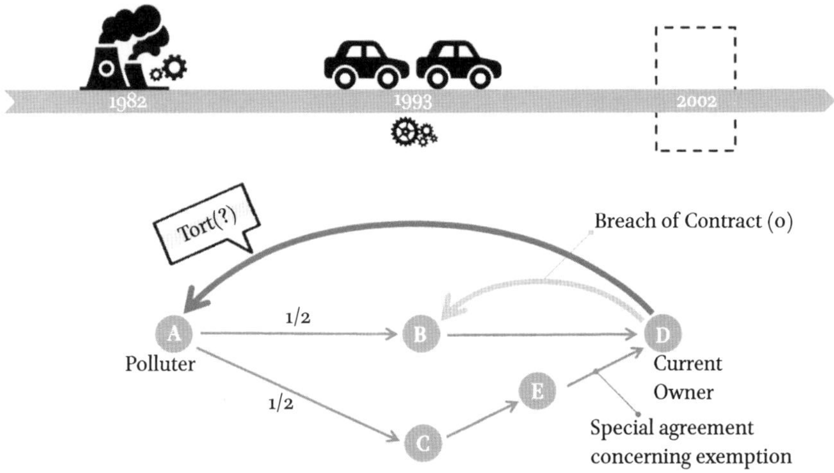


DIAGRAM 1 *Fact pattern*

that in this case, the Supreme Court recognized tort liability borrowing from principles of environmental rights under the constitution and environmental laws.

## II Facts of the Case and Issue

### 1 *Facts of the 2016 Supreme Court Case (As illustrated in Diagram 1 above)*

A. Company A ("Defendant Company A") had been operating a casting foundry for roughly twenty years since 1973 and caused soil contamination. On 21 December 1993, Company A sold one-half of the land to Company B ("Defendant Company B") and Company D ("Plaintiff"), respectively.

B. In 1993, Company C demolished the casting foundry and underwent reclamation works (project outsourced by Defendant Company A), and proceeded to perform works such as surface grading in order to build an automobile shipment factory (project outsourced by Defendant Company B). Company C tore down the surface structures, excluding the subterranean structures located below the surface of the land and buried the construction waste. Company C then proceeded to carry out surface grading and asphalt overlaying works. From around July 1994,

Defendant Company B had been using the land as an automobile shipment factory.

C. On June 28, 2000 Company E purchased Company C's share of the land.

D. In planning to build a multi-electronics distribution center on the land, Company D purchased one-half of the land from Company E in December 2001 and purchased the remaining half from Defendant Company B in February, 2002. Company D purchased the Instant Land without being aware of the soil contamination.

E. The price paid by Company D (Plaintiff) for the land was 24,500,000,000 KRW (approximately 21.5 million USD). However, on top of that, Company D (Plaintiff) paid an additional 10,879,199,388 KRW (approximately 9.6 million USD) in clean up costs for the disposal of contaminated soil and waste on the land during construction. As a result, Company D (Plaintiff) was made to bear unexpected clean up costs amounting to almost half of the purchase price.

## 2 *Issue*

The main issue of this case is whether Company D (Current Landowner) can claim damages against Company A (Polluter) despite not having a direct relationship?

### a Need to Find Tort Liability for the Current Landowner (Company D)

In cases where the current landowner, without having been aware of the land contamination at the time of purchase, incurs costs from the purification of contamination or from the removal of waste, he may impose liability on the former owner, the vendor of the contaminated land, for the default of obligation or warranty for defects derived from imperfect fulfillment. However, it is often difficult for the purchaser to become aware of the existence of latent defects, such as "hidden" contaminated soil or waste buried underground, particularly in cases where there is no cause of doubt giving rise to a reason to know of the contamination. It is common in such situations that the purchaser would not have an opportunity to reach a reasonable agreement for such conditions at the time of signing the contract, or that the purchaser may fail to seek compensation within the appropriate time period for default of obligation or warranty for defects. In the present case, the Supreme Court recognized the contractual liability of Company B. However, due to the existence of an agreement of exemption with regards to liability between Company D and Company E, Company D was unable to bring a lawsuit against Company E. Therefore, Company D was unable to recover half of the purification fee, which is why Company D commenced litigation against Company A, the original polluter.

#### b The Difficulty of Finding Liability against Original Polluter (Company A)

In cases where the landowner causes soil contamination on the landowner's own land and the contaminated land is then sold to two different owners who subsequently sell the land, there is no contractual relationship between the very first landowner (the polluter) and the current landowner. Thus, the current landowner cannot hold the first owner liable for the default of obligation or responsible for a warranty against defects. However, as mentioned above, considering the difficulty in seeking compensation for damages incurred by "hidden" contamination and the burden of costs incurred by the current owner for the actions of another in contaminating the land, it is justifiable to establish the liability of the first landowner to compensate the current owner. However, problems arise from two elements; on what grounds and to what extent may the current landowner hold the first landowner liable for compensation?

## III Decisions of the Supreme Court

### 1 *The Supreme Court Decision of 2002 Resulted in "No Finding of Tort Liability."*

Prior to the present case, cases with similar facts had been brought to court. In each instance, there was an initial polluter (Defendant) who polluted the land, sold the contaminated land to a buyer, who in turn subsequently sold the land to the current owner (Plaintiff), who later discovered that the land had been contaminated. Following numerous cases, the Supreme Court Decision 99Da16460 decided on 11 January 2002 held that:

1. Setting aside the fact that the Defendant, without obtaining approval from the Minister of Environment, etc. as prescribed by the Wastes Control Act, buried waste on the land of the instant case which was owned by the Defendant, and thereby having received administrative sanction or criminal punishment, the Defendant's act was committed against oneself rather than a third party and thus, tort is not established. In addition, as the Defendant's act in and of itself cannot be deemed to have caused any damages whatsoever to the Plaintiff, it cannot be concluded that the Defendant committed an unlawful act against the Plaintiff who obtained ownership of this case's land after the Defendant buried the waste.

2. Although tort can be established in cases where the Defendant's act of burying the waste caused damages to owners of nearby land or residents, the Defendant cannot be said to be liable for tort committed against the Plaintiff (new buyer) and the Plaintiff does not have the right to claim damages incurred therefrom.[2]

The Supreme Court expressed that, even if a person buried waste in one's own or another's land, the said person could not be held liable for tort committed against the buyer of the relevant land. In short, there was no finding of tort between the original polluter and the current owner. This ruling remained the established precedent for fourteen years until 2016 and the ruling of the present case.

### 2 *Decision of 2016 in Which "Tort Liability was Established"*

#### a Decisions of the Court of First Instance[3] and the Appellate Court[4]

Following established precedent, the first trial held that the case did not establish tort since the unlawful act was not committed against a third party. The act of contaminating the soil or burying the waste in and of itself could not be deemed to have caused damages to the one who acquired ownership of the land after the contamination had been carried out. In addition, it also stated that because the Waste Control Act regulates administrative duties, civil compensation for damages cannot be acknowledged directly under the abovementioned regulations; as long as general tort is not established, special tort, based upon the Soil Environment Conservation Act and Framework Act on Environmental Policy, also cannot be established.

However, on appeal, the Appellate Court held that tort could be established in this case. When the first landowner, who had contaminated the land, sold the land without notifying the subsequent owner of such conditions, the costs expended in land purification and the removal of waste were deemed to be foreseeable. The court also stated that the actions of the first landowner harmed the safety of transactions concerning the land and that it could be deemed the equivalent of creating a defective product and selling it to others, thereby damaging the trust of those who would acquire the land in the future.

Moreover, cause and effect was established by the court between the contamination caused by the polluter which resulted in damages in the form of waste disposal and land purification costs for which the current owner was

2 Supreme Court Decision 99Da16460.

3 Seoul Central District Court Decision 2006GaHap7988.

4 Seoul High Court Decision 2008Na92864.

left to bear. Such tort, established on the basis of one's illegal act, yields damages over time and when those potential damages become actualized, the tort could be said to be established upon the discovery of the land contamination and the duty to remove such contamination by the new landowner.

#### b The Decision of the Supreme Court[5]

In accordance with the decision of the Appellate Court, the Supreme Court determined that its 2002 ruling had been incorrect and sought to overturn it decision. The present case was heard before the entire bench of the Supreme Court of fourteen judges. The Majority held that where a previous landowner sells land after either:

i. causing soil pollution by discharging, leaking, dumping; or
ii. neglecting soil contaminants without subsequently purifying the contaminated soil, or
iii. illegally burying waste without subsequently treating the waste, the said act could be regarded a tort committed against the current owner of the land in question.[6]

Furthermore, the previous landowner, as the tortfeasor, could also be liable for compensating the current landowner for damages, in the form of costs incurred or to be incurred for purifying the contaminated land or treating the buried waste. In reaching their conclusion, the Majority referred to Article 35(1) of the Constitution, the former Framework Act on Environmental Policy, the former Soil Environment Conservation Act, and the former Wastes Control Act.

## IV Impact of the 2016 Decision

### 1 *Heavier Responsibility of the Polluter*

As discussed above, the change in position of the Supreme Court allows the current landowner to hold the former landowner (polluter) responsible for tort committed in civil law. It could be said that the responsibility of the former landowner (polluter) has been aggravated in many ways.

5 Supreme Court en banc Decision 2009Da66549, Decided 19 May 2016 (First Draft), available at: http://library.scourt.go.kr/SCLIB_data/decision/22-2009Da66549_soil%20contamination_jh.htm.

6 *Ibid.*

It is possible for the Polluter to be held liable in tort even without direct contractual relationship. Moreover, regardless of a special agreement concerning the exemption of the duty of land purification at any stage in the chain of land transactions, the current landowner can still bring an action in tort against the Polluter to recover the cost of land purification. Thus, even if the Polluter sells the contaminated land at a lower price to factor in the purification costs, as long as the waste remains on the land, the Polluter is potentially at risk of paying purification costs to landowners further down the chain. Therefore, this doubles the Polluter's burden.

### 2 *Risk of Infringement on the Freedom of Contracts*

Up until now, the Polluter was able to exercise his right to negotiate the terms of a contract and could sell contaminated land at a cheaper price to reflect the purification costs. However, after this decision, even if such negotiations have taken place, the Polluter may still be liable to future land owners who succeed in bringing a case against the Polluter, rendering validly contracted provisions ineffective. This could present a threat to the freedom of contracts. Also, the dissenting opinion of this decision pointed out that it was possible for contaminated land to be the subject of a contract. Therefore, it is arguable that this decision infringed upon property rights as prescribed under Article 23(1) of the Constitution.

### 3 *The Incapacitation of the Statute of Limitations and Resulting Uncertainty with Regard to Potential Liability*

The Supreme Court held that the point in time the buyer of contaminated land incurs purification costs is when actual damages are incurred. On this point, the dissenting opinion was concerned that the requisite point in time could be arbitrarily determined by the buyer, which in turn made it possible for the buyer to arbitrarily set the starting period for the calculation of the statute of limitation.[7] This is the equivalent of excluding the application of the statute of limitations clause with regards to unlawful acts involving soil contamination.

The Soil Environment Conservation Act, Article 10-4(3) states that the one who must carry the responsibility of the land purification includes "the one who started the land contamination due to merger or inheritance or for any other reason, the one who owned or possessed a land contamination management facility which caused the land contamination at the time of land

7 *Ibid.*

contamination, or the one who inherited the rights and the duty of an operator of the land contamination management facility."[8]

In accordance with the abovementioned article, the current owner may impose liability on the heir of the polluter for the tort committed and may also claim the associated compensation for costs incurred in the disposal of waste on the relevant land, incurred during the development of the land that the current owner decided to carry out even after a hundred years from the date of purchase of the land.

This results in the opposite of what the policy of the statute of limitation intends, which is to seek the stability of one's right in time.

## V Conclusion

### 1 *The Intent of the Supreme Court in its 2016 Decision*

In effect, the Supreme Court established the doctrine of strict liability with regard to environmental pollution. This is in line with the "polluter pays principle," the widely accepted principle which holds those responsible for producing pollution for bearing the costs of damage done to the environment. It is part of a broader set of principles designed to provide guidance in a move towards worldwide sustainable development. In overturning established precedent and interpreting existing regulations to hold the polluter liable for environmental contamination, it can be demonstrated that the Supreme Court is realizing its intent to align national practices with those of the wider global community with its aim of using a legal framework to manage the impact of human activity on the environment.

### 2 *Negative Effects of Overly Austere Environmental Laws on Environment Conservation*

The other aspect that needs to be discussed is whether the changed decision of the Supreme Court indeed has a solely positive effect on environmental conservation. When the Comprehensive Environmental Response, Compensation, and Liability Act (CERCLA) of the United States imposed heavy responsibility placed upon polluters, people appointed by the government as being potentially responsible for contamination spent more time and financial resources on different investigation and litigation to avoid responsibility, rather than

8 *Ibid.*

cooperating with one another to restore the land.[9] In addition, industrial facilities on which hazardous substances had once been used were turned down by investors who took precautions by utilizing land which had never been used before, destroying green tracts of land to build new industrial facilities in order to avoid even the remote possibility of potential responsibility for existing pollution on brownfield sites.[10]

In the same vein, the Soil Environment Conservation Act of Korea Article 10-3, Section 1 states no-fault liability, Section 2 states that in cases whereby there are two persons or more who have caused soil contamination and there are no means to accurately apportion blame for the damage done, they both share joint responsibility to compensate, as well as the sharing of the duty to purify the land.[11] In accordance with this, land owners who operate businesses that could be deemed to have caused contamination will not attempt to sell land to a buyer who may potentially use hazardous substances. As a result, there is a possibility that new facilities which could be harmful to the environment may only be built on greenfield sites, thus yielding negative effects on the environment.

### 3 *Necessity of Presenting an Alternative Solution, Other than Relying on Tort Liability*

In accordance with the purport of the Framework Act on Environmental Policy which states, "all citizens must put effort in reducing the environmental pollution and damage and in conserving national land and the natural

---

9 "Polluter Pays Principle" in Reality: concerning Cleanup Responsibility under CERCLA, Young-geun Chae, JOURNAL OF ENVIRONMENTAL LAW 23-2 (In Korean).

10 *Ibid.*

11 Soil Environment Conservation Act of Korea Article 10-3 (Strict Liability, etc. for Damages Resulting from Soil Contamination).

"(1) Where any damage occurs due to the soil contamination, a person who has caused the contamination shall compensate for such damage and take measures, such as purifying the contaminated soil: Provided, That the same shall not apply to cases where the soil contamination has been caused by a natural disaster, war, or force majeure. <Amended by Act No. 12522, 24 March 2014>

(2) Where at least two persons have caused the contamination, and it is impracticable to find out which one has caused the damage under paragraph (1), each one shall jointly and severally compensate for such damage and take measures, such as purifying the contaminated soil. <Amended by Act No. 12522, 24 March 2014>"

[This Article wholly Amended by Act No. 10551, 5 April 2011].

environment,"[12] the changed decision of the Supreme Court is a welcome one. It puts a heavier responsibility on the land polluter on the grounds that, unlike general consumer goods in which the owner can use and dispose of it at his or her will, land should not be subject to environmental pollution even if it is carried out by the owner of the land.

However, there are major concerns caused by the finding of tort liability, which could lead to other problems in addition to those mentioned above. For example, in relation to the incapacitation of the statute of limitations, another potentially unfair consequence for the heir of the polluter would be that of inflation; the costs incurred from the cleanup would be incomparably high in comparison to the value of the land at the time of the sale. To resolve such inadequacies, the Supreme Court needs to make decisions in a more detailed manner, clearly and specifically stating who is responsible and the appropriate prescription. Moreover, aside from the law of torts, it is necessary to consider the enactment of new legislation that does not subject the polluter to crushing liability, but allows the polluter to be subject to a burden proportionate to the action.

---

12 Framework Act on Environmental Policy Article 6 (Rights and Duties of Citizens)

"(1) All citizens shall have the right to live in a healthy and agreeable environment.

(2) All citizens shall cooperate in environmental preservation policies of the State and local governments.

(3) All citizens shall endeavor to reduce any environmental pollution and environmental damage that may result from their daily lives and to preserve the national land and natural environment."

# *Legal Materials*

# Participation in Multilateral Treaties*

*Karin Arts*

## Editorial Introduction

This section records the participation of Asian States in open multilateral law-making treaties which mostly aim at world-wide adherence. It updates the treaty sections of earlier Volumes until 31 December 2015. New data are preceded by a reference to the most recent previous entry in the multilateral treaties section of the *Asian Yearbook of International Law*. In case no new data are available, the title of the treaty is listed with a reference to the last Volume containing data on the treaty involved. For the purpose of this section, States broadly situated west of Iran, north of Mongolia, east of Papua New Guinea and south of Indonesia will not be covered.

### *Note*

- Where no other reference to specific sources is made, data were derived from *Multilateral Treaties Deposited with the Secretary-General*, https://treaties.un.org/pages/participationstatus.aspx
- Where reference is made to the Hague Conference on Private International Law (HccH), data were derived from https://www.hcch.net/en/instruments/conventions
- Where reference is made to the International Atomic Energy Agency (IAEA), date were derived from http://ola.iaea.org/ola/treaties/multi.html
- Where reference is made to the International Civil Aviation Organization (ICAO), data were derived from https://www.icao.int/Secretariat/Legal/Pages/TreatyCollection.aspx
- Where reference is made to the International Committee of the Red Cross (ICRC), data were derived from https://www.icrc.org/applic/ihl/ihl.nsf/
- Where reference is made to the International Labor Organization (ILO), data were derived from http://www.ilo.org/dyn/normlex/en/f?p=NORMLEXPUB:1:0

* Compiled by Dr. Karin Arts, Professor of International Law and Development at the International Institute of Social Studies of Erasmus University Rotterdam (ISS), based in The Hague, The Netherlands.

- Where reference is made to the International Maritime Organization (IMO), data were derived from http://www.imo.org/en/About/Conventions/StatusOfConventions/Documents/Status%20-%202017.pdf
- Where reference is made to the Secretariat of the Antarctic Treaty, data were derived from http://www.ats.aq/devAS/ats_parties.aspx?lang=e
- Where reference is made to the United Nations Educational, Scientific and Cultural Organization (UNESCO), data were derived from http://portal.unesco.org/en/ev.php-URL_ID=12024&URL_DO=DO_TOPIC&URL_SECTION=201.html
- Where reference is made to WIPO, data were derived from http://www.wipo.int/treaties/en
- Where reference is made to the Worldbank, data were derived from http://www.worldbank.org/en/about/leadership/members#4 and https://www.miga.org/who-we-are/member-countries/
- Reservations and declarations made upon signature or ratification are not included.
- Sig. = Signature; Cons. = Consent to be bound; Eff. date = Effective date; E.i.f. = Entry into force; Rat. = Ratification or accession.

## Table of Headings

## Antarctica

**Antarctic Treaty, Washington, 1959**
(Continued from Vol. 6 p. 234 and corrected)
(Status as provided by the Secretariat of the Antarctic Treaty)

| *State* | *E.i.f.* |
|---|---|
| China | 8 Jun 1983 |
| India | 19 Aug 1983 |
| Japan | 23 Jun 1961 |
| Kazakhstan | 27 Jan 2015 |
| Korea (DPR) | 21 Jan 1987 |
| Korea (Rep.) | 28 Nov 1986 |
| Malaysia | 31 Oct 2011 |
| Mongolia | 23 Mar 2015 |
| Pakistan | 1 Mar 2012 |
| Papua New Guinea | 16 Mar 1981 |

## Commercial Arbitration

Convention on the Recognition and Enforcement of Foreign Arbitral Awards, 1958: *see* Vol. 20 p. 194.

## Cultural Matters

Agreement for Facilitating the International Circulation of Visual and Auditory Materials of an Educational, Scientific and Cultural Character, 1949: *see* Vol. 7 pp. 322–323.
Agreement on the Importation of Educational, Scientific and Cultural Materials, 1950: *see* Vol. 12 p. 234.
Convention concerning the International Exchange of Publications, 1958: *see* Vol. 6 p. 235.
Convention concerning the Exchange of Official Publications and Government Documents between States, 1958: *see* Vol. 6 p. 235.
International Agreement for the Establishment of the University for Peace, 1980: *see* Vol. 16 p. 157.

Regional Convention on the Recognition of Studies, Diploma's and Degrees in Higher Education in Asia and the Pacific, 1983: *see* Vol. 14 p. 227.
Revised Asia-Pacific Regional Convention on the Recognition of Qualifications in Higher Education, 2011: see Vol. 20 p. 195.

## Cultural Property

Convention for the Protection of Cultural Property in the Event of Armed Conflict, 1954: *see* Vol. 13 p. 263.
Protocol for the Protection of Cultural Property in the Event of Armed Conflict, 1954: *see* Vol. 13 p. 263.
Convention concerning the Protection of the World Cultural and Natural Heritage, 1972: *see* Vol. 18 p. 100.
Second Protocol for the Protection of Cultural Property in the Event of Armed Conflict, 1999: *see* Vol. 19 p. 178.
Convention for the Safeguarding of the Intangible Cultural Heritage, 2003: *see* Vol. 20 p. 196.
Convention on the Protection and Promotion of the Diversity of Cultural Expressions, 2005: *see* Vol. 18 p. 100.

**Convention on the Means of Prohibiting and Preventing the Illicit Import, Export and Transfer of Ownership of Cultural Property, 1970**
(Continued from Vol. 19 p. 178)
(Status as provided by UNESCO)

| *State* | *Sig.* | *Cons.* |
|---|---|---|
| Laos | | 22 Dec 2015 |

## Development Matters

Charter of the Asian and Pacific Development Centre, 1982: *see* Vol. 7 pp. 323–324.
Agreement to Establish the South Centre, 1994: *see* Vol. 7 p. 324.
Amendments to the Charter of the Asian and Pacific Development Centre, 1998: *see* Vol. 10 p. 267.

**Multilateral Agreement for the Establishment of an International Think Tank for Landlocked Developing Countries, 2010**
(Continued from Vol. 19 p. 101)

| *State* | *Sig.* | *Cons.* |
|---|---|---|
| Kazakhstan | | 3 Feb 2015 |

## Dispute Settlement

Convention on the Settlement of Investment Disputes between States and Nationals of Other States, 1965: *see* Vol. 11 p. 245.

| *State* | *Sig.* | *Cons.* |
|---|---|---|
| Japan | | 6 Oct 2015 |

**Declarations Recognizing as Compulsory the Jurisdiction of the International Court of Justice under Article 36, paragraph 2, of the Statute of the Court**
(Continued from Vol. 18 p. 101)

## Environment, Fauna and Flora

International Convention for the Prevention of Pollution of the Sea by Oil, as amended, 1954: *see* Vol. 6 p. 238.
International Convention on Civil Liability for Oil Pollution Damage, 1969: *see* Vol. 15 p. 215.
International Convention Relating to Intervention on the High Seas in Cases of Oil Pollution Casualties, 1969: *see* Vol. 9 p. 284.
Convention on Wetlands of International Importance especially as Waterfowl Habitat, 1971: *see* Vol. 18 p. 103.

International Convention on the Establishment of an International Fund for Compensation for Oil Pollution Damage, 1971: *see* Vol. 12 p. 237.
Convention on the Prevention of Marine Pollution by Dumping of Wastes and Other Matter, 1972, as amended: *see* Vol. 7 p. 325.
Protocol Relating to Intervention on the High Seas in Cases of Pollution by Substances Other Than Oil, 1973: *see* Vol. 6 p. 239.
Protocol to the 1969 International Convention on Civil Liability for Oil Pollution Damage, 1976: *see* Vol. 10 p. 269.
Protocol Relating to the 1973 International Convention for the Prevention of Pollution from Ships 1978, as amended: *see*
Vol. 15 p. 225.
Protocol to amend the 1971 Convention on Wetlands of International Importance especially as Waterfowl Habitat, 1982: *see* Vol. 13 p. 265.
Convention for the Protection of the Ozone Layer, 1985: *see* Vol. 15 p. 215.
Protocol on Substances that Deplete the Ozone Layer, 1987: *see* Vol. 16 p. 161.
Amendments to Articles 6 and 7 of the 1971 Convention on Wetlands of International Importance especially as Waterfowl Habitat, 1987: *see* Vol. 13 p. 266.
International Convention on Oil Pollution Preparedness, Response, and Cooperation, 1990: see Vol. 20 p. 199.
Amendment to the Montreal Protocol, 1990: *see* Vol. 15 p. 216.
Amendment to the Montreal Protocol, 1992: *see* Vol. 18 p. 103 Framework Convention on Climate Change, 1992: *see* Vol. 13 p. 266.
Convention on Biological Diversity, 1992: *see* Vol. 14 p. 229.
Protocol to Amend the 1969 International Convention on Civil Liability for Oil Pollution Damage, 1992: *see*
Vol. 16 p. 161.
Protocol to Amend the 1972 International Convention on the Establishment of an International Fund for Compensation for Oil Pollution Damage, 1992: *see* Vol. 19 p. 181.
UN Convention to Combat Desertification in those Countries Experiencing Serious Drought and/or Desertification, Particularly in Africa, 1994: *see* Vol. 11 p. 247.
Amendment to the Convention on the Control of Transboundary Movements of Hazardous Wastes and Their Disposal, 1995: *see* Vol. 12 p. 238.
Amendment to the Montreal Protocol, 1997: *see* Vol. 19 p. 182.
Protocol to the Framework Convention on Climate Change, 1997: *see* Vol. 19 p. 182.

Rotterdam Convention on the Prior Informed Consent Procedure for Certain Hazardous Chemicals and Pesticides in International Trade, 1998: *see* Vol. 19 p. 182.
Amendment to the Montreal Protocol, 1999: *see* Vol. 19 p. 182.
Cartagena Protocol on Biosafety to the Convention on Biological Diversity, 2000: *see* Vol. 19 p. 183.
Stockholm Convention on Persistent Organic Pollutants, 2001: *see* Vol. 19 pp. 183.
International Convention on Civil Liability for Bunker Oil Pollution Damage, 2001: see Vol. 20 p. 199.

**Convention on the Control of Transboundary Movements of Hazardous Wastes and Their Disposal, 1989**
(Continued from Vol. 19 p. 181)

| *State* | *Sig.* | *Rat.* |
|---|---|---|
| Myanmar | | 6 Jan 2015 |

**International Convention on the Control of Harmful Anti-Fouling Systems on Ships, 2001**
(Continued from Vol. 20 p. 199)
(Status as provided by IMO)

| *State* | *Cons. (dep.)* | *E.i.f.* |
|---|---|---|
| India | 24 Apr 2015 | 24 Jul 2015 |
| Vietnam | 27 Nov 2015 | |

**International Convention for the Control and Management of Ships' Ballast Water and Sediments, 2004**
(Continued from Vol. 20 p. 199)
(Status as provided by IMO)

| *State* | *Cons. (dep.)* | *E.i.f.* |
|---|---|---|
| Indonesia | 24 Nov 2015 | |

**Nagoya Protocol on Access to Genetic Resources and the Fair and Equitable Sharing of Benefits Arising from their Utilization to the Convention on Biological Diversity**
Nagoya, 29 October 2010
Entry into force: 12 October 2014

| *State* | *Sig.* | *Rat.* |
|---|---|---|
| Bangladesh | 6 Sep 2011 | |
| Bhutan | 20 Sep 2011 | 30 Sep 2013 |
| Cambodia | 1 Feb 2012 | 19 Jan 2015 |
| India | 11 May 2011 | 9 Oct 2012 |
| Indonesia | 11 May 2011 | 24 Sep 2013 |
| Japan | 11 May 2011 | |
| Kazakhstan | | 17 Jun 2015 |
| Kyrgyzstan | | 15 Jun 2015 |
| Laos | | 26 Sep 2012 |
| Mongolia | 26 Jan 2012 | 21 May 2013 |
| Myanmar | | 8 Jan 2014 |
| Pakistan | | 23 Nov 2015 |
| Philippines | | 29 Sep 2015 |
| Korea (Rep.) | 20 Sep 2011 | |
| Tajikistan | 20 Sep 2011 | 12 Sep 2013 |
| Thailand | 31 Jan 2012 | |
| Vietnam | | 23 Apr 2014 |

**Nagoya – Kuala Lumpur Supplementary Protocol on Liability and Redress to the Caratagena Protocol on Biosafety**
Nagoya, 15 October 2010
Entry into force: not yet

| *State* | *Sig.* | *Rat.* |
|---|---|---|
| Cambodia | | 30 Aug 2013 |
| India | 11 Oct 2011 | 19 Dec 2014 |
| Japan | 2 Mar 2012 | |
| Mongolia | 26 Jan 2012 | 21 May 2013 |
| Thailand | 6 Mar 2012 | |
| Vietnam | | 23 Apr 2014 |

**Minamata Convention on Mercury**
Kumamoto, 10 October 2013
Entry into force: not yet

| *State* | *Sig.* | *Rat.* |
|---|---|---|
| Bangladesh | 10 Oct 2013 | |
| Cambodia | 10 Oct 2013 | |
| China | 10 Oct 2013 | |
| India | 30 Sep 2014 | |
| Indonesia | 10 Oct 2013 | |
| Iran | 10 Oct 2013 | |
| Japan | 10 Oct 2013 | |
| Malaysia | 24 Sep 2014 | |
| Mongolia | 10 Oct 2013 | 28 Sep 2015 |
| Nepal | 10 Oct 2013 | |
| Pakistan | 10 Oct 2013 | |
| Philippines | 10 Oct 2013 | |
| Korea (Rep.) | 24 Sep 2014 | |
| Singapore | 10 Oct 2013 | |
| Sri Lanka | 8 Oct 2014 | |
| Vietnam | 11 Oct 2013 | |

## Family Matters

Convention on the Recovery Abroad of Maintenance, 1956: *see* Vol. 11 p. 249.
Convention on the Law Applicable to Maintenance Obligations Towards Children, 1956: *see* Vol.6 p. 244.
Convention on the Conflicts of Law Relating to the Form of Testamentary Dispositions, 1961: *see* Vol. 7 p. 327.
Convention on Consent to Marriage, Minimum Age for Marriage and Registration of Marriages, 1962: *see* Vol. 8 p. 178.
Convention on the Law Applicable to Maintenance Obligations, 1973: *see* Vol. 6 p. 244.
Convention on Protection of Children and Co-operation in Respect of Intercountry Adoption, 1993: *see* Vol. 19 p. 184.

### Finance

Agreement Establishing the Asian Development Bank, 1965: *see* Vol. 7 p. 327.
Convention Establishing the Multilateral Investment Guarantee Agency, 1988: *see* Vol. 19 p. 184

### Health

Protocol Concerning the Office International d'Hygiène Publique, 1946: *see* Vol. 6 p. 245.
World Health Organization Framework Convention on Tobacco Control, 2003: *see* Vol. 19 p. 185.

### Human Rights, Including Women and Children

Convention on the Political Rights of Women, 1953: *see* Vol. 10 p. 273.
Convention on the Nationality of Married Women, 1957: *see* Vol. 10 p. 274.
Convention against Discrimination in Education, 1960: *see* Vol. 16 p. 164.
International Covenant on Economic, Social and Cultural Rights, 1966: *see* Vol. 14 p. 231.
International Covenant on Civil and Political Rights, 1966: *see* Vol. 16 p. 165.
Optional Protocol to the International Covenant on Civil and Political Rights, 1966, *see*: Vol. 15 p. 219.
Convention on the Elimination of All Forms of Discrimination against Women, 1979: *see* Vol. 11 p. 250.
International Convention against Apartheid in Sports, 1985: *see* Vol. 6 p. 248.
Convention on the Rights of the Child, 1989: *see* Vol. 11 p. 251.
Second Optional Protocol to the International Covenant on Civil and Political Rights, Aiming at the Abolition of the Death Penalty, 1989: *see* Vol. 18 p. 106.
International Convention on the Protection of the Rights of All Migrant Workers and Members of Their Families, 1990: *see* Vol. 18 p. 106.
Amendment to article 8 of the International Convention on the Elimination of All Forms of Racial Discrimination, 1992, *see* Vol. 12 p. 242.
Optional Protocol to the Convention on the Elimination of All Forms of Discrimination against Women, 1999: see Vol. 17 p. 170.

Optional Protocol to the Convention on the Rights of the Child on the Sale of Children, Child Prostitution and Child Pornography, 2000: *see* Vol. 20 p. 202.

Optional Protocol to the Convention on the Rights of Persons with Disabilities, 2008: *see* Vol. 18 p. 107.

**International Convention on the Elimination of All Forms of Racial Discrimination, 1966**

(Continued from Vol. 8 p. 179)

| *State* | *Sig.* | *Cons.* |
|---|---|---|
| Singapore | 19 Oct 2015 | |

**Convention Against Torture and Other Cruel, Inhuman or Degrading Treatment or Punishment, 1984**

(Continued from Vol. 19 p. 186)

| *State* | *Sig.* | *Cons.* |
|---|---|---|
| Brunei | 22 Sep 2015 | |

**Optional Protocol to the Convention on the Rights of the Child on the Involvement of Children in Armed Conflict, 2000**

(Continued from Vol. 18 p. 106)

| *State* | *Sig.* | *Cons.* |
|---|---|---|
| Myanmar | 28 Sep 2015 | |

**Optional Protocol to the Convention Against Torture and Other Cruel, Inhuman or Degrading Treatment or Punishment, 2002**

(Continued from Vol. 19 p. 186)

| *State* | *Sig.* | *Cons.* |
|---|---|---|
| Mongolia | 24 Sep 2013 | 12 Feb 2015 |

**Convention on the Rights of Persons with Disabilities, 2008**
(Continued from Vol. 20 p. 202)

| *State* | *Sig.* | *Cons.* |
|---|---|---|
| Kazakhstan | 11 Dec 2008 | 21 Apr 2015 |
| Vietnam | 22 Oct 2007 | 5 Feb 2015 |

**International Convention for the Protection of All Persons from Enforced Disappearance, 2010**
(Continued from Vol. 19 p. 187)

| *State* | *Sig.* | *Cons.* |
|---|---|---|
| Mongolia | 6 Feb 2007 | 12 Feb 2015 |
| Sri Lanka | 10 Dec 2015 | |

## Humanitarian Law in Armed Conflict

International Conventions for the Protection of Victims of War, I–IV, 1949: *see* Vol. 11 p. 252.
Protocol I Additional to the Geneva Conventions of 12 August 1949, and Relating to the Protection of Victims of International Armed Conflicts, 1977, *see:* Vol. 18 p. 107.
Protocol II Additional to the Geneva Conventions of 12 August 1949, and Relating to the Protection of Victims of Non-International Armed Conflicts, 1977, *see:* Vol. 12 p. 244.
Protocol III Additional to the Geneva Conventions of 12 August 1949, and Relating to the Adoption of an Additional Distinctive Emblem, 2005: *see* Vol. 17 p. 171.

## Intellectual Property

Convention for the Protection of Industrial Property, 1883 as amended 1979: *see* Vol. 12 p. 244.

Convention for the Protection of Literary and Artistic Works, 1886 as amended 1979: *see* Vol. 18 p. 108.
Madrid Union Concerning the International Registration of Marks, including the Madrid Agreement 1891 as amended in 1979, and the Madrid Protocol 1989: *see* Vol. 16 p. 168.
Universal Copyright Convention, 1952: *see* Vol. 6 p. 251.
Protocols 1, 2 and 3 annexed to the Universal Copyright Convention, 1952: *see* Vol. 6 p. 251.
Nice Agreement Concerning the International Classification of Goods and Services for the Purposes of the Registration of Marks, 1957 as amended in 1979: *see* Vol. 13 p. 271.
International Convention for the Protection of Performers, Producers of Phonograms and Broadcasting Organizations, 1961: *see* Vol. 18 p. 109.
Convention Establishing the World Intellectual Property Organization, 1967: *see* Vol. 12 p. 245.
Patent Cooperation Treaty, 1970 as amended in 1979 and modified in 1984 and 2001: *see* Vol. 15 p. 221.
Convention for the Protection of Producers of Phonograms against Unauthorized Duplication of their Phonograms, 1971: *see* Vol. 18 p. 109.
Multilateral Convention for the Avoidance of Double Taxation of Copyright Royalties, 1979: *see* Vol. 6 p. 252.
Trademark Law Treaty, 1994: *see* Vol. 15 p. 222.
WIPO Performances and Phonograms Treaty, 1996: *see* Vol. 18 p. 109.
WIPO Copyright Treaty, 1996: *see* Vol. 18, p. 109.
Patent Law Treaty, 2000: *see* Vol. 17 p. 172.
Singapore Treaty on the Law of Trademarks, 2006: *see* Vol. 20 p. 204.

**Beijing Treaty on Audiovisual Performances**
Beijing, 24 June 2012
Entry into force: not yet

| *State* | *Sig.* | *Rat.* |
|---|---|---|
| China | 26 Jun 2012 | 9 Jul 2014 |
| Indonesia | 18 Dec 2012 | |
| Japan | | 10 Jun 2014 |
| Korea (DPR) | 26 Jun 2012 | |
| Mongolia | 26 Jun 2012 | |

**Marrakesh Treaty to Facilitate Access to published Works for Persons who are Blind, Visually Impaired or Otherwise Print Disabled**
Marrakesh, 27 June 2013
Entry into force: not yet

| *State* | *Sig.* | *Rat.* |
|---|---|---|
| Afghanistan | 28 Jun 2013 | |
| Cambodia | 28 Jun 2013 | |
| China | 28 Jun 2013 | |
| India | 30 Apr 2014 | 24 Jun 2014 |
| Indonesia | 24 Sep 2013 | |
| Iran | 27 Jun 2014 | |
| Korea (DPR) | 28 Jun 2013 | |
| Korea (Rep.) | 26 Jun 2014 | 9 Oct 2015 |
| Mongolia | 28 Jun 2013 | 23 Sep 2015 |
| Nepal | 28 Jun 2013 | |
| Singapore | | 30 Mar 2015 |

## International Crimes

Slavery Convention, 1926 as amended in 1953: *see* Vol. 15 p. 223.
Supplementary Convention on the Abolition of Slavery, the Slave Trade, and Institutions and Practices Similar to Slavery, 1956: *see* Vol. 14 p. 236.
Convention on Offences and Certain Other Acts Committed on Board Aircraft, 1963: *see* Vol. 9 p. 289.
Convention on the Non-Applicability of Statutory Limitations to War Crimes and Crimes Against Humanity, 1968: *see* Vol. 6 p. 254.
Convention for the Suppression of Unlawful Seizure of Aircraft, 1970: *see* Vol. 8 p. 289.
Convention for the Suppression of Unlawful Acts Against the Safety of Civil Aviation, 1971: *see* Vol. 8 p. 290.
International Convention on the Suppression and Punishment of the Crime of Apartheid, 1973: *see* Vol. 7 p. 331.
Convention on the Prevention and Punishment of Crimes Against Internationally Protected Persons Including Diplomatic Agents, 1973: *see* Vol. 14 p. 236.
International Convention Against the Taking of Hostages, 1979: *see* Vol. 20 p. 206.

Convention for the Suppression of Unlawful Acts Against the Safety of Maritime Navigation, 1988: *see* Vol. 18 p. 111.
Protocol for the Suppression of Unlawful Acts of Violence at Airports Serving International Civil Aviation, Supplementary to the Convention for the Suppression of Unlawful Acts Against the Safety of Civil Aviation, 1988, *see* Vol. 12 p. 247.
International Convention against the Recruitment, Use, Financing and Training of Mercenaries, 1989: *see* Vol. 11 p. 254.
Convention on the Marking of Plastic Explosives for the Purpose of Detection, 1991: *see* Vol. 15 p. 224.
Convention on the Safety of United Nations and Associated Personnel, 1994: *see* Vol. 11 p. 255.
International Convention for the Suppression of Terrorist Bombings, 1997: *see* Vol. 20 p. 206.
Statute of the International Criminal Court, 1998: *see* Vol. 16 p. 171.
International Convention for the Suppression of the Financing of Terrorism, 1999: *see* Vol. 17 p. 174.
United Nations Convention Against Corruption, 2003: *see* Vol. 17 p. 175.
International Convention for the Suppression of Acts of Nuclear Terrorism, 2005: *see* Vol. 20 p. 207.
Protocol for the Suppression of Unlawful Acts Against the Safety of Fixed Platforms Located on the Continental Shelf, 2005: *see* Vol. 18 p. 112.

**Convention on the Prevention and Punishment of the Crime of Genocide, 1948**
(Continued from Vol. 8 p. 182)

| *State* | *Sig.* | *Rat.* |
|---|---|---|
| Tajikistan | | 3 Nov 2015 |

**United Nations Convention Against Transnational Organized Crime, 2000**
(Continued from Vol. 19 p. 191)

| *State* | *Sig.* | *Rat.* |
|---|---|---|
| Korea (Rep.) | 13 Dec 2000 | 5 Nov 2015 |

**Protocol to Prevent, Suppress and Punish Trafficking in Persons, Especially Women and Children, supplementing the United Nations Convention Against Transnational Organized Crime, 2000**
(Continued from Vol. 20 p. 207)

| *State* | *Sig.* | *Rat.* |
|---|---|---|
| Korea (Rep.) | 13 Dec 2000 | 5 Nov 2015 |
| Singapore | | 8 Sep 2015 |
| Sri Lanka | 13 Dec 2000 | 15 Jun 2015 |

**Protocol against the Smuggling of Migrants by Land, Sea and Air, supplementing the United Nations Convention Against Transnational Organized Crime, 2000**
(Continued from Vol. 15 p. 224)

| State | Sig. | Rat. |
|---|---|---|
| Korea (Rep.) | 13 Dec 2000 | 5 Nov 2015 |

**Protocol against the Illicit Manufacturing of and Trafficking in Firearms, Their Parts and Components and Ammunition, supplementing the United Nations Convention Against Transnational Organized Crime, 2001**
(Continued from Vol. 17 p. 174)

| State | Sig. | Rat. |
|---|---|---|
| Korea (Rep.) | 4 Oct 2001 | 5 Nov 2015 |

### International Representation
(*see also*: Privileges and Immunities)

Vienna Convention on the Representation of States in their Relations with International Organizations of a Universal Character, 1975: *see* Vol. 6 p. 257.

### International Trade

Convention on Transit Trade of Land-locked States, 1965: *see* Vol. 17 p. 176.
Convention on the Limitation Period in the International Sale of Goods, 1974: *see* Vol. 6 p. 257.
UN Convention on the Liability of Operators of Transport Terminals in International Trade, 1991: *see* Vol. 6 p. 257.

**UN Convention on Contracts for the International Sale of Goods, 1980**
(Continued from Vol. 14 p. 239)

| State | Sig. | Rat. |
|---|---|---|
| Vietnam | | 18 Dec 2015 |

**United Nations Convention on the Use of Electronic Communications in International Contracts, 2005**
(Continued from Vol. 16 p. 173)

| State | Sig. | Rat. |
|---|---|---|
| Sri Lanka | 6 Jul 2006 | 7 Jul 2015 |

### Judicial and Administrative Cooperation

Convention on Civil Procedure, 1954: *see* Vol. 20 p. 208.
Convention Abolishing the Requirement of Legalisation for Foreign Public Documents, 1961: *see* Vol. 17 p. 176.
Convention on the Service Abroad of Judicial and Extrajudicial Documents in Civil or Commercial Matters, 1965: *see* Vol. 9 p. 291.
Convention on the Taking of Evidence Abroad in Civil or Commercial Matters, 1970: *see* Vol. 16 p. 173.

### Labor

Forced Labor Convention, 1930 (ILO Conv. 29): *see* Vol. 19 p. 192.
Freedom of Association and Protection of the Right to Organise Convention, 1948 (ILO Conv. 87): *see* Vol. 19 p. 192.

Right to Organise and Collective Bargaining Convention, 1949 (ILO Conv. 98): *see* Vol. 19 p. 193.
Equal Remuneration Convention, 1951 (ILO Conv. 100): *see* Vol. 19 p. 193.
Abolition of Forced Labor Convention, 1957 (ILO Conv. 105): *see* Vol. 19 p. 193.
Discrimination (Employment and Occupation) Convention, 1958 (ILO Conv. 111): *see* Vol. 19 p. 193.
Employment Policy Convention, 1964 (ILO Conv. 122): see Vol. 8 p. 186.
Minimum Age Convention, 1973 (ILO Conv. 138): *see* Vol. 19 p. 193.
Worst Forms of Child Labor Convention, 1999 (ILO Conv. 182): *see* Vol. 19 p. 194.

**Promotional Framework for Occupational Safety and Health Convention (ILO Conv. 187), 2006**
(Continued from Vol. 20 p. 209)
(Status as provided by the ILO)

| *State* | *Rat. Registered* |
|---|---|
| Indonesia | 31 Aug 2015 |
| Kazakhstan | 3 Feb 2015 |

## Narcotic Drugs

Protocol Amending the Agreements, Conventions and Protocols on Narcotic Drugs, concluded at The Hague on 23 January 1912, at Geneva on 11 February 1925 and 19 February 1925 and 13 July 1931, at Bangkok on 27 November 1931 and at Geneva on 26 June 1936, 1946: *see* Vol. 6 p. 261.
Agreement Concerning the Suppression of the Manufacture of, Internal Trade in, and Use of, Prepared Opium and amended by Protocol, 1925, amended 1946: *see* Vol. 6 p. 261.
International Opium Convention, 1925, amended by Protocol 1946: *see* Vol. 7 p. 334.
Agreement Concerning the Suppression of Opium Smoking, 1931, amended by Protocol, 1946: *see* Vol. 6 p. 261.
Convention for Limiting the Manufacture and Regulating the Distribution of Narcotic Drugs, 1931, and amended by Protocol, 1946: *see* Vol. 7 p. 334.
Protocol bringing under International Control Drugs outside the Scope of the Convention of 1931, as amended by the Protocol of 1946: *see* Vol. 6 p. 262.
Convention for the Suppression of the Illicit Traffic in Dangerous Drugs, 1936, amended 1946: *see* Vol. 6 p. 262.

Protocol for Limiting and Regulating the Cultivation of the Poppy Plant, the Production of, International and Wholesale Trade in, and Use of Opium, 1953: *see* Vol. 6 p. 262.
Single Convention on Narcotic Drugs, 1961: *see* Vol. 13 p. 276.
Convention on Psychotropic Substances, 1971: *see* Vol. 13 p. 276.
United Nations Convention Against Illicit Traffic in Narcotic Drugs and Psychotropic Substances, 1988: *see* Vol. 20 p. 210.

**Single Convention on Narcotic Drugs, 1961, as Amended by Protocol 1972**
(Continued from Vol. 15 p. 227)

| *State* | *Sig.* | *Cons.* |
|---|---|---|
| Afghanistan | | 19 Feb 2015 |

**Protocol amending the Single Convention on Narcotic Drugs, 1972**
(Continued from Vol. 15 p. 227)

| *State* | *Sig.* | *Cons.* |
|---|---|---|
| Afghanistan | | 19 Feb 2015 |

## Nationality and Statelessness

Convention relating to the Status of Stateless Persons, 1954: *see* Vol. 17 p. 178.
Optional Protocol to the Vienna Convention on Diplomatic Relations concerning Acquisition of Nationality, 1961: *see* Vol. 6 p. 265.
Optional Protocol to the Vienna Convention on Consular Relations concerning Acquisition of Nationality, 1963: *see* Vol. 8 p. 187.

## Nuclear Material

Convention on Civil Liability for Nuclear Damage, 1963: *see* Vol. 17 p. 179.
Joint Protocol Relating to the Application of the Vienna Convention (and the Paris Convention on Third Party Liability in the Field of Nuclear Energy), 1980: *see* Vol. 6 p. 265.

Convention on Early Notification of a Nuclear Accident, 1986: *see* Vol. 19 p. 196.
Convention on Assistance in the Case of a Nuclear Accident or Radiological Emergency, 1986: *see* Vol. 19 p. 196.
Convention on Nuclear Safety, 1994: *see* Vol. 18 p. 117.
Joint Convention on the Safety of Spent Fuel Management and on the Safety of Radioactive Waste Management, 1997: *see* Vol. 19 p. 196.
Convention on Supplementary Compensation for Nuclear Damage, 1997: *see* Vol. 16 p. 178.
Protocol to Amend the 1963 Convention on Civil Liability for Nuclear Damage, 1997: *see* Vol. 17 p. 180.
Amendment to the 1980 Convention on the Physical Protection of Nuclear Material, 2005: *see* Vol. 20 p. 212.

**Convention on the Physical Protection of Nuclear Material, 1980**
(Continued and corrected from Vol. 18 p. 116)
(Status as provided by IAEA)

| *State* | *Sig.* | *Cons. (deposit)* |
|---|---|---|
| Kyrgyzstan | | 15 Sep 2015 |

## Outer Space

Treaty on Principles Governing the Activities of the States in the Exploration and Use of Outer Space, Including the Moon and Other Celestial Bodies, 1967: *see* Vol. 16 p. 178.
Agreement governing the Activities of States on the Moon and other Celestial Bodies, 1979: *see* Vol. 10 p. 284.
Convention on Registration of Objects launched into Outer Space, 1974: *see* Vol. 15 p. 229.

## Privileges and Immunities

Convention on the Privileges and Immunities of the United Nations, 1946: *see* Vol. 19 p. 197.
Convention on the Privileges and Immunities of the Specialized Agencies, 1947: *see* Vol. 7 p. 338.
Vienna Convention on Diplomatic Relations, 1961: *see* Vol. 19 p. 197.

Optional Protocol to the Vienna Convention on Diplomatic Relations concerning the Compulsory Settlement of Disputes, 1961: *see* Vol. 6 p. 269.
Vienna Convention on Consular Relations, 1963: *see* Vol. 19 p. 197.
Optional Protocol to the Vienna Convention on Consular Relations concerning the Compulsory Settlement of Disputes, 1963: *see* Vol. 6 p. 269.
Convention on Special Missions, 1969: *see* Vol. 6 p. 269.
Optional Protocol to the Convention on Special Missions concerning the Compulsory Settlement of Disputes, 1969: *see* Vol. 6 p. 269.
United Nations Convention on Jurisdictional Immunities of States and Their Property, 2004: *see* Vol. 15 p. 230.

### Refugees

Convention relating to the Status of Refugees, 1951: *see* Vol. 12 p. 254.
Protocol relating to the Status of Refugees, 1967: *see* Vol. 12 p. 254.

### Road Traffic and Transport

Convention on Road Traffic, 1968: *see* Vol. 12 p. 254.
Convention on Road Signs and Signals, 1968: *see* Vol. 20 p. 213.

### Sea

Convention on the Territorial Sea and the Contiguous Zone, 1958: *see* Vol. 6 p. 271.
Convention on the High Seas, 1958: *see* Vol. 7 p. 339.
Convention on Fishing and Conservation of the Living Resources of the High Seas, 1958: *see* Vol. 6 p. 271.
Convention on the Continental Shelf, 1958: *see* Vol. 6 p. 271.
Optional Protocol of Signature concerning the Compulsory Settlement of Disputes, 1958: *see* Vol. 6 p. 272.
United Nations Convention on the Law of the Sea, 1982: *see* Vol. 19 p. 198.
Agreement relating to the Implementation of Part XI of the United Nations Convention on the Law of the Sea of 10 December 1982, 1994: *see* Vol. 19 p. 199.
Agreement for the Implementation of the Provisions of the United Nations Convention on the Law of the Sea (…) relating to the Conservation and Management of Straddling Fish Stocks and Highly Migratory Fish Stocks, 1995: *see* Vol. 20 p. 214.

### Sea Traffic and Transport

Convention Regarding the Measurement and Registration of Vessels employed in Inland Navigation, 1956: *see* Vol. 6 p. 273.
International Convention for the Safety of Life at Sea, 1960: *see* Vol. 6 p. 273.
Convention on Facilitation of International Maritime Traffic, 1965 as amended: *see* Vol. 12 p. 255.
International Convention on Load Lines, 1966: *see* Vol. 15 p. 230.
International Convention on Tonnage Measurement of Ships, 1969: *see* Vol. 15 p. 231.
Special Trade Passenger Ships Agreement, 1971: *see* Vol. 6 p. 275.
Convention on the International Regulations for Preventing Collisions at Sea, 1972: *see* Vol. 19 p. 200.
International Convention for Safe Containers, as amended 1972: *see* Vol. 20 p. 215.
Protocol on Space Requirements for Special Trade Passenger Ships, 1973: *see* Vol. 6 p. 275.
Convention on a Code of Conduct for Liner Conferences, 1974: *see* Vol. 6 p. 276.
International Convention for the Safety of Life at Sea, 1974: *see* Vol. 15 p. 231.
Protocol Relating to the International Convention for the Safety of Life at Sea, 1974 as amended 1978: *see* Vol. 12 p. 256.
UN Convention on the Carriage of Goods by Sea, 1978: *see* Vol. 6 p. 276.
International Convention on Standards of Training, Certification and Watchkeeping for Seafarers, as amended, 1978: *see* Vol. 19 p. 200.
Protocol Relating to the International Convention on Load Lines, 1988: *see* Vol. 17 p. 183.
Protocol Relating to the International Convention for the Safety of Life at Sea, 1988: *see* Vol. 18 p. 120.

**Nairobi International Convention on the Removal of Wrecks, 2007**
Nairobi, 19 May 2007
Entry into force: 14 April 2015
(Status as provided by IMO)

| *State* | *Cons. (dep.)* | *E.i.f.* |
|---|---|---|
| India | 23 Mar 2011 | 14 Apr 2015 |
| Iran | 19 Apr 2011 | 14 Apr 2015 |
| Malaysia | 28 Nov 2013 | 14 Apr 2015 |

## Social Matters

International Agreement for the Suppression of the White Slave Traffic, 1904, amended by Protocol 1949: *see* Vol. 6 p. 278.
International Convention for the Suppression of the White Slave Traffic, 1910, amended by Protocol 1949: *see* Vol. 6 p. 278.
Agreement for the Suppression of the Circulation of Obscene Publications, 1910, amended by Protocol 1949: *see* Vol. 6 p. 278.
International Convention for the Suppression of the Traffic in Women and Children, 1921: *see* Vol. 6 p. 277.
Convention for the Suppression of the Traffic in Women and Children, 1921, amended by Protocol in 1947: *see* Vol. 6 p. 277.
International Convention for the Suppression of the Circulation of and Traffic in Obscene Publications, 1923: *see* Vol. 6 p. 277.
Convention for the Suppression of the Circulation of, and Traffic in, Obscene Publications, 1923, amended by Protocol in 1947: *see* Vol. 6 p. 277.
International Convention for the Suppression of the Traffic in Women of Full Age, 1933: *see* Vol. 6 p. 277.
Convention for the Suppression of the Traffic in Women of Full Age, 1933, amended by Protocol, 1947: *see* Vol. 6 p. 277.
Convention for the Suppression of the Traffic in Persons and of the Exploitation of the Prostitution of Others, 1950: *see* Vol. 12 p. 257.
Final Protocol to the Convention for the Suppression of the Traffic in Persons and of the Exploitation of the Prostitution of Others, 1950: *see* Vol. 12 p. 257.
International Convention Against Doping in Sports, 2005: *see* Vol. 20 p. 217.

## Telecommunications

Constitution of the Asia-Pacific Telecommunity, 1976: *see* Vol. 13 p. 280.
Convention on the International Maritime Satellite Organization (INMARSAT), 1976 (as amended): *see* Vol. 19 p. 202.
Agreement establishing the Asia-Pacific Institute for Broadcasting Development, 1977: *see* Vol. 10 p. 287.
Amendment to Article 11, Paragraph 2(a), of the Constitution of the Asia-Pacific Telecommunity, 1981: *see* Vol. 8 p. 193.
Amendments to articles 3(5) and 9(8) of the Constitution of the Asia-Pacific Telecommunity, 1991: *see* Vol. 9 p. 298.
Tampere Convention on the Provision of Telecommunication Resources for Disaster Mitigation and Relief Operations, 1998: *see* Vol. 15 p. 232.

Amendments to the Agreement establishing the Asia-Pacific Institute for Broadcasting Development, 1999: *see* Vol. 10 p. 288.
Amendments to the Constitution of the Asia-Pacific Telecommunity, 2002: *see* Vol. 13 p. 280.

**Treaties**

Vienna Convention on the Law of Treaties, 1969: see Vol. 19 p. 203.
Vienna Convention on the Law of Treaties Between States and International Organizations or Between International Organizations, 1986: *see* Vol. 6 p. 280.

**Weapons**

Protocol for the Prohibition of the Use in War of Asphyxiating, Poisonous or other Gases, and of Bacteriological Warfare, 1925: *see* Vol. 6 p. 281.
Treaty Banning Nuclear Weapon Tests in the Atmosphere, in Outer Space and Under Water, 1963: *see* Vol. 6 p. 281.
Treaty on the Non-Proliferation of Nuclear Weapons, 1968: *see* Vol. 11 p. 262.
Treaty on the Prohibition of the Emplacement of Nuclear Weapons and Other Weapons of Mass Destruction on the Sea-Bed and the Ocean Floor and in the Subsoil Thereof, 1971: *see* Vol. 6 p. 282.
Convention on the Prohibition of the Development, Production and Stockpiling of Bacteriological (Biological) and Toxin Weapons and on Their Destruction, 1972: *see* Vol. 20 p. 220.
Convention on Prohibitions or Restrictions on the Use of Certain Conventional Weapons which may be Deemed Excessively Injurious or to have Indiscriminate Effects, and Protocols, 1980: *see* Vol. 11 p. 263.
Comprehensive Nuclear Test Ban Treaty, 1996: *see* Vol. 19 p. 204.
Convention on the Prohibition of the Use, Stockpiling, Production and Transfer of Anti-Personnel Mines and on Their Destruction, 1997: *see* Vol. 13 p. 281.
Amendment of Article 1 of the 1980 Convention on Prohibitions or Restrictions on the Use of Certain Conventional Weapons which may be Deemed Excessively Injurious or to have Indiscriminate Effects, 2001: *see* Vol. 12 p. 259.
Convention on Cluster Munitions, 2008: *see* Vol. 19 p. 204.
Arms Trade Treaty, 2013: *see* Vol. 20 p. 220.

**Convention on the Prohibition of Military or any other Hostile Use of Environmental Modification Techniques, 1976**
(Continued from Vol. 12 p. 258)

| *State* | *Sig.* | *Cons.* |
|---|---|---|
| Kyrgyzstan | | 15 Jun 2015 |

**Convention on the Prohibition of the Development, Production, Stockpiling and Use of Chemical Weapons and on Their Destruction, 1993**
(Continued from Vol. 12 p. 259)

| *State* | *Sig.* | *Cons.* |
|---|---|---|
| Myanmar | 14 Jan 1993 | 8 Jul 2015 |

# State Practice of Asian Countries in International Law

*Bangladesh*

*Sumaiya Khair**

## Legislation

### *Bilateral Or Multilateral Treaty – Money-Laundering – Mutual Legal Assistance – Anti-Corruption—Asset Freezing*

**The Money Laundering Prevention (Amendment) Act 2015 (Act 25 of 2015)** – an Act that imbues the spirit and standards articulated in international instruments namely, the International Convention for the Suppression of the Financing of Terrorism 1999, the United Nations Convention against Transnational Organized Crime 2000, and the United Nations Convention Against Corruption 2003.

The Bangladesh Parliament passed the Money Laundering Prevention (Amendment) Act 2015 on 26 November 2015 with immediate effect. This Act amends some provisions of the Money Laundering Prevention Act 2012 in order to strengthen the effectiveness of the latter. While the amending law does not make direct reference to any international instrument, its enactment reflects attempts at alignment of national legislation with related international law instruments.

#### Definitions

"Definitions" articulated in Section 2 of the Act of 2012 have undergone some changes. 'Bangladesh Financial Intelligence Unit' has replaced 'Bangladesh Bank'. While the 2012 law primarily vested investigative functions on the Anti-Corruption Commission and officers of any other investigating agency, the term 'investigating agency' in the amending Act signifies any agency authorized to investigate 'predicate offences' listed in this Act. However, the Criminal Investigation Department of Bangladesh Police shall investigate offences that are subject to investigation by the Bangladesh Police. The Bangladesh Financial

* University of Dhaka, Bangladesh.

Intelligence Unit, in consultation with the Government, can also authorize other investigating agencies to conduct investigations. Whereas the 2012 law included the laundering of or attempt to launder money or property derived from "human trafficking" in the list of offences, the amending Act has extended the ambit by adding to the offence of human trafficking the receipt of or attempting to receive money or any valuable object from anyone with false promises of overseas employment.

Monetary Punishment

The amending Act changed the monetary punishment structure prescribed in Section 4 of the 2012 Act by increasing the amount of the fine and permitting the Court to extend the period of imprisonment in the event of non-payment of the fine within the stipulated time.

Investigation and Trial of Offences

Section 9 of the 2012 Act regarding investigation and trial of predicate offences has been replaced. Now officials of the Investigating Agencies or joint investigating forces constituted by the Bangladesh Financial Intelligence Unit in consultation with the Government may investigate the offences under this Act. In addition to this law, investigating officials will be entitled to exercise their authority provided by other laws in force to investigate and identify property of the accused individual or entity. In undertaking investigation, the Investigating Agency shall be entitled to obtain information on client accounts from banks or financial institutions or from Bangladesh Financial Intelligence Unit.

A Special Judge appointed under Section 3 of the Criminal Law (Amendment) Act (Act XL of 1958) 1958 shall try offences under this Act. By changing Section 12 of the 2012 Act, the amending law enables the Court to freeze or issue croak order against property situated in or outside Bangladesh linked to money laundering or illegally obtained income or property based on a written application of the Investigating Agency. Where it is not possible to identify such property or income, the Court may freeze income or issue croak order against property of equivalent value from other resources belonging to the accused individual or entity.

### *Consumer Protection—Food Safety – Right To Life – Protection Against Particular Hazards*

**The Formalin Control Act 2015 [Act 5 of 2015]** – an Act enacted to protect the health and well-being of the public by preventing the misuse of preservative substances.

The right to food is explicitly mentioned in different international instruments, namely, the International Covenant on Economic, Social and Cultural Rights 1966; the Convention on the Elimination of All Forms of Discrimination against Women 1979; the Convention on the Rights of the Child 1989; the Convention Relating to the Status of Refugees 1951; and the Convention on the Rights of Persons with Disabilities 2006. The United Nations Guidelines for Consumer Protection (as expanded in 1999) encourages "high levels of ethical conduct for those engaged in the production and distribution of goods and services to consumers" for the protection of populations.

The unrestricted use of formalin to preserve and increase the shelf life of fruits, vegetables, fish, meat and other food items by unscrupulous traders has become pervasive in Bangladesh, which poses grave threats to the life, health and well-being of consumers. Recognizing the seriousness of the matter, the Government has enacted The Formalin Control Act, 2015 for containing the misuse of formalin and bringing its production, import, sale and use under a regulatory framework. The law shall be applicable to formalin, formaldehyde and any other government-approved chemicals used for the manufacture of formalin.

The Act introduces a licensing system under which anyone who wishes to import, produce, ship, stock, sell, or use formalin will require a license from the Government (Sections 4–5). The licensing authority or an official duly authorized by it shall have the power to enter into any premises that produce or stock the substance and any shop that sells it for inspection. The authority can confiscate the preservative on the discovery of errors in the books of account and/or faults in the equipment, or if the amount of formalin is found to exceed the permissible limit (Section 7). If deemed necessary, the Authority may close down the stores engaged in trade or transport of the substance for a maximum of 15 days (Section 8). The Act provides for the formation of Formalin Control Committees in every district and sub-district for overseeing the implementation of the law at the local level (Section 9).

Based on the nature of the offence, the Act provides penalties of varying degrees ranging from fines to life imprisonment. Penalties shall apply if someone is found to possess, import, produce, stock, sell, use, and transport formalin without a proper (Section 23). Anyone breaching the conditions of the license shall be liable for a maximum of 7 years imprisonment but not less than 3 years or a fine of Taka 5,00,000 but not less than Taka 2,00,000 or with both (Section 21). The Act also imposes penalties against anyone who is in possession of equipment and raw material or who permits the use of property and equipment for formalin production (Sections 24–25) without proper authorization.

### *Worker's Rights—Service Rules – Working Conditions—Health And Safety—Non-Discrimination – Collective Bargaining—Employment Of Adolescents*

**The Bangladesh Labor Rules 2015** – rules formulated by dint of the powers given in Section 351 of the Bangladesh Labor Act, 2006 (Act No. 42 of 2006).

Long after the enactment of the Bangladesh Labor Act in 2006 and following lengthy consultations with employers and workers groups, the Government of Bangladesh introduced the Bangladesh Labor Rules in September 2015 through an official gazette. The Rules encapsulate a wide range of operational matters starting from the introduction of service rules and disciplinary actions to health and safety. The Rules are intended to better conform to the fundamental rights at work as envisaged in the Covenant on Social, Economic and Cultural Rights 1966 and international labor standards on workers' welfare, health and safety underpinned in various International Labor Organisation (ILO) conventions on freedom of association; collective bargaining; abolition of forced or compulsory labor; non-discrimination and equality of opportunity and treatment in employment and occupation; elimination of child labor; and conditions of employment of young persons. The Labor Rules comprise 367 sections. The key provisions are highlighted below.

#### Service Rules

The Rules lay out comprehensive conditions of appointment and services in Chapter 2. If any owner of any establishment wishes to introduce Service Rules, he must furnish the Inspector General with a draft copy for approval (Section 3). The provisions in the Service Rules must correspond to the rights of the workers envisaged in The Labor Act 2006. The Service Rules must go through an elaborate vetting process before formal approval (Section 4).

#### Contracting Firms

Contracting firms that wish to supply workers to any firm or establishment require registration and a formal license in the due process (Section 7). Each contracting firm must deposit security money in order to get the license (Section 11). The Rules impose certain restrictions on licensees and receivers of services. For example, conditions, which are less favorable as described in the law, must not be inserted in the appointment letter executed between the contracting organization and the worker (Section 8).

#### Conditions of Work

The Labor Rules expound a wide range of issues that are essential for strengthening good governance in the workplace and ensuring workers' rights.

These include inter alia an organogram on workers (Section 18); appointment letters containing necessary information including wages/salary and other financial benefits (Section 19); photo identity cards (Sections 20–24); measures for lay-off, curtailment and discharge from service (Sections 25–28) and procedures for investigating misconduct by workers and related punishments (Sections 29–33).

### Employment of Adolescents

Certification of age and competence is essential for employment of adolescents. In the absence of birth and school certificates, a registered physician (Section 34) shall give such certification. The Inspector shall approve working hours for adolescents (Section 35). Adolescents are prohibited from engaging in dangerous and hazardous work (Section 36).

### Pregnant Workers

Special provisions are in place for pregnant workers. A pregnant worker shall not be subjected to any behavior or comment that may be construed as derogatory or humiliating; shall not be engaged in any hazardous work or work which potentially constitutes a threat to her health; shall be given priority in terms of using the elevator at work; and shall be provided with congenial facilities for breast-feeding after delivery (Section 37).

### Health and Safety

The Rules cover workers' health protection and security issues in Sections 40–67. Workers must use prescribed safety gears while undertaking dangerous works (Section 67). The Rules also provide elaborate welfare measures for first aid and treatment of workers, cleaning and washing facilities, canteen, and children's crèche (Sections 76–98). Sections 40–53 focus on healthy working conditions that include issues that range from waste removal, washing, dust and smoke, ventilation, temperature, drinking water, toilet and washroom to building structures, emergency exits, adequate supply of water to fire extinguishers.

### Working Hours

The Rules permit adult workers to work for 8 (eight) hours daily (excluding the time for having meals and break period) and maximum of 10 hours provided the workers agree to work overtime on payment (Section 99). Workers employed in construction, re-rolling, steel mills, ship-breaking industry and hazardous works shall be entitled to half an hour's break after every two hours of work against which the owner cannot deduct any wage (Section 99). Night work for female workers from 10.00 pm to 6.00 am is permissible only if they consent to it (Section 103).

Leave

Workers are entitled to different categories of leave—weekly, casual, sick, festival and annual leave (Sections 100–101, 106–110). Festival leave shall be fixed in consultation with the Joint Bargaining Representative (if any). In the absence of a Joint Bargaining Representative, the owner shall fix the festival leave by discussing the matter with the workers to the extent possible.

Wages

A Wage Board, constituted by representatives of workers, the owner, owner associations, trade union federations or highest representative unions in the absence of federations (Section 121), shall recommend the rate of minimum wage by way of a Government Gazette. Workers must be informed about their wages before they are formally employed (Section 111[4]). A worker who resigns or is laid off, discharged, terminated, or expelled must be paid his/her wages within 7 (seven) working days after his/her separation from the job; compensation and other dues must be paid within a maximum 30 (thirty) working days from the date of separation (Section 112).

### *Public Sector Procurement—Concession Law-Partnering Contracts—Competition—Market Access—Trade and Service—Anti-Corruption*

**The Bangladesh Public-Private Partnership Act, 2015 (Act 18 of 2015)** – a law enacted with the objective of fulfilling the fundamental needs of citizens and improving their standard of living by accelerating socio-economic development through increased investment in public sector infrastructure for sustainable economic growth. The law provides a robust legal framework to attract national and international private sector investors to partner with the Government and help create opportunities for Bangladesh to successfully participate in the world economy.

The Act reinforces select provisions of the UNCITRAL Guidance on Public-Private Partnership/ Concession Laws (2000), UNCITRAL – Legislative Guide on Privately Finance Infrastructure Projects, 2001, Guidance on PPP/ Concession Laws, OECD Principles for Public Governance of Public-Private Partnerships, the WTO Agreement, the General Agreement on Tariffs and Trade (GATT), and the General Agreement on Trade in Services (GATS).

The Act provides for the establishment of a Public-Private Partnership Authority (PPP Authority) (Section4 [1]), to be chaired by the Prime Minister (Section 7[1][a]) and overseen by a Board of Governors (Section 6). The PPP Authority, an entity that can sue and be sued in its name, shall be neutral and independent in terms of its financial and administrative activities (Section 4[3]). Section 9 spells out the powers and functions of the PPP

Authority at length. Among other things, the PPP Authority is empowered to promulgate and implement PPP related policies, regulations, directives and guidelines; provide decisions on the financial participation and provision of incentives for PPP projects by the Government; frame technical and best practice requirements, pre-qualification and bid documents; develop and vet model PPP contracts; determine the process for selecting private partners; approve the selected bidder for PPP projects; approve the termination of PPP projects; frame the Terms of Reference (ToR) for the appointment of consultants and experts; determine and approve the organogram and salary structure of officers and employees; and oversee and monitor PPP activities.

Chapter 3 sets out the provisions for the identification and approval of PPP projects. The contracting authority or the PPP Authority may take up a project for implementation on a PPP basis by identifying any project from within or outside the Annual Development program of the Government (Section 13). It may declare any project as a national priority for socio-economic development of the country or for urgently mitigating effects of a major adversity faced by the general public (Section 15). The Cabinet Committee has the mandate to grant the in-principle and final approval for PPP projects (Section 14). Under the Act, the Government can provide financing in respect of technical assistance and viability gap, against equity and loan, against linked component and any other activities as may be determined by the PPP Authority (Section 16). Besides, the Government may by general or special order, declare incentives to encourage private sector investment in PPP projects (Section 17).

Chapter 4 highlights the selection process of a private partner for PPP projects in accordance with the regulations as approved by the Board of Governors (Section 20). Any private organization may, in accordance with the prescribed regulations, submit to the contracting authority or the PPP Authority, a PPP project proposal for the construction and operation of new infrastructure or the reconstruction and operation of existing infrastructure of the public sector (Section 20[1]). Unsolicited proposals shall be evaluated in accordance with the said regulations (Section 20[2]). Once finally selected, the private partner shall, either prior to or after the execution of the PPP contract, incorporate a limited company in accordance with provisions of existing laws pertaining to formation of companies (Section 22 [1]).

The Act contains clear provisions to guard against corruption and conflict of interest. The law makes any person found directly or indirectly engaging in any corrupt, fraudulent, coercive or collusive practice in the selection process of a private partner or implementation of a PPP project, liable for corruption or misconduct, or both. The penalty in such cases is prosecution including departmental disciplinary action in line with service rules (Section 24[1]).

Furthermore, if any organization is found to be involved in corrupt activities, its pre-qualification, bid or PPP contract, shall be cancelled and declared ineligible, either permanently or temporarily (Section 24[2]). If a person involved in the evaluation of bids for selecting a private partner finds that he has a direct or indirect conflict of interest with any person or organization associated with any concerned project, he shall voluntarily withdraw from such process, failing which he will be held liable for collusive practice (Section 25).

The Act provides a comprehensive checklist of the key issues that must be incorporated in a PPP contract (Section 26). The terms and conditions of partnerships includes the granting the private partner the right to access the land of the project and to impose levy on users in consideration of the supply of public goods and services (Section 28). The law envisages dispute resolution mechanisms to settle differences between contracting parties, which include amicable settlement, mediation and arbitration (Section 30).

## Judicial Decisions

### *War Crimes—Crimes Against Humanity—Genocide—Persecution On Religious & Political Grounds*

***Salahuddin Qader Chowdhury v. The Chief Prosecutor, International Crimes Tribunal***, 8 ALR (AD) 2016(2)[Criminal Appeal No. 122 of 2013, Judgement on 29 July, 2015, Appellate Division of the Supreme Court of Bangladesh]

In October 2013, the International Crimes Tribunal (hereafter ICT) convicted the appellant, Salahuddin Qader Chowdhury, on charges of crimes against humanity and war crimes committed in 1971 during the Bangladesh war of liberation. The Tribunal sentenced him to death. The appellant took a plea of alibi claiming that he was not present at the scene in Chittagong during the alleged incidents, as he had left for erstwhile West Pakistan for studies at the beginning of the liberation struggle and subsequently went to London where he stayed until 1974.

Considering the materials on record and testimonies of the witnesses, the Court was convinced that the plea of alibi taken by the appellant was concocted and had no basis and that the ICT had rightly found the accused guilty of the charges with the exception of one charge. In view of the appellant's complicity in the incidents of torture and murder, the Court considered the award of death sentence by the ICT as appropriate and observed:

> [The accused] persecuted civilian and unarmed people, tortured them to death, caused disappearance of innocent people … solely on religious

> and political grounds … he had [committed] all these brutal offences with [the] specific intention to exterminate the Hindu religious community and his political opponents from that locality. And he eventually accomplished his killing mission of mass people, … [the] rarest of atrocities so far committed with the collaboration of occupying [armed] forces and local allies. Accordingly, it is one of the fittest cases to award such sentences. We find no cogent ground to interfere with the sentences of death.

The verdict clearly resonates with the core principles of international humanitarian laws, human rights against torture and non-discrimination based on religion.

### *War Crimes—Genocide—Judicial Notice*

***Ali Ahsan Muhammad Mujahid v. The Chief Prosecutor, International Crimes Tribunal***, 24 BLT (AD) 2016 [Criminal Appeal No. 103 of 2013, judgement on 16 June, 2015, Appellate Division of the Supreme Court of Bangladesh]

The International Crimes Tribunal (hereafter ICT) convicted the appellant, Ali Ahsan Muhammad Mujahid, on charges of crimes against humanity during the Bangladesh war of liberation in 1971. The Tribunal sentenced him to 5 year imprisonment and to life imprisonment on some charges and to death on charges of killing intellectuals. On appeal, the Court considered the oral and documentary evidence together with the appellant's activities and conduct prior to, during and after the war of liberation. It found the appellant liable for the instigation, abetment and commission of the crime of genocide by planning, proposing and provoking the *Al Badr Bahini* to kidnap and kill the intellectuals of the country only days before Bangladesh achieved victory in the war of liberation.

Recognizing that this case carried the burden of establishing the historical context in which the alleged crimes occurred, the Court acknowledged the necessity of taking judicial notice of adjudicated facts. By way of reference, the Court drew upon observations of the International Criminal Tribunal for Rwanda (hereafter ICTR) in *Prosecutor v. Semanza* (ICTR-97-20-A, Appeal Judgement on 20th May, 2005) where it was held that taking judicial notice of the facts of common knowledge is a matter of an obligation and not discretionary. In determining what constitutes common knowledge, the ICTR stated that these are facts that are so notorious or clearly established or susceptible to determination by references to readily obtainable or authoritative sources, and as such, evidence of their existence is unnecessary. The ICTR maintained that common knowledge concerns facts that are generally known in the Tribunal's jurisdiction and are reasonably undisputable.

Alluding to the brutality with which *Al Badr Bahini* committed the killings at the instigation of the appellant, the Court observed that such acts were "comparable with Hitler's gas chamber genocide". Upholding the death sentence awarded by the ICT, the Court commented:

> [The] motive of the killings of intellectuals was cold-blooded with the deliberate design … to cripple the future of this newborn country. It is the duty of the Court to award proper sentence having regard to the nature of the offence, … the degree of criminality, the manner in which it was committed and all attend[ing] circumstances. The occurrences of [the] killing of intellectuals were committed [in an] extremely cruel and beastly manner which demonstrated … the depraved character of the perpetrators. It will be a mockery of justice to permit the accused to escape the extreme penalty of law when faced with such evidence and such cruel acts…. The sentence awarded by the Tribunal for [the killing of] intellectuals is not disproportionate in view of the nature of [the] charge and [the] evidence adduced. The people of this earth did not forget Hiroshima and Nagasaki. This Nation did not and shall never forget 1971.

### *Indemnity—Human Rights Violation—Torture—Custodial Deaths—Equality before Law—Non-Discrimination—Reparation*

***Z. I. Khan Panna v. Bangladesh represented by the Secretary, Ministry of Law, Justice and Parliamentary Affairs and others*** **[Writ Petition No. 7650 of 2012, judgement on 13-09-2015, High Court Division of the Supreme Court of Bangladesh (Special Original Jurisdiction)]**

The petitioner filed an application challenging an impugned Act that was promulgated in 2003 which provided indemnity for all disciplined forces and public functionaries for the detention, arrest, search, interrogation and such other actions taken against the citizens between 16th October, 2002 and 9th January, 2003 pursuant to an order dated 16 October 2002. The Government issued the order on the pretext of maintaining law and order in the country, curbing terrorism and recovering illegal arms from miscreants pursuant to which drives under "Operation Clean Heart" was conducted all over the country until 9th January, 2003.

The said Act provided that no legal proceeding shall lie in any Court due to any harm to one's life, liberty or property or any mental or physical damage stemming therefrom, if such injury was caused by the actions taken by the disciplined forces pursuant to the order dated 16th October, 2002 and other subsequent orders made by the Government. The Act further stipulated that any proceeding initiated in any Court relating to the actions taken pursuant to the above-mentioned orders within the said period and any decision rendered by such Court shall be considered void, ineffective and abated.

Allegations of human rights violations and unlawful acts during the drives by the joint forces during the said period were rife. Both electronic and print media at the time widely reported these crimes, which included harassment, illegal arrests, trespass, illegal seizure of property, torture, mutilation and custodial killings.

The petitioner maintained that the law should be scrapped as being *ultra vires* the Constitution and the losses suffered by the victims of the so-called 'Operation Clean Heart' be redressed by offering compensation to their families.

In arriving at its decision, the Court referred to international law standards on human rights and fundamental freedoms and various case law of the Indian Supreme Court. The Court emphasised that "no one is above law and everybody is subject to law.... In this respect, we are reminded of an oft quoted legal dictum— 'Be you ever so high, the law is above you." Reiterating Bangladesh's commitment under international law, the Court stated:

> Indisputably Bangladesh is a signatory to the United Nations Universal Declaration of Human Rights, 1948, International Covenant on Civil and Political Rights, 1976 and Convention against Torture and Other Cruel, Inhuman or Degrading Treatment or Punishment, 1987. Apart from the provisions of our Constitution [.....], as a State Party [...] Bangladesh is committed to translate into reality the provisions of those international instruments and to see that no one is subjected to torture, intimidation, coercion, degrading treatment, brutality or custodial death save in accordance with law.

Drawing on the above, the Court found the indemnity law to be void *ab initio* and *ultra vires* the Constitution and observed:

> Any sort of deliberate torture on the victims in the custody of the joint forces or law-enforcing agencies is ex-facie illegal, unconstitutional and condemnable. In that event, they have the right to seek the protection of the law in any independent and impartial Court or Tribunal, as the case may be.... The law-enforcing agencies or the joint forces cannot take

> the law into their own hands and by doing so, they have infringed the relevant provisions of the Constitution.... By providing blanket indemnity ... to the members of the joint forces and all their actions during the period under reference, a clear discriminatory situation has been created amongst the citizenry which is violative of their fundamental rights as embodied and guaranteed in the Constitution.

On the issue of compensation, the Court observed that the assessment of the quantum of compensation would vary from case to case depending on the facts and circumstances; therefore, no hard and fast rule could be laid down. Since this is a Public Interest Litigation and no affected individual or victim has personally invoked the writ jurisdiction of the High Court Division claiming compensation, the Court refrained from passing any wholesale order of payment of compensation to the victims or their families. However, the Court ruled that they would be entitled to "call in aid the writ jurisdiction of the High Court Division for reparations by way of pecuniary compensation to be paid to them by the State for the unlawful and unconstitutional State actions during the 'Operation Clean Heart'." Accordingly, the affected persons/victims of brutalities or torture or the dependents/family members of the deceased in case of custodial deaths during the 'Operation Clean Heart' may file cases against concerned members of the joint forces/law-enforcing agencies both under civil and criminal laws of the land. They may also invoke the writ jurisdiction of the High Court Division for compensation, in addition to the reliefs sought for under prevalent civil as well as criminal laws of Bangladesh.

In conclusion, the Court recommended that the State may consider enacting enact a law like the *Philippines Human Rights Victims' Reparation and Recognition Act of 2013* in order to compensate victims/affected persons of human rights violations during Operation Clean Heart.

### *International Agreements*

**Promotion and Reciprocal Protection of Investments between the Government of the People's Republic of Bangladesh and the Government of the Kingdom of Bahrain, 22 December, Manama, Bahrain**

The Government of Bangladesh entered into a bilateral agreement with the Government of Bahrain on 22nd December, 2015 in Manama, Bahrain. The purpose of the Agreement is to "expand and deepen economic cooperation on a long-term basis" and "create and maintain favourable conditions for investments" by both countries in each other's territories.

The Agreement emphasises that investment objectives must be achieved without harming the environment and public health of either state [Article 4].

The Agreement also stipulates that neither of the Contracting Parties shall take any measures for expropriation, nationalization or dispossession against investors of the other party except where such measures (i) are necessary to protect public interest and are taken in due process of the law; (ii) are non-discriminatory; and (iii) are accompanied by payment of prompt, adequate and effective compensation in line with internationally recognized principles of valuation on the basis of the fair market value at the time when the action was taken [Article 6].

According to Article 8 of the Agreement, disputes between a Contracting Party and the investor of the other Contracting Party shall be resolved amicably failing which the matter may be submitted to (i) a competent court in the territory of the Contracting Party where the investment was made; or (ii) the International Center for Settlement of Investment Disputes (ICSID); or (iii) an ad hoc tribunal established under the arbitration rules of the United Nations Commission On International Trade Law (UNCITRAL). The arbitral decisions shall be final and binding on the Parties to be executed in accordance to their laws and United Nations Conventions on the Recognition and Enforcement of Foreign Arbitral Awards (New York Convention) 1955.

In the event of a dispute between the Contracting Parties, the matter should be settled through diplomatic channels failing which the matter shall be referred to an arbitral tribunal [Article 9 (1)(2)]. If any problem arises with regard to the appointment of members of the tribunal, the President of the International Court of Justice shall make the necessary arrangements [Article 9(4)].

**Promoting Social Dialogue and Harmonious Industrial Relations in the Bangladesh Ready-Made Garment Industry—Initiative Signed by ILO, Sweden and Bangladesh in New York on 26 September 2015**

An agreement to launch a project to enhance rights in the workplace and industrial relations in the Bangladesh ready-made garment sector in line with relevant international labor standards was signed in New York on the margins of the United Nations General Assembly meeting on 26 September 2015. The signatories were the Swedish Minister for International Development Cooperation, the ILO Director General and the Bangladesh Minister of Labor and employment.

The initiative, which will run from November 2015 to December 2020, will receive US$5.4 million from Sweden. In addition to improving dialogue between workers and employers, the initiative seeks to strengthen conciliation and arbitration mechanisms to enhance the capacity of employers and workers to engage in collective bargaining and social dialogue to effectively prevent and resolve workplace disputes. Given that nearly 80% of the workers in this sector are women, this initiative will focus on empowerment of women workers by incorporating their rights and interests in the workplace.

**The 1974 India-Bangladesh Land Boundary Agreement Enters into Force on 6 June 2015**

Bangladesh and India have resolved a decades-old border dispute through a land exchange agreement that started with a physical exchange of enclaves on July 31, 2015. The exchange of instruments of ratification by Prime Minister Narendra Modi of India and Prime Minister Sheikh Hasina of Bangladesh finally paved the way for the long-standing India-Bangladesh Land Boundary Agreement to enter into force on 6 June 2015 during the Indian Prime Minister's State visit to Bangladesh.

India and Bangladesh have a land boundary of approximately 4,100 km, which was determined by the 1947 Radcliffe Award as the India-East Pakistan land boundary. However, disputes arose regarding some border issues. Following the independence of Bangladesh in 1971, India and Bangladesh signed the Land Boundary Agreement in 1974 in an attempt to settle the outstanding issues. This Agreement was amended in 2011 by an additional Protocol. The Agreement provides for the exchange of pockets of Indian and Bangladeshi territories and the clarification of the India-Bangladesh border, which remained unresolved following partition in 1947. The implementation of the Land Boundary Agreement deals with three major border issues pertaining to (a) adverse possessions, (b) enclaves, and (c) an un-demarcated land boundary of approximately 6.1 km. The implementation of the Agreement was on hold for various reasons primarily on the part of India.

In October 2009, Bangladesh initiated arbitration proceedings under Annex VII of the of the United Nations Convention on the Law of the Sea 1982. It requested the Tribunal to identify the land boundary between Bangladesh and India and delimit each State's territorial sea, exclusive economic zone (EEZ) and continental shelf within and beyond 200 nautical miles, where both States had competing claims. On 7 July 2014, the Arbitral Tribunal issued an award granting approximately 106,613km to Bangladesh and 300,220 km to India, out of a total relevant area of 406,833km. Both India and Bangladesh accepted the decision.

While lending a much-needed clarity in terms of maritime entitlements of both countries, this development is an exemplary example of how States can amicably resolve sovereignty issues and convert them into opportunities for economic and political cooperation.

**Agreement between the European Union and the People's Republic of Bangladesh on Certain Aspects of Air Services, February 2015**

An agreement was initiated in February 2015 to strengthen aviation relations between the EU and Bangladesh and to restore bilateral air services agreements between Bangladesh and EU Member States.

The Agreement aims to modernise the legal framework for air services between the Parties and allow any EU airline to operate flights between Bangladesh and any EU Member State where it is established and where a bilateral agreement with Bangladesh exists. The Agreement shall enter into force when the Parties have notified each other in writing that their respective internal procedures necessary for its entry into force have been completed (Article 8). Both Parties are committed to completing the necessary formalities as soon as possible.

**Memorandum of Understanding on Education the People's Republic of Bangladesh and the People's Republic of China Signed on 24 May 2015**

Bangladesh and China signed an MOU to promote and strengthen exchanges and cooperation in the field of education, research, and intellectual development between the two countries. Such exchanges will take place at both basic and higher education levels and will extend to technical and vocational training. Under the MOU, opportunities will be available for staff learning, research, and scholarships for under-graduate and post-graduate students. The MOU also provides for refresher programmes and seminars, conferences and symposiums for capacity development through cross learning.

**Agreement between the Government of the Kingdom of Bahrain and the Government of the People's Republic of Bangladesh for the Avoidance of Double Taxation and the Prevention of Fiscal Evasion with Respect to Taxes on Income Signed in Manama on 22 December 2015**

According to this Agreement, where a resident of a Contracting State earns an income in accordance with the provisions of this Agreement, may be taxed in the other Contracting State, the first-mentioned Contracting State shall allow as deduction from the tax on the income of that resident, an amount equal to the income tax paid in that other Contracting State. However, such deduction shall not exceed that part of the income tax as computed before the deduction is made, which is attributable, as the case may be, to the income, which may be taxed in that Contracting State.

**Bilateral Agreements, Protocols and MOUs between the Governments of Indian and Bangladesh Signed on 6 June 2015**

India and Bangladesh signed several bilateral agreements, protocols and MOUs to promote mutual cooperation in the fields of trade, communication, energy, tourism and education and culture on 6 June 2015 during the Indian Prime Minister's State visit to Bangladesh.

The two nations signed an Agreement on coastal shipping to promote 2-way trade and commerce through ports of both countries; a Protocol on inland water transit and trade (renewal) for mutual use of waterways for trade and passage of goods; an Agreement between Bangladesh Standards and Testing Institution (BSTI) and Bureau of Indian Standards (BIS) on cooperation in the field of standardisation to eliminate technical barriers to trade and enhance reciprocal market access of products to each other's countries.; Agreements and Protocols on bus service through Dhaka-Shillong-Guwahati and Kolkata-Dhaka-Agartala for facilitate passenger services; an Agreement between Submarine Cable Company Limited (BSCCL) and Bharat Sanchar Nigam Limited (BSNL) for leasing of international bandwidth to boost signal strength of the internet in the North-East of India.

Both countries signed MOUs between coast guards of both countries to ensure joint marine security and prevent crimes at sea; on the prevention of human trafficking and ensuring speedy rescue, recovery, prosecution and re-integration; on the prevention of smuggling and circulation of fake currency notes; the extending of a new line of credit (LoC) of USD 2 billion by the Indian Government to the Government of Bangladesh for social and infrastructure development; on blue economy and maritime cooperation in the Bay of Bengal and the Indian Ocean for capacity building, training and joint research collaborations; on the use of Chittagong and Mongla ports for the movement of goods to and from India; for a project under IECC (India Endowment for Climate Change of SAARC) for supplying efficient and improved cook stoves to 70000 rural households in Bangladesh; on the establishment of Indian special economic zone in Bangladesh to encourage investment; on cultural exchange programme for the years 2015–17; for joint research by the University of Dhaka, Bangladesh and Council of Scientific and Industrial Research, India on Oceanography of the Bay of Bengal; for education and cultural exchange between the University of Rajshahi, Bangladesh and the University of Jamia Millia Islamia, India.

A statement of intent on Bangladesh-India Education Cooperation (adoption) was made which envisages a broad framework to enhance bilateral co-operation in the field of education. A letter of consent was handed over by the Insurance Development and Regulatory Authority (IDRA), Bangladesh to Life Insurance Corporation (LIC) of India to start commercial business operations in Bangladesh through joint ventures.

# State Practice of Asian Countries in International Law

*Japan*

*Kanami Ishibashi**

## Environment

### *Act on Preventing Environmental Pollution on Mercury and the Amendment to the Air Pollution Control Act*

Since 2009, Japan had taken significant leadership as one of the countries which had a bitter experience from toxicity of mercury (well known as Minamata disease which cause methylmercury (MeHg) poisoning to those who ingest fish or shellfish contaminated by the waste discharge of Chisso Co. Ltd. chemical plant). As a result, the text of the Minamata Convention on Mercury was adopted at the Conference in Kumamoto, Japan on 10 October 2013 and opened for signature for one year. It will enter into force on 16 August 2017.

To implement this convention, Japan enacted the Act on Preventing Environmental Pollution on Mercury (Act No. 42 of 2015) and the amendment of the Air Pollution Control Act (Act No. 97 of 1968; Amendment Act No. 41 of 2015). The Convention obliges the parties "to protect the human health and the environment from anthropogenic emissions and releases of mercury and mercury compounds" (Article 1) and requires the parties to prohibit, phase out and control, uses, mining, manufacturing, trades, release and storage of mercury and mercury added products (including wastes). Therefore, the Act on Preventing Environmental Pollution on Mercury prohibits mining of mercury itself (Article 4) and mining and extracting gold using mercury (Article 20). The Act prohibits uses of "designated mercury added products" such as battery, lamp, medical and industrial measuring equipment including thermometer and blood-pressure meter and dental amalgam unless it accords with the usages defined in the Convention (Articles 5–11). Moreover, the Act provides to expand the scope of "designated mercury added product" to include the products which have less mercury rather than the Convention requires or to phase out such use itself by providing deadlines. After such deadlines, the trade of those will also be strictly regulated. Besides, the Act requires the person or

* Associate Professor, Tokyo University of Foreign Studies, Japan.

DOI 10.1163/9789004344556_017

the enterprise to assess risks of new mercury added products which is not designated by the Convention if he/she manufactures or sells such products (Articles 13–15).

To ensure the safe and proper storage of mercury, the Act requires the person or enterprise that possesses mercury to report the status of its storage to the Authority periodically (Article 22). And, the Act requires the manufacturing enterprises to indicate voluntarily if products are mercury added product (Article 18) to facilitate the reuse or recycle of such products. The Act provides the reuse or recycle of mercury added products should be subject to environmentally sound control guidelines and should be reported to the Authority periodically (Articles 23–24).

Furthermore, the Air Pollution Act is amended and ensures to implement the part of emission of mercury in the air. Since mercury is liquid at normal temperature and is highly volatile, the regulation of emission to air is very important. Such emission occurs, for example, in coal combustion and incineration of mercury added products as wastes.

Concerning the air pollution caused by mercury, the Convention draws special attention to five "point sources of emissions of mercury and mercury compounds to the atmosphere" as follows: coal-fired power plants; coal-fired industrial boilers; smelting and roasting processes used in the production of non-ferrous metals; waste incineration facilities; cement clinker production facilities (Annex D). Therefore, the Act firstly provides the enterprise to report in advance about new establishment of such facilities (Article 18 (23, 24)), secondly to regulate concentrations of emissions at the outlet of such emissions by using standard set up with best available technology (Article 18 (22)) and the Act even requires the facilities which are not designated by the Convention to make voluntary framework to reduce emissions of mercury, by setting up the standard, measuring concentrations, keeping record and cooperating with the Authority to join the national policy (Article 18 (32, 33)).

## Security

### *Significant Reform of Security Acts: The Role of the Japanese SDF (Self Defense Forces) is Expanded*

There were comprehensive reforms of the Japanese Security System and International Peace Support Act (Law Concerning Cooperation and Support Activities to Armed Forces of Foreign Countries, etc. in Situations where the International Community is Collectively Addressing for International

Peace and Security (Act No. 77 of 2015)). The Act is newly legislated and major amendments to the security issues are carried out in the ten Acts, the amendment part of which are bundled and named as Peace and Security Legislation Development Act (Act No. 76 of 2015).

The International Peace Support Act includes amendments to existing laws as follows (Act No. of all amendment to the original Acts is No. 76 of 2015):

1. Self-Defense Forces Act (Act No. 165 of 1954);
2. International Peace Cooperation Act (Act on Cooperation with United Nations Peacekeeping Operations and Other Operations) (Act No. 79 of 1992);
3. Act Concerning Measures to Ensure Peace and Security of Japan in Situations that Will Have an Important Influence on Japan's Peace and Security (Act. No. 60 of 1999);
4. Ship Inspection Operations Act (Law Concerning Ship Inspection Operations in Situations that Will Have an Important Influence on Japan's Peace and Security and Other Situations) (Act No. 145 of 2000);
5. Armed Attack Situations Response Act (Law for Ensuring Peace and Independence of Japan and Security of the State and the People in Armed Attack Situations, etc., and Survived-Threatening Situation) (Act No. 79 of 2003);
6. The US and Others' Military Actions Related Measures Act (Law Concerning the Measures Conducted by the Government in Line with US and Other Countries' Military Actions in Armed Attack Situations, etc., and Survival-Threatening Situation) (Act. No. 113 of 2004);
7. Act Regarding the Use of Specific Public Facilities (Law Concerning the Use of Specific Public Facilities and Others in Situations including Where an Armed Attack against Japan Occurs) (Act No. 114 of 2004);
8. Maritime Transportation Restriction Act (Law Concerning the Restriction of Maritime Transportation of Foreign Military Supplies and Others in Armed Attack Situations, etc., and Survived-Threatening Situation) (Act No. 116 of 2004);
9. Prisoners of War Act (Law Concerning the Treatment of Prisoners of War and Other Detainees in Armed Attack Situations, etc., and Survived-Threatening Situation) (Act No. 117 of 2004); and
10. Act for Establishment of the National Security Council (Act No. 71 of 1986).

In the above legislation, Japan changed its interpretation of Article 9 of the Constitution and adopted new conditions which allow Japan to invoke the use of force as follows:

(1) When an armed attack against Japan has occurred, or when an armed attack against a foreign country that is in a close relationship with Japan occurs and as a result threatens Japan's survival and poses a clear danger to fundamentally overturn people's right to life, liberty, and pursuit of happiness;
(2) When there is no appropriate means available to repel the attack, and ensure Japan's survival and protect its people; and
(3) Use of force to the minimum extent necessary.

Firstly, the new Act, International Peace Support Act (Law Concerning Cooperation and Support Activities to Armed Forces of Foreign Countries, etc. in Situations where the International Community is Collectively Addressing for International Peace and Security) established the permanent system for dispatch of the SDF to support the armed forces operating in conflict areas. This Act brings important differences as follows: Japan does not need any special legislation to dispatch the SDF to the to the conflict areas anymore (which was needed in the past), the Act allows to dispatch the SDF not only under the traditional UN resolution (resolutions that decide, call upon, recommend or authorize foreign countries to respond to the situation that threatens the peace and security of the international community) but also under the resolution that regard the situations as a threat to peace or a breach of the peace and call on UN member States to respond to the situation concerned. While the dispatch of the SDF needs "resolution" of either UNSC or UNGA, it expands the possibility for the SDF to be dispatched.

Since the Japanese Constitution in principle prohibits the use of force (Article 9 provides "the Japanese people forever renounce ... the threat or use of force as a means of settling international disputes"), the use of force had been permitted only as a self-defense measure. However, the Act admits rescue activities such as "Kaketsuke-Keigo" (coming to protection of individuals related to operations in response to urgent request) of the SDF to be commenced by the commanding officers on site and thereby allows the SDF dispatched to use force not only for self-defense but also for accomplishing its mission. The Act cautions that such use of force is not merged with the normal "use of force" and, to avoid any risk for Japan to be dragged into war, provides that such activities are only allowed in the area where combat operations are not actually being conducted.

Secondly, the bundled amendments to the existing laws, named as Peace and Security Legislation Development Act is established.

The key amendments are follows:

(1) **Revision of the Self-Defense Forces Law: Rescue missions and use of force not for self defense**
The SDF can operate rescue activities to Japanese nationals overseas involving the use of weapons on the condition that (a) the competent authorities of the country concerned are maintaining public safety and order at the time; (b) no act of combat will be conducted in that area; (c) the country concerned consents to the SDF; (d) there are expected coordination and cooperation between the units of the SDF and the competent authority of the country concerned (Article 84-3); and (e) the SDF personnel are permitted to use weapons, depending on the situation when there are adequate grounds to use weapons to protect the lives and bodies of Japanese nationals and others (Article 94-5).

(2) **Revision of the Law Concerning Measures to Ensure the Peace and Security of Japan in Situations in Areas Surrounding Japan**
The amendment to this Act deletes the limits of the previous law related to the area as "in areas surrounding Japan." The SDF will be operated to respond to such situation and to carry out logistics support activities, search and rescue activities, ship inspection operations, and other measures necessary to respond to situations that will have an important influence on Japan's peace and security. In addition, one of the significant changes from the previous act is added mission: the New Act allows the "provision of ammunition" and "refueling and maintenance of aircraft ready to takeoff for combat operations."

(3) **Revision of the Ship Inspection Operations Law**
The previous law limits the place as to be conducted only in situations in areas surrounding Japan, but the new Act allows ship inspection in situations threatening international peace and security that the international community is collectively addressing (discussed below) set forth in the International Peace Support Act.

(4) **Amendment to the International Peace Cooperation Act**
The previous International Peace Cooperation Act requires five conditions to be met in order to authorize the dispatch of the SDF to the UN peacekeeping operations and its task should be limited only to the logistical aspects of PKO such as surveillance of election and protection of refugees.

The above five conditions are:
(a) a cease-fire must be in place;
(b) the parties to the conflict must have given their consent to the operation;
(c) the activities must be conducted in a strictly impartial manner;
(d) participation may be suspended or terminated if any of the above conditions ceases to be satisfied; and
(e) the use of weapons shall be limited to the minimum necessary to protect life or person of the personnel.

The new Act expands the scope of the SDF's mission to include so-called "safety-ensuring" operations including "Kaketsuke-Keigo" (coming to protection of individuals related to operations in response to urgent request) and allows the SDF personnel to use force to accomplish such missions. On the other hand, the Act adds extra conditions to be fulfilled. These are, (f) based on resolutions of the General Assembly, the Security Council or the Economic and Social Council of the UN; (g) at the request by any international organizations including the UN Organs established by the UN General Assembly and regional organizations; and (h) at the request of the countries to which the area where those operations are to be conducted belongs.

(5) **Revision of Legislation for Responses to Armed Attack Situations**

In addition to the armed attack situations, etc., (an armed attack situation and an anticipated armed attack situation), the Act introduces "Survival-Threatening Situation" ("a situation where an armed attack against a foreign country that is in a close relationship with Japan occurs and as a result threatens Japan's survival and poses a clear danger to fundamentally overturn people's right to life, liberty and pursuit of happiness") and provides a necessary response to such situations.

Consequently, the relevant acts are also amended to introduce new articles concerning "Survival-Threatening Situation," such as the Act Related to the Actions of the US Forces and Others, Maritime Transportation Restriction Act, Prisoners of War Act, and Act Regarding the Use of Specific Public Facilities.

# State Practice of Asian Countries in International Law

*Korea*

*Buhm-Suk Baek**

## Municipal Law

### *Treaties – Jurisdiction Civil*

**Decision of Supreme Court Decision on the 'Revocation of Disposition Imposing Corporate Tax'**

*Supreme Court Decision 2013Du7711 (decided on 26 March 2015)*

Issues

One of the main legal issues in this case is the applicability of the Korea–Germany Tax Treaty and the tax rate applicable towards dividend income accrued in the source country (Korea), in the event a German based corporation is not liable for tax in the residence country (Germany).

Judgment

The Court ruled as follows:

> A tax treaty is purported to apply to any person who is generally liable to pay tax in the country of domicile by reason of his/her address, residence, place of headquarters or main office, or any other criterion of a similar nature, and as such, any person who is not generally liable to pay tax in the country of residence is not subject to the application of the treaty with respect to income that he/she earned in the source country, as a matter of principle .... [E]ven if the fiscally transparent entity falls under a "foreign corporation" in accordance with Korean corporate tax law but is not subject to general taxation, such as corporate income tax according to German tax law, it cannot be deemed as a corporation under the Korea–Germany Tax Treaty. Thus, with respect to dividend income earned in Korea (the source country), the limited tax rate of 15% is only applicable in accordance with Article 10(2) Item b under the Korea–Germany.

* Kyung Hee University, Korea.

© Buhm-Suk Baek, 2018 | DOI 10.1163/9789004344556_018

Comment

The Korea–Germany Tax Treaty states that a tax treaty is applicable to any person who is generally liable to pay tax in the country of residence. But this treaty does not stipulate provisions on the applicability as a resident in the case of the so-called fiscally transparent entity, in which its constituent partner rather than the entity itself pays taxes on income deriving from the entity's activity. Therefore, the Court confirmed in this case that the Korea–Germany Tax Treaty is not applicable to the entity to the extent that its constituent partner does not pay German tax on income earned in the source country.

## State Responsibility

### *Treaties – Jurisdiction – Human Rights*

**Decision of Supreme Court concerning 'Damages'**

*Supreme Court Decision 2013Da208388 (decided on 11 June 2015)*

Facts

The plaintiff, who was born in Japan in 1943 as a national of Korea, became a naturalized Japanese citizen and lost Korean nationality in 2006. In 1975, when he/she was a college student, the plaintiff was arrested without a warrant and was detained by the investigators of the Korean Central Intelligence Agency, an institution affiliated with Korean government (Defendant). His/her trial ran for three years on charges of espionage under the National Security Act, and during this trial he/she was detained for one and a half years. The Supreme Court finally remanded the case on grounds of insufficient evidence other than the plaintiff's confession, and the plaintiff was released. In 2010, the Truth and Reconciliation Commission of Korea confirmed that the Korean Central Intelligence Agency unlawfully detained the plaintiff for a prolonged period subjected to cruel and inhumane treatment. But as the defendant failed to take any affirmative action in spite of the Commission's finding, the plaintiff brought a lawsuit for State compensation. The defendant responded that such an action was unlawful because the plaintiff is an alien and State compensation was only applicable in cases where a mutual guarantee with a corresponding nation existed. In addition, the defendant argued that in any event, the statute of limitations had run.

Issues

One of the main legal issues was the standard for determining whether a mutual guarantee exists as stipulated in Article 7 of the State Compensation Act, and whether such a mutual guarantee exists between Korea and Japan.

Judgment

The Supreme Court decided as follows:

> With a view to preventing any disadvantages to which the Republic of Korea may be unilaterally put and promoting equity in international relations, Article 7 of the State Compensation Act sets out as a prerequisite for an alien's claim for State compensation.... Demanding that the corresponding nation's prerequisites for an alien's claim for State compensation be identical with, or even more lenient than, those of the Republic of Korea would result in an excessive restriction of an alien's claim for State compensation. It might even have the irrational effect of making foreign countries refuse to protect Korean nationals. Nor would it sit well with today's realities featuring frequent international exchanges. *In this regard, it is reasonable to deem foreign prerequisites to have met the mutual guarantee requirement under Article 7 of the State Compensation Act, so long as: (a) the respective prerequisites for a State compensation claim in Korea and the foreign country are not manifestly disproportionate; (b) the foreign prerequisites are not excessively onerous overall than those of Korea; and thus (c) the foreign prerequisites hardly entail any substantive difference in major aspects. It is sufficient to recognize mutual guarantee by comparison of pertinent prerequisites based on such sources as foreign statutes, precedents, and custom....* [A] treaty does not necessarily have to be in place with the corresponding nation. Even in the absence of a concrete case in which the corresponding nation has recognized the State compensation claim of a Korean national, it is sufficient to have the expectation of recognition of such a claim.

Comment

As the plaintiff was a Japanese national who claimed for State compensation for damages inflicted through the unlawful performance of official duties by a public official of Korea, the court should first review whether a mutual guarantee exists between the Republic of Korea and Japan. And the Court held that such a mutual guarantee exists between the two States.

### *International Agreements*

**Free Trade Agreement between the Republic of Korea and Canada**

- Signed on 22 September 2014 in Ottawa, Canada
- Entered into force on 1 January 2015 (Treaty No. 2216)

Brief Description

- Consistent with Article XXIV of GATT 1994 and Article V of GATS, the Parties agree to establish a free trade zone in accordance with the provisions of this Agreement.
- Article 2.3-2, Tariff Elimination except as otherwise provided in this Agreement, each Party shall progressively eliminate its customs duties on originating goods in accordance with its Schedule to Annex 2-D and notwithstanding Article 2.3, a Party may impose an agricultural safeguard measure in the form of a higher import duty.
- Each Party shall accord to service, service providers, investment and investors of the other Party with national treatment and treatment no less favorable than that it accords.

**Agreement for Cooperation on Climate Change between the Government of the Republic of Korea and the Government of the People's Republic of China**

- Signed on 29 January 2015 in Beijing, China
- Entered into force on 28 February 2015 (Treaty No. 2223)

Brief Description of the Purpose and Content of the Agreement

It is adopted with a purpose to strengthen bilateral dialogue and cooperation regarding international negotiations on climate change, and promote joint cooperative projects to combat climate change.

- To strengthen bilateral dialogue and cooperation on climate change negotiations including implementation of the UN Framework Convention on Climate Change.
- To facilitate and coordinate the implementation of this Agreement, the Parties shall establish a Joint Committee on Climate Change Cooperation.
- The Parties shall bear the expenses to be incurred in conjunction with the implementation of the cooperative programs and projects between government agencies or institutes under this Agreement on the basis of equality, subject to the availability of resources and in accordance with the applicable national laws and regulations of each Party.

**Maritime Labor Convention 2006**

- Signed on 23 February 2006 in Geneva, Switzerland

- Entered into force on 20 August, 2013
- Entered into force on 9 January 2015 (in Republic of Korea)

Brief Description of the Purpose and Content of the Agreement

- This convention applies to ships, whether publicly or privately owned, ordinarily engaged in commercial activities, other than one which navigate exclusively in inland waters or waters within or closely adjacent to, sheltered waters or areas where port regulations apply.
- Each member shall satisfy itself that the provisions of its laws and regulations respect, in the context of this Convention, the fundamental rights of freedom of association and the effective recognition of the right to collective bargaining, the elimination of all forms of forced or compulsory labor, the effective abolition of child labor and the elimination of discrimination in respect of employment and occupation.
- Every seafarer has the right to a safe and secure workplace that complies with safety standards, right to fair terms of employment and right to decent working and living conditions on board ship.
- The employment, engagement or work of seafarers under the age of 18 shall be prohibited where the work is likely to jeopardize their health or safety. The types of work in concern shall be determined by national laws or regulations or by the competent authority, after consultation with the ship owners' and seafarers' organizations concerned, in accordance with relevant international standards.
- The terms and conditions for employment of a seafarer shall be set out or referred to in a clear written legally enforceable agreement and shall be consistent with the standards set out in the code and each member shall ensure that seafarers are paid for their services, the hours of work or hours of rest for seafarers are regulated, adequate leave, right to be repatriated.

**Exchange of Notes between the Government of the Republic of Korea and the Office of the High Commissioner for Human Rights Permitting the Operation of the Field-Based Structure of the Office of the High Commissioner for Human Rights in the Republic of Korea**

- Signed on 22 May 2015 and exchange of notes in Geneva, Switzerland
- Entered into force 22 May 2015 (Treaty No. 2241)

Brief Description of the Purpose and Content of the Agreement

- The Convention on the Privileges and Immunities of the United Nations of 13 February 1946 shall be applicable to the OHCHR's Field-based Structure, as part of the United Nations.
- The relevant authorities of the Government shall take all appropriate measures to ensure the security and protection of the premises of the Field-based Structure.
- The Government, in accordance with the relevant United Nations principles and practices and the present exchange of notes, shall respect the freedom of expression of all participants of meetings, seminars, training courses, symposiums, and workshops organized by the Field-based Structure, to which the Convention shall be applicable.
- The Government shall take all necessary measures, without undue delay, to facilitate the entry into and exit from, and movement.
- Without prejudice to the privileges, immunities, and facilities accorded by the present exchange of notes, it is the duty of all persons enjoying such privileges, immunities, and facilities to observe the laws and regulations of the Host Country.

**Agreement for Cooperation between the Government of the Republic of Korea and the Government of the United States of America concerning Peaceful Uses of Nuclear Energy**

- Signed on 15 June 2015 at Washington, D.C., USA
- Entered into force on 25 November 2015 (Treaty No. 2262)

Brief Description of the Purpose and Content of the Agreement

- It is confirmed that the Treaty on the Non-Proliferation of Nuclear Weapons, done on 1 July 1968, to which the Republic of Korea and the United States of America are parties, is the cornerstone of the global nuclear nonproliferation regime and reaffirming their desire to promote universal adherence to the NPT.
- The Parties shall confirm related cooperation process and facilitating routes to enhance cooperation in the areas of reliable nuclear fuel supply, spent fuel management, and storage and retransfers.

- The Parties shall form a High Level Bilateral Commission to facilitate the Parties' strategic cooperation and dialogue regarding areas of mutual interest in peaceful nuclear cooperation.
- The 1972 Agreement shall terminate on the date this Agreement enters into force and nuclear material, moderator material, equipment and components subject to the 1972 Agreement shall become subject to this Agreement upon its entry into force and shall be considered to have been transferred pursuant to this Agreement.

**Free Trade Agreement between the Government of the Republic of Korea and the Government of the People's Republic of China**

- Signed on 1 June 2015 in Seoul
- Entered into force on 20 December 2015 (Treaty No. 2269)

Brief Description of the Purpose and Content of the Agreement

- Consistent with Article XXIV of GATT 1994 and Article V of GATS, the Parties hereby establish a free trade zone.
- Each Party shall facilitate and liberalize by progressively reducing or eliminating its customs duties on originating goods of the other Party in accordance with its Schedule to Annex 2-A.
- Each Party shall accord to service, service providers, investment and investors of the other Party with national treatment and treatment no less favorable than that it accords.
- The Parties shall enhance cooperation in agriculture, forestry, steel industry, SMEs, telecommunication, government supply, energy, resources, etc.

**Free Trade Agreement between the Government of the Republic of Korea and the Government of the Socialist Republic of Viet Nam**

- Signed on 5 May 2015 at Hanoi
- Entered into force on 20 December 2015 (Treaty No. 2270)

Brief Description of the Purpose and Content of the Agreement

- Except as otherwise provided for in this Agreement, each Party shall progressively reduce or eliminate its customs duties on originating goods in accordance with its Schedule.

- Each Party shall accord to service, service providers, investment and investors of the other Party with national treatment and treatment no less favorable than that it accords.

**United Nations Convention against Transnational Organized Crime**

- Adopted on 15 November 2000 in New York, USA
- Entered into force on 29 September 2003
- (in Republic of Korea) Entered into force on 5 December 2015

Brief Description of the Purpose and Content of the Agreement

- This Convention shall apply, except as otherwise herein, to the prevention, investigation and prosecution of transnational organized criminal groups.
- Each State party shall adopt such legislative and other measures as may be necessary to establish as criminal offences, when involved in an organized criminal group, money-laundering, corruption, illicit trafficking are committed intentionally.
- State Parties shall adopt, to the greatest extent possible within their domestic legal system, such measures as may be necessary to enable confiscation of proceeds of crime derived from offences covered by thins Convention or property the value of which corresponds to that of such proceeds and property, equipment or other instrumentalities used in or destined for use in offences covered by this Convention.
- States Parties shall afford one another the widest measure of mutual legal assistance in jurisdiction, extradition, mutual legal assistance, joint investigations.
- Each State Party shall take appropriate measures within its means to provide assistance and protection to victims of offences covered by this Convention, in particular in cases of threat of retaliation or intimidation and shall establish appropriate procedures to provide access to compensation and restitution for victims of offences covered by this Convention.

**Free Trade Agreement between the Republic of Korea, of the One Part, and the European Union and Its Member States, of the Other Part**

- Signed on 6 October 2010 in Brussels, Belgium
- Entered into force on 13 December 2015 (Treaty No. 2263)

Brief Description of the Purpose and Content of the Agreement

- This agreement is to establish a free trade area in accordance with Article XXIV of the General Agreement on Tariffs and Trade 1994 and Article V of the General Agreement on Trade in Services to liberalize and facilitate trade in goods, services and investment between Parties.
- Each Party shall eliminate its customs duties on originating goods of the other Party in accordance with its Schedule and enhance cooperation in the non-tariff measures on goods from the application of a Party's regulation in the areas of electronics, motor vehicles and parts, pharmaceutical products and medical devices and chemicals.
- Each Party shall accord to service, service providers, investment and investors of the other Party with national treatment and treatment no less favorable than that it accords and prohibit market restricted access.
- The parties shall achieve an adequate and effective level of protection and enforcement of intellectual property rights particularly in copyright, the rights related to patents, trademarks, service marks, designs, layout- designs (topographies) of integrated circuits, geographical indications, plant varieties and protection of undisclosed information.
- Recognizing the right of each Party to establish its own levels of environmental and labor protection, and to adopt or modify accordingly its relevant laws and policies, each Party shall seek to ensure that those laws and policies provide for and encourage high levels of environmental and labor protection, consistent with the internationally recognized standards or agreements and shall strive to continue to improve those laws and policies.
- Establishing the Committee on Outward Processing Zones (OPZ) on the Korean Peninsula in accordance with Annex IV of the Protocol concerning the Definition of 'Originating Products' and Methods of Administrative Cooperation and at the request of the applicant authority, the requested authority shall inform to it whether good imported or exported from the territory of one of the Parties have been properly imported or exported into the territory specifying the customs procedure applied to the goods.

**Articles of Agreement of the Asian Infrastructure Investment Bank**

- Adopted on 22 May 2015 in Singapore/People's Republic of China
- Entered into force on 25 December 2015
- Entered into force on 25 December 2015 (Treaty No. 2274) (in Republic of Korea)

Brief Description of the Purpose and Content of the Agreement

- The purpose of the Bank is to create wealth and improve infrastructure connectivity in Asia by investing in infrastructure and other productive sectors.
- Membership in the Bank shall be open to members of the International Bank for Reconstruction and Development or the Asian Development Bank.
- The Bank will be conducted through loan, capital stock, guarantee, and technical assistance.
- The principle office of the Bank shall be located in Beijing, People's Republic of China.
- This Agreement shall enter into force when instruments of ratification acceptance or approval have been deposited by at least ten (10) Signatories whose initial subscriptions in the aggregate comprise not less than fifty (50) per cent of total of such subscription.

# State Practice of Asian Countries in International Law

*Malaysia*

*Shaun Kang**

## Human Rights

### *Human Rights – Peaceful Assembly – Prior Notice – European Convention on Human Rights – European Court of Human Rights – OSCE Guidelines on Freedom of Peaceful Assembly*

**Public Prosecutor v. Yuneswaran a/l Ramaraj**
**Court:** Court of Appeal
**Date:** 1 October 2015
**Published:** Malaysian Law Journal, 2015, Volume 6, p. 47.

Facts

The Respondent Mr. Yuneswaran Ramaraj was prosecuted in his capacity as organizer of an unlawful assembly under the Peaceful Assembly Act 2012 (PAA). The PAA required *inter alia*, for the organizer of an assembly to notify the police of an intended assembly, 10 days before the taking place of such an assembly. In this appeal, the issue before the Court of Appeal included the question of, whether the 10 days advance notice was a restriction of the constitutional right of assembly, which is provided for by Article 10(1) (b) of the Malaysian Federal Constitution and is a well-recognized right, internationally.

Decision

The Court of Appeal examined whether the requirement of 10 days advance notice was in consonant with international standards. Firstly, the Court expressly recognized the freedom of assembly as an established right under international human rights law. The Court then turned to examine the status of advance notices for peaceful assembly in the European Union. In particular, the Court underlined that Article 11 of the European Convention of Human Rights and Fundamental Freedoms protects the right to assembly, albeit not in an absolute manner. The Convention imposes certain restrictions on the exercise of this right. That said, the Convention does not provide for any

---

* Research Associate, Centre for International Law, National University of Singapore.

DOI 10.1163/9789004344556_019

requirement of advance notice. The Court then examined the position in several other European countries, and found that the requirement of advance notice was present in all surveyed countries, except in Sweden.

Having accepted that advance notice was consistent with international standards, the Court turned to examine whether the 10-day advance notice was acceptable. The Court examined the legislative intent, and found guidance from the Malaysian Parliament Hansard, where the Minister during the debate of the PAA bill underlined that the OSCE, Guidelines on Freedom of Peaceable Assembly, Europe allows respective States to decide on a reasonable period of advance notice. The purpose of this is to allow adequate time for the relevant State authorities to make the necessary plan and preparation to satisfy their positive obligation.

The Court proceeded to examine three European Court of Human Rights (ECHR) decisions, a European Commission of Human Rights case, and a communication examined by the UN Human Rights Committee (UNHRC).

The European Commission on Human Rights, in the case of *Reassemblement Jurassien and Unite Jurassienne v. Switzerland* found that the giving of a prior or advance notice is consistent with Article 11 of the European Convention on Human Rights. Similarly, in the three ECHR cases examined, *Bukta & Other v. Hungary*, ECHR Application No 25691/04, *Eva Molnar v. Hungary*, ECHR Application No. 10346/05 and Sikba Polan, ECHR Application No. 10659/03 (Dec), the respective courts concluded that even though there is a possibility for spontaneous demonstrations, that is, a demonstration without prior notice, this is only acceptable in exceptional cases. The requirement of prior notice is consistent with the right to freedom of peaceful assembly under Article 11 of the European Convention on Human Rights.

In the UNHRC's examination of the communication of *Kivenmaa v Finland*, Communication No 412/1990, the Committee found that a requirement to notify the police of a demonstration, 6 hours prior to the demonstration may be compatible with the limitations laid down in Article 21 of the International Convention on Civil and Political Rights (ICCPR). In all, the Court held that the imposition of the 10 days prior notice by the PAA was in accordance with international norms and that it was constitutional.

## Amendment to the Malaysian Child Act in Compliance with the 1989 Convention on the Rights of the Child

### *Human Rights – UN Convention on the Rights of the Child – Corporal Punishment – Child Protection*

The 1989 Convention on the Rights of the Child (CRC) prohibits the use of corporal punishment against a child. In 2006, the Committee on the Rights of the Child in General Comment No.8 (2006), called upon States Parties to take "all appropriate legislative, administrative, social and educational measures to eliminate …" the corporal punishment against children.

Malaysia enacted the Child Act 2001 (Act 611) giving effect to its treaty obligations under the CRC, which was ratified in 1995. On 2 December 2015, in line with its obligations under the CRC, the Malaysian Government introduced an amendment bill to the Child Act 2001. The amendment *inter alia*, proposes to abolish whipping of a child offender, focusing on enforcing community service for child offenders and improving child protection through the National Council for Children and Child Welfare Teams. Further, the amendments called for an increase in fine from RM 20,000 to RM 50,000 for child abuse and neglect cases. The amendment was passed by the Malaysian Parliament on 4 May 2016.

## Criminal Law

### *Human Rights – Extradition Treaty between the United States and Malaysia – Dual Criminality – Writ of Habeas Corpus*

**Amin Ravan v. Menteri Dalam Negeri & Ors.**
**Court:** Federal Court
**Date:** 14 September 2015
**Published:** Malaysian Law Journal, 2015, Volume 5, p. 577.

Facts

The appellant is an Iranian national who travelled to Malaysia on 1 October 2012, on a tourist visa. On 5 October 2012, the United States Government requested the Malaysian Government to issue a provisional warrant against the appellant pursuant to Article 11 of the Extradition Treaty between the Government of Malaysia and the Government of the United States of America ("Treaty"). The appellant is wanted by the US authorities for allegedly committing the following offences extraterritorially: smuggling, illegal export and attempted illegal exports as well as for conspiracy to defraud the US Government. The Malaysian authorities acted on this request and obtained a court order to arrest the appellant. The appellant applied for *inter alia*, a writ of habeas corpus, on the grounds that the dual criminality requirement as provided for by both Article 2 of the Treaty and Section 6 of the Extradition Act was not met. The issue before the Federal Court was whether the requirement of dual criminality was fulfilled, allowing for the committal and extradition of the appellant. The appellant argued that in order to fulfil this requirement, the offences which are extraterritorial in the US must also be offences which are extraterritorial in Malaysia. Both the Sessions Court and High Court disagreed with the appellant, leading to an appeal before the Federal Court.

Decision

The Court examined Article 2(5) of the Treaty which states: "If the offence has been committed outside the territory of the requesting State, extradition shall be granted if the laws of the requested State provided for punishment of an offence committed outside its territory in similar circumstances …". The prosecutor advanced the argument that by applying the effect approach, the broad conduct approach and the continuing approach, Article 2(5) was inapplicable in the present case, as the appellant was charged within the jurisdiction of the US District Court for the District of Columbia.

Disagreeing with the prosecutor's argument, the Court found that the central issue was whether the corresponding offences in Malaysia had extraterritorial effect. The Court underlined that in Malaysia, extraterritorial offences are limited to offences committed under the Official Secrets Act, Sedition Act, and to offences under certain chapters of the Penal Code. The Court found that the offences in which the appellant allegedly committed were extraterritorial offences in the US, but not in Malaysia. Article 2(5) of the Treaty, also provides for a requested State to refuse an extradition request in situations where there is no corresponding extraterritorial jurisdiction in that State. On that basis, the Court allowed the appeal and granted the appellant a writ of habeas corpus.

## UN Security Council

### Draft UN Security Resolution to establish an Ad Hoc International Criminal Tribunal in relation to the downing of Malaysian Airlines Flight MH 17

*International Criminal Law – International Criminal Tribunal- International Criminal Law – UN Security Council- Air Crash*

Malaysia Airlines Flight MH 17 was a scheduled international civilian flight from Amsterdam, the Netherlands to Kuala Lumpur, Malaysia. On 17 July 2014, the aircraft was shot down by a BUK surface-to-air missile while flying over Eastern Ukraine.

Following this, on 29 July 2015, Malaysia, a non-permanent member of the Security Council, introduced a draft resolution (S/2015/562), alongside Australia, Belgium, the Netherlands and Ukraine. In presenting the draft resolution, the Malaysian delegate (Transport Minister) recalled the resolve of the

Security Council in demanding accountability for the downing of the flight in an earlier resolution, 2166 (2014). He continued by underlining that the establishment of this tribunal will "… send a clear message to the growing number of non-State actors with the ability to target civilian aircraft that such attacks are unacceptable …". He cautioned that the failure to hold the perpetrators to account would place those who travel by air at greater risk.

In essence, the draft resolution proposes *inter alia*, for the Security Council to act under Chapter VII of the Charter of the United Nations to establish an International Criminal Tribunal which has jurisdiction over individuals involved in the downing of flight MH 17. The draft resolution also attached a comprehensive statute of the tribunal.

Angola, China and Venezuela abstained from the vote, while all remaining members of the Security Council, with the exception of Russia voted for the adoption of the draft resolution. The Russian Federation exercised its veto as permanent member of the Security Council, resulting in the failure of the Security Council to adopt the resolution.

## Terrorism

### Report of the Government of Malaysia to the United Nations in Fulfilment of Its Obligations under UNSC Resolution 2140 (2014)

*Terrorism – UN Security Council – Chapter VII UN Charter – Yemen – Travel Bans – Assets Freezing*

In 2014, the UNSC responded to the ongoing political, security, economic and humanitarian challenges in Yemen, adopting UN Security Council Resolution 2140 under Chapter VIII of the Charter of the United Nations. In that regard, the UNSC adopted a further resolution, 2204 (2015). The resolution requires States to ensure that any funds, financial assets or economic resources are prevented from being made available by their nationals or individuals or entities within their territories to or for the benefit of identified individuals who were involved in acts threatening the peace, security, or stability of Yemen. Further, the obligation extends to States preventing entry into or transit through their territories. The resolution established the Sanctions Committee which exercises monitoring functions including, to monitor the implementation of measures proscribed by the Resolution and to examine any violations and non-compliance of such measures.

On 8 July 2015, pursuant to this UNSC Resolution, Malaysia through its Permanent Mission presented its report to the Chair of the Sanctions Committee.

In its report, Malaysia underlined that it had imposed travel bans under the Immigration Act 1959/63, preventing the entry of identified persons from entering, leaving and transiting Malaysia. Pursuant to Section 82 of the Central Bank of Malaysia Act 2009, Malaysia had also instructed relevant financial institutes to freeze assets owned directly or indirectly by individuals identified by the Committee. Malaysia confirmed that it had undertaken investigations into the allegation that there might be assets disguised in Malaysia, related to the designated individuals. The investigation found no such evidence.

## Shipping

### Implementation of the 2007 Nairobi Convention

*Shipping – Treaties – Nairobi Convention – Wrecks Removal – Liability – Financial Security – Insurance – Imo*

The 2007 Nairobi International Convention on the Removal of Wrecks (Nairobi Convention) aims to provide the first set of uniform international rules for the prompt and effective removal of wrecks located beyond the territorial sea. The Convention provides the legal basis for coastal States to remove, or have removed, from their coastlines, wrecks which pose a hazard to the safety of navigation or to the marine and coastal environments, or both.

Malaysia ratified the Convention on 28 November 2013. On 14 April 2015, the Convention entered into force and was implemented in Malaysia on the same date. To implement the provisions of this Convention, Malaysia amended the Merchant Shipping Ordinance 1952, inserting Section 381A. The provision requires all ships measuring above 300GT entering or leaving port in Malaysia or any part of Malaysia waters to maintain a contract of insurance or other financial security to cover liability under the Convention. The penalty for failing to comply with the provisions of this section is a minimum fine of 2,000 Malaysian Ringgit, and not exceeding 500,000 Malaysian Ringgit.

## Aviation Law

### Proclamation of Malaysia Airlines MH 370 as an Accident According to the 1944 Chicago Convention on International Civil Aviation

*Aviation – accident investigation – search and rescue – 1944 Chicago convention – Declaration*

Malaysian Airlines Flight MH 370 was a scheduled international civilian flight from Kuala Lumpur, Malaysia to Beijing, China. On 8 March 2014, the flight lost contact with air traffic control. Investigations in to the fate and location of the wreckage begun on the same date. Following this, on 29 January 2015, the Malaysian Department for Civil Aviation (DCA) officially declared the loss of the aircraft as an accident. The DCA made the declaration according to standards set out by Annex 12 and 13 to the Convention on International Civil Aviation 1944 (Chicago Convention), in which Malaysia acceded to on 7 April 1958.

An accident is defined in Annex 13, to include a situation where the aircraft is missing and that, the official search has been terminated. Search is defined in Annex 12 as an operation to locate persons in distress. According to the DCA, the search and rescue operations were terminated on 13 April 2014, marking an end to the official search. Accordingly, given that the aircraft remains missing, the definition of an accident for the purposes of Annex 13 to the Chicago Convention, were met.

# State Practice of Asian Countries in International Law

*Philippines*

*Jay L. Batongbacal**

## Jurisprudence

### *Environmental Law – Biosafety – Precautionary Principle*

***International Service for the Acquisition of Agri-Biotech Applications v Greenpeace*** **[G.R. Nos. 209271, 209276, 209301 & 209430. 8 December 2015]**
Greenpeace Southeast Asia and a coalition of farmers, scientists, and non-government organizations filed a petition for the issuance of a writ of *kalikasan* against the International Service for the Acquisition of Agri-Biotech Applications (ISAAA), various regulatory agencies of the Philippine government, and the University of the Philippines to stop and prevent the field testing of *Bt talong*, a genetically modified type of eggplant. The field trials were made pursuant to Administrative Order (DAO) 08 – 2002 which prescribed guidelines for the import and release of genetically modified organisms (GMOs) in the Philippines. The Court issued a temporary environmental protection order and referred the case to the Court of Appeals for hearing, reception of evidence, and judgment.

The Court of Appeals invalidated DAO 08-2002 and permanently enjoined the conduct of field trials after finding that the government's regulations were insufficient to guarantee the safety of the environment and the health of the people. It invoked the precautionary principle in environmental law and incorporated into the Rules of Procedure in Environmental Cases, noting that the overall safety of *Bt talong* was not guaranteed, found the introduction of GMOs to be an "ecologically imbalancing act" that may cause irreparable and irreversible damage, and considered it a clear and present danger to the people's right to healthful and balanced ecology. ISAAA, as well as several intervenors, sought judicial review of the Court of Appeal's decision on numerous procedural and substantive grounds. Among the latter, they argued that the Court of Appeals misapplied the precautionary principle.

* University of the Philippines.

After reviewing studies and expert testimonies, and summarizing the global debate over GMO crops, the Supreme Court upheld the validity of the injunction until the government took concrete action to perform its regulatory mandates. The Court found that DAO 08-2002 only provided the permitting process for GMO field testing and use, and merely supplemented the National Biosafety Framework (previously enacted in Executive Order 514) which in turn required the conduct of detailed risk assessment in accordance with the Cartagena Protocol on Biosafety signed and ratified by the Philippines. The Court determined that while the government adhered to the procedure, it did not properly comply with the requirements for risk assessment necessary to protect against possible environmental damage from GMO crops. Notably, the procedures were not sufficiently transparent, meaningful and participatory, in light of the finding that the government lacked mechanisms to ensure that applicants for GMO testing complied with international biosafety protocols, and yet also previously allowed the entry and use of all GMOs as requested by multinational companies. The Court also required the conduct of an environmental impact assessment since GMO testing and use involved new and emerging technologies subject to the Environment Impact Statement System.

The Court also detailed the application of the precautionary principle in the Philippine context. It cited Articles 10 and 11, and Annex III of the Cartagena Protocol on Biosafety in relation to Rule 20 of the Philippines' Rules of Procedure in Environmental Cases. It considered the precautionary principle as a principle of last resort for purposes of evidence where application of the regular rules would cause inequity for an environmental plaintiff. These cases include those in which (a) the risks of harm are uncertain, (b) the harm might be irreversible and what is lost is irreplaceable, and (c) the harm that might result would be serious. The case for application of the precautionary principle was deemed strongest when all three features coincide, and in case of doubt, it must be resolved in favor of the constitutional right to a balanced and healthful ecology. This also justified the Court's decision to affirm the Court of Appeals' decision.

### *Criminal Jurisdiction – Immunity from Jurisdiction – Human Rights – International Covenant on Civil and Political Rights*

***Laude v Ginez-Jabelde* [G.R. No. 217456. 24 November 2015]**

On 15 December 2014, US Marine Lance Corporal Joseph Scott Pemberton was charged with the crime of murder of Jennifer Laude in Olongapo City. He was detained in Camp Aguinaldo, the general headquarters of the Armed Forces of the Philippines, in accordance with the terms of the Visiting Forces Agreement

(VFA) in force between the Philippines and the United States. Marilou Laude, sister of the victim Jennifer, filed a motion for the Armed Forces to surrender custody of Pemberton to the Olongapo City Jail and to allow media coverage of the trial. Judge Ginez-Jabelde denied the motion on procedural grounds, having been filed less than three days before the date of hearing and without the approval of the Public Prosecutor. Laude then brought the matter before the Supreme Court on the argument that the procedural obstacles should be dispensed with, invoking the International Covenant on Civil and Political Rights (ICCPR) to which the Philippines is a State party. She also argued that the VFA should be declared unconstitutional for impairing the Court's power to promulgate rules of procedure because its contains provisions concerning the custody and detention of military personnel undergoing criminal prosecution.

The Court denied the petition, stating that compliance with the procedural due process cannot be justified by general exhortations of human rights. It clarified that the obligations in Article 2 of the ICCPR pertain to the establishment of accessible and effective remedies through judicial and administrative mechanisms. Since the existence of the trial itself affirmed a legal system for redress, the petitioner could not use the ICCPR to excuse its failure to adhere to simple procedural rules intended to protect the rights of the accused, which are likewise human rights. With respect to the VFA, the Court noted that the issue had previously been adjudicated in the case of *Nicolas v. Secretary Romulo et al.*, [G.R. No. 175888, 11 February 2009], where it declared that international law recognized that foreign armed forces permitted to enter another State's territory are immune from local jurisdiction except to the extent agreed upon by the parties. Thus, the provisions for custody and detention of visiting military personnel did not impair the Court's power to promulgate rules of procedure but were normally encountered under similar arrangements around the world. Nothing in the Philippine Constitution prevented such arrangements, and in fact it expressly adopts the generally accepted principles of international law as part of the law of the land.

### *Nationality – Naturalization – Refugees*

***Republic v Karbasi* [G.R. Nos. 210412. 29 July, 2015]**

Kamran Karbasi was born in Iran but fled the country after the fall of the Shah of Iran and during the Iran-Iraq War in 1986. After spending three years in Pakistan, in 1990 he arrived in the Philippines where he was recognized as a person of concern by the United Nations High Commissioner for Refugees. Thereafter he settled, finished college, set up a small business, got married to a Philippine citizen, and applied for and was granted naturalization as a Philippine citizen. His naturalization was opposed by the Office of the Solicitor General (OSG) on several grounds, one of them being the lack of reciprocity between the Philippines and Iran in the grant of citizenship through naturalization.

In deciding the case, the Court agreed that the Naturalization Law disqualified subjects from countries who do not give reciprocal rights of naturalization, but also noted that Karbasi successfully established refugee status upon arriving in the Philippines. The country's obligations as a signatory of the 1951 Convention Relating to the Status of Refugees therefore apply. The Court concluded that since Article 7 of the Convention expressly provides for exemption from reciprocity, while Articles 6 and 34 state a duty to facilitate the assimilation and naturalization of refugees, Karbasi's status as a refugee must end with the attainment of citizenship. It also stated that the Naturalization Law should be read in light of developments in international human rights law, especially with respect to the status of refugees and stateless persons.

### *Human Rights – International Covenant on Civil and Political Rights – Right to Run for Public Office*

***Risos-Vidal v Commission on Elections*** **[G.R. No. 206666, 21 January 2015]**

On 12 September 2007, former-President Joseph Ejercito Estrada was convicted of the crime of "plunder," an offense committed by public officials under Philippine criminal law. The penalties for the crime included life imprisonment, civil interdiction, forfeiture, and a perpetual absolute disqualification from public office. A little more than a month later on 25 October, his successor former-President Gloria Macapagal Arroyo granted a pardon to Estrada. The full text of the pardon stated that Estrada "has publicly committed to no longer seek any elective position or office" and was granted executive clemency and "restored to all his civil and political rights." Subsequently, he re-entered local politics and ran for the Office of the Mayor of the City of Manila. Petitioner Risos-Vidal filed a case to disqualify Estrada from the election on the ground of his previous conviction for plunder, arguing that the pardon was a conditional pardon that did not remove his disqualification to vote and be voted for public office under the Local Government Code, and that the restoration of such rights needed to be stated in explicit and positive language rather than a simple general statement of restoration to unspecified "civil and political rights".

The issue in this case is whether the unqualified grant of pardon restored Estrada's right to vote and be voted for public office. The Court dismissed the petition, viewing the pardon issued by former-President Arroyo to be an absolute pardon that was complete, unqualified, and unambiguous. It rejected the argument that restoration of the right to vote and be voted for public officer needed to be expressly stated on grounds that the power to grant executive clemency could not be limited by legislative action. In support of its conclusion, the Court noted that the International Covenant on Civil and Political Rights, to which the Philippines is a signatory, acknowledges the existence of the right to seek public office as a civil and political right. Hence, the pardon extended to Estrada conferred upon him the ability to again seek an elective position.

## International Agreements

### *Treaties – Agreements Concurred by the Philippine Senate in 2015*

25 May 2015

The Philippines issued Resolution No. 85 concurring with the Nagoya Protocol on Access to Genetic Resources and the Fair and Equitable Sharing of Benefits Arising from their Utilization to the Convention on Biological Diversity. The Protocol supplements the Convention on Biological Diversity by providing a framework for the equitable distribution of benefits from genetic resources. In the concurring resolution, the Philippines affirms the role of the Protocol in allowing biodiversity to contribute to development, particularly by promoting incentives for sustainable use.

10 Aug 2015

The Philippines issued Resolution No. 94 concurring with a Protocol Relating to an Amendment to the Convention on International Civil Aviation, which was ratified by the Philippines on 5 May 2014. The Protocol inserts an Article 3 *bis* to the original Convention, enjoining States from using weapons against civil aircraft. It also enjoins Contracting Parties to take measures to prevent aircraft from flying into its territory without authority.

On the same day, Resolution No. 95 was issued concurring with the 1999 Montreal Convention for the Unification of Certain Rules for International Carriage by Air, acceded to by the Philippines on 26 May 2014. The Convention modifies the liability regime for accidental death or injury to passengers of aircraft, and for destruction, loss, damage or delay of baggage or cargo, as well as the jurisdiction for bringing claims therein. The concurring resolution emphasizes the need to ratify the Convention particularly in light of ASEAN integration.

14 December 2015

The Philippines issued three resolutions to concur with agreements for the avoidance of double taxation with respect to taxes on income and capital. The said agreements were made with Turkey (concurred via Resolution No. 107), Italy (Resolution No. 108), and Germany (Resolution No. 109). Among other effects, the agreements allocate taxing jurisdiction between the contracting parties.

## Legislative and Administrative Regulations

### *Human Rights – Rights of the Child – An Act Declaring November of Every Year as National Children's Month*

On 29 May 2015, an Act Declaring November of Every Year as National Children's Month was enacted. The declaration in the said statute commemorates the adoption of the Convention on the Rights of the Child by the United Nations General Assembly, and seeks to instill its significance in the Philippine consciousness.

Towards that end, several agencies, including the Department of Social Welfare and Development and the Council for the Welfare of Children are tasked to prepare and implement activities to implement and observe National Children's Month. Local government units and private organizations are similarly encouraged to participate in the commemorative activities.

### *International Economic Law – Nomenclature and Rates of Duty on Certain Articles – Asia Pacific Economic Cooperation – WTO Decision on Waiver Relating to Special Treatment for Rice of the Philippines*

On 26 June 2015, the Philippines enacted Executive Order No. 185, titled 'Modifying the Nomenclature and Rates of Duty on Certain Imported Articles as Provided for Under the Tariff and Customs Code of the Philippines, as Amended, in Order to Implement the Philippine Tariff Commitments on Certain Products Included in the Environmental Goods List under the Asia – Pacific Economic Cooperation'. The Order amended the Tariff and Customs Code of the Philippines by subjecting imported articles to reduced Most Favored Nation rates of duty. It covers articles included in the APEC List of Environmental Goods, as endorsed under the 2012 Vladivostok Declaration.

This was followed on 5 November by Executive Order No. 190, an Order 'Modifying the Most Favored Nation Rates of Duty on Certain Agricultural Products under the Tariff and Customs Code of the Philippines, as Amended, in Order to Implement the Philippine Tariff Commitments under the WTO Decision on Waiver Relating to Special Treatment for Rice of the Philippines'.

Under the Order, certain rates of duty as listed in the Tariff and Customs Code were amended to apply Most Favored Nation rates. Similarly, on the same date Executive Order No. 191 was issued 'Modifying the Rates of Duty on Certain Agricultural Products under EO No. 851 (s. 2009) in Order to Implement the Philippines' ASEAN – Australia – New Zealand Free Trade Area (AANZFTA) Tariff Commitments Relating to the WTO Decision on Waiver Relating to Special Treatment for Rice of the Philippines'. EO No. 191 adjusts the rates of duty on selected agricultural products to comply with the AANZFTA rates on import duty. Both Orders were issued in compliance with a WTO decision reinstating special treatment for rice, which allowed the Philippines to impose restrictions on rice importation.

# State Practice of Asian Countries in International Law

*Singapore*

*Jaclyn Neo* and Rachel Tan Xi'En***

## Dispute Resolution Clause in the FIDIC 1999 Conditions of Contract ("The Red Book") – International Arbitration Act

### *PT Perusahaan Gas Negara (Persero) TBK v CRW Joint Operation* [2015] 4 SLR 364 [27 May 2015]

Facts

The dispute between the parties arose in respect to claims made by CRW. The contract between the parties adopted the standard provisions of the 1999 edition of the *Conditions of Contract for Construction: For Building and Engineering Works Designed by the Employer* ("the Red Book") published by the International Federation of Consulting Engineers ("FIDIC"), including the Dispute Resolution Clause.

The Red Book's Dispute Resolution Clause provides for the following steps:

(a) A dispute arising out of the contract must first be referred to a Dispute Adjudication Board ("DAB") for resolution by any party.

(b) The DAB must issue a decision within 84 days from the referral of the dispute. This decision would be binding on both parties who shall promptly give effect to it, unless and until it shall be revised in an amicable settlement or an arbitral award.

(c) Any party unsatisfied with the decision can issue a Notice of Dissatisfaction. If no Notice of Dissatisfaction is issued within 28 days, the decision is final and binding.

(d) If a Notice of Dissatisfaction is issued, the parties have up to 56 days to reach an amicable settlement, failing which, parties may commence arbitration pursuant to the parties' arbitration agreement set out at clause 20.6 of the Dispute Resolution Clause.

---

* Assistant Professor, Faculty of Law, National University of Singapore.

** Research Assistant, Centre for International Law, National University of Singapore.

 | DOI 10.1163/9789004344556_021

(e) The arbitration agreement provides that any dispute in respect of which the DAB's decision is not final and binding shall be resolved by arbitration. Additionally, clause 20.7 provides that the failure to comply with a decision, if it becomes final and binding, may be referred to arbitration directly without first being referred to the DAB or amicable settlement attempts.

After the DAB rendered several decisions on CRW's claims to payment, PT Perusahaan Gas Negara ("PGN") accepted all the decisions except a decision ordering it to pay CRW US$17,298,834.57 ("the US$17 million award"). PGN issued a notice of dissatisfaction against this award and did not comply with payment.

CRW thus commenced arbitration ("the 2009 arbitration") against PGN in respect of the US$17 million award, seeking a declaration that PGN had an immediate obligation to pay CRW. The Arbitral Tribunal found that PGN was required to comply. On appeal, the Singapore High Court set aside the Tribunal's award. This was upheld by the Court of Appeal, which held that the Tribunal should not have granted a final award requiring compliance without revisiting the merits of the Dispute Resolution Board's US$17 million award. It further held that compliance with the DAB's decision should have been dealt with by an interim or partial award after which, in the same arbitration, the merits of the US$17 million award should have been dealt with by way of a final award.

In 2011, CRW commenced a second arbitration against PGN ("the 2011 arbitration") seeking a final determination that PGN was liable to (a) pay CRW the US$17 million award, and (b) pending that final determination, a partial or interim award for the same sum with interest. The majority of the Tribunal in the 2011 arbitration found in favour of CRW and decided that PGN was obliged to comply with the US$17 million award notwithstanding the issuance of the notice of dissatisfaction and the pending resolution of the primary dispute (the merits of the US$17 million award). The majority also found that compliance with the US$17 million award could be enforced by way of an "interim award" ordering immediate payment of the sum and issued an award in those terms. The dissenting arbitrator in the 2011 arbitration reached the opposite conclusion and viewed that such an award would be provisional in nature and could not be enforced in Singapore.

CRW then applied to enforce the 2011 interim award in the Singapore courts and was granted leave to do so by an enforcement order. PGN applied to set aside both the enforcement order and the 2011 interim award. The High Court dismissed PGN's applications and this dismissal was the subject of appeal in *PT Perusahaan*.

Judgment

The Court of Appeal unanimously held that once a DAB decision was issued, the parties were contractually obliged to give effect to the decision by making timely payments of money notwithstanding the notice of dissatisfaction.

The Court of Appeal had to further decide on whether a DAB decision could be enforced by way of an arbitral award notwithstanding that the merits of the decision would be reviewed in an arbitration. First, the majority of the Court of Appeal found that the enforcement of the US$17 million award fell within the scope of the Dispute Resolution Clause, while the minority's view was that the enforceability dispute was not referable to arbitration. Second, the majority of the Court of Appeal also found that the 2011 interim award was a final award within the meaning of s19B(1) of the International Arbitration Act and was enforceable. The Dispute Resolution Clause imposed an obligation on the parties to comply with a decision of the DAB regardless of whether a notice of dissatisfaction was issued and whether the decision would eventually be reversed in part or whole. Further, the 2011 interim award would not be revised by any future awards pertaining to the primary dispute, which was a separate question on the state of final accounts between the parties. Hence, the enforceability dispute was a dispute in its own right, which was capable of being settled by international arbitration.

## Prima Facie Standard for Obtaining a Stay Of Court Proceedings in Favour of Arbitration – Whether Minority Oppression Claims are Arbitrable – International Arbitration Act

***Tomolugen Holdings Ltd and another v Silica Investors Ltd and other appeals*** **[*2015*] *1 SLR 373* [*26 October 2015*]**

Facts

The dispute arose out of a share sale agreement entered into by Silica Investors Limited and Lionsgate Holdings Pte Ltd (the second defendant) to purchase approximately 4.2% of the shareholding in Auzminerals Resource Group Limited (the eighth defendant). The share sale agreement contained an arbitration clause. Silica Investors Limited alleged that it had been oppressed as a minority shareholder and sought various reliefs. Some of the defendants applied to stay the proceedings under Section 6 of the International Arbitration Act and/or the inherent jurisdiction of the court. The matter was heard by an Assistant Registrar, who refused to stay the proceedings. The defendants appealed to the

High Court, which dismissed their appeal. The defendants appealed again to the Singapore Court of Appeal.

Judgment

The Singapore Court of Appeal held that a court should adopt a *prima facie* standard of review when hearing an application for a stay under s6 of the International Arbitration Act. The court hearing such a stay application should grant it in favour of arbitration, if the applicant was able to establish *prima facie* that:

(a) there was a valid arbitration agreement;
(b) the dispute in the court proceedings (or any part thereof) fell within the scope of the arbitration agreement; and
(c) the arbitration agreement was not null and void, inoperative, or incapable of being performed.

The Court of Appeal then dealt with the question of whether minority oppression claims were arbitrable. It referenced English decisions that held that oppressive or unfairly prejudicial conduct were arbitrable. It decided that Silica Investors Limited's claims were arbitrable and, with reference to decisions from England and Hong Kong, found that there was nothing in principle precluding a Tribunal from resolving the underlying dispute with parties subsequently applying to court for relief that the Tribunal could not award. Furthermore, the Court opined that procedural complexity was not sufficient reason to preclude a dispute from being arbitrable.

## Whether Caning Unconstitutional because it Violates Prohibition against Torture at International Law – Whether Torture is Jus Cogens – Dualist And Monist Systems of International Law

*Yong Vui Kong v Public Prosecutor* [2015] sgca 11 [*4 March 2015*]

Facts

The Appellant, Yong Vui Kong, had been charged with trafficking in 47.27g of diamorphine, which is an offence under the Misuse of Drugs Act ("MDA"). He was convicted after trial and sentenced to death on 14 November 2008. Yong's sentence of death was held in abeyance as he brought a series of legal challenges against the constitutionality of the mandatory death penalty, the integrity of the clemency process, and the decision to prosecute him for a capital offence while applying for a discontinuance not amounting to an acquittal of various charges under the MDA against Yong's alleged principal and supplier. While these proceedings were ongoing, the Government began a review of the mandatory death penalty and all executions were suspended from July 2011 pending its completion. The review culminated in various pieces of legislation including the amended MDA. Under the new s33B of the MDA, a person convicted of a drug trafficking offence punishable with death could instead be sentenced to imprisonment for life with caning, or imprisonment for life if the person was only a courier and was suffering from abnormality of mind which substantially impaired his mental responsibility.

### Judgment

The Singapore Court of Appeal, in response to submissions made by Yong's counsel, dealt with the following questions:

(a) whether caning constituted a form of torture that was *jus cogens*;
(b) whether international law obligations undertaken either by custom or treaty would automatically be incorporated into domestic law;
(c) whether caning was indeed a form of torture at all.

In relation to the first question, the Court accepted that there was strong evidence that the prohibition against torture was *jus cogens,* noting that there were 155 State parties to the *Convention against Torture and Other Cruel, Inhuman or Degrading Treatment or Punishment* ("CAT"), and that numerous international courts and tribunals had held that the prohibition of torture was *jus cogens.*

In relation to the second question, the Court found that there was no automatic incorporation of an international obligation into the domestic sphere. It endorsed a strict dualist approach to the relationship between international and domestic law. As per the dualist theory, the domestic and international law systems were separate and a norm under one system did not automatically cause it to exist and take precedence over laws that existed in another legal system. Hence, a *jus cogens* norm only admitted of no derogation in the international sphere and did not dictate the position in the domestic sphere.

The Court also endorsed the transformation doctrine in international law, noting that it was logically consistent with the dualist system of international law. Customary international law rules did not have effect domestically until specifically adopted by the legislature or domestic courts. The court also held that even treaty obligations, which arguably possessed greater force than custom, could not be "interpretively incorporated" into domestic law without express adoption by legislation or the domestic courts. Hence, there was essentially no distinction between treaty law and customary international law for the purposes of incorporation into domestic law – both were insufficient to automatically trump a domestic law that was clear and unambiguous on its face.

In any event, the Court's position was that caning in Singapore did not constitute torture. It noted that the definition of torture in the CAT drew a distinction between torture and inhuman punishment. In line with jurisprudence from the European Court of Human Rights, the key difference was in the intensity of the suffering inflicted. Hence, while caning inflicted a considerable level of pain and suffering, it was not of "severe and indiscriminate brutality" which would amount to torture in international law.

## International Agreements – Avoidance of Double Taxation

Singapore signed several bilateral treaties concerning double taxation in 2015:

- *15 January 2015:* Singapore and Uruguay signed an Agreement for the Avoidance of Double Taxation, which clarifies the taxing rights of both countries on all forms of income flows arising from cross-border business activities, and minimizes the double taxation of such income. This aims to lower barriers to cross-border investment and boost trade and economic flows between the two countries.
- *16 January 2015:* Singapore and France signed a revised Agreement for the Avoidance of Double Taxation, which offers improved terms for businesses, such as lower withholding tax rates for dividends and includes anti-abuse provisions.
- *11 June 2015:* Singapore and Thailand signed a new Avoidance of Double Taxation Agreement to replace an existing one that has been in force since 15 September 1975. The new Agreement lengthens the threshold period for determining the presence of a permanent establishment and lowers the withholding tax rates for dividends, interest and royalties. It will enter into force after ratification by both countries.
- *17 November 2015:* Singapore and Russia signed a Protocol on 17 November 2015 to amend the existing Singapore-Russia Avoidance of Double Taxation Agreement. The Protocol lengthens the threshold period for determining the presence of a permanent establishment and lowers the withholding tax rates for dividends, interest and royalties, amongst other changes.

- *18 December 2015:* Singapore's respective bilateral agreements with Ecuador, San Marino and Seychelles for the avoidance of double taxation entered into force on 18 December 2015. The DTAs provide clarity on tax matters and eliminate double taxation relating to cross-border transactions between Singapore and the respective contracting jurisdictions.
- *28 December 2015:* The Agreement between the Government of the Republic of Singapore and Government of the Grand Duchy of Luxembourg for the Avoidance of Double Taxation and the Prevention of Fiscal Evasion with Respect to Taxes on Income and on Capital entered into force on 28 December 2015.

## International Agreements – Free Trade Agreement

On 14 November 2015, Turkey and Singapore signed a comprehensive *Free Trade Agreement* on the sidelines of the G20 Summit in Antalya, Turkey. This is Turkey's first comprehensive agreement in a single undertaking and comprises Turkey's first treaty commitments in government procurement and newer elements such as intellectual property rights, e-commerce, competition and transparency.

## International Agreements – Strategic Partnerships

On 29 June 2015, Singapore and Australia signed a *Joint Declaration on the Comprehensive Strategic Partnership*. The partnership will, *inter alia*, enhance relations in the following ways:

(a) Review the Singapore-Australia Free Trade Agreement;
(b) Establish a Closer Economic Relationship (CER) that will remove regulatory obstacles and enhance an enabling environment for businesses;
(c) Increase consultation and cooperation on regional and global issues including those relating to the ASEAN Regional Forum (ARF) and East Asia Summit (EAS);
(d) Strengthen the defence and security partnership through military and civilian exchanges and postings, access to training areas, and collaboration on transnational crime including on foreign terrorist fighters and deradicalisation; and
(e) Enhance people-to-people ties through collaboration in the arts, culture, heritage, sports, and education.

Further, on 24 November 2015, Singapore and India concluded a Joint Declaration establishing a "Strategic Partnership" between India and Singapore to elevate bilateral relations to a higher level. This was against the backdrop of the 50th anniversary of diplomatic relations between India and Singapore, in conjunction with Prime Minister Narendra Modi's Official Visit to Singapore from 23 to 24 November 2015. Amongst other aims, the "Strategic Partnership" seeks to increase political exchanges between Singapore and India, enhance defence and security cooperation through regular consultations, scale up trade and investment, strengthen air transport and maritime cooperation, and strengthen legal and judicial cooperation.

### International Treaties – International Convention on the Elimination of All Forms of Racial Discrimination

On 19 October 2015, Singapore signed the *International Convention on the Elimination of All Forms of Racial Discrimination* ("ICERD") in New York and is expected to ratify it in 2017. The government views the signing of the ICERD as further entrenching its commitment to eliminate racial discrimination in the country, which it sees as necessary for racial and religious harmony. Under the Singapore constitution, racial discrimination is specifically prohibited under article 12(2).

### United Nations Convention on the Law of the Sea – Domestic Incorporation – Deep Seabed Mining Act

The Singapore Parliament passed the *Deep Seabed Mining Act 2015* on 12 February 2015, which came into force on 1 April 2015. The purpose of the Act is to fulfil Singapore's obligations under the United Nations Convention on the Law of the Sea ("UNCLOS") in relation to deep seabed mining activities. It establishes a licensing regime to ensure that Singaporean companies undertake exploration and exploitation activities in a responsible manner to protect the marine environment.

### International Agreement – Hague Convention on Choice of Court Agreements

Singapore signed the *Hague Convention on Choice of Court Agreements* on 25 March 2015. The Convention aims to ensure that exclusive choice of court agreements in favour of Contracting States are effectively enforced, and that judgments rendered by the chosen courts are recognized and enforced in Contracting States. This enhances Singapore's position as a dispute resolution hub in Asia as a dispute must be heard in Singapore if a Singapore court is the chosen court of an exclusive choice of court agreement covered by the Convention. Further, courts of other Contracting States will be obliged to recognize and enforce Singapore court judgments on that dispute, enhancing the enforceability of Singapore court judgments, including those of the Singapore International Commercial Court.

## Asian Infrastructure Investment Bank Act 2015

The Singapore Parliament passed the *Asian Infrastructure Investment Bank Act 2015* on 17 August 2015, and the Act came into force on 22 August 2015. The Act is to implement the *International Agreement* for the establishment and operation of the Asian Infrastructure Investment Bank ("AIIB"), to enable Singapore to become a member of the Bank and for connected purposes. The *AIIB* is an initiative by the Chinese government to set up a multilateral development bank that aims to support the building of infrastructure in the Asia-Pacific region. Singapore is one of the first few countries to be involved in the establishment of the AIIB and will subscribe US$250 million to the bank. Other countries that have signed the AIIB Articles of Agreement include other ASEAN member States and major European economies such as France, Germany and the UK.

## Regional Organizations – ASEAN Economic Community

As a Member State of the Association of Southeast Asian Nations, Singapore became part of the ASEAN Economic Community ("AEC") that was established on 31 December 2015. In a press statement issued on the formation of the Community, Singapore's Minister for Foreign Affairs noted that the AEC was a significant milestone in ASEAN's history and was aimed at enhancing the region's growth and developmental opportunities, as well as to expand the operations of businesses beyond national boundaries to the wider region to serve ASEAN's growing middle class. The AEC is one of ASEAN's three Community Pillars, the other two being the ASEAN Political-Security Community (APSC) and the ASEAN Socio-Cultural Community (ASCC).

# State Practice of Asian Countries in International Law

*Sri Lanka*

*Danushka S. Medawatte**

## Freedom to Seek, Receive, and Impart Information

### *19th Amendment – 1978 Constitution of the Democratic Socialist Republic of Sri Lanka*

The 19th Amendment to the 1978 Constitution of the Democratic Socialist Republic of Sri Lanka was adopted on 15 May 2015. By virtue of Article 14A (1) of the Amendment, right of access to information was incorporated into the Fundamental Rights Chapter of the Constitution. The enforceability of this right is dependent on whether the right of access to information is provided for by law, and whether such access paves way for the protection of a citizen's right.

Providing the right to access information is consistent with the obligations that Sri Lanka has undertaken under Article 19(2) of the International Convention on Civil and Political Rights (ICCPR) which requires State parties to grant *inter alia* the freedom to seek, receive and impart information as an integral component of the freedom of expression.

## Commitment to the Purposes and Principles of the Charter of the United Nations and International Law

### *President's Duty to Act in Accordance with International Law*

Section 5 of the 19th Amendment reiterates that the President should exercise his powers and functions *inter alia* in accordance with the international law. This obligations is stated in Article 33 (2) (h) of the Constitution and is a continuation of the constitutional guarantee that was embodied in Article 33(f) of the Constitution pre-19th Amendment. This is consistent with General Assembly Resolution 66/102 (2012) which reaffirmed the commitment of the members of the United Nations General Assembly to guarantee the protection of the rule of law at national and international levels.

* Faculty of Law, University of Colombo.

 | DOI 10.1163/9789004344556_022

## United Nations Convention against Corruption and United Nations Convention against Transnational Organized Crime

### *Chapter XIXA of the Constitution of Sri Lanka*

Chapter XIXA of the Constitution that was introduced by the 19th Amendment provides the legal framework for the establishment of a Commission to Investigate Allegations of Bribery or Corruption. Article 156A(c) of Chapter XIXA states that the Parliamentary law establishing such a Commission shall provide for 'measures to implement the United Nations Convention Against Corruption and any other international Convention relating to the prevention of corruption, to which Sri Lanka is a party'. Sri Lanka has ratified UN Convention against Corruption and UN Convention against Transnational Organized Crime

## United Nations Convention against Transnational Organized Crime

### *Assistance to and Protection of Victims of Crime and Witnesses Act, No 4 of 2015*

By virtue of Articles 24 and 25, the UN Convention against Transnational Organized Crime requires State parties to provide assistance and protection to witnesses and victims of crime. The Assistance to and Protection of Victims of Crime and Witnesses Act No. 4 of 2015 was certified on 7 March 2015 to give effect to obligations undertaken under the aforementioned UN Convention which was ratified by Sri Lanka on 22 September 2006.

The preamble to the Assistance to and Protection of Victims of Crime and Witnesses Act provides as follows:

> An Act to provide for the setting out of rights and entitlements of victims of crime and witnesses and the protection and promotion of such rights and entitlements; *to give effect to appropriate international norms, standards and best practices relating to the protection of victims of crime and witnesses*; the establishment of the National Authority for the Protection of Victims of Crime and Witnesses; constitution of a Board of Management, the Victims of Crime and Witnesses Assistance and Protection Division of the Sri Lanka Police Department; payment of compensation to victims of crime; establishment of the Victims of Crime and Witnesses Assistance and Protection Fund and for matters connected therewith or incidental thereto. [emphasis added]

## Arbitrary Deprivation of Life, Torture, Ill Treatment, Lack of Proper Investigation, Right to an Effective Remedy, Right to Liberty and Security of Person, Respect for the Inherent Dignity of the Human Person

*Misilin Nona Guneththige and Piyawathie Guneththige (represented by the Asian Legal Resource Centre and Redress) v. Sri Lanka.* Communication No. 2087/2011, Human Rights Committee, 113th Session, 16 March – 2 April 2015, CCPR/C/113/D/2087/2011, 7 May 2015.

The communication was submitted on behalf of Thissera Sunil Hemachandra who was the son of Misilin Nona and nephew of Piyawathie. The authors of the communication alleged that the following provisions of the International Covenant on Civil and Political Rights were violated by the State party: Articles 2(3),[1] 6,[2] 7,[3] 9(1),[4] 9(2),[5] 9(4),[6] and 10 (1).[7]

The facts of the case indicate that the victim – Sunil had won a lottery worth over three million Sri Lankan rupees. A lottery sales agent and a policeman had visited Sunil's house on the following day and had attempted to compel him to visit the police. On 21July 2003, Sunil had been requested to visit Moragahahena Police Station even though no reasons necessitating such a visit had been explained to him. Sunil had then been compelled to pay Rs.25,000 to cover the expenses of a procession of a temple. Although Sunil was initially released upon agreeing to make the payment, he was taken into police custody on the following day, i.e., 22 of July 2003.

Sunil had been beaten in police custody and been deprived of medical attention claiming that he was merely suffering from an epileptic fit. After this was brought to the attention of the police by the second author, Sunil had been admitted to hospital. Two police officers had recorded a statement from Sunil while he was in hospital. During this time, Sunil had only been able to utter his name and place his thumb print on the alleged 'statement' that was recorded by the police. His thumb print had so been obtained even though he was capable of placing his signature.

1 Right to an effective remedy.
2 Inherent right to life.
3 Right to be free from torture, cruel, inhuman and degrading treatment or punishment.
4 Right to liberty and security of person, right to be free from arbitrary arrests or detention.
5 Right to be informed of the reasons for arrest and charges at the time of the arrest.
6 Entitlement to take proceedings before a court, in order that the court may decide without delay on the lawfulness of an arrested person's detention and order such person's release if the detention is not lawful.
7 Right to be treated with humanity and with respect for the inherent dignity of the human person during the period of deprivation of liberty.

On 24 July, Sunil had been transferred to the National Hospital in Colombo where he was subject to brain surgery and was treated in the Intensive Care Unit. Sunil succumbed to the injuries on the 26July 2003. There were inconsistencies in the Judicial Medical Officer's Report. The authors of the communication filed a petition to move the Supreme Court (SC) concerning the violated fundamental rights in September 2003. Simultaneously, the possibility of raising criminal charges against alleged perpetrators were considered by the Attorney General (AG), and on 29April 2004, the AG decided that no charges can be filed as there was no evidence of an assault against the victim. This decision was made even though the Magistrate had noted that the circumstances surrounding the victim's death were suspicious.

The authors had also filed a petition at the Human Rights Commission of Sri Lanka (HRCSL) soon after the death of the victim. This remained unanswered until 21August 2008 and the authors were later informed that the proceedings were suspended. On the 6tAugust 2010, the SC dismissed the fundamental rights application on the ground that Sunil's fall was due to a fit arising from alcohol withdrawal. The SC abstained from assessing whether the victim was subject to assault in custody. The authors therefore claim that domestic remedies have been exhausted and that the State party is liable for the violation of Articles 2(3), 6(1), 7, 9 (1, 2, and 4), and 10.

The Human Rights Committee requested information from the State party in four different instances regarding the admissibility of the case. However, the committee noted with regret that the State has not cooperated and the requested information was not received. The Committee noted that Sri Lanka is obliged by virtue of Article 4(2) of the Optional Protocol to the ICCPR to examine in good faith all allegations levelled against the State party, and to make available to the Committee all information at the disposal of the State party. The Committee decided to give due weight to the allegations of the authors to the extent substantiated in the absence of a reply from the State party. The Committee declared the communication admissible due to domestic remedies being unduly prolonged and due to the absence of a response from the State party.

The Committee noted that the inherent right to life as stipulated in Article 6 of the ICCPR also means that the State party bears the responsibility to care for the life of arrested and detained individuals and that 'a death in any type of custody should be regarded prima facie as a summary or arbitrary execution'. The Committee further stated that 'consequently, there should be a thorough, prompt, and impartial investigation to confirm or rebut [the above] presumption especially when complaints by relatives or other reliable reports suggest unnatural death.' The very officers of the Moragahahena Police Station where the victim was detained being involved in the investigation, the

Attorney General's refusal to conduct a criminal prosecution and the seven year duration taken by the Supreme Court of Sri Lanka to make a ruling on the fundamental rights petition filed by the authors of the communication were regarded by the Committee as factors invoking State responsibility concerning its failure to protect the victim's life. The Committee considered this as resulting in the breach of Article 6(1) read alone and in conjunction with Article 2(3) of the ICCPR. The Committee further found a violation of Article 7 by the State as there was evidence of severe beatings on the head and abdomen of the victim and because the authorities failed to provide timely and effective medical assistance to the victim. The Committee further concluded that the arrest of the victim without informing of reasons for arrest deprived the victim of any possibility of seeking legal assistance and that in the absence of any rebuttal by the State party, there is sufficient evidence to conclude that the victim's rights under Article 9 have been violated by the State.

The Committee noted that despite the lapsing of nearly 12 years since the victim's death, the authors are still unaware of the circumstances surrounding the death due to the State party's inaction. The continued stress and mental anguish caused upon the authors of the communication by such inaction was considered as amounting to a breach of Article 2(3) read in conjunction with Article 7.

The Committee noted in conclusion that the State party has recognized the competence of the Committee to determine whether or not there has been a violation of the provisions of the ICCPR and that the State has undertaken the obligation of providing an effective and enforceable remedy when a violation has been established. The State party was requested to provide information to the Committee within 180 days and to widely disseminate the views concerning this violation after having them translated into the official languages of Sri Lanka.

## Promoting Reconciliation, Accountability and Human Rights In Sri Lanka

### *Human Rights Council Resolution 30/L.29 on Promoting Reconciliation, Accountability and Human Rights in Sri Lanka, A/HRC/30/L.29, 29 September 2015*

The United Nations Human Rights Council adopted Resolution 30/1 on Promoting Reconciliation, Accountability and Human Rights in Sri Lanka on 29 September 2015. The Human Rights Council welcomed the steps taken by the Government of Sri Lanka since 2015 to advance respect for human rights, and to strengthen good governance and democratic institutions. The Council further welcomed the efforts of the government to investigate into allegations of bribery, corruption, fraud and abuse of power. Clause 3 of the Resolution states as follows:

> Supports the commitment of the Government of Sri Lanka to strengthen and safeguard the credibility of the process of truth-seeking, justice, reparations and guarantees of non-recurrence by engaging in broad national with the inclusion of victims and civil society, including non-governmental organizations, from all affected communities, which will inform the design and implementation of these processes, drawing on international expertise, assistance and best practices.

## Convention on the Elimination of All Forms of Discrimination against Women

### *Sri Lankan State Party Report to the CEDAW Committee, Eighth Periodic Report of State Parties Due in 2015 (received on 30 April 2015), CEDAW/C/LKA/8, 29 May 2015*

In this report, the absence of a Women's Right Bill and minimal female representation at elected political bodies was cited. However, the State party noted that the number of women in Sri Lanka Administrative Services has increased. Since the approval of the budget in January 2015, the State has implemented a system of paying Rs. 20,000 to pregnant women for purchase of nutritious food recommended by doctors. This was targeted at avoiding anemia, low birth weight and malnutrition affecting both mothers and babies.[8] This is consistent with the obligations that Sri Lanka has undertaken under Article 12(2) of CEDAW.

Section 13K of the Assistance to and Protection of Victims of Crime and Witnesses Act No 4 of 2015 seeks to lay a framework to take measures to sensitize police officers, Prison Department, government medical officers, public officers associated with probation and social services and other officers on matters concerning *inter alia* gender.[9] This is in line with Article 2(b) of CEDAW.

Paragraph 94 of the State Report records that the State has adopted measures to abolish the concept of "head of household" in administrative practice and recognize joint or co-ownership of land. This is consistent with the obligations that Sri Lanka has undertaken under Article 16(1)(h) of CEDAW.

8 Paragraph 24.

9 See also paragraph 28 and 29 of the State Report to CEDAW.

# State Practice of Asian Countries in International Law

*Thailand*

*Kitti Jayangakula**

## Human Rights

### *Children's Rights – the Protection of Children Born through Assisted Reproductive Technologies – Surrogacy Law*

On 19 February 2015, the National Legislative Assembly of Thailand enacted the Protection for Children Born through Assisted Reproductive Technologies Act (ART Act), which is a significantly protect children born through Assisted Reproductive Technologies (ART) and sets the legal procedures that spouses must follow in order to have such children.

The purposes of the ART Act are: to specify the parent's legal status; to control and specify the rights and duties of related parties during and after surrogacy; to control and set boundaries on the proper use of enhanced technology, specifically for achieving pregnancy in procedures; and to prohibit surrogacy involving a business or profit-making enterprise.

Section 3 of the ART Act defines "Assisted Reproductive Technologies (ART)" as "any medical procedure which allows extracting sperm and egg from a human body and achieving pregnancy without sexual intercourse, including artificial insemination" and defines surrogacy as "pregnancy by ART."

However, ART applicants must be lawful spouses, and the wife cannot be pregnant as stipulated in Section 21 of the ART Act that

> … [p]ermission for the act of surrogacy shall meet the following criteria:
>
> (1) the legally married husband and wife who apply for surrogacy because the wife is not able to get pregnant shall be both Thai nationals. In case either a husband or a wife is not a Thai national, the couple must have been married for at least three years prior to the application.

* Eastern Asia University, Thailand.

 | DOI 10.1163/9789004344556_023

(2) The surrogate mother shall not be either the parent or the descendant of any of the applicants under the Clause (1);
(3) The surrogate mother shall be a blood relative of one of the applicants under the Clause (1); in case the applicants have no blood relatives, the surrogate mother shall be chosen in accordance with the rules, methods and terms prescribed by the regulations issued by the Minister of Public Health as advised by the Committee;
(4) The surrogate mother shall have had a pregnancy before the surrogacy; in case the surrogate mother is legally married or stays in a civil union she shall obtain the consent of her legitimate spouse or partner.

Regarding this, same-sex couples cannot seek surrogacy, because Thai law has not yet provided for legally sanctioned same-sex marriage.

According to the ART Act, the applicants and the surrogate mother must have a written agreement before the pregnancy occurs, indicating that the applicants will be the legal parents of the child (Section 3). The Act also clearly states that the applicants will be the legal parents of the surrogate child and cannot deny the parentage of a child born through ART (Sections 29[10] and 33[11]), and it will be applied retroactively to those children of surrogacy born before the Act's entry into force, through a process of the parents' seeking court approval (Section 56[12]).

---

10 Section 29 provides that "The child born with the usage of the sperm or the egg of a donor through the Assisted Reproductive Technologies (ART) under this Act, regardless of whether the birth was given by the legitimate wife of the applicant or by the surrogate mother, is the legitimate child of this legally married couple. This is also true in case the wife or the husband die prior to the fact of birth. The man or the woman whose reproductive cells were used in the process of the embryo formation with the purpose of achieving pregnancy or the person who donate the embryo or the infant born from his/her sperm, egg or embryo have no rights and liabilities over the child, in accordance with the provisions of the Civil and Commercial Code concerning family and legacy matters."

11 Section 33 provides that "It is prohibited to the husband, wife or both of the applicants for surrogacy to deny the parentage of the child born through surrogacy."

12 Section 56 provides that "In case the child was born through surrogacy before the day on which the present Act comes into force regardless of whether the agreement was drawn up or not, the wife or the husband who applied for surrogacy or the Public Prosecutor have the right to plead the Court to issue an order which allows the child born before the day on which this Act comes into force to become a legitimate child of the couple who applied for surrogacy since the day of his/her birth. Therefore, regardless of whether the couple who applied for surrogacy was legally married or not, this order will not eliminate

The ART Act provides that the surrogacy shall not be performed for commercial purposes (Section 24) then, if anyone is involved in surrogacy for profit, he/she will be sentenced upon conviction to imprisonment for up to ten years or a fine of up to THB 200,000 (Section 48). To act as an intermediary or an agent as well as to claim, receive or agree to receive assets or other advantage as the reward for organizing or advising on the matter of surrogacy is also prohibited under the ART Act (Section 27) then if anyone acts as an agent by requesting or accepting money, property, or other benefits in return for managing or giving advice about surrogacy, he/she will be sentenced upon conviction to imprisonment for up to five years and/or a fine of up to THB 100,000 (Section 49).

### *Children's rights – Child pornography – Implementation of Optional Protocol to the Convention on the Right of the Child on the Sale of Children, Child Prostitution and Child Pornography*

On 14 May 2015, the National Legislative Assembly of Thailand voted unanimously to amend the Penal Code of Thailand to criminalise child pornography. On 8 September 2015, the Amendments to the Penal Code Act (24th edition) B.E. 2558 (2015) were published in the Royal Thai Government Gazette and came into effect 90 days after its publication (7 December 2015). The Amendments define the term 'child pornography' in complying with international agreement and criminalize criminal acts concerning child pornography. As a party to the Convention on Rights of the Child (CRC) and the Optional Protocol to the Convention on the Rights of the Child on the Sale of Children, Child Prostitution and Child Pornography, the Amendments fulfill the obligations under such international agreements.

According the Act, the meaning of child pornography is added to Section 1(17) of the Penal Code as defined the Act as "being a material or thing showing or displaying any sexual activities of a child or with a child who is under 18 year olds by picture or text or by any means whatsoever, any document, painting, print, printed matter, picture, poster, symbol, photograph, cinematograph film, magnetic sound-recording tape, magnetic picture-recording tape or any other similar things, including any aforementioned subject or thing which is recorded in computers or electronic devices which can be shown or displayed. "

---

the rights of legally acting third parties since the day of the child's birth and until the date of the issue of the relevant Court order."

The Amendments have prescribed the penalty regarding *"Child Pornography"*, as separate from the current pornography penalty specified in the Penal Code of Thailand. Having any child pornography for sexual benefits to oneself or other persons, shall be subject to an imprisonment not exceeding 5 years or a fine not exceeding THB 100,000, or both. (Section 287/1, para. 1)

If the person who committed the above activity disseminated such child pornography to other persons, that person shall be subject to a term of imprisonment not exceeding 7 years or a fine not exceeding THB 140,000, or both (Section 287/1, para. 2); and Section 287/2 provides:

> Whoever:
> For the purpose of trade or by trade, for public distribution or exhibition, makes, produces, possesses, brings or causes to be brought into Thailand, sends or causes to be sent out of Thailand, takes away or causes to be taken away, or circulates by any means whatever, any Child Pornography; or
>
> Carries on trade, or takes part or participates in the trade concerning any Child Pornography, or distributes or exhibits to the public, or hires out such Child Pornography; or
>
> Assists in the circulation or trading of any Child Pornography, propagates or spreads the news by any means whatsoever that there is a person committing the acts prescribed above, or propagates or spreads the news that the Child Pornography may be obtained from any person or by any means,

Such person shall be subject to an imprisonment from 3 to 10 years with a fine from THB 60,000 to THB 200,000.

### *Human Rights and Labor Rights – Human Trafficking and Forced Labor in the Fisheries Sector – Regularization and Protection of Migrant Workers*

2015 marked a major turning point for Thai fisheries. The Thai government embarked on a comprehensive fisheries reform, guided by Food and Agriculture Organization (FAO) and other relevant international standards, to tackle deep-seated problems in the fisheries sector. The reform aims to revamp fisheries management and governance, with a view to rooting out illegal, unreported and unregulated (IUU) fishing as well as human trafficking and forced labor in the fisheries sector. The end goal is to ensure sustainable and responsible practices in all aspects of Thailand's fisheries sector.

As the first steps of the reform, Thailand has overhauled the legal and policy frameworks governing the fisheries sector, grounded in international principles and standards relating to sustainable and responsible fisheries. A new fisheries law, the Royal Ordinance on Fisheries B.E. 2558 (2015), was enacted and entered into force on 14 November 2015. The law significantly empowers relevant authorities to combat IUU fishing and unlawful labor practices in the fishing and seafood industries (Section 4).

The Royal Ordinance introduces *proportionate and deterrent penalties*, with a maximum fine of 30 million baht as stipulated in Section 123 that:

> Any person violating Section 10 shall be subject to a fine of between ten thousand baht and one hundred thousand baht, or to a fine of three times the value of the aquatic animals obtained through the fishing operation. In whichever case, the higher fine shall apply.
>
> Any offender pursuant to paragraph one using a vessel of a size from ten gross tonnage up to less than twenty gross tonnage shall be subject to a fine of between one hundred thousand baht and two hundred thousand baht, or to a fine of five times the value of the aquatic animals obtained from the fishing operation. In whichever case, the higher fine shall apply.
>
> Any offender pursuant to paragraph one using a vessel of a size from twenty gross tonnage up to less than sixty gross tonnage shall be subject to a fine of between two hundred thousand baht and six hundred thousand baht, or to a fine of five times the value of the aquatic animals obtained from the fishing operation. In whichever case, the higher fine shall apply.
>
> Any offender pursuant to paragraph one using a vessel of a size from sixty gross tonnage up to less than one hundred and fifty gross tonnage shall be subject to a fine of between six hundred thousand baht and five million baht, or to a fine of five times the value of the aquatic animals obtained from the fishing operation. In whichever case, the higher fine shall apply.
>
> Any offender pursuant to paragraph one using a vessel of a size from one hundred and fifty gross tonnage onwards shall be subject to a fine of between five million baht and thirty million baht, or to a fine of five times the value of the aquatic animals obtained from the fishing operation. In whichever case, the higher fine shall apply.

The infringement could lead to serious administrative sanctions, including the revocation of the fishing license and vessel registrar, as well as the suspension or closure of seafood processing factories with illegal migrant workers.

## International Trade Law

### *International Air Carriage – 1999 Montreal Convention for the Unification of Certain Rules for International Carriage by Air*

On 13 February 2015, the new law on air carriage passed by the National Legislative Assembly of Thailand was announced in the Royal Thai Government Gazette. It came into effect 90 days after its publication on 14 May 2015. The law, called the International Air Carriage Act B.E. 2558 (Air Carriage Act), covers air carrier liability for accidents, delays, and cargo losses. The Air Carriage Act therefore provides a welcome degree of certainty for air carriers and passengers alike. The Act is also generally consistent with the 1999 Montreal Convention for the Unification of Certain Rules for International Carriage by Air, the international airline liability treaty, of which Thailand is not a member. The Air Carriage Act brings Thailand closer to international standards, and may signal a new willingness by the Thai government to ratify the Montreal Convention.

The Air Carriage Act provides liability for bodily injury or death of the passengers when the accident occurred either on board the aircraft or during embarkation or disembarkation (Section 10). The liability level is determined, in part, by a plaintiff's contributory negligence (Section 14). The Air Carriage Act sets statutory limitations to liability, including liability for bodily injury or death.

For liability for checked baggage and delays, the Act also provides liability for damage arising from the destruction or loss of checked baggage. Liability attaches only if the event that caused the destruction occurred on board the aircraft or if the carrier controls the checked baggage. The Air Carriage Act does not define these terms, so they will be interpreted differently by the national courts. The air carrier is automatically liable for damage to or loss of unchecked baggage when the damage is due to the carrier's agents (Section 11). An air carrier is also liable for damage caused by flight delays. To escape liability, the carrier must prove that it took measures to avoid the damage (Section 12).

The Air Carriage Act contains provisions governing liability for air cargo. A carrier is liable for damages caused by the loss or damage to cargo when the event causing the damage took place during the carriage by air. The carrier is also liable for damage to cargo that resulted from delays, unless the carrier can prove that it "took all measures" to avoid the damage.

The Air Carriage Act applies equally to domestic carriage and international carriage. All cases brought in relation to domestic carriage by air must be brought before the Central Intellectual Property and International Trade Court in Bangkok.

Section 58 provides that "Cases on domestic carriage by air shall fall within the jurisdiction of the Intellectual Property and International Trade Court."

But strangely, the Air Carriage Act does not mention jurisdiction for cases involving international carriage. This deviates from the Montreal Convention, which has specific provisions on jurisdiction. Moreover, the Air Carriage Act makes no mention of handling disputes by arbitration—another difference with the Montreal Convention. Issues involving jurisdiction over cases related to international carriage will therefore be decided by the individual court.

## Judicial Decision

### *The Right to Refuse Treatment of Patient – the Right to Die – Patient's Living Will – Legitimacy of Ministerial Regulation on Living Wills*

*Thapanawong Tang-uraiwan, Oraphan Methadilokkul, and Cherdchoo Ariyas-riwattana v. Prime Minister PM Yingluck Shinawatra and Public Health Minister Wittaya Buranasiri [Supreme Administrative Court, Black Case No. For.147/2554, Red Case No. For.11/2558, 18 June 2015]*

Facts

Three doctors submitted a petition before the Supreme Administrative Court claimed to abrogate Section 12, Paragraph 2 of the National Health Act B.E. 2550 (2007) (NHA). They tried to get this regulation nullified, as they believe it goes against the Medical Practice Act and is unethical because the regulation requires doctors to stop treating patients, when doctors have been taught to never stop saving a life.

Section 12 of the NHA, which states that

> A person shall have the right to make a living will in writing to refuse the public health service which is provided merely to prolong his/her terminal stage of life or to make a living will to refuse the service as to cease the severe suffering from illness.
>
> The living will under paragraph one shall be carried out in accordance with the rules and procedure prescribed in the Ministerial Regulation.
>
> An act done by public health personnel in compliance with the living will under paragraph one shall not be held an offence and shall not be liable to any responsibility whatsoever.

The provision recognizes patients' living wills, in which they can spell out their preferences for medical care at a time when they are unable to make decisions for themselves. In their living wills, they can state what kind of treatments they would or would not want to receive when they reach a terminal stage while Ministerial Regulation on Rule and Procedure for Implementing a Living Will to Refuse Public Health Services that Prolong Dying in the Terminal Stage of Illness or to End Suffering from Illness B.E. 2557 (2010), which allows public health professionals to accord the patient's living wills without having to worry about legal consequences.

The plaintiffs claimed that doctors have been taught and practiced to save patient's life. The definitions and meanings of "public health services that prolong dying in the terminal stage of illness or to end suffering from illness," "terminal stage of life," and "suffering from illness", stipulated in the Ministerial Regulation, have never been taught in medical school. In addition, the plaintiffs as well as others doctors have been acknowledged and taught concerning "mercy killing" or "euthanasia" which means letting the patient dies by withholding or withdrawing all medical measures. Regarding this, to comply with his/her living will, pursuant to Section 12 of the NHA, would be the omission from professional healthcare standard and the doctors have to responsible for those consequences. The plaintiffs also claimed that patient's self determination to live or to die is his/her freedom, not right and the right to die is not recognized under the Constitution of the Kingdom of Thailand B.E. 2550 (2007) (the 2007 Constitution).

Judgment

The Supreme Administration Court (the Court) stated that the right to commit a living will is the right and freedom over his/her life and body, which is recognized by the 2007 Constitution. The draft of Ministerial Regulation has already taken into account the opinions of professional bodies and various organizations under the process of public hearing stipulated by the 2007 Constitution. A person has right over his/her life and body; doctors have to respect the decision of the patient through his/her living will without legal consequences, which lead to criminal liability for his/her omission under the Penal Code.

The Court affirmed that rules and procedure under the Ministerial Regulation is not the rejection of taking professional healthcare, or using of medicine or medical equipment to end a life of patient, but it remains the taking of palliative care for the patient to die naturally without suffering complying with his/her living will to refuse the service as to cease the severe suffering from illness. The Court dismissed a petition of the plaintiffs, in effect, gives patients "the right to die."

# State Practice of Asian Countries in International Law

*Vietnam*

*Tran Viet Dung**

## Economic – Trade

### *Ratification of the Protocol Amending the Marrakesh Agreement establishing the World Trade Organization (WTO)*

On 26 November 2015, the National Assembly of Vietnam ratified the Protocol Amending the Marrakesh Agreement Establishing the World Trade Organization ("Protocol").[13]

The Protocol was adopted by the General Council of the WTO on 27 November 2014 to insert the new Agreement on Trade Facilitation ("TFA") and the commitments of developing countries that are incorporated as an Annex to the Marrakesh Agreement Establishing the World Trade Organization. The TFA was the first newly established agreement adopted by all Members since the foundation of the WTO in 1995.

The purpose of the amendments to TFA is to further simplify and modernize procedures for the movement, release and clearance of goods and to enhance transparency of trade related procedures. It aims to help smaller businesses exploit export opportunities and to facilitate developing countries' participation in international trade. These amendments are also expected to help the developing countries to reduce the bureaucracy, promote trade and investment by reducing the trade transaction costs as well as to prevent illegal imports and to improve the collection of customs duties.

By ratifying the Protocol, Vietnam has committed to further improve the foreign trade environment. It is expected that in coming years the Vietnamese government will amend and revise the trade rules and regulations, such as unclear trade rules, procedures and fees; unjust discretion of officials; unreasonable requests for documents for import; and the long period of time from the arrival of goods to the permission of import etc., and thus support trade and

* Associate Professor, Ho Chi Minh City University of Law, Vietnam.

13 Resolution No. 108/2015/QH13 dated 26 November 2015 of the National Assembly, ratifying the Protocol Amending the Marrakesh Agreement Establishing the World Trade Organization.

 | DOI 10.1163/9789004344556_024

other economic activities of companies from WTO members, which not only export finished goods, but also develop supply chains on a global scale.

## International Economic Law

### *International Economic Cooperation – Free Trade Agreements*

In 2015, the Government of the Socialist Republic of Vietnam completed negotiations and signed a number of important free trade agreements, including with the European Union – Vietnam Free Trade Agreement, Korea – Vietnam Free Trade Agreement, Vietnam – Eurasia Economic Union Free Trade Area. The initiative of Vietnam towards the conclusion of free trade agreements in 2015 has brought the country to the position of one the most active supporters of regional economic integration in Southeast Asia alongside Singapore.

### *The Free Trade Agreement between the European Union and the Socialist Republic of Vietnam*

On 4 December 2015, the Free Trade Agreement between European Union and the Socialist Republic of Vietnam (EUVFTA) was officially signed by the two parties to establish the free trade area. The FTA, for which negotiations started in October 2012, is one the most ambitious and comprehensive FTA that the EU has ever concluded with a developing country, the second in the ASEAN region after Singapore, and a further building block towards the EU's ultimate objective of an ambitious and comprehensive region-to-region EU-ASEAN FTA. The EUVFTA shall eliminate nearly all tariffs (over 99%), except for a small number of tariff lines for which the EU and Vietnam agreed on partial liberalization through zero-duty Tariff Rate Quotas (TRQs):[14] Vietnam will liberalize 65% of import duties on EU exports to Vietnam at entry into force, with the remainder of duties being gradually eliminated over a 10-year period; and EU duties will be eliminated over a 7-year period.

Pursuant to the EUVFTA, almost all EU exports of machinery and appliances will be fully liberalized at entry into force and the rest after 5 years. Motorcycles (with engines larger than 150 cc) will be liberalized after 7 years and cars after 10 years, except those with large engines (>3000cc for petrol, > 2500cc for diesel) which will be liberalized one year earlier. Roughly half of EU pharmaceuticals exports will be duty free at entry into force and the rest after 7 years. Close to 70% of EU chemicals export will be duty free at entry into force and the rest after 3, 5 and 7 years. Wines and spirits will be liberalized after 7 years.

14 Ministry of Industry and Trade, Foreign Trade Development, Annual Report, (2016).

Frozen pork meat will be duty free after 7 years, beef after 3 years, dairy products after a maximum of 5 years and food preparations after a maximum of 7 years. Chicken will be fully liberalized after 10 years.[15]

The EU will eliminate duties for textile and footwear products of Vietnam within 5 to 7[16] years for the more sensitive items and 3 years and entry into force for less sensitive goods. With regard to garment products, the EUVFTA applies very strict rules of origin, which require the products to use of fabrics produced in Vietnam, with the only exception being of fabrics produced in South Korea, another FTA partner of the EU. Some sensitive agricultural products will not be fully liberalized, but the EU has offered access to Vietnamese exports via tariff rate quotas (TRQs) for rice, sweet corn, garlic, mushrooms, sugar and high-sugar-containing products, manioc starch, surimi and canned tuna.

The EU and Vietnam have also agreed to strengthen the disciplines of the WTO Technical Barriers to Trade (TBT) agreement. In particular, Vietnam has committed to increasing the use of international standards in drafting its regulations. The agreement also contains a chapter addressing Sanitary and Phytosanitary measures (SPS), specifically aimed at facilitating trade in plant and animal products, where the parties agreed on some important principles such as regionalization and the recognition of the EU as a single entity. These provisions will facilitate access for EU companies producing a large variety of products, including electrical appliances, IT, and food and drinks to the Vietnamese market.

The agreement will also contain a specific annex with far-reaching provisions to address non-tariff barriers in the automotive sector, including, five years after its entry into force, the recognition of the EU vehicle whole certificate of conformity.

Vietnam and EU also established a list mutually accepted Geographical Indications (GIs). Accordingly, farmers and small businesses of the two parties producing food with traditional methods will benefit from the recognition and protection on this GI regime. As result of the EUVFTA the use of 169 European GIs such as Champagne, Feta, Parmigiano Reggiano, Rioja, Roquefort or Scotch Whisky will be reserved in Vietnam for products imported from the European regions in which they originate. Meanwhile, 39 Vietnamese GIs, too, will be recognized and protected as such in the EU, providing the adequate framework for further promoting imports of quality products such as Phú Quốc fish sauce,

15 Ibid.

16 On footwear, Vietnam agreed on a solution based on an ex-out definition, which enables liberalization of athletic/sports footwear either at entry into force or in three years; the rest of the footwear products will be liberalized in seven years.

Mộc Châu tea or Buôn Ma Thuột coffee. The agreement will allow new GIs to be added in the future.

The EUVFTA also deals with the issue of treatment of the State-Owned Enterprises (SOEs) The Agreement contains rules regarding state-owned enterprises (SOEs). This achievement is significant as SOEs have traditionally been a backbone of Vietnamese economy and create around 40% of GDP. Core rules related to SOEs include:

(a) Non-discrimination and commercial considerations: rules applicable to SOEs will put SOEs and private enterprises on an equal footing when engaged in commercial transactions (sales and purchases with a profit making objective).
(b) Transparency: Parties can request information on a case-by-case basis on corporate structures and finances of the companies.
(c) Corporate governance: regulatory functions will treat SOEs and private enterprises in the same way and that all laws and regulations will be applied in a non-discriminatory manner.

Public services are fully safeguarded under the agreement and nothing in the SOE chapter will affect the Parties' ability to continue providing services of general economic interest.

In the area of trade in services, Vietnam has committed to substantially improve market access for EU service suppliers to a broad range of services sectors, including business services; environmental services, postal and courier services, financial services, insurance, maritime transport, higher education services, distribution services.

The result of this chapter goes largely beyond both WTO commitments and any other FTA that Vietnam has concluded, thereby giving EU companies the best possible access to the Vietnamese service market.

With regards to investment promotion, Vietnam has committed to open up to investments in manufacturing in a number of key sectors:

- food products and beverages
- fertilizers and nitrogen composites
- tires and tubes
- gloves and plastic products
- ceramics
- construction materials

On investment protection, the FTA has set the key provisions on protection such as Most Favorite Nation treatment, National Treatment, "minimum standard of treatment" for investments, rules on expropriation (the expropriation shall only be applied for a public purpose, in accordance with due process of law, and subject to prompt, adequate and fully realizable and transferable compensation).

The FTA also includes a chapter on cooperation, as a means to contribute to the efficient implementation of the economic tide of the parties. Boosting sustainable development in all its dimensions is a key objective for such cooperation, for which areas of particular importance include labor and environmental matters, trade facilitation, and SMEs. This chapter is placed under the existing EU-Vietnam Framework Cooperation Agreement.

### *The Free Trade Agreement between the Socialist Republic of Vietnam and the Eurasian Economic Union*

On 29 May 2015, after two years of negotiation, the Free Trade Agreement between the Socialist Republic of Vietnam and the Eurasian Economic Union (EAEU – including the Russian Federation, the Republic of Belarus, the Republic of Kazakhstan, the Republic of Armenia, and the Kyrgyz Republic) was signed. The EAEU-Vietnam FTA is now under the domestic ratification process of the Parties (expected to be completed before October 2016). This is the first free trade agreement of the EAEU with external partner and is expected to create preferences for Vietnamese enterprises when exporting to EAEU countries.

The EAEU-Vietnam FTA regulates the trade in goods, trade in service, investment, rules on economic cooperation and other related issues of mutual interest to be considered in flexible principle, for development goals, benefit – demand balancing, and in conformity with common practices and WTO commitments.

Under the framework of the EAEU-Vietnam FTA, parties agreed to grant each other the market access for 90% in tariff-line, equivalent to over 90% of bilateral trade coverage.[17] Accordingly, the EAEU shall apply duties of 0% on all sea-products originating from Vietnam at the time of coming into force of the FTA. Together with tariff reduction and elimination, two parties will implement Sanitary and Physo Sanitary (SPS) mechanism which includes mutual recognition on SPS measures and management system in the relevant sector, verification on satisfying the regional requirements, auditing report and information of the international organizations; promoting cooperation in implementing trade facilitation, technical support and establishment of the effective consultation mechanism. Meanwhile, Vietnam also set a roadmap to open market for the products of husbandry, number of industrial products including machineries, equipment, vehicles .... originating from the EAEU. Such items are not

17 Ministry of Industry and Trade, Foreign Trade Development, Annual Report, (2016).

competitive to similar products of Vietnam and help to diversify the domestic market. For agricultural products such as milk, milk-based products and cereal products in category of priority offered with free access at agreement enforcement mainly for local demand and not for export promotion.

It should be noted that the Chapter on trade in services, investment and movement of natural persons of the EAEU-Vietnam FTA is only applied only to Vietnam and Russia.[18] The chapter has set out the rules on liberalization and market access of a number of service sectors. The rules on investment provides the basic investment protections rules which could be found in other investment-related agreements, including national treatment; most-favored-nation treatment; "minimum standard of treatment" for investments in accordance with customary international law principles; prohibition of expropriation that is not for public purpose, without due process, or without compensation; prohibition on "performance requirements" such as local content or technology localization requirements; free transfer of profit; and freedom to appoint senior management positions of any nationality.

### *Free Trade Agreement between Republic of Korea and the Socialist Republic of Vietnam*

On 5 May 2015, the Government of the Socialist Republic of Vietnam and the Government of Republic of Korea signed the Korea-Vietnam Free Trade Agreement (KVNFTA). The agreement has become affective as of 20 December 2016 and is expected to further contribute to boosting trade and investment cooperation between the two countries. The bilateral trade between Vietnam and Korea has increased 57 folds over the past decades, from 500,000 million USD in 1992 to 28.8 billion USD in 2014.[19] In 2014, the Korea is the 3rd largest trading partner of Vietnam, after China and the US, while Vietnam is the Korea's 6th largest export market.

The KVNFTA is a comprehensive trade agreement with high level of commitment and benefit balance. The agreement covers Trade in goods (tariff elimination and reduction), trade in service (annexes on telecommunication, finance.), Investment, Intellectual Property, Sanitary and Phyto-sanitary (SPS), Rule of Origin, Custom Facilitation, Trade Safeguard, Technical Barriers to Trade (TBT), E-Commerce, Competition, Institutional, Legislative and Horizontal Issues, Economic Cooperation.

18 Article 8.2, EAEU-Vietnam FTA

19 Department of Foreign Affairs of Hanoi [http://www.dfa.gov.vn/foreign-central/Vietnam-RoK-free-trade-agreement-becomes-effective-3452.htm], last visited 10/10/2016.

Tariff reduction and elimination by Korea are expected to offer new opportunity for export of Vietnam's important export-categories such as agro-products, pivotal aqua-products of shrimp, fish, tropical fruits, industrial products of garment, mechanical instruments. Korea also commits to grant market access in service and investment and agreed to promote economic co-operation, technical support in diversified sectors.

Korea, for the first time, opens its market for some agricultural products of high sensitivity such as garlic, ginger, honey, shrimp, offering considerable opportunities for Vietnam producers.

Vietnams, on the other hand, commits to offer concession for Korea in categories of industrial products such as garment materials and accessories, plastic materials, electronic accessories, trucks and cars (having capacity of 2500cc) and car-parts, electrical home appliances, steel products, and cables.

All other commitments on service, investment, intellectual property, competition, trade safeguard, dispute settlement, economic cooperation, sanitary and phyto-sanitary measures, technical barriers to trade ensure benefit-balance and in conformity with domestic legal regulation, having no negative impacts on other ongoing FTA negotiations.

With commitments on service, investment, transparent policy environment, fair competition in accordance to the international regulations, the KVNFTA is expected to attract investment from Korea, especially in high-technology, manufacturing and processing industries, and, at the same time, to promote economies linking, to consolidate and tighten Vietnam – Korea strategic co-operation relation.

## Criminal Law

*Criminal Law – Law Enforcement – Mutual Legal Assistance in Criminal Matters – Execution*

**Treaty between the Socialist Republic of Vietnam and the Kingdom of Spain Concerning Mutual Legal Assistance in Criminal Matters**

On 18 September 2015, the Prosecutor General of the Supreme People's Procuracy Nguyen Hoa Binh and Spanish Minister of Justice Rafael Catala Polo signed the Treaty on mutual legal assistance in criminal matters between Vietnam and Spain (MLAT). The agreement is intended to better mutual legal assistance activities relating to criminal issues between the two countries' relevant agencies.

Vietnam and Spain shall, in accordance with this Agreement and their respective laws, grant to each other assistance in investigations or proceedings in respect of criminal matters, especially the transnational crimes such offences against a law relating to taxation, customs duties, foreign exchange control and other revenue matters.[20]

Legal assistance granted under this Agreement shall include:

(a) locating and identifying persons
(b) providing documents, records, and evidence;
(c) taking evidence and obtaining statements of persons (including the execution of letters rogatory);
(d) executing requests for search and seizure;
(e) locating, restraining and forfeiting the proceeds and/or instruments of crime;
(f) service of documents;
(g) seeking the consent of persons to be available to give evidence or to assist in investigations in the Requesting Party, and where such persons are in custody, arranging for their temporary transfer to that Party;
(h) collection of forensic material;
(i) examining, freezing, seizuring and confiscating the proceeds of crime and the tools and means of crime;
(j) exchanging of assets and evidence to presented before the court;
(k) exchanging on information on crimes and criminals;
(l) exchanging information on the criminal records;
(m) other assistance consistent with the objects of this Treaty which is not inconsistent with the laws of the Requested Party.[21]

The Central Authority of the Requested Party may refuse assistance if: (a) the execution of the request would prejudice the sovereignty, security, order public or other essential interests of the Requested Party; (b) the request relates to a person who, if proceeded against in the Requested Party for the offence for which assistance is requested, would be entitled to be discharged on the grounds of a previous acquittal or conviction; (c) the request relates to an offence that is regarded by the Requested Party as a military offence; (d) the request relates to criminal proceedings which are politically motivated; or (e) the conduct to which the request relates fails to satisfy a requirement of the domestic law of the Requested Party requiring the establishment of dual criminality.

---

20 Article 1, Spain-Vietnam MLAT.

21 Article 3, Spain-Vietnam MLAT.

## ASEAN

### *Regional Integration – ASEAN Community*

**Declaration on Establishment of ASEAN Community**

On 22 November 2015, the Southeast Asian leaders signed a Declaration to formally establish an ASEAN Community in Kuala Lumpur to a milestone for regional integration. ASEAN Community has come to existence since 31 December 2015.

The move is a landmark development for ASEAN, which was originally formed in 1967 with just five members. It is a step towards realizing the idea of a three-pillared community to deepen regional integration first proposed in 2003 comprising an ASEAN Political and Security Community; an ASEAN Economic Community; and an ASEAN Socio-Cultural Community.

Vietnam and other ASEAN members intend to establish a rules-based Community of shared values and norms; a cohesive, peaceful, stable and resilient region with shared responsibility for comprehensive security including a dynamic and outward-looking region. The full development of ASEAN Community is expected to bring about prosperity in the region and protects the interests and wellbeing of ASEAN peoples.

## International Economic Law

### *Import–Export – WTO Dispute Settlement System – Anti-dumping Law and Practices*

**Agreement on settlement of disputes relating to United States—Anti-Dumping Measures on Certain Shrimp from Viet Nam**

On the 18 July 2015, the United States and Vietnam signed an agreement to resolve the two WTO disputes which brought by Vietnam to the WTO, namely the *United States – Anti-dumping Measures on Certain Shrimp from Viet Nam* (DS404) and *United States – Anti-dumping Measures on Certain Shrimp from Viet Nam* (DS429). The agreement also provides a framework for the settlement of certain U.S. court litigation, as well as the resolution of certain outstanding duty claims covering various administrative reviews of the warm water shrimp antidumping duty order.

One of the central issues of the disputes was the US DOC's use of the "zeroing" methodology, in administrative reviews on the application of the anti-dumping measures, which Viet Nam argued was, "as such" and "as applied" in the fourth, fifth and sixth administrative reviews under the anti-dumping order, inconsistent with Article 2.4 and 9.3 of the Anti-Dumping Agreement and Article VI:2 of the GATT 1994. The US DOC's zeroing is a controversial method of calculating dumping margin, which involves ignoring certain data when calculating them. The mutual agreement has been reached after the Appellate Body of the WTO found in the *US – Anti-dumping Measures on Certain Shrimp from Viet Nam* (DS429)[22] that zeroing practices of the US DOC were inconsistent with the WTO anti-dumping law.

According to the agreement, DOC must revisit prior administrative determinations to bring their decisions into compliance with the WTO dispute findings. As a result, some Vietnamese exporters would no longer be subject to the antidumping duty order. In addition, certain domestic litigation has been resolved and duty deposits were refunded.

This case is also important to world trade system because it addresses the sometimes nebulous question of what exactly is fair in determining the proper prices of exports from non-market economies into market economies like the United States. Vietnam and China are the only two countries considered by the WTO to be non-market economies.

22 Appellate Body Report, *United States – Anti-dumping Measures on Certain Shrimp from Viet Nam*, WT/DS429/AB/R.

# *Literature*

# *Book Review*

∵

**Seokwoo Lee and Warwick Gullet (eds.)**

*Asia-Pacific and the Implementation of the Law of the Sea: Regional Legislative and Policy Approaches to the Law of the Sea Convention* (Brill Nijhoff, 2015) Hardcover: 230pp.

There is no shortage of books on the law of the sea, an enduring topic of scholarly inquiry in international law. On the occasion of the 20th anniversary of the entry into force of the United Nations Convention on the Law of the Sea (LOSC) in 2014, presented an opportune time to examine the successes and shortcomings of the "constitution of the oceans" since its adoption in 1982.

In this book, Seokwoo Lee and Warwick Gullett review the legislative and implementation approaches to the LOSC of nine Asia-Pacific States: China, Japan, Korea, Malaysia, Singapore, Vietnam, Australia, Canada and the United States. Each chapter, written by an expert in the law of the sea from that country, focuses on a single country. The authors make a compelling assessment of the LOSC implementation, dispute settlement and maritime cooperation practices of the countries examined, with a concise discussion of current issues and future challenges faced by these countries. The chapters in this book provide an insightful, kaleidoscopic spectrum of State practice in respect of the LOSC, hinting at the genesis of a regional practice which supports a stable albeit disparate implementation of the LOSC across the Asia-Pacific.

In the opening chapter on China, Zou Keyuan of the University of Central Lancashire, discusses and examines contentious issues faced by China: innocent passage for warships, military activities in the EEZ, and the controversial "U-shaped line" in the South China Sea. The chapter examines China's maritime delimitation challenges with its neighbors and clarifies the position of China to delimit its overlapping EEZ and continental shelf claims in accordance with the equitable principle and on the basis of international law, which is rendered more complicated in the context of China's territorial disputes over islands, for instance, over the Spratly Islands in the South China Sea and Diaoyu (Senkaku) Islands in the East China Sea. Zou's honest assessment, that China's implementation of the LOSC reveals areas of passivity and inconsistencies in its maritime legislation, is tempered by his optimism that China has generally supported the LOSC and is prepared to comply with its provisions.

The next chapter, Chie Kojima of Musashino University, examines the LOSC implementation in Japan. Kojima's paper begins with an historical overview of the Japanese government's ocean policies during the incipient stages of the development of the law of the sea and recounts Japan's active participation and engagement in the UN Conferences on the Law of the Sea (UNCLOS) as well as its implementation since Japan ratified the LOSC in 1996. Then, the paper gives an analysis of Japan's domestic legislation implementing the LOSC and their enforcement. The final section of the chapter focuses on Japan's initiatives to establish regional cooperation frameworks such as the Regional Cooperation Agreement on Combatting Piracy and Armed Robbery against Ships in Asia (ReCAAP); and Japan's use of international courts and tribunals. Kojima observes that the four cases where Japan appeared before the ICJ and ITLOS involved a law of the sea issue.

The LOSC implementation in Korea, which ratified the LOSC in 1996, is examined in the third chapter written by Young Kil Park of the Korea Maritime Institute and Seokwoo Lee of Inha University. Park and Lee note that, domestically, the Korean Constitution treats the LOSC, as a ratified treaty, as having the same effect of domestic laws without need of any further step in terms of legislation. However, the authors acknowledge as unrealistic an examination of Korea's implementation of all 320 articles of LOSC, which they admit not every single provision has been incorporated into Korean domestic law. The chapter limited its focus on regulations regarding the various LOSC maritime jurisdiction zones and concluded with a brief assessment of Korea's implementation of the LOSC by identifying several missing legislation which need to be enacted or existing laws which need to be amended in order to fully comply with the LOSC.

In Chapter 4, Mary George of the University of Malaya, provides a thorough examination of Malaysia's domestic implementation of the LOSC interwoven with Malaysia's participation at UNCLOS, highlighting the country's particular interests and concerns on issues crucial to Malaysia such as navigation and passage regimes, piracy, fisheries governance and offshore installations. The chapter recognizes Malaysia's contribution to the peaceful settlement of disputes with its use of the ICJ and ITLOS to resolve its maritime disputes with Indonesia and Singapore. The chapter concludes with a thoughtful list of unresolved law of the sea issues for Malaysia.

The port city of Singapore, which signed the LOSC on the day it opened for signature and ratified it in 1994, is the focus of the next chapter written by Zhen Sun of the Centre of International Law, National University of Singapore. The author, notes at the outset, Singapore's reputation for its adherence to and observation of international law in its foreign policy. The chapter begins with an examination of measures taken by Singapore to implement its flag and port State rights and duties; it then examines Singapore's maritime boundary agreements with neighbors Malaysia and Indonesia and potential maritime claims in the Singapore Strait. The chapter then considers the legal status of the Straits of Malacca and Singapore under the LOSC and the IMO's navigational rules and regimes, exploring cooperative efforts by bordering States to promote the safety of navigation and environmental protection in the Straits of Malacca and Singapore. The chapter concludes that Singapore's implementation of the LOSC is consistent with its adherence to international law in general and a demonstration of its confidence on the rule of law in the governance of the world's oceans.

In Chapter 6, Nguyen Thai Giang of the Diplomatic Academy of Vietnam analyses Vietnam's legislative implementation of the LOSC especially in the context of the various maritime jurisdiction zones under the convention, then it discusses Vietnam's policy in the settlement of maritime disputes and maritime delimitation agreements with Thailand and China. Giang also discusses fishery cooperation and law enforcement policy, Vietnam's participation in forums and entities in organizations established under LOSC such as the IMO and ISA and related agreements, as well as ASEAN agreements related to shipping and maritime services. The chapter concludes that Vietnam has made considerable efforts and expressed its full commitment to fully apply and harmonize its domestic law with LOSC since it has implemented the landmark treaty.

Warwick Gullett of the School of Law and Australian National Centre for Ocean Resources and Security, University of Wollongong commences his examination of the implementation of the LOSC in Australia with an observation that the international law of the sea is a priority for Australia given its vast coastline and dependence on the peaceful and lawful order of the sea. Gullett premises Australia's interest in the law of the sea on its heavy reliance on seaborne trade as well as its extensive marine resources and sensitive marine environments, which explain Australia's active contribution in all three UNCLOS culminating in its signature to LOSC in 1982 and 1994 when it became a party, the year the convention entered into force. The chapter gives a detailed discussion of how Australia has incorporated into its domestic laws the sea rights and obligations in LOSC, including a discussion of contentious issues involving fisheries such as hot pursuit, automatic forfeiture, and domestic measures which regulate innocent and transit passage in Australia. Gullett finishes his analysis with his observation of Australia's innovative interpretation of the LOSC against the backdrop of a number of areas of textual disparity between Australia's domestic law and the LOSC across several areas which do not mean Australia is in breach of LOSC obligations.

In the penultimate chapter, Jeffrey Smith of McGill University emphasises the comparative success of Canada in its implementation of the LOSC since its accession to the convention. Smith recounts Canada's participation in the making of the LOSC and eventual accession and ratification of the LOSC which provides historical context to the chapter. The chapter observes that the domestic definition of Canada's maritime zones is consistent with the LOSC and State practice. The chapter concludes with some prescient identification of future challenges to Canada's ocean policy and governance, including shipping, pollution and navigation issues in the Arctic and Canada's role in the making of the IMO Polar Code; climate change, maritime security and defence, and even intergovernmental conflicts over maritime jurisdiction ownership and division of revenues from seabed petroleum extraction.

In the final chapter, Anastasia Telesetsky of the College of Law, University of Idaho, in examining the implementation of the LOSC by the United States, argues that US laws and practices, with the exception of the dispute settlement provisions, are largely in conformity with the obligations of LOSC. Telesetsky maintains that ratification of the LOSC by the US is a concrete opportunity for the US to demonstrate its long-term commitment to global cooperation in oceans governance. However, many US stakeholders who further their interests and a policy of American isolationalism halt US ratification. Telesetky proposes that the way around the ongoing political stalemate may be a new government approach to accession. The chapter concludes with the option of the US becoming a full party to the LOSC through either a Congressional-Executive agreement requiring a simple majority of each Congressional chamber or a sole Executive agreement.

The book has significant strengths. It is clear that the editors as well as authors of the individual chapters in the book have sound and solid understanding of their topics. The principal strength of this manuscript lies in its presentation of domestic legislative and enforcement of LOSC provisions of key countries in the Asia-Pacific, written by leading legal scholars of international repute. Whilst not exactly novel, the subject matter covered in the book is definitely of importance, timely, interesting, and a valuable addition to existing academic literature. Throughout the work, the authors maintain a balanced outlook and a clear, strictly objective voice that matches their lifetime worth of rigorous research and solid scholarship. The book is a joy to read and does not have the pretentious tones of a tedious text, despite its apparent scholarly nature.

Whilst understandable to an extent, and especially since the book attempts to cover a wide range of countries across the Asia-Pacific, the vast scope of the book did lend itself to the chapters appearing a bit discordant, and noticeably lacking some coherent unifying conceptual or theoretical thread except for the putative reference to the domestic implementation of the LOSC. A somewhat deeper engagement and analysis or critique of State practice and conformity with the letter and spirit of the LOSC underpinned by any relevant theory – albeit not necessarily a serious flaw – might have given the book stronger theoretical foundations.

The market for this book is quite broad, principally university libraries and the academic community, in particular those in the areas of international relations, political science and international law. It may also be useful to policy makers and government departments. Since the book is written in an academic yet accessible language, it is suitable for a wider audience including government officials, officials of global and regional organizations, members of non-government organizations, researchers, the media and the general public. Despite its regional focus, the book's appeal is actually global rather than being confined to the Asia-Pacific as the issues it covers are of international concern.

*Lowell Bautista*
Senior Lecturer, School of Law, University of Wollongong, Australia; Executive Editor, Asian Yearbok of International Law.

# International Law in Asia: A Bibliographic Survey – 2015

*Lowell Bautista**

## Introduction

This bibliography provides information on books, articles, notes, and other materials dealing with international law in Asia, broadly defined. Only English language publications are listed. In the preparation of this bibliography, good use has been made of the list of acquisitions of the Peace Palace Library, the Washington & Lee University law journal rankings, as well as book reviews in journals of international law, Asian studies, and international affairs. Most of the materials can be listed under multiple categories, but to save space each item is listed under a single category. (Edited books however may appear more than once if multiple chapters from the book are listed under different categories). Readers are advised to refer to all categories relevant to their research.

The bibliography is limited to new materials published in 2015 or previously published materials that have updated editions in 2015. The headings used in this year's bibliography are as follows:

1. General
2. States and statehood
3. IGOs
4. NGOs
5. Territory and jurisdiction
6. Seas and marine resources
7. Maritime security
8. Jus ad bellum and jus in bello
9. International criminal law and transnational crime
10. Peace and transitional justice
11. Security
12. Environment
13. Climate change
14. Development

* Senior Lecturer, School of Law, University of Wollongong; Executive Editor, Asian Yearbook of International Law.

15. Human rights – General
16. Human rights – Institutions and Organizations
17. Humanitarian law
18. Nationality, migration and refugees
19. Colonialism and self determination
20. International economic and business law – General
21. WTO and trade
22. Investment
23. Intellectual property
24. Cultural property and heritage
25. Dispute settlement
26. Arbitration
27. Private International law
28. Air and Space
29. Miscellaneous

## 1 General

Menon, Sundaresh, *The Impact of Public International Law in the Commercial Sphere and Its Significance to Asia,* 16 The Journal of World Investment and Trade 772–799 (2015).

Miyazawa, Setsuo, et al. (Eds.), East Asia's Renewed Respect for the Rule of Law in the 21st Century (Brill, 2015).

Port, Kenneth L., Gerald Paul McAlinn, and Salil Mehra, Comparative law: law and the process of law in Japan (2015).

Rao, Pemmaraja Sreenivasa, *The Nature And Function Of International Law: An Evolving International Rule Of Law,* 55 Indian Journal of International Law 459–491 (2015).

Sharma, S.K. and Welsh, J.M. (eds.), The Responsibility to Prevent: Overcoming the Challenges of Atrocity Prevention (2015).

Vanhullebusch, M., *Regime Change, the Security Council and China,* 14 Chinese Journal of International Law 665–707 (2015).

## 2 States and Statehood

Chan, Phil C W, China, State Sovereignty and International Legal Order (Brill Nijhoff, 2015).

Gordon, Gregory S., *When 'One Country, Two Systems' Meets 'One Person, One Vote': The Law of Treaties and the Handover Narrative through the Crucible of Hong Kong's Election Crisis* 16 (2) MELBOURNE JOURNAL OF INTERNATIONAL LAW 1–54 (2015).

Seah, Daniel, *The CFSP as an Aspect of Conducting Foreign Relations by the United Kingdom: With Special Reference to the Treaty of Amity & Cooperation in Southeast Asia,* 2015 INTERNATIONAL REVIEW OF LAW 1–20 (2015).

Takashi, Miyazaki, *Sovereignty vs International Cooperation: Major Problems Facing East Asia at Present,* 12 (3) INDONESIAN JOURNAL OF INTERNATIONAL LAW 280–285 (2014–2015).

Tomoko, Yamashita, *Do Jus Cogens Norms Invalidate State Immunity? International Restorative Justice and Japanese War Compensation Cases,* 31 CHINESE (TAIWAN) YEARBOOK OF INTERNATIONAL LAW AND AFFAIRS 160–194 (2015).

## 3 IGOs

Chesterman, Simon, *Asia's Ambivalence about International Law and Institutions: Past, Present and Futures* 27 (4) EUROPEAN JOURNAL OF INTERNATIONAL LAW 945–978 (2016).

CHESTERMAN, SIMON, FROM COMMUNITY TO COMPLIANCE: THE EVOLUTION OF MONITORING OBLIGATIONS IN ASEAN (Cambridge University Press, 2015).

CHESTERMAN, SIMON, FROM COMMUNITY TO COMPLIANCE? THE EVOLUTION OF MONITORING OBLIGATIONS IN ASEAN (Cambridge University Press, 2015).

INAMA, STEFANO AND SIM, EDMUND W., THE FOUNDATION OF THE ASEAN ECONOMIC COMMUNITY: AN INSTITUTIONAL AND LEGAL PROFILE (Cambridge University Press, 2015).

INAMA, STEFANO, THE FOUNDATION OF THE ASEAN ECONOMIC COMMUNITY: AN INSTITUTIONAL AND LEGAL PROFILE (Cambridge University Press, 2015).

KUIJPER, PIETER JAN, FROM TREATY-MAKING TO TREATY-BREAKING: MODELS FOR ASEAN EXTERNAL TRADE AGREEMENTS (Cambridge University Press, 2015).

Loevy, Karin, *The Legal Politics of Jurisdiction: Understanding ASEAN's Role in Myanmar's Disaster, Cyclone Nargis (2008),* 5 (1) ASIAN JOURNAL OF INTERNATIONAL LAW 55–93 (2015).

Mohamad, Rahmat, *International Criminal Court in the Development of International Rule of Law: a Reflection of Asian-African Views,* in CHARLES SAMPFORD AND RAMESH THAKUR, INSTITUTIONAL SUPPORTS FOR THE INTERNATIONAL RULE OF LAW (Routledge, Taylor & Francis Group, 2015) 59–73.

Nguitragool, Paruedee, ASEAN as an Actor in International Fora: Reality, Potential and Constraints (Cambridge University Press, 2015).

Piris, Jean-Claude and Woon, Walter, Towards a Rules-Based Community: An ASEAN Legal Service (Cambridge University Press, 2015).

Roberts, C.B., *ASEAN: The Challenge of Unity in Diversity*, in Buszynski, L.; and Roberts, C.B. (eds.), The South China Sea Maritime Dispute: Political, Legal and Regional Perspectives (2015), 130–149.

Schuldt, Lasse, *Southeast Asian Hesitation: ASEAN Countries and the International Criminal Court*, 16 German Law Journal75–104 (2015).

Zhu, Dan, *China, the Crime of Aggression, and the International Criminal Court*, 5 (1) Asian Journal of International Law 94–122 (2015).

## 4 NGOs

Baird, Natalie, *The Role of International Non-Governmental Organisations in the Universal Periodic Review of Pacific Island States: Can 'Doing Good' Be Done Better?* 16 (2) Melbourne Journal of International Law 1–37 (2015).

## 5 Territory and jurisdiction

Anderson, D.H., *Recent Judicial Decisions Concerning Maritime Delimitation*, in L. del Castillo (ed.), Law of the Sea, from Grotius to the International Tribunal for the Law of the Sea: Liber Amicorum Judge Hugo Caminos (2015), 495–511.

Charlermpalanupap, T., *Review of the ASEAN-China Declaration of the Conduct of Parties in the South China Sea and Prospects of a Code of Conduct in the South China Sea: an ASEAN Perspective*, in Tran Truong Thuy and Le Thuy Trang (eds.), Power, Law, and Maritime Order in the South China Sea (2015) 37–48.

Chesterman, S., *The International Court of Justice in Asia: Interpreting the Temple of Preah Vihaer Case*, (2015) 5 Asian Journal of International Law 1–6.

Chesterman, Simon, *The International Court of Justice in Asia: Interpreting the Temple of Preah Vihear Case*, 5 (1) Asian Journal of International Law 1–6 (2015).

Eiriksson, G., *The "Bay of Bengal" Case before the International Tribunal for the Law of the Sea*, in L. del Castillo (ed.), Law of the Sea, from Grotius to the International Tribunal for the Law of the Sea: Liber Amicorum Judge Hugo Caminos (2015) 512–528.

Huang, J., and Billo, A. (eds.), Territorial Disputes in the South China Sea: Navigating Rough Waters (2015).

Kattan, V., *The Ghost of the Temple of Preah Vihaer/Phra Viharn in the 2013 Judgment*, 5 Asian Journal of International Law 16–25 (2015).

Kattan, Victor, *The Ghosts of the Temple of Preah Vihear/Phra Viharn in the 2013 Judgment*, 5 (1) Asian Journal of International Law 16–25 (2015).

Lalonde, S., *The Role of the "Uti Possidetis" Principle in the Resolution of Maritime Boundary Disputes*, in C. Chinkin and F. Baetens (eds.), Sovereignty, Statehood and State Responsibility: Essays in Honour of James Crawford (2015), 248–272.

McCullough, Shaun, *In a Rising Sea of Uncertainty: A Call for a New International Convention to Safeguard the Human Rights of Citizens of Deterritorialized Asia-Pacific Small Island-States*, 26 (1) Colorado Natural Resources, Energy & Environmental Law Review 109–138 (2015).

Ming, L., *The Paradox of Economic Integration and Territorial Rivalry in the South China Sea*, in Togo, K. and Naidu, G. (eds.), Building Confidence in East Asia: Maritime Conflicts, Interdependence and Asian Identity Thinking (2015) 27–43.

Oral, N., *Law of the Sea, Naval Blockades, and Freedom of Navigation in the Aftermath of "Gaza Flotilla" Incident of 31 May 2010*, in L. del Castillo (ed.), Law of the Sea, from Grotius to the International Tribunal for the Law of the Sea: Liber Amicorum Judge Hugo Caminos (2015), 356–376.

Pham Lan, Dung and Nguyen Ngoc, Lan, *Some Legal Aspects of the Philippines-China Arbitration under Annex VII of the United Nations Convention on the Law of the Sea*, in Tran Truong, Thuy and Le Thuy, Trang (eds.), Power, Law, and Maritime Order in the South China Sea (2015) 331–348.

Phan, Hao Duy, *Institutional Design and Its Constraints: Explaining ASEAN's Role in the Temple of Preah Vihear Dispute*, 5 (1) Asian Journal of International Law 7–15 (2015).

Poling, G., *US Interests in the South China Sea: International Law and Peaceful Dispute Resolution*, in Tran Truong, Thuy and Le Thuy, Trang (eds.), Power, Law, and Maritime Order in the South China Sea (2015) 61–75.

Togo, Kazuhiko, *Japan and the South China Sea in the Context of New East Asian Power Relations*, in Tran Truong Thuy and Le Thuy Trang (Eds.), Power, Law, and Maritime Order in the South China Sea (2015).

Yu, M., *China's Informal Participation in the Annex VII Philippines v. China Arbitral Tribunal's Proceedings*, 30 International Journal of Marine and Coastal Law 54–92 (2015).

Zou, K., *The South China Sea*, in D.R. Rothwell, A.G. Oude Elferink, K.N. Scott, and T. Stephens (eds.), The Oxford Handbook of the Law of the Sea (2015), 626–646.

## 6 Seas and marine resources

Clapham, P.J., *Japan's Whaling Following the International Court of Justice Ruling: Brave New World – or Business as Usual?*, 51 Marine Policy 238–241 (2015).

Jia, B.B., *The Curious Case of Article 281: A "Super" Provision within UNCLOS*, 46 Ocean Development and International Law 266–280 (2015).

Kim, Suk Kyoon, *Marine Pollution Response in Northeast Asia and the NOWPAP Regime,* 46 (1) Ocean Development and International Law17–32 (2015).

Peel, J., (*Introductory Note to*) *Whaling in the Antarctic* (*Australia v. Japan: New Zealand intervening*) (*ICJ*), 54 International Legal Materials 1–52 (2015).

Popovski, V., *UNCLOS and the Peaceful Use of the Sea,* in Wu, S., Valencia, M. and Hong, N. (eds.), UN Convention on the Law of the Sea and the South China Sea (2015) 73–83.

Riesenberg, D.P., (*Introductory Note to*) '*Request for Interpretation of the Judgment of 15 June 1962 in the Case Concerning the Temple of Preah Vihear* (*Cambodia v. Thailand*) (*ICJ*), 54 International Legal Materials 53–82 (2015).

Ringbom, Henrik, *The European Union and International Maritime Law – Lessons for the Asia Pacific Region,* 30 (1) Australian and New Zealand Maritime Law Journal 1 67–77 (2016).

Togo, K. and Naidu, G.V.C. (eds.), Building Confidence in East Asia: Maritime Conflicts, Interdependence and Asian Identity Thinking (2015).

Tran Truong, Thuy, *Code of Conduct and the Prevention and Management of Incidents in the South China Sea,* in Tran Truong, Thuy and Le Thuy, Trang (eds.), Power, Law, and Maritime Order in the South China Sea, (2015) 317–330.

Treves, T., *Coastal States' Rights in the Maritime Areas under UNCLOS*, 12 Revista de Direito Internacional 40–48 (2015).

Tuerk, H., *UNCLOS and the Contributions of ITLOS*, in Wu, S., Valencia, M. and Hong, N. (eds.), UN Convention on the Law of the Sea and the South China Sea (2015) 15–30.

Wang, K.-H., Peaceful Settlement of Disputes in the South China Sea through Fisheries Resources Cooperation and Management (2015).

Wu, Sh., Valencia, M. and Hong, N. (eds.), UN Convention on the Law of the Sea and the South China Sea (2015).

## 7 Maritime security

Iwamoto, S. and Togo, K., *Three Complementary, Simultaneous Approaches to Maritime Security in the East China Sea: International Law, Crisis Management, and Dialogue*, in Togo, K. and Naidu, G. (eds.), Building Confidence in East Asia:

MARITIME CONFLICTS, INTERDEPENDENCE AND ASIAN IDENTITY THINKING (2015) 87–102.

Tran Viet, Thai and Naidu, G.V.C., *The Maritime Security Environment in East Asia: The Need for Strengthening Maritime Regimes, Greater Cooperation, and Dialogues*, in TOGO, K. AND NAIDU, G. (EDS.), BUILDING CONFIDENCE IN EAST ASIA: MARITIME CONFLICTS, INTERDEPENDENCE AND ASIAN IDENTITY THINKING (2015) 74–86.

## 8 Jus ad bellum and jus in bello

Nadarajah, S., and Rampton, D., *The Limits of Hybridity and the Crisis of Liberal Peace*, (2015) 41 REVIEW OF INTERNATIONAL STUDIES 49–72.

Orakhelashvili, A., *The Impact of Unilateral EU Economic Sanctions on the UN Collective Security Framework: the Cases of Iran and Syria*, in A.Z. MAROSSIAND AND M.R. BASSETT (EDS.), ECONOMIC SANCTIONS UNDER INTERNATIONAL LAW (2015) 3–21.

Orakhelashvili, A., *Undesired, yet Omnipresent: "Jus ad Bellum" in Its Relation to Other Areas of International Law*, 2 JOURNAL ON THE USE OF FORCE AND INTERNATIONAL LAW 238–256 (2015).

Zhang, T., *Conflict-Sensitive Approach to Climate Change Mitigation and Adaption in the Urbanizing Asia-Pacific*, 15 ENVIRONMENTAL LAW REVIEW OF EASTERN AND CENTRAL EUROPE 1–66 (2015).

## 9 International criminal law and transnational crime

Babb, Nathaniel H., *Don't forget the Far East : a modern lesson from the Chinese prosecution of Japanese war criminals after World War II*, 222 MILITARY LAW REVIEW 129–155 (2014).

Conway-Lanz, Sahr, *Bombing Civilians After World War II : The Persistence Of Norms Against Targeting Civilians in the Korean War*, in THE AMERICAN WAY OF BOMBING : CHANGING ETHICAL AND LEGAL NORMS, FROM FLYING FORTRESSES TO DRONES (Cornell University Press, 2014) 47–63.

Fernandes, Clinton, *The maxim of Thucydides : transparency, fact-finding, and accountability in East Timor*, in INVESTIGATING OPERATIONAL INCIDENTS IN A MILITARY CONTEXT : LAW, JUSTICE, POLITICS (Brill Nijhoff, 2015) 51–70.

Kumar, K.S., *The European Union and Conflict Resolution in Sri Lanka*, in R.K. JAIN (ED.), THE EUROPEAN UNION AND SOUTH ASIA (2015) 111–128.

Meisenberg, Simon M., *Complying with Complementarity? The Cambodian Implementation of the Rome Statute of the International Criminal Court*, 5 (1) ASIAN JOURNAL OF INTERNATIONAL LAW 123–142 (2015).

Mohamad, Rahmat, *An Afro-Asian Perspective on the International Criminal Court*, 4 HISTORICAL ORIGINS OF INTERNATIONAL CRIMINAL LAW 729–748 (2015).

SELLARS, KIRSTEN (ED.), TRIALS FOR INTERNATIONAL CRIMES IN ASIA (Cambridge University Press, 2015).

TOTANI, YUMA, JUSTICE IN ASIA AND THE PACIFIC REGION, 1945–1952: ALLIED WAR CRIMES PROSECUTIONS (Cambridge University Press, 2015).

## 10 PEACE AND TRANSITIONAL JUSTICE

Bass, G.J., *Indian Way of Humanitarian Intervention*, 40 YALE JOURNAL OF INTERNATIONAL LAW 227–294 (2015).

King, A., *The EU and Multilateral Peace Operations: after Afghanistan*, in M.G. GALANTINO AND M.R. FREIRE (EDS.), MANAGING CRISES, MAKING PEACE: TOWARDS A STRATEGIC EU VISION FOR SECURITY AND DEFENSE (2015) 255–274.

Kumar, K.S., *The European Union and Conflict Resolution in Sri Lanka*, in R.K. JAIN (ED.), THE EUROPEAN UNION AND SOUTH ASIA (2015) 111–128.

PERSSON, A., EU AND THE ISRAELI–PALESTINIAN CONFLICT, 1971–2013: IN PURSUIT OF A JUST PEACE (2015).

## 11 SECURITY

Andersson, R. and Weigand, F., *Intervention at Risk: the Vicious Cycle of Distance and Danger in Mali and Afghanistan*, 9 JOURNAL OF INTERVENTION AND STATEBUILDING 519–541 (2015).

Delahunty, R.J., *Towards a Concert of Asia: A Proposed International Security Regime*, 11 (1) UNIVERSITY OF PENNSYLVANIA ASIAN LAW REVIEW 1–80 (2015–2016).

Fuchs, I., and H. Borowski, *The New World Order: Humanitarian Interventions from Kosovo to Libya and perhaps Syria?*, 65 SYRACUSE LAW REVIEW 304–343 (2015).

Mastroianni, M.A., *Growing Numbers of Chinese Blue Helmets: China's changing Role within the Security Council*, 27 FLORIDA JOURNAL OF INTERNATIONAL LAW 121–161 (2015).

Musiol, Marek, *Post-Soviet Central Asia as a Unique Regional Security Complex*, 24 (4) POLISH QUARTERLY OF INTERNATIONAL AFFAIRS 59–78 (2015).

Reiterer, Michael, *The NAPCI in the Volatile Security Environment of North-East Asia: Which Role for the European Union*, 20 (4) EUROPEAN FOREIGN AFFAIRS REVIEW 573–590 (2015).

Schulz, M., 'The League of the Arab States, the Gulf Co-operation Council, and the Arab Civil Uprisings, 2011–13', in P. WALLENSTEEN AND A. BJURNER (EDS.), REGIONAL ORGANIZATIONS AND PEACEMAKING: CHALLENGERS TO THE UN? (2015), 202–216.

Sloan, Elinor, *America's Rebalance to the Asia-Pacific: The Impact on Canada's Strategic Thinking and Maritime Posture*, 70 (2) INTERNATIONAL JOURNAL 268–285 (2015).

Timmoneri, S., *Responsibility to protect and "peacetime atrocities": the case North Korea*, 19 THE INTERNATIONAL JOURNAL OF HUMAN RIGHTS 1290–1302 (2015).

Vanhullebusch, M., *Regime Change, the Security Council and China*, 14 CHINESE JOURNAL OF INTERNATIONAL LAW 665–707 (2015).

Whyte, Leon; Weltz, Richard, *Enough to Go around: Money Matters Complicate U.S. Strategic Rebalance to Asia-Pacific*, 2 (1) FLETCHER SECURITY REVIEW 39–42 (2015).

## 12 ENVIRONMENT

Atapattu, Sumudu, *The Role of Human Rights Law in Protecting Environmental Rights in South Asia*, in LADAWN HAGLUND AND ROBIN STRYKER (EDS.) CLOSING THE RIGHTS GAP: FROM HUMAN RIGHTS TO SOCIAL TRANSFORMATION (University of California Press, 2015) 105–126.

Boer, Ben, *Environmental Law and Human Rights in the Asia-Pacific*, BEN BOER (ED.), ENVIRONMENTAL LAW DIMENSIONS OF HUMAN RIGHTS (Oxford University Press, 2015) 135–179.

MARSDEN, SIMON AND BRANDON, ELIZABETH, TRANSBOUNDARY ENVIRONMENTAL GOVERNANCE IN ASIA: PRACTICE AND PROSPECTS WITH THE UNECE AGREEMENTS (Edward Elgar, 2015).

MARSDEN, SIMON, TRANSBOUNDARY ENVIRONMENTAL GOVERNANCE IN ASIA: PRACTICE AND PROSPECTS WITH THE UNECE AGREEMENTS (Edward Elgar Publishing, 2015).

## 13 CLIMATE CHANGE

Das, Kasturi; and Bandyopadhyay, Kaushik Ranjan, *Climate Change Adaption in the Framework of Regional Cooperation in South Asia*, 2015 (1) CARBON & CLIMATE LAW REVIEW 40–54 (2015).

Lin, Jolene, *Climate Change Litigation in Asia and the Pacific*, in GEERT VAN CALSTER, WIM VANDENBERGHE, LEONIE REINS (EDS.) RESEARCH HANDBOOK ON CLIMATE CHANGE MITIGATION LAW (Edward Elgar Publishing, 2015) 578–599.

## 14 DEVELOPMENT

ESLAVA, LUIS, LOCAL SPACE, GLOBAL LIFE: THE EVERYDAY OPERATION OF INTERNATIONAL LAW AND DEVELOPMENT (Cambridge University Press, 2015).

HINTJENS, H., AND D. ZARKOV (EDS.), CONFLICT, PEACE, SECURITY AND DEVELOPMENT: THEORIES AND METHODOLOGIES (2015).

## 15 HUMAN RIGHTS – GENERAL

Ghosh, Pritam, *Teaching and Research of International Humanitarian Law in Asia: Efforts, Issues and Prospects*, 2 (1) ASIAN JOURNAL OF LEGAL EDUCATION 1–16 (2015).

Lai, Gloria, *Asia: Advocating for Humane and Effective Drug Policies*, 21 SUR – INTERNATIONAL JOURNAL ON HUMAN RIGHTS 1–6 (2015).

## 16 HUMAN RIGHTS – INSTITUTIONS AND ORGANIZATIONS

CHAMBERLAIN, CYNTHIA, CHILDREN AND THE INTERNATIONAL CRIMINAL COURT (Intersentia, 2015).

ELIAS-BURSAC, ELLEN, TRANSLATING EVIDENCE AND INTERPRETING TESTIMONY AT A WAR CRIMES TRIBUNAL: WORKING IN A TUG-OF-WAR (Palgrave Macmillan, 2015).

FEIGHERY, TIMOTHY J; GIBSON, CHRISTOPHER S.; AND RAJAH, TREVOR M., (EDS.), WAR REPARATIONS AND THE UN COMPENSATION COMMISSION: DESIGNING COMPENSATION AFTER CONFLICT (Oxford University Press, 2015).

KUCZYŃSKA, HANNA, THE ACCUSATION MODEL BEFORE THE INTERNATIONAL CRIMINAL COURT (Springer, 2015).

MARINIELLO, TRIESTINO (ED.), THE INTERNATIONAL CRIMINAL COURT IN SEARCH OF ITS PURPOSE AND IDENTITY (Routledge, 2014).

RAMCHARAN, BERTRAND G., THE LAW, POLICY AND POLITICS OF THE UN HUMAN RIGHTS COUNCIL (Brill Nijhoff, 2015).

ROBERTS, CHRISTOPHER N J, THE CONTENTIOUS HISTORY OF THE INTERNATIONAL BILL OF HUMAN RIGHTS (Cambridge University Press, 2015).

## 17 Humanitarian Law

Alexander, Amanda, *A Short History of International Humanitarian Law*, 26 (1) European journal of international law 109–138 (2015).

Arai-Takahashi, Y., *The intervention brigade within the MONUSCO. The legal challenges of Applicability and Application of IHL*, (2015) Questions of International Law 5–23 (2015).

Bass, G.J., *The Indian Way of Humanitarian Intervention*, 40 Yale Journal of International Law 227–294 (2015).

Bazirake, J.B. and Bukuluki, P., *A Critical Reflection on the Conceptual and Practical Limitations of the Responsibility to Protect*, 19 (2015) The International Journal of Human Rights 1017–1028 (2015).

Corten, O., *The Russian Intervention in the Ukrainian Crisis: Was Jus Contra Bellum "Confirmed Rather than weakened"?* 2 Journal on the Use of Force and International Law 17–41 (2015).

Philip, Diana, *Humanitarian Assistance and the Right to Water: an ASEAN Region Perspective*, in Andrej Zwitter, Christopher K. Lamont, Hans-Joachim Heintze, Joost Herman (Eds.), Humanitarian Action: Global, Regional and Domestic Legal Responses (Cambridge University Press, 2015) 302–329.

Sterio, M., *The Applicability of the Humanitarian Intervention "Exception" to the Middle Eastern Refugee Crisis: Why the International Community Should Intervene Against ISIS*, 38 Suffolk Transnational Law Review 325–357 (2015).

Tan, K.C., *Humanitarian Intervention as a Duty*, 7 Global Responsibility to Protect 121–141 (2015).

## 18 Nationality, migration and refugees

Davies, Sara E., *The 1989 Comprehensive Plan of Action (CPA) and Refugee Policy in Southeast Asia: Twenty Years Forward What Has Changed?*, in Ademola Abass & Francesca Ippolito (Eds.), Regional Approaches to the Protection of Asylum Seekers: An International Legal Perspective (Ashgate Publishing, 2014) 325–346.

Human Rights Watch Staff, Persecuting "Evil Way" Religion: Abuses Against Montagnards in Vietnam (Human Rights Watch, 2015).

Jones, Martin, *Moving Beyond Protection Space: Developing a Law of Asylum in South-East Asia*, in Susan Kneebone, Dallal Stevens and Loretta Baldassar (Eds.), Refugee Protection and the Role of Law: Conflicting Identities (Routledge, 2014) 251–270.

Kingston, L.N., *Protecting the world's most prosecuted: the responsibility to protect and Burma's Rohingya minority*, (2015) 19 THE INTERNATIONAL JOURNAL OF HUMAN RIGHTS 1163–1175 (2015).

Kneebone, Susan, *ASEAN and the Conceptualization of Refugee Protection in Southeastern Asian States*, in ADEMOLA ABASS & FRANCESCA IPPOLITO (EDS.), REGIONAL APPROACHES TO THE PROTECTION OF ASYLUM SEEKERS: AN INTERNATIONAL LEGAL PERSPECTIVE (Ashgate Publishing, 2014) 295–323.

Lombardo, G., *The responsibility to protect and the lack of intervention in Syria between the protection of human rights and geopolitical strategies*, 19 THE INTERNATIONAL JOURNAL OF HUMAN RIGHTS 1190–1198 (2015).

Loper, Kelley, *The Protection of Asylum Seekers in East Asian State Parties to the 1951 Convention Relating to the Status of Refugees and Its 1967 Protocol*, in ADEMOLA ABASS & FRANCESCA IPPOLITO (EDS.), REGIONAL APPROACHES TO THE PROTECTION OF ASYLUM SEEKERS: AN INTERNATIONAL LEGAL PERSPECTIVE (Ashgate Publishing, 2014) 347–376.

Orchard, Cynthia, *Almaty Process: Improving Compliance with International Refugee Law in Central Asia*, 28 (1) THE INTERNATIONAL JOURNAL OF REFUGEE LAW 55–84 (2016).

## 19 COLONIALISM AND SELF DETERMINATION

RAJARAM, PREM KUMAR, RULING THE MARGINS: COLONIAL POWER AND ADMINISTRATIVE RULE (Routledge, 2015).

## 20 INTERNATIONAL ECONOMIC AND BUSINESS LAW – GENERAL

Buckley, Ross P., *From Regional Fragmentation to Coherence: a Way forward for East Asia* in C.L. LIM, BRYAN MERCURIO (EDS.), INTERNATIONAL ECONOMIC LAW AFTER THE GLOBAL CRISIS : A TALE OF FRAGMENTED DISCIPLINES (Cambridge University Press, 2015) 107–133.

CHIA, SIOW YUE, ASEAN ECONOMIC COOPERATION AND INTEGRATION: PROGRESS, CHALLENGES AND FUTURE DIRECTIONS (Cambridge University Press, 2015).

Irish, Leon E.; and Simon, Karla W., *Legal and Fiscal Innovations in East Asia: Update* 13 (1) INTERNATIONAL JOURNAL OF CHARITY SECTOR LAW 43–58 (2015).

Lee, Eric Yong Joong, *Trans-Pacific Partnership (TPP) as a US Strategic Alliance Initiative under the G2 System: Legal and Political Implications*, 8 JOURNAL OF EAST ASIA AND INTERNATIONAL LAW 323–352 (2015).

Liu, O. & Shan, W. (eds.), China and International Commercial Dispute Resolution (2015).

Liu, Q., Shan, W. & Ren, X. (eds.), China and International Commercial Dispute Resolution (2015).

Paparinskis, Martins, *The Schizophrenia of Countermeasures in International Economic Law: the Case of the ASEAN Comprehensive Investment Agreement,* in C.L. Lim, Bryan Mercurio (Eds.), International Economic Law after the Global Crisis: a Tale of Fragmented Disciplines (Cambridge University Press, 2015) 263–278.

Parra, A.A., *The Convention and Centre for Settlement of Investment Disputes*, Recueil des cours / Collected courses of The Hague Academy of International Law. 2014: Tome 374 de la collection (2015) 313–410.

Paswan, Nawal K., India and Central Asia: Deepening Economic Cooperation (A.P.H. Publishing Corporation, 2015).

Sabhasri, Chayodom, *Regional Economic and Financial Integration in Asia: Challenges from the Global and Financial Crisis,* in Friedl Weiss, Armin J. Kammel, (Eds.) The Changing Landscape of Global Financial Governance and the Role of Soft Law (Brill Nijhoff, 2015) 337–367.

## 21 WTO and Trade

Allen, Nathan W., *Keeping Rising Asia at a Distance: Canadian Attitudes towards Trade Agreements with Asian Countries*, 70 (2) International Journal 286–308 (2015).

Bolongaita, Emil P. and Oshikawa, Maika, *The Future of Asia: Unleashing the Power of Trade and Governance,* in Uri Dadush and Chiedu Osakwe (eds.) WTO Accessions and Trade Multilateralism 161–186 (Cambridge University Press, 2015).

Brown, Ronald C., *Asian and US Perspectives on Labor Rights under International Trade Agreements Compared,* in Axel Marx, Jan Wouters, Glen Rayp, Laura Beke (Eds.) Global Governance of Labour Rights : Assessing the Effectiveness of Transnational Public and Private Policy Initiatives (Edward Elgar Publishing, 2015).

Garcia, Maria and Masselot, Annick, *The Value of Gender Equality in EU-Asian Trade Policy: an Assessment of the EU's Ability to implement its Own Legal Obligations,* in Annika Björkdahl, Natalia Chaban, John Leslie, Annick Masselot, (Eds.), Importing EU Norms : Conceptual Framework and Empirical Findings (Springer, 2015) 191–209.

Ghori, Umair, *An Epic Mess: 'Exhaustible Natural Resources' and the Future of Export Restraints after the China — Rare Earths Decision* 16 (2) Melbourne Journal of International Law 1–34 (2015).

Hsieh, Pasha L., *APEC's Soft-law Mechanism and the Multilateral Trading System*, in Choi, Won-mog (Ed.), International Economic Law: the Asia-Pacific Perspectives (Cambridge Scholars Publishing, 2015) 74–102.

Hsieh, Pasha L., *Liberalizing Trade in Legal Services under Asia-Pacific FTAs: The ASEAN Case,* 18 (1) Journal of International Economic Law 153–186 (2015).

Kubo, Hiromasa, *EU-Asia Trade Relations*, in Christiansen, Thomas, Kirchner, Emil and Murray, Philomena (Eds.), The Palgrave Handbook of EU-Asia Relations (Palgrave Macmillan, 2015) 247–262.

Menon, Sundaresh, *The Impact of Public Law in the Commercial Sphere and Its Significance to Asia*, 16 Journal of World Investment & Trade 772–799 (2015).

Neuwirth, Rostam J.; and Svetlicinii, Alexandr, *The Regulation of Trade and Public Health in Asia-Pacific: A Case for Inter-Regime Regulatory Co-Opetition*, 10 (2) Asian Journal of WTO and International Health Law and Policy 349–380 (2015).

Smith, Michael, *The EU, Asia and the Governance of Global Trade*, in Christiansen, Thomas, Kirchner, Emil and Murray, Philomena (Eds.), The Palgrave Handbook of EU-Asia Relations (Palgrave Macmillan, 2015) 377–391.

Weber, Rolf H., Digital Trade and E-Commerce: Challenges and Opportunities of the Asia-Pacific Regionalism, 10 (2) Asian Journal of WTO and International Health Law and Policy 321–348 (2015).

## 22 Investment

Brimer, Jeffrey A.; Hang, Mai Thi Minh; Hara, Etsuko; Wong, S.F.; Harto, Nadia; Zeidman, Philip F., *Government Regulation of Franchising, Licensing, and Distribution in Asia – Too Much, Too Little, or Just Right*, 13 (3) International Journal of Franchising Law 11–48 (2015).

Chaisse, Julien, *The Shifting Tectonics of International Investment Law – Structure and Dynamics of Rules and Arbitration on Foreign Investment in the Asia-Pacific Region*, 47 (3) George Washington International Law Review 563–638 (2015).

Choukroune, Leila, *Indian and Chinese FDI in Developing Asia: The Standards Battle beyond Trade*, 7 Indian Journal of International Economic Law 89–116 (2015).

Mohan, Mahdev, *Corporate Accountability in Southeast Asia: National Action Plans for Responsible Business Conduct Under International Law*, 8 (1) Journal of East Asia and International Law 9–28 (2015).

Petersmann, E.U., *Judicial Administration of Justice in Multilevel Commercial, Trade and Investment Adjudication?*, in Shan, W. and Su, J. (eds.), China and International Investment Law: Twenty Years of ICSID Membership (2015), 56–115.

Sattorova, Mavluda, *International Investment Law in Central Asia*, 16 JOURNAL OF WORLD INVESTMENT & TRADE 1089–1124 (2015).

## 23 Intellectual property

ANTONS, CHRISTOPH AND HILTY, RETO M. (EDS.) INTELLECTUAL PROPERTY AND FREE TRADE AGREEMENTS IN THE ASIA-PACIFIC REGION (Springer, 2015).

Son, Min, *Defining Architectural Works in East Asia: Intellectual Property Protection for Local and Transnational Architectural Works*, 1(2) JOURNAL OF GLOBAL JUSTICE AND PUBLIC POLICY 319–344 (2014–2015).

## 24 Cultural property and heritage

Hwa, Gregory, *Breaking out of the West, Advancing into Asia: Cultural Considerations for Brand Management in China*, 25 MARQUETTE SPORTS LAW 399–412 (2014–2015).

Mun, Juliet Y., *The Impact of Confucianism on Gender (In)Equality in Asia*, 16 (3) GEORGETOWN JOURNAL OF GENDER AND THE LAW 633–657 (2015).

Patel, Simin, Mitra Sharafi, *Law and Identity in Colonial South Asia: Parsi Legal Culture*, 1772–1947, 33(4) LAW AND HISTORY REVIEW 1015–1017 (2015).

ROODT, C., PRIVATE INTERNATIONAL LAW, ART AND CULTURAL HERITAGE (2015).

## 25 Dispute settlement

Buszynski, L., *The Origins and Development of the South China Sea Maritime Dispute*, in L. BUSZYNSKI AND C.B. ROBERTS (EDS.), THE SOUTH CHINA SEA MARITIME DISPUTE: POLITICAL, LEGAL, AND REGIONAL PERSPECTIVES (2015), 1–23.

Buszynski, L. and Roberts, C.B., *The South China Sea: Stabilisation and Resolution*, in L. BUSZYNSKI AND C.B. BUSZYNSKI (EDS.), THE SOUTH CHINA SEA MARITIME DISPUTE: POLITICAL, LEGAL, AND REGIONAL PERSPECTIVES (2015), 187–208.

BUSZYNSKI, L., AND C.B. ROBERTS (EDS.), THE SOUTH CHINA SEA MARITIME DISPUTE: POLITICAL, LEGAL AND REGIONAL PERSPECTIVES (2015).

Clapham, P.J., *Japan's Whaling Following the International Court of Justice Ruling: Brave New World – or Business as Usual?*, 51 MARINE POLICY 238–241 (2015).

Kamara, O.K., *An Analysis of the Adequacy of the Dispute Settlement Mechanism under UNCLOS: Maritime Boundary Delimitation Disputes*, in C. JALLOH AND O. ELIAS (EDS.), SHIELDING HUMANITY: ESSAYS IN INTERNATIONAL LAW IN HONOUR OF JUDGE ABDUL G. KOROMA (2015) 187–229.

Keith, K., *The Peaceful Settlement of International Disputes: the Rainbow Warrior Affair – Experiences of a Small State*, in C. Jalloh and O. Elias (eds.), Shielding Humanity: Essays in International Law in Honour of Judge Abdul G. Koroma (2015) 21–34.

Subedi, S.P., *An Innovative Solution to an Ambitious Project: Dispute Resolution in the 1982 Convention on the Law of the Sea*, in C. Jalloh and O. Elias (eds.), Shielding Humanity: Essays in International Law in Honour of Judge Abdul G. Koroma (2015) 163–186.

Supancana, I.B.R., *Maritime Boundary Disputes between Indonesia and Malaysia in the Area of Ambalat Block: Some Optional Scenarios for Peaceful Settlement*, 8 Journal of East Asia and International Law 195–211 (2015).

Taylor, B., *The South China Sea as a "Crisis"*, in L. Buszynski and C.B. Roberts (eds.), The South China Sea Maritime Dispute: Political, Legal, and Regional Perspectives (2015), 173–186.

Young, Margaret A. and Sullivan, Sebastián Rioseco, *Evolution through the Duty to Cooperate: Implications of the Whaling Case at the International Court of Justice* 16 (2) Melbourne Journal of International Law 1–33 (2015).

Zhang, J., *China's South China Sea Policy: Evolution, Claims and Challenges*, in L. Buszynski and C.B. Roberts (eds.), The South China Sea Maritime Dispute: Political, Legal and Regional Perspectives (2015), 60–82.

## 26 Arbitration

Allsop, James, *International Commercial Arbitration – the Courts and the Rule of Law in the Asia Pacific Region*, 81 Arbitration 169–175 (2015).

Bhatia, Vijay K. and Gotti, Maurizio (Eds.) Arbitration Discourse in Asia (Peter Lang, 2015).

Mannan, Morshed, The prospects and challenges of adopting the UNCITRAL Model Law on Cross-Border Insolvency in South Asia (Bangladesh, India and Pakistan), (Universiteit Leiden, 2015).

Salomon, Claudia T. and Friedrich, Sandra, *Investment Arbitration in East Asia and the Pacific*, 16 Journal of World Investment & Trade 800–842 (2015).

## 27 Private International law

Carballo Leyda, Alejandro, Asian Conflict of Laws: East and South East Asia (Kluwer Law International, 2015).

Chen, W., Chinese Civil Procedure and the Conflict of Laws (2013).

Hanotiau, Bernard, *Non-signatories, Groups of Companies and Groups of Contracts in Selected Asian Countries: A Case Law Analysis*, 32 JOURNAL OF INTERNATIONAL ARBITRATION 571–620 (2015).

MINAMIKATA, SATOSHI, FAMILY AND SUCCESSION LAW IN JAPAN (KLUWER LAW INTERNATIONAL, 2015).

Okano, Yuko, *Japanese Court Cases Involving East Asian Citizens and Corporations – Law Applicable to International Transactions with Chinese, Taiwanese, and Korean Parties before Japanese Courts*, 57 THE JAPANESE YEARBOOK OF INTERNATIONAL LAW 243–286 (2015).

RAMSEYER, J. MARK, SECOND-BEST JUSTICE: THE VIRTUES OF JAPANESE PRIVATE LAW (University of Chicago Press, 2015).

## 28 AIR AND SPACE

Kaiser, Stefan A., *Legal Considerations about the Loss of Malaysia Airlines Flight MH 17 in Eastern Ukraine,* 2 AIR AND SPACE LAW Issue 107–121 (2015).

Lee, Jae Woon and Dy, Michelle, *Mitigating Effective Control Restriction on Joint Venture Airlines in Asia: Philippine AirAsia Case,* 40 (3) AIR AND SPACE LAW 231–254 (2015).

## 29 MISCELLANEOUS

Chopra, Surabhi, *Legislating Safety Nets: Comparing Recent Social Protection Laws in Asia,* 22 (1) INDIANA JOURNAL OF GLOBAL LEGAL STUDIES 573–630 (2015).

Fryberg, H.G., *Legal Innovations in Asia: Judicial Lawmaking and the Influence of Comparative Law,* 2015 LAWASIA JOURNAL 109–116 (2015).

Godwin, Andrew, *Barriers to Practice by Foreign Lawyers in Asia: Exploring the Role of Lawyers in Society,* 22 (3) INTERNATIONAL JOURNAL OF THE LEGAL PROFESSION 299–322 (2015).

HAHM, CHAIHARK, & SUNG HO KIM. MAKING WE THE PEOPLE: DEMOCRATIC CONSTITUTIONAL FOUNDING IN POSTWAR JAPAN AND SOUTH KOREA (Cambridge University Press, 2015).

HANAMI, TADASHI, FUMITO KOMIYA, AND RUICHI YAMANAKA, LABOUR LAW IN JAPAN (Kluwer Law International, 2015).

Laverack, Peter J., *The Rise of Asia and the Status of the French Language in International Law,* 14 CHINESE JOURNAL OF INTERNATIONAL LAW 567–583 (2015).

Moon, Hyoungjin and Nam, Jongho, *The Great Ming Code and International Custom of Medieval East Asia: An Analysis of Korea's Policies regarding Japanese Crimes in the*

*Fifteenth Century,* 8 JOURNAL OF EAST ASIA AND INTERNATIONAL LAW 133–148 (2015).

Rieu-Clarke, Alistair, *Notification and Consultation Procedures Under the Mekong Agreement: Insights from the Xayaburi Controversy,* 5 (1) ASIAN JOURNAL OF INTERNATIONAL LAW 143–175 (2015).

Rong, Hu, *China's Challenges and Its Countermeasures to Hunt the Fugitives Who Are Involved in Corruption and Fled to the Asia Pacific Region,* 2015 (4) ACTUAL PROBLEMS OF ECONOMICS AND LAW 84–95 (2015).

Saul, Ben; and Stephens, Tim, *Responsive Antarctic Law-Making in the Asian Century,* 7 THE YEARBOOK OF POLAR LAW 55–82 (2015).

Singh, Prabhakar, *India Before and After the Right of Passage Case,* 5 (1) ASIAN JOURNAL OF INTERNATIONAL LAW 176–208 (2015).

SUGINO, YOSHIKAZU, LABOUR AND EMPLOYMENT COMPLIANCE IN JAPAN. INTERNATIONAL LABOUR AND EMPLOYMENT COMPLIANCE HANDBOOK (Wolters Kluwer Law & Business, 2015).

VANOVERBEKE, DIMITRI, JURIES IN THE JAPANESE LEGAL SYSTEM: THE CONTINUING STRUGGLE FOR CITIZEN PARTICIPATION AND DEMOCRACY (Routledge, 2015).

WILSON, MATTHEW J., HIROSHI FUKURAI, AND MARUTA TAKASHI, JAPAN AND CIVIL JURY TRIALS: THE CONVERGENCE OF FORCES (Edward Elgar Publishing, 2015).

Yanagihara, Masaharu, *Significance of the History of the Law of Nations in Europe and East Asia,* 371 RECUEIL DES COURS (2015).

# DILA *Events*

# 2015 DILA International Conference and 2015 DILA Academy & Workshop

The Foundation for the Development of International Law in Asia (DILA) was founded in 1989, in the words of its charter, for the:

(1) promotion of the study and analysis of topics and issues in the field of international law, in particular from an Asian perspective;
(2) promotion of the study of, and the dissemination of knowledge of, international law in Asia;
(3) promotion of contacts and cooperation between persons and institutions actively dealing with questions of international law relating to Asia.

In pursuit of these purposes, DILA has regularly organized international conferences bringing together international legal scholars from around the world to present on issues and topics pertinent to the Asian continent.

The 2015 DILA International Conference was held on 16 October 2015 at the Faculty of Law, Hasanuddin University (UNHAS) in Makassar, Indonesia. The theme of the conference was "Asian Perspectives on the Role and Impact of Non-State Actors in International Law: From Westphalia to World Community?" While States are the principal actors in international relations and have international legal personality, non-State actors have taken on a more prominent role within the international system. The conference was intended to provide Asian perspectives on the impact of non-State actors, particularly within the Asian context.

The conference commenced with welcome addresses by Professor Seokwoo Lee as Chairman of DILA, Professor of International Law, Inha University Law School in Korea and Dr. Dwia Ariestina Pulubuhu, Rector of Hasanuddin University.

Session 1 which focused on the impact of non-State actors in relation to Indonesia was chaired by Kevin Y.L. Tan, Professor (Adjunct), Faculty of Law, National University of Singapore and formerly Editor-in-Chief of the Asian Yearbook of International Law. In his remarks, Professor Tan mentioned that the international system has come a long way from Brierly's description of international law being a law of nations. The presentations from session 1 and the other sessions that followed reflect the reality that international law does not only concern nation-States, but also the growing importance of non-State actors within the international system. Dr. Winner Sitorus, Senior Lecturer at the Faculty of Law of Hasanuddin University presented his paper on the "Judicial Control of Foreign Arbitral Awards in Indonesia." He was followed by Dr. Laode M. Syarif of the Faculty of Law of Hasanuddin University looking at "The Role of CSOs in the Implementation of UNCAC in Indonesia."

Session 2 was moderated by Dr. Maskun Zulkifli of the Faculty of Law of Hasanuddin University which examined the role of non-State actors in the context of human rights on conflict resolution. Professor Buhm-Suk Baek who teaches in the College of International Studies of Kyung Hee University in Korea presented on "International Human Rights and Role of NGOs: The Experience of Korea." His presentation was followed by Dr. Dwia Ariestina Pulubuhu, the Rector of Hasanuddin University on "The Role of Non-State Actors in Conflict Resolution in the ASEAN Countries."

Session 3 was chaired by Hee Eun Lee who is Associate Dean and Professor of Law at Handong International Law School in Korea and was the Executive Editor of the Asian Yearbook of International Law. Following up on Professor Tan's comments in session 1, Professor Lee observed that implicit in Brierly's description is that legal personality is accorded only to nations or what we call States today. From this older perspective, States are the only object and subject of international law. He remarked that the object and subject of the international legal system are not only States, but also includes non-State actors. The focus of this session was examining the role of non-State actors in the context of human rights and also environmental protection. Kanami Ishibashi, associate professor at Tokyo University of Foreign Studies in Japan presented on "The Role of Non-State Actors in Human Rights and Environmental Protection" while Mr. Rafendi Djamin, Representative of Indonesia to the ASEAN Intergovernmental Commission on Human Rights looked at "The Role of CSOs in Mainstreaming Human Rights Values in ASEAN Countries."

The final session on the role of non-State actors in the territorial and boundary disputes was moderated by Hikmahanto Juwana who is Professor of International Law, Faculty of Law, Universitas Indonesia. Professor Seokwoo Lee described "The Role of Non-State Actors in Territorial and Boundary Disputes." His presentation was followed by I Made Andi Arsana of the Faculty of Geodesy, Gajah Mada University, Indonesia who presented on "The Role of Non-State Actors in the Settlement of Territorial Boundaries Disputes in Indonesia." Professor Seokwoo Lee concluded the conference with his closing remarks.

The following day on 17 October DILA opened the 2015 DILA Academy and Workshop entitled "The Making Of International Law In Indonesia." The purpose of the academy and workshop is to provide an opportunity for faculty and students at the host institution to learn about the important international legal issues of the country where the host institution is located from local scholars and experts.

Session 1 of the DILA Academy and Workshop was entitled "Indonesia's Encounter with the Modern International Legal System" and was moderated by Kevin Y.L. Tan. Dr. R. Herlambang and P. Wiratraman of Airlangga University in Indonesia spoke on "Indonesia's Encounter with 'Modern' International Legal System and its Impact toward the Indonesian Legal System."

The focus of Session 2 was on the "The Legacy and Impact of Colonialism," which was chaired by Professor Seokwoo Lee. Dr. Shidarta of Bina Nusantara University in Indonesia presented on "The Legacy of Colonialism in Shaping the Indonesian Legal System."

Session 3 was entitled "Indonesia's Contribution to the Development of International Law" and was moderated by Professor Hee Eun Lee. Professor Hikmahanto Juwana explained the "Making of Archipelagic State Concept in the UNCLOS" while Dr. Andri G. Wibisana, Professor of International Law of the Faculty of Law, Universitas Indonesia, discussed "The Role of Indonesia in Shaping Legal Basis to Reduce Emission from Deforestation and Forest Degradation."

The final session, "Other International Legal Issues Affecting Indonesia" was chaired by Professor Kevin Y.L. Tan. Mr. Anang Noegroho of the Ministry of Marine Affairs and Fisheries of Indonesia looked at "The Indonesian Government Efforts to Include IUU-Fishing as Trans-national Organized Crimes." Afterwards, Professor Seokwoo Lee closed the 2015 DILA Academy and Workshop with some concluding thoughts and final remarks.

*Seokwoo Lee*, Inha University Law School
Co-Editor-in-Chief

*Hee Eun Lee*, Handong International Law School
Co-Editor-in-Chief

# Articles from Volume 1 to Volume 20 of the *Asian Yearbook of International Law*

In recognition of the past 20 volumes of the *Asian Yearbook of International Law*, we have listed the articles that have appeared in the pages of the Yearbook.

## Volume 1 – 1991 Ko Swan Sik, M.C.W. Pinto, J.J.G. Syatauw, General Editors (Martinus Nijhoff Publishers)

Jamshed A. Hamid, Conduct of Foreign Relations, including Treaty-making Powers, under the Constitution of the Islamic Republic of Pakistan

Patricia Hyndman, Developing International Refugee Law in the Asian Pacific Region; Some Issues and Prognoses

Roda Mushkat, Balancing Western Legal Concepts, Asian Attitudes and Practical Difficulties – A Critical Examination of Hong Kong's Response to the Refugee Problem

Sompong Sucharitkul, ASEAN Society, A Dynamic Experiment for South-East Asian Regional Co-operation

## Volume 2 – 1992 Ko Swan Sik, M.C.W. Pinto, J.J.G. Syatauw, General Editors (Martinus Nijhoff Publishers)

E. Valencia-Ospina, The International Court of Justice and International Environmental Law

Rahmatullah Khan, Environment v. Development Revisited: Contributions of India's Judiciary to the Conflict Resolution

N. Jasentuliyana, The International Regulatory Regime for Satellite Communications: The Meaning for Developing Countries

Allahyar Mouri, Aspects of the Iran-United States Claims Tribunal

Yu Hui, Joint Development of Mineral Resources – An Asian Solution?

Roda Mushkat, Environmental Problems and Policy Response in Hong Kong: An Evaluation from an International Legal Perspective

Peter B. Payoyo, Philippine Marine Resources Policy in the Exclusive Economic Zone

### Volume 3 – 1993 Ko Swan Sik, M.C.W. Pinto, J.J.G. Syatauw, General Editors (Martinus Nijhoff Publishers)

Shigeru Oda, The International Court of Justice – Retrospective and Prospects

Antonio Augusto Cançado Trindade, Environment and Development: Formulation and Implementation of the Right to Development as a Human Right

K.I. Vibhute, Transnational Trade Transactions of a Foreign State and Sovereign Immunity in India: an Appraisal

Allahyar Mouri, Treatment of the Rules of the International Law of Money by the Iran–U.S. Claims Tribunal

Edward L. Miles, Towards more Effective Management of High Seas Fisheries

J.J.G. Syatauw, The Non-Aligned Movement at the Crossroads – the Jakarta Summit adapting to the Post Cold War Era

Bharat Desai, The Bhopal Gas Leak Disaster Litigation: an Overview

### Volume 4 – 1994 Ko Swan Sik, M.C.W. Pinto, J.J.G. Syatauw, General Editors (Kluwer Law International)

Subrata Roy Chowdry, Outer Space without Arms: Substratum of a Peaceful Regime for Common Benefit

Francis A. Boyle, The Decolonization of Northern Ireland

S. Mullally, Separate Spheres: Protective Legislation for Women in Pakistan

M. Sornarajah, ICSID Involvement in Asian Foreign Investment Disputes: The AMCO and AAPL Cases

C.G. Weeramantry, Access to Information: A New Human Right. The Right to Know

### Volume 5 – 1995 Ko Swan Sik, M.C.W. Pinto, J.J.G. Syatauw, General Editors (Kluwer Law International)

F. Danelius, De Maximis Non Curat Praetor or Judicial Review: The Hague Court in a Time of Transition

Charika Marasinghe, The Right to Legal Assistance and International Law with Special Reference to the ICCPR, ECHR and the ACHR

Paul Peters, Recent Developments in Expropriation Causes of Asian Investment Treaties

M.C.W. Pinto, Democratization of International Relations and its Implications for Development and Application of International Law

Ando Nisuke, Some Critical Observations on The International Law Commission's Draft Articles on State Responsibility

V.S. Mani, Effectuation of International Law in the Municipal Legal Order – The Law and Practice In India

Said Mahmoudi, The United Nations Environment Programme (UNEP): An Assessment

### Volume 6 – 1996 Ko Swan Sik, M.C.W. Pinto, J.J.G. Syatauw, General Editors (Kluwer Law International)

Miyoshi Masahiro, Recent Trends in the Jurisprudence of the International Court of Justice and International Arbitral Tribunals, with Special Reference to Territorial and Boundary Cases

Zou Keyuan, An Environmental Regime for the Arctic and the Antarctic Analogy

*Symposium on the Law of International Civil Procedure in Asian Countries*

Antonio R. Bautista, Philippine Civil Procedure in Transboundary Disputes

Sudargo Gautama, International Civil Procedure in Indonesia;

Kono Toshiyuki, International Civil Procedure in Japan

Li Shuangyuan and Lü Guoming, The Law of International Civil Procedure in China

Suh Chul Won, Transboundary Civil Litigation in Korea

### Volume 7 – 1997 Ko Swan Sik, M.C.W. Pinto, Surya P. Subedi, General Editors (Kluwer Law International)

Florentino P. Feliciano, Reflections on Good Governance, Development and Judicial Reform: Some Perspectives on the Problem of Judicial Corruption

Onuma Yasuaki, Towards an Intercivilizational Approach to Human Rights

J. Castellino, The Succession of Bangladesh in International Law: Setting New Standards?

Su Wei, Reservations to Treaties and Some Practical Issues

V. Crnic-Grotic, Object and Purpose of Treaties in the Vienna Convention on the Law of Treaties

Suzuki Eisuke, The Review and Repudiation of Judgments of International Administrative Tribunals

Raul C. Pangalangan, The Asian Development Bank Administrative Tribunal: Constitutive Instruments and Case-Law

T.L. MacDorman, Port State Control: A Comment on the Tokyo MOU and Issues of International Law

Zou Kenyuan, Maritime Jurisdiction over Vessels-Source Pollution in the Exclusive Economic Zone: The Chinese Experience

### Volume 8 – 1998/1999 B.S. Chimni, Ko Swan Sik, Miyoshi Masahiro, M.C.W. Pinto, Surya P. Subedi, General Editors (Martinus Nijhoff Publishers)

Zhao Yun, Liberalization of Air Transport Services under the Framework of the WTO: Confronting the Challenge of the Twenty-First Century

Alberta Fabbricotti, The ASEAN Free Trade Area (AFTA) and its Compatibility with the GATT/WTO

Mizukami Chiyuki, The Fisheries Policy of Japan under the New Law of the Sea

Eric Yong-Joong Lee, The Establishment of a *De Jure* Peace on the Korean Peninsula: Inter-Korean Peace Treaty-making under International Law

Kong Qingjiang, Bilateral Investment Treaties: The Chinese Approach and Practice

Nguyen Hong Thao, Vietnam and Joint Development in the Gulf of Thailand

### Volume 9 – 2000 B.S. Chimni, Miyoshi Masahiro, Surya P. Subedi, General Editors (Martinus Nijhoff Publishers)

Scott Davidson, Dangerous Waters: Combating Maritime Piracy in Asia

V.S. Mani, An Indian Perspective on the Evolution of International Law on the Threshold of the Third Millennium

Sakai Tetsuya, Idealism and Realism in the Post-War Foreign Policy Debate in Japan

Richard A. Barnes, Objective Regimes Revisited

Shigeta Yasuhiro, Some Reflections on the Relationship between the Principle of Equitable Utilization of International Watercourses and the Obligation Not to Cause Transfrontier Pollution Harm

Steve Allen, Statehood, Self-Determination and the 'Taiwan Question'

### Volume 10 – 2001/2002 B.S. Chimni, Miyoshi Masahiro, Surya P. Subedi, General Editors (Martinus Nijhoff Publishers)

Anthony Carty, The Japanese Seizure of Korea from the Perspective of the United Kingdom National Archive, 1904–1910

Annapurna Waughray, Human rights in South Asia: Abuse and Degradation

Azmi Sharom, Appreciating Compliance with International Environmental Law Treaties: Lessons from a Developing Country – Malaysia

M.T. Karoubi, Unilateral Use of Armed Force and the Challenge of Humanitarian Intervention in International Law

Tahmina Karimova, Universal Permissive Jurisdiction for the Violation of Common Article 3 to the Geneva Conventions for the Protection of the Victims of War of 12 August 1949

### Volume 11 – 2003/2004 B.S. Chimni, Miyoshi Masahiro, Surya P. Subedi, General Editors (Martinus Nijhoff Publishers)

C.L. Lim, Non-Recognition of Putative Foreign States (Taiwan) under Singapore's State Immunity Act

Duncan French, The Heroic Undertaking? The Separate and Dissenting Opinions of Judge Weeramantry during His Time on the Bench of the International Court of Justice

Palitha T.B. Kohona, Implementing Global Environmental Standards: Is the Non-State Sector a Reluctant Convert or an Eager Devotee?

Sugiyama Kanako, Genuine Protection of International Refugees: A Study of the Influence of Western States on the Mandate of the UNHCR

Abraham Mohit, The Customary Law of International Abductions: Limits and Boundaries

### Volume 12 – 2005/2006 B.S. Chimni, Miyoshi Masahiro, Thio Li-ann, General Editors (Martinus Nijhoff Publishers)

Mary George, Maritime Terrorism and Security Challenges in the Straits of Malacca and Singapore

Katak B. Malla, UN Security Council Reform and Global Security

Jaemin Lee, The United Nations Security Council and the International Court of Justice: Co-operation, Co-existence, and Co-involvement

Naazima Kamardeen, The Erosion of Community Rights to Intellectual Property: An Asian Perspective

### Volume 13 – 2007 B.S. Chimni, Miyoshi Masahiro, Thio Li-ann, General Editors (Routledge)

Ben Chigara, The Unfinished Business of Human Rights Protection and the Increasing Threat of International Terrorism

*Special Feature: Selected Papers, International Symposium of the Asian Society of International Law, 7–8 April 2007*

Jean d'Aspremont, International law in Asia: The Limits to the Western Constitutionalist and Liberal Doctrines

Richard Burchill, Regional Integration and the Promotion and Protection of Democracy in Asia: Lessons from ASEAN

H. Harry L. Roque, Jr., Export of War: Issues of Individual Criminal and State Responsibility

Sakai Hironobu, "As if" Acting under Chapter VII of the UN Charter?: Rigidity of the Threshold Between Chapter VII and non-Chapter VII

Mary George, The Role of IMO Resolutions in Ocean Law and Policy in the Asia-Pacific

### Volume 14 – 2008 B.S. Chimni, Miyoshi Masahiro, Thio Li-ann, General Editors (Routledge)

Takashi Miyazaki, Japan-Alcoholic Beverages Case Revisited: A Case of Treaty Interpretation or Formation of International Law?

Michael Ewing-Chow and Ng Wuay Teck, Caveat Emptor: Three Aspects of Investment Protection Treaties

Zhu Lijiang, Some Asian States' Opposition to the Concept of War Crimes in Non-International Armed Conflicts and its Legal Implications

Sanzhuan Guo, Effectiveness of National Human Rights Institutions in International Human Rights Law: Problems and Prospects

### Volume 15 – 2009 B.S. Chimni, Miyoshi Masahiro, Javaid Rehman, General Editors (Routledge)

Sergey Sayapin, International law, the Use of Force and the Crime of Aggression: From the Charter of the United Nations to the Rome Statute of the International Criminal Court

Chen Yifeng, The Treaty-Making Power in China: Constitutionalisation, Progress and Problems

Dik Dik Sodik, Post–LOSC Legal Instruments and Measures to Address Illegal IUU Fishing

Amin Ghanbari Amirhandeh, An Examination of the Plea of Self-Defence vis-à-vis Non-State Actors

Rishav Banerjee, Destruction of Environment During an Armed Conflict and Violation of International Law: A Legal Analysis

**Volume 16 – 2010 Kevin Y.L. Tan, Editor-in-Chief; Hee Eun Lee, Managing Editor (Foundation for the Development of International Law in Asia (DILA) in collaboration with Handong International Law School)**

Fort Fu-Te Liao, Partly Virtual, Partly Real: Taiwan's Unique Interaction with International Human Rights Instruments

Hee Eun Lee and Seokwoo Lee, Positivism in International Law: State Sovereignty, Self-Determination, and Alternative Perspectives

Kevin Y.L. Tan, International Law in the Courts of the Straits Settlement

Prabhakar Singh, Why Wield Constitutions to Arrest Universal International Law?

**Volume 17 – 2011 Kevin Y.L. Tan, Editor-in-Chief; Hee Eun Lee, Executive Editor (Foundation for the Development of International Law in Asia (DILA) in collaboration with Handong International Law School)**

Surya P. Subedi, Land Rights in Countries in Transition: A Case Study of Human Rights Impact of Economic Land Concessions in Cambodia

Sumaiya Khair, Bringing International Human Rights Law Home: Trends and Practices of Bangladeshi Courts

Rhona Smith, Form over Substance? – China's Contribution to Human Rights through Universal Periodic Review

Mario Gomez, Keeping Rights Alive: Reform and Reconciliation in Post-War Sri Lanka

### Volume 18 – 2012 Kevin Y.L. Tan, Editor-in-Chief; Hee Eun Lee, Executive Editor (Foundation for the Development of International Law in Asia (DILA) in collaboration with Handong International Law School)

Jaclyn Neo, Incorporating Human Rights: Mitigated Dualism and Interpretation in Malaysian Courts

Koesrianti Koesrianti, An Overview of Indonesia's Protection on Women Migrant Workers

Abdullah Al Faruque, Judgment in Maritime Boundary Dispute between Bangladesh and Myanmar: Significance and Implications under International Law

### Volume 19 – 2013 Kevin Y.L. Tan, Editor-in-Chief; Hee Eun Lee, Executive Editor (Foundation for the Development of International Law in Asia (DILA) in collaboration with Handong International Law School)

Thio Li-ann, International Law in the Courts of Singapore: No longer a 'Little Island'?

V.G. Hegde, International Law in the Courts of Asia: The Indian Experience

Tom Temprosa, Reflections on a Legal Confluence: International Law in the Philippine Court, 1940–2000

Jamal Seifi and Kamal Javadi, The Consequences of the "Clean Hands" Concept in International Investment Arbitration

### Volume 20 – 2014 Kevin Y.L. Tan, Editor-in-Chief; Hee Eun Lee, Executive Editor (Foundation for the Development of International Law in Asia (DILA) in collaboration with Handong International Law School)

Surya Subedi, Life as a UN Special Rapporteur

Patrick C.R. Terry, The Recognition of New States in Times of Secession: Is State Recognition Turning into Another Means of Intervention?

Sumaiya Khair, Civil Society Activism Against Corruption: Practices, Problems, and Prospects

Matthew Seet, China's Suspended Death Sentence with a Two-Year Reprieve: Humanitarian Reprieve or Cruel, Inhuman and Degrading Punishment?